The Instructional Design Trainer's Guide

The Instructional Design Trainer's Guide provides foundational concepts and actionable strategies for training and mentoring instructional design and educational technology students to be effective across contexts. ID faculty are charged with bridging the gap between research and practice preparing graduate students for the real-world workforce. This book provides trainers and university programs with authentic learning experiences that better articulate the practices of and demands on design and technology professionals in the field. Through this enhanced perspective, learners will be better positioned to confidently embrace constraints, work among changing project expectations, interact with multiple stakeholders, and convey to employers the skills and competencies gleaned from their formal preparation.

Jill E. Stefaniak is Associate Professor in the Department of Career and Information Studies at the University of Georgia, USA.

Rebecca M. Reese is Director of Online Learning at Rocky Mountain College of Art + Design, USA.

The Instructional Design Trainer's Guide

Authentic Practices and Considerations for Mentoring ID and Ed Tech Professionals

Edited by
Jill E. Stefaniak and Rebecca M. Reese

NEW YORK AND LONDON

Cover image: © Shutterstock

First published 2022
by Routledge
605 Third Avenue, New York, NY 10158

and by Routledge
4 Park Square, Milton Park, Abingdon, Oxon, OX14 4RN

Routledge is an imprint of the Taylor & Francis Group, an informa business

© 2022 selection and editorial matter, Jill E. Stefaniak and Rebecca M. Reese;
individual chapters, the contributors

The right of Jill E. Stefaniak and Rebecca M. Reese to be identified as the authors
of the editorial material, and of the authors for their individual chapters, has been
asserted in accordance with sections 77 and 78 of the Copyright, Designs and
Patents Act 1988.

All rights reserved. No part of this book may be reprinted or reproduced or
utilized in any form or by any electronic, mechanical, or other means, now
known or hereafter invented, including photocopying and recording, or in any
information storage or retrieval system, without permission in writing from the
publishers.

Trademark notice: Product or corporate names may be trademarks or registered
trademarks, and are used only for identification and explanation without intent to
infringe.

Library of Congress Cataloging-in-Publication Data
Names: Stefaniak, Jill E., 1984- editor. | Reese, Rebecca M., editor.
Title: The instructional design trainer's guide : authentic practices and
considerations for mentoring ID and ED tech professionals / edited by
Jill E. Stefaniak and Rebecca M. Reese.
Description: New York, NY : Routledge, 2022. | Includes bibliographical
references and index. | Summary: "The Instructional Design Trainer's
Guide provides foundational concepts and actionable strategies for
training and mentoring instructional design and educational technology
students to be effective across contexts. ID faculty are charged with
bridging the gap between research and practice preparing graduate
students for the real-world workforce. This book provides trainers and
university programs with authentic learning experiences that better
articulate the practices of and demands on design and technology
professionals in the field. Through this enhanced perspective, learners
will be better positioned to confidently embrace constraints, work among
changing project expectations, interact with multiple stakeholders, and
convey to employers the skills and competencies gleaned from their
formal preparation"-- Provided by publisher.
Identifiers: LCCN 2021048553 (print) | LCCN 2021048554 (ebook) | ISBN
9780367626129 (hardback) | ISBN 9780367619879 (paperback) | ISBN
9781003109938 (ebook)
Subjects: LCSH: Instructional systems--Design. | Educational technology.
Classification: LCC LB1028.38 .I5725 2022 (print) | LCC LB1028.38 (ebook)
| DDC 371.33--dc23/eng/20211109
LC record available at https://lccn.loc.gov/2021048553
LC ebook record available at https://lccn.loc.gov/2021048554

ISBN: 978-0-367-62612-9 (hbk)
ISBN: 978-0-367-61987-9 (pbk)
ISBN: 978-1-003-10993-8 (ebk)

DOI: 10.4324/9781003109938

Access the Support Material: www.routledge.com/9780367619879

Typeset in Baskerville
by SPi Technologies India Pvt Ltd (Straive)

To Dolly Parton.– JES
To my pack.– RMR

Contents

About the Editors	ix
List of Contributors	x

1 **A Holistic Approach to Teaching Instructional Design**   1
JILL E. STEFANIAK AND REBECCA M. REESE

2 **An Overview of the Competencies and Career Outcomes in Educational Technology**   9
FLORENCE MARTIN, SWAPNA KUMAR, AND ALBERT D. RITZHAUPT

3 **Inscribing a Designer Mindset to Instructional Design Students**   18
ELIZABETH BOLING, COLIN M. GRAY, AND AHMED LACHHEB

4 **Preparing Instructional Design Students for Reflective Practice**   29
JASON K. MCDONALD

5 **Creativity and Design Thinking: Crucial Mindsets in Instructional Design Education**   38
WILLIAM CAIN AND DANAH HENRIKSEN

6 **Learning Experience Design in Practice: "Theoretically, We Did Everything Right"**   48
MATTHEW SCHMIDT

7 **Empathy for Action in Instructional Design**   58
JOHN BAAKI AND MONICA W. TRACEY

8 **Designed Failure in Instructional Design and Technology**   67
T. LOGAN ARRINGTON AND ANDREW A. TAWFIK

9 **Instructional Design from the Lens of Self-Regulated Ill-Structured Problem Solving: Research and Practical Applications**   77
XUN GE, ALI CEYHUN MUFTUOGLU, AND SPENCER BRICKELL

10 **Designing for Service-Learning Experiences**   90
LUANN BATSON-MAGNUSON, BETH SOCKMAN, LAURENE CLOSSEY, AND OLIVIA CARDUCCI

viii *Contents*

11 Inclusive Online Courses: Universal Design for Learning Strategies that Impact Faculty Buy-In 101

AMY LOMELLINI AND PATRICK R. LOWENTHAL

12 Systems Thinking in Instructional Design 112

ANGELA DOUCET RAND

13 Integrating Ethics into the Curriculum: A Design-Based Approach for Preparing Professionals to Address Complex Problem Spaces 121

STEPHANIE L. MOORE AND GABRIELLE GRIFFIN

14 Instructional Design Embedded in Culture 135

BETH SOCKMAN AND LAURA KIESELBACH

15 Preparing Instructional Designers to Scale Needs Assessment 147

JILL E. STEFANIAK, LISA A. GIACUMO, AND STEVE VILLACHICA

16 The Value of Human Performance Improvement in Instructional Design and Technology 161

T. LOGAN ARRINGTON, ALISON L. MOORE, KAILA STEELE, AND JAMES D. KLEIN

17 Preparing Instructional Designers to Apply Human Performance Technology in Global Context 170

LISA A. GIACUMO AND TUTALENI I. ASINO

18 Integrating Evaluation in Instructional Design Practice 180

PHILENA DEVAUGHN

19 Project Management for Instructional Designers: Navigating People, Processes, and Politics 189

SHAHRON WILLIAMS VAN ROOIJ

20 Supporting Instructional Design Graduate Education through Networked Learning and Institutional Social Media 206

ENILDA ROMERO-HALL

21 Creating and Cultivating a Regional Community of Practice for Instructional Design and Faculty Development Practitioners 219

SAMANTHA J. BLEVINS, TRACEY W. SMITH, CHARLEY COSMATO, M. AARON BOND, AND EMORY MAIDEN

22 Developing Consulting Skills in Novice Instructional Designers 229

BARBARA B. LOCKEE AND MIRIAM B. LARSON

Index 245

Editors

Jill E. Stefaniak is Associate Professor in the Learning, Design, and Technology program in the Department of Career and Information Studies at the University of Georgia, USA. Her research interests focus on the professional development of instructional designers, designer decision-making processes, and contextual factors influencing design in situated environments.

Rebecca M. Reese is Director of Online Learning for Rocky Mountain College of Art + Design, USA. Her research primarily focuses on the application of Universal Design for Learning to improve online accessibility, and the incorporation of game theory in online environments to enhance knowledge transfer and reduce cognitive load.

Contributors

T. Logan Arrington is an Assistant Professor of Instructional Technology in the Department of Educational Technology and Foundations at the University of West Georgia, where he teaches graduate-level courses on Instructional Design and Human Performance Improvement. Logan's research interests focus on failure-based instructional strategies, professional issues in the field of Instructional Design and Technology, and authentic learning opportunities for underrepresented groups, specifically rural students.

Tutaleni I. Asino is an Associate Professor of Educational Technology and Director of the Emerging Technology and Creativity Research Lab at Oklahoma State. His research agenda includes Comparative and International Education, mobile learning, diffusion of innovations, Open Education, and how culture, agency and representation manifest themselves and interplay in learning settings. He is an active member of the Association for Educational Communications and Technology where he served as president of the Culture, Learning and Technology Division and the Comparative International Education Society where he served as Chair of the Indigenous Knowledge Special Interest Group.

John Baaki is an Associate Professor of Instructional Design & Technology at Old Dominion University. Baaki has interests in both instructional design and performance improvement. His research interests include how designers open themselves to their audience's feelings and experiences and use an empathic link to make design decisions considering how it impacts the audience of focus.

LuAnn Batson-Magnuson is an Associate Professor at East Stroudsburg University in the Department of Communication Sciences and Disorders. She completed her Ph.D. at Rutgers University (University of Medicine and Dentistry of New Jersey). She has over 30 years of clinical experience in educational and medical settings and 12 years of experience using the service-learning pedagogy at the university level. Her research and publications are in the areas of service learning, test validity, the connections between oral language and reading, and the impact of rheumatic disease on cognitive-linguistic function.

Samantha J. Blevins is currently an Instructional Designer & Learning Architect at Radford University within the Center for Innovative Teaching and Learning. She has broad design and teaching experience in various educational settings, including K-12, higher education, and professional development. She has served in various roles for the Systems Thinking and Change division of AECT including Board Representative. Her research focus areas include: Diffusion of innovation theory, electronic portfolio implementation; systems thinking and change; integrated learning practices; and faculty development.

Elizabeth Boling is a Professor of Instructional Systems Technology in the School of Education at Indiana University. Her prior experience includes 10 years in design practice, five with Apple Computer, Inc. Her research interests include visual design for information and instruction, and design theory, pedagogy, and practice. She is past editor-in-chief of TechTrends, founding editor and current Editor-In-Chief of the International Journal of Designs for Learning, lead editor of the 2016 Routledge title Studio Teaching in Higher Education: Selected Design Cases and a co-editor of the AECT Handbook of Research in Educational Communications and Technology, 5th Edition.

M. Aaron Bond has worked in the field of instructional technology, distance education, and professional development for more than 20 years.

Spencer Brickell is a doctoral student in the Learning Sciences program at the University of Oklahoma. She holds a Master's of Education in Adult and Higher Education also from the University of Oklahoma. Her interests are in expertise development, metacognition in adult learners, and instructional design. Spencer currently works as an Instructional Systems Designer and Project Manager for a company that develops e-Learning for the government.

William Cain is an Assistant Professor of Learning, Design, & Technology in the College of Education at the University of Wyoming, Laramie, USA. His current research interests include the design and use of technology in educational settings, emphasizing instructional design challenges as catalysts for learning, creativity, and innovation. Dr. Cain has published and presented his work in regional, national, and international forums such as TechTrends, International Journal for Designs for Learning, the Association for Educational Communications and Technology, and the American Educational Research Association. He is co-Chair of the Creativity SIG for the Society of Information Technology in Education.

Olivia Carducci is a Professor of Mathematics at East Stroudsburg University. Her research interest is combinatorial optimization and graph theory. Since 2008 she has included a significant service-learning project in her Mathematical Modeling class. Example projects include investigating the value of undeveloped land for the Pocono Environmental Education Center and the viability of a community kitchen for Meals on Wheels of Monroe County. She has been a member of the Service-Learning Initiative Committee since 2007.

Laurene Clossey is a Professor of Social Work at East Stroudsburg University. Her research focuses on mental health recovery. Caring deeply about learning transfer, her students experience authentic projects mostly in the realm of service learning with a systems perspective. Some of her past course partnerships include Meals on Wheels and Head Start. Laurene has been a long-time advocate and leader of service-learning curriculum development and has co-chaired the university service-learning committee since 2017.

Charley Cosmato is the Director of Radford University's Center for Innovative Teaching and Learning [CITL] where he explores solutions to teaching and learning challenges with a team of instructional designers, technologists, and new media developers. The CITL team leads the Radford University campus in brave exploration of learning science, instructional technology, instructional design, and innovative teaching methodology.

xii *Contributors*

Philena DeVaughn has over 20 years of experience in instructional design, facilitation, training, and management. She received a B.A. in Psychology from Michigan State University, an M.A. in Education from the University of Chicago, and her Ph.D. in Instructional Design and Technology from Old Dominion University.

Angela Doucet Rand is director of the Marx Library and Biomedical Library at the University of South Alabama. She holds an MLIS from University of Southern Mississippi and a Ph.D. in Instructional Design and Development from the University of South Alabama. Additionally, Angela holds a certificate in Human Performance Improvement and teaches in an online graduate program. Her professional interests led her from librarianship to instructional design and human performance improvement. In her current position she leads, manages, and supervises library policies and operations for both libraries. Her research interests include systems thinking, design thinking, and media and information literacy.

Xun Ge is Professor of Learning Sciences in the Department of Educational Department at the University of Oklahoma. She has been serving as the President of the Association of Educational Communications and Technology (2020–2021). Dr. Ge's research involves ill-structured problem solving, scaffolding, and designing technology-supported learning environments. Her scholarly work is committed to supporting learners' skill development in problem representation, developing strategies for solutions, constructing argument, and self-regulation. Her scholarly work intersects cognition, motivation, design, and assessment in various educational contexts. Dr. Ge has been widely recognized in the field of learning, design, and technology through her scholarly publications and awards.

Lisa A. Giacumo is an Associate Professor of Organizational Performance and Workplace Learning at Boise State University. Her research and teaching interests include mentoring systems in organizations, design to support global and cross-cultural workplace learning needs, the use of technology for workplace learning and performance improvement, and the preparation of instructional designers. She has worked internationally as an instructional designer, trainer, and manager for businesses, universities, non-profits, and NGOs.

Colin M. Gray is an Associate Professor at Purdue University in the Department of Computer Graphics Technology and Associate Professor (by courtesy) of Learning Design & Technology in the Department of Curriculum and Instruction. He is program lead for an undergraduate major and graduate concentration in UX Design. His research focuses on the ways in which the pedagogy and practice of designers informs the development of design ability, particularly in relation to ethics, design knowledge, and professional identity formation. His work crosses multiple disciplines, including engineering education, instructional design and technology, design theory and education, and human-computer interaction.

Gabrielle Griffin is a secondary social studies educator with over 20 years of classroom experience. She is currently an Ed.D. Instructional Design and Technology student at the University of Virginia.

Danah Henriksen is an Associate Professor of Leadership and Innovation at Arizona State University. Her research examines creativity, transdisciplinary thinking skills, and design thinking in education. Her work has been published in academic journals such as Teachers College Record, Educational Technology & Society, Thinking Skills & Creativity, and practitioner venues such as Educational Leadership or Phi Delta Kappan. She is co-Chair of the Creativity SIG for the Society of Information Technology in Education. Dr. Henriksen has taught on topics in educational psychology, systems change, leadership, design thinking, or creativity in education. More information can be found at http://danah-henriksen.com.

Laura Kieselbach is a Professor in English and serves as the Education Specialist for the department. She is passionate about the practice of culturally relevant pedagogical practices in the classroom that are intended to celebrate, honor, and embrace diverse lived experiences. Making necessary curricular changes and embedding strategies that offer student choice and voice can reshape the learning experience for students.

James D. Klein is the Walter Dick Distinguished Professor of Instructional Systems Design at Florida State University (FSU) and Professor Emeritus at Arizona State University. He also serves as chair or the Department of Educational Psychology and Learning Systems at FSU. He has authored numerous journal articles, books, chapters, and conference papers, wining several awards for his scholarship. He was identified one of the most productive authors in both ETR&D and Performance Improvement Quarterly. Dr. Klein's research, teaching, and consulting activities are in the areas of instructional design, strategies for active learning, and performance improvement.

Swapna Kumar is a Clinical Associate Professor and coordinates the online doctoral program in Educational Technology at the College of Education, University of Florida, USA. Her current research is focused on quality in online programs, online teaching, and online mentoring/ supervision. Details of her publications are at http://www.swapnakumar.com

Ahmed Lachheb is a Learning Experience Designer at the University of Michigan's Center for Academic Innovation. As an early-career design scholar, an experienced design practitioner, and a design educator, Ahmed's research work crosses design practice, designers' design knowledge and actions, design theory, and design pedagogy. Ahmed has a Ph.D. in Instructional Systems Technology from Indiana University Bloomington with a minor in Human-Computer Interaction & Design. He serves on the Editorial Board of the International Journal of Designs for Learning (IJDL). More about his work can be found on his website: https://lachheb.me

Miriam B. Larson is an instructional designer and researcher at the University of Tennessee, Knoxville, supporting faculty in their efforts to create and deliver online instruction. She is also an adjunct Assistant Professor in the Instructional Technology graduate program, and has 35+ years of experience designing instruction for organizations in a variety of career environments. She is co-author with Barbara Lockee of the popular and award-winning text, Streamlined ID: A Practical Guide to Instructional Design (2nd edition, 2020), and has published articles and book chapters on the preparation of instructional designers for different career environments.

Barbara B. Lockee is a Professor of Instructional Design and Technology in the School of Education at Virginia Tech. Her research and teaching are centered at the intersection of instructional design and distance learning, with the goal of advancing knowledge regarding the creation of effective distance courses and programs based on the principles of human learning. Dr. Lockee is Past President of the Association for Educational Communications and Technology. She earned her Ph.D. in 1996 from Virginia Tech in Curriculum and Instruction (Instructional Technology), and M.A. (1991, Curriculum and Instruction) and B.A. (1986, Communication Arts) from Appalachian State University.

Amy Lomellini is an instructional designer at Molloy College. She provides individual instructional design consultations and facilitates faculty development courses and webinars to promote high-quality web-enhanced, hybrid, and online learning experiences. Her research focuses on accessible and inclusive online course design strategies for higher education.

Patrick R. Lowenthal is an Associate Professor in the Department of Educational Technology at Boise State University. He specializes in designing and developing online learning environments. His research focuses on how people communicate using emerging technologies – with a specific focus on issues of presence, identity, and community – in online learning environments.

Emory Maiden serves as Director for Learning Technology Services for the Center for Academic Excellence at Appalachian State University. He holds a master's degree in Instructional Technology from AppState and previously served as the Associate Director for Online Learning and Quality Assurance. In this role he led quality online course development efforts and supported faculty development in online teaching and learning. Before that, he was as an Instructional Technology Consultant for the Reich College of Education. Emory has taught online as an adjunct instructor in the Department of Curriculum and Instruction since 2014.

Florence Martin is a Professor in Learning, Design and Technology at University of North Carolina Charlotte. She received her doctorate and master's degrees in Educational Technology from Arizona State University. She teaches 100% online. Dr. Martin engages in research to create transformative learning experiences through effective design and integration of digital teaching and learning innovations. She has conducted several studies focusing on designing and integrating online learning environments to improve learner achievement and engagement. Dr. Martin is currently serving as a Director for the International Board of Standards for Training, Performance and Instruction. For more details visit https://www.florencemartin.net

Jason K. McDonald is an Associate Professor in the Department of Instructional Psychology and Technology at Brigham Young University. His research interests include the use of practical knowledge in instructional design, reflective design practices, and instructional design education.

Alison L. Moore is a Clinical Assistant Professor of Learning Design and Technologies in the Educational Studies Department at the University of South Carolina. She teaches graduate courses and advises dissertations focused on educational technology.

Stephanie L. Moore is an Assistant Professor in Organization, Information, and Learning Sciences at the University of New Mexico. Her research and development interests include the integration of ethics into learning design, development, and decision making.

Ali Ceyhun Muftuoglu is a Fulbright recipient and a Ph.D. student in Instructional Psychology & Technology Program at the University of Oklahoma. His specialization is in the intersection of linguistics, psychology, and technology. His current research interests are exploring learning experiences in virtual and augmented reality environments.

Albert D. Ritzhaupt is a Professor at the University of Florida. His primary research areas focus on the design and development of technology-enhanced learning environments, professionals in educational technology, and operationalizing and measuring technology integration in education.

Enilda Romero-Hall is an Associate Professor in the Department of Education at The University of Tampa. She is also the Graduate Coordinator of the Instructional Design and Technology program. Dr. Romero-Hall is particularly interested in the design and development of interactive multimedia, faculty and learners' digital literacy and preparedness, and networked learning in online social communities. Other research areas include innovative research methods in learning design and technology; culture, technology, and education; and feminist pedagogies.

Matthew Schmidt is Associate Professor at the University of Florida in the Educational Technology program, Faculty in the Institute for Advanced Learning Technologies, and Director of the Advanced Learning Technologies Studio. His primary research interest includes design and development of innovative educational courseware and computer software with a particular focus on individuals with disabilities and their families/caregivers. His secondary research interests include immersive learning and learning experience design.

Tracey W. Smith is Professor in the Department of Curriculum and Instruction at Appalachian State University. She is also the Faculty Fellow for Mentoring Initiatives for the College of Education. For her fellowship, Smith designed a developmental community model of mentorship. In 2017, Smith was awarded the UNC Board of Governors Excellence in Teaching Award. Her research interests include mentoring and educational development in higher education, middle level education, and teacher preparation. She has had articles published in journals such as To Improve the Academy: A Journal of Educational Development, Journal of Teacher Education, and Middle School Journal.

Beth Sockman is a Professor in Professional and Secondary Education. She is passionate about designing learning environments with authentic learning experiences in undergraduate and graduate education. Using systems thinking, Beth researches pedagogical development and uses service learning as a key strategy to meet learning goals. Her students solve problems with their evolving knowledge interwoven with reflective formative assessments.

Kaila Steele began her career in education in 2006 and has served as a teacher, Instructional Technology Specialist, Student Information Coordinator, and is currently the Director of Accountability at Mountain Education Charter High School. Kaila earned both her Master of Education and Education Specialist degrees at the University of West Georgia, where her research led her to utilize Human Performance Technology as a basis for school improvement.

Andrew A. Tawfik is an Assistant Professor of Instructional Design & Technology at the University of Memphis, where he also serves as the director for the Instructional Design & Technology Studio. His research interests include problem-based learning, case-based reasoning, case library instructional design, and computer-supported collaborative learning.

Monica W. Tracey is a Professor of Learning Design and Technology in the College of Education at Wayne State University. Tracey embraces a teaching and research focus on the designer, including developing designer professional identity, empathic design, and the designer's use of a localized context for design action. She has over 60 publications concentrating on design including a Brown Book Award-winning book, The instructional design knowledge base: Theory, research, and practice.

Shahron Williams van Rooij is Associate Professor in the Learning Design and Technology program, Learning Technologies Division of the College of Education and Human Development at George Mason University. She holds the Project Management Professional (PMP) credential from the Project Management Institute, Inc. Prior to joining George Mason University, Dr. Williams van Rooij worked for a software development company where she facilitated the engineering of new e-learning technology solutions. Her book The Business Side of Learning Design and Technologies, a Routledge–Taylor & Francis publication, was released in September 2018.

Steve Villachica has consulted and worked in business, government, and non-profit settings over 35 years. He joined the Department of Organizational Performance and Workplace Learning in the College of Engineering at Boise State University in 2007. Prior to that, Steve collaborated with colleagues and clients at DLS Group, Inc., to create large-scale performance support systems, training, job aids, and other solutions. At Boise State, Steve teaches courses in performance foundations, instructional design, needs assessment, and workplace performance improvement. Steve is co-principal investigator of the Process Management Lab, which provides affordable process planning, redesign, and implementation services to the non-profit community.

1 A Holistic Approach to Teaching Instructional Design

Jill E. Stefaniak and Rebecca M. Reese

Chapter Overview

The practice of instructional design consists of applying strategies to analyze, design, and development solutions that best address the needs of a situation. Experienced instructional designers apply an iterative approach to design where they take a systemic view of the situation and use that information to inform their design. While several books have been written that outline the fundamental practices of instructional design, many of these imply that instructional design is simply a systematic and linear process. The purpose of this chapter is to provide our view of instructional design and explain the impetus for this book, which is focused on *how* to teach instructional design.

Guiding Questions

1. What is instructional design?
2. What challenges do I observe my students encountering while learning instructional design?
3. What holistic skills do my students need to be taught to be successful?
4. How can I promote a designer mindset in my classes?
5. How can I prepare my students to consider the systemic implications of their design decisions?

What is Instructional Design?

Instructional design is commonly recognized by practitioners and academics as "the systematic and reflective process of translating principles of learning and instruction into plans for instructional materials, activities, information resources, and evaluation" (Smith & Ragan, 2005, p. 4). Richey et al. (2011) expanded on this definition to recognize the role and responsibility instructional designers have for *facilitating* and *maintaining* a variety of activities that support learning and improve performance.

Over the decades, a number of books have been written to provide an overview of the instructional design process (Brown & Green, 2016; Cennamo & Kalk, 2019; Dick et al., 2009; Larson & Lockee, 2020; Morrison et al., 2013; Seels & Richey, 1994). Many of these have been used as textbooks in several learning, design, and technology programs. While there may be slight differences to approaching instructional design, they all present prescriptive strategies for applying a systematic approach to instructional design.

Applying a systematic approach to instructional design does not necessarily equate to linearity. While most designers will adopt some systematic steps to designing instruction, expert designers recognize that design is recursive (Ertmer & Stepich, 2005; Rowland,

DOI: 10.4324/9781003109938-1

2 *Jill E. Stefaniak and Rebecca M. Reese*

1992; Hardré et al., 2005; Perez & Emery, 1995). Experienced designers will approach every project with two things:

- Sustainable instructional design solutions require consideration of the systemic factors contributing to the project needs;
- Design requires an iterative approach to interpreting and meeting the needs of a project.

Recognizing that instructional design does not occur in a vacuum, it is important that instructional designers are trained to recognize the systemic nature that is instructional design (Kowch, 2019; Nelson, 2020; Stefaniak, 2020). In a systemic review conducted by Stefaniak and Xu (2020) to examine the extent that instructional design models address systemic considerations, they found three models addressed strategies to promote systemic design (Cennamo, 2003; Gibbons, 2014; Tessmer & Wedman, 1990).

Applications of Instructional Design

Instructional design extends to a variety of sectors such as business and industry, healthcare, higher education, government, K-12 education, military, and not-for-profit. Each sector has its own nuanced expectations, organizational culture, and factors that must be attended to by instructional designers. Several organizations such as the International Board of Standards for Training Performance and Instruction (ibstpi), the Association for Educational Communications and Technology, the E-Learning Guild, the Online Learning Consortium, and the International Society for Performance Improvement have established competencies and guidelines expected of instructional design professionals.

Several studies have been conducted exploring competencies expected of instructional designers. Table 1.1 provides an overview of these studies. These studies have explored which competencies, knowledge, skills, and attitudes are most prevalent in the field. A common theme among a number of the studies outlined in Table 1.1 is that they stress the need for instructional designers to extend their skillset beyond "ADDIE" to include attitudes and soft skills needed to facilitate instructional design activities. These soft skills include the ability to communicate with clients and team members, engage in project management, work independently and within a team, and demonstrate leadership (Koszalka et al., 2013; Visscher-Voerman, 2017; Williams van Rooij, 2010).

Upon our review of the scholarship on instructional design and the professional development of instructional designers in addition to our own personal experience as designers in the field, we suggest that the training and preparation of instructional designers expand beyond the prescriptive approaches focused on applying ADDIE and address constituent skills identified by experts in the field. Examples of these additional topics include, but are not limited to, the following:

- Adopting a designer mindset;
- Promoting equity and inclusive in design;
- Employing inclusive design;
- Recognizing systemic factors influencing work and learning environments;
- Espousing creativity in design;
- Project management and leadership.

This is not intended to be an exhaustive list, but it does emphasize the need for instructional designers to be training other key aspects of design and educational pedagogy.

Table 1.1 Overview of Studies Exploring ID Competencies Needed in the Field

Author(s) and Year	Audience	Purpose of Study
Kline et al. (2020)	Educational technologists in higher education (project management)	Exploration of project management competencies of educational technologists in higher education.
Martin et al. (2021)	Instructional designers in higher education	Overview of learning and development roles in higher education.
Martin and Ritzhaupt (2021)	Instructional designers	Overview of standards and competencies expected of instructional design and technology professionals.
Ritzhaupt and Kumar (2015)	Instructional designers in higher education	Study explored the knowledge, skills, and attitudes required of instructional designers in higher education.
Ritzhaupt and Martin (2014)	Educational technologists	Development of a multimedia competency survey to evaluate competencies required of educational technologists.
Rozitis (2017)	High school teachers	Examination of instructional design competencies required of high school teachers responsible for teaching online courses.
Sugar et al. (2007)	Instructional designers (multimedia production)	Identification of multimedia production competencies in instructional design practices.
Sugar et al. (2012)	Instructional designers (multimedia production)	Analysis of job postings to identify multimedia production competencies and skills expected of instructional designers.
Williams van Rooij (2011)	Instructional design (project management)	Study explored the convergence and divergence between instructional design and project management competencies.
Yalçın et al. (2021)	Instructional designers	Study explored the construct validity of the ibstpi standards.
York and Ertmer (2011)	Instructional designers	An exploratory study to establish instructional design heuristics to support the professional development of instructional designers.
Wang et al. (2021)	Instructional designers	Exploratory study comparing job announcement analyses with instructional design competencies.

Promoting Equity and Inclusive Through Design

Instructors often approach course design, the question of who they're designing for comes last. Instructional design approaches designing with equity at the center of the process, to anticipate the unique needs of the target learners for each course. Putting learners at the heart of course design gives more of them the opportunity to successfully complete the course. When design does not interrogate assumptions about learner differences/needs it can end up reinforcing inequalities. Putting equity at the heart of instructional design confronts and removes barriers to learning.

Equity-centered design is typically described as the practice of intentional inclusivity throughout the design process thereby addressing inequity and barriers to success (Indar, 2018; Oliveri et al., 2020; Poe et al., 2018). Equity-centered design expands on the concept of human-centered design and relevant methodologies through intentional identification and addressing barriers for learners that are or could be minoritized within the learning environment. Equitable learning environments must be intentionally designed to create spaces in which all students have equitable access, and feel valued and supported. Without such considerations, the design could perpetuate or deepen systemic inequalities in the teaching and learning space. Equitable design explicitly works to provide opportunities for success that are not impacted by learner differences. Instructional designers should consider the following when designing with equity in mind:

- A course should promote a sense of belonging, respect for diversity, and path for successful learning for all learners;
- Create space for meaningful discussions that challenge learners on issues related to individual identities and current events as they relate to course content. Create a positive and growth environment around difficult topics by setting guidelines for appropriate dialogue;
- Remove barriers to learning, by utilizing the principles of Universal Design for Learning (UDL). Consider synchronous and asynchronous activities in online courses and how they may create or remove barriers to learning.

Instructional Designers (ID) seek to understand the learner(s) before beginning the design process. The very first questions to ask is, who could the learners be? Along with traditional demographics, consider that most learners are juggling multiple roles in their lives as well as course work. They may be a parent, a caregiver, or working multiple jobs. Then ask yourself: How do learner variables contribute to their unique needs? Will any of the variables affect the learner's ability to be successful? What barriers are often or immediately associated with specific learner variables?

Creating Options for Learner Participation and Engagement

Because our learners have varying needs, IDs should observe the guidelines provided UDL when designing. This includes providing multiple pathways for: learner engagement, representation, and ways to respond or demonstrate knowledge/skills. UDL guidelines provide methods for learners to engage in a way that is most effective for them and meet the learning goals. Providing multiple pathways empower and increase success for all learners. For example, allowing learners choices for summative assessment reduces anxiety often experienced by some learners when presented with a traditional exam.

Check for Barriers to Learning Resources

When designing courses, consider the materials learners will be required to use. Ask yourself: are there accessible alternatives to the current resources, and do learners have multiple options to choose from? This is especially important with online learning. Learners will have varying degrees of access to technologies and ultimately course resources. Consider providing the option to download content, including the time needed to complete tasks so that students can work offline and better manage their time.

Growing from and Giving Feedback

Learner data and feedback is the best way of knowing whether or how things are going for learners. The most difficult part of gaining feedback is knowing if it is authentic to the tasks or experience learners are having, or if they are just checking the boxes to tell us what we want to hear. Therefore, it becomes important for instructors and designers to find ways that build trust so learners will share authentic feedback.

The way to do this is by building in opportunities throughout the course for learners to offer feedback which is then used for continuous improvement purposes in the course design. The addition of reflective discussion or assignments that ask leaners; what about an assignment they liked/disliked, or what barriers they ran into while completing an activity. You might even ask them how they might approach the activity differently.

Consider how autogenerated systems provide feedback. Typically, there is an acknowledgment of correct or incorrect based on simplistic built-in feedback fields. Instead, work with instructors, or SMEs to design informative feedback for autogenerated items. Feedback messaging could recognize an incorrect answer while providing information on why it is incorrect. This then allows learners to further engage their existing schemas to create new understanding.

Represent Diversity in the Learning Environment

Every design choice is an opportunity to send a message of equity and access to learners. Our goal with this section is to start a dialogue around how diverse and inclusive practices extend to learning and the learning environment during course design. In doing so, we hope that designers to give designers a reference point to work from and toward. The messages that we send through our design choices directly impact learners and the learning process in a variety of ways. By looking through the lens of equity when designing learning content, we move toward a more equitable, inclusive, and accessible learning experience for all learners.

The Impetus for This Book

The idea for an edited book was inspired from a Panel Presentation at AECT 2018 entitled "Design Considerations for Bridging the Gap Between Pedagogy and Practice." Faculty and practitioners from six instructional design programs collaborated to discuss ways in which we need to adjust classroom instruction to meet the demands of real-world instructional design needs. All panelists had instructional design experience in industry and higher education and hold advanced degrees in the field.

The panel discussed the challenges that many IDs face on the job and identify strategies to mitigate the challenges students face entering the workforce. Research has shown, however, that there is a gap between employers' expectations of instructional designers' roles and responsibilities and what designers are actually doing on the job (Kenny et al., 2005; Sugar & Moore, 2015; Villachica et al., 2010). There is an inherent need, then, for instructional design programs in higher education to develop a better understanding of the practices of instructional designers in the field. Not only will this help programs address workforce development needs as they relate to instructional design, but it will also better position academic programs to prepare their learners for the expectations of the workplace. In turn, learners will be better positioned to articulate and educate employers on the skills and competencies possessed by formally prepared instructional designers.

Unclear expectations are not the only challenge facing new designers. It is important that new instructional designers feel confident embracing constraints, working among changing project expectations, and interacting with multiple stakeholders on a variety of projects. Not only is it important for ID programs to provide new designers a solid foundation in fundamental instructional design concepts, but they must also work toward cultivating their learners' interpersonal skills (Visscher-Voerman, 2017).

It is important that educators take inventory of how they are facilitating authentic learning experiences for their learners, so these new designers are ready for the wide variety of contextual factors that may impact the results of their projects (Bannan-Ritland, 2001; Quinn, 1994, 1995; Stefaniak et al., 2021; Tracey & Boling, 2014). As educators provide these situated experiences, learners will be able to develop abilities as

6 *Jill E. Stefaniak and Rebecca M. Reese*

designers, and artifacts that showcase their skills, making them more competitive, and viable for the workforce.

While there are number of resources that outline systematic processes for engaging in instructional design activities, there are limited resources addressing *how* to teach instructional design. We have sought scholars in the field of learning, design, and technology to provide recommendations for how educators can facilitate learning experiences that prepare instructional designers to address this expanded focus and view of instructional design. Our book has been structured to address themes such as design thinking, learner-centered instruction, equality and inclusion, instructional strategies, human performance technology, project management, and consulting. Our intent is to provide a resource to individuals teaching and mentoring instructional designers. Each chapter provides an overview of the topic and suggestions for best ways to facilitate learning experiences that take a holistic approach to teaching instructional design.

Each chapter of the book follows a similar format including the following:

- Chapter overview;
- Guiding questions to assist the reader with topics they should reflect on throughout the chapter reading and activities;
- Identification of key terms and concepts;
- A presentation of a case study at the beginning of the chapter that would be revisited at the end of the chapter. Case studies would explore examples of how concepts outlined in chapters can be carried out in the real world;
- Content addressing theory and processes related to the chapter;
- A section entitled Professional Practice (the case study presented at the beginning of the chapter is revisited and content from the chapter is applied);
- A section entitled Connecting Process to Practice Activities (questions and activities to forward discussion related to content in chapter).

Additionally, a set of recommended readings relevant to each of the book's chapters can be downloaded from www.routledge.com/9780367619879.

References

Bannan-Ritland, B. (2001). Teaching instructional design: An action learning approach. *Performance Improvement Quarterly, 14*(2), 37–52. doi:10.1111/j.1937-8327.2001.tb00208.x

Brown, A. H., & Green, T. D. (2016). *The essentials of instructional design: Connecting fundamental principles with process and practice.* Routledge.

Cennamo, K. (2003). Design as knowledge construction model: Constructing knowledge design. *Computers in the Schools, 20*(4), 13–35. doi:10.1300/J025v20n04_03

Cennamo, K., & Kalk, D. (2019). *Real world instructional design: An iterative approach to designing learning experiences* (2nd ed.). Routledge.

Dick, W., Carey, L., & Carey, J. (2009). *The systematic design of instruction* (7th ed.). Upper Saddle River.

Ertmer, P. A., & Stepich, D. A. (2005). Instructional design expertise: How will we know it when we see it? *Educational Technology, 45*(6), 38–43.

Gibbons, A. S. (2014). Eight view of instructional design and what they should mean to instructional designers. In B. Hokanson & A. S. Gibbons (Eds.), *Design in educational technology* (pp. 15–36). Springer.

Hardré, P. L., Ge, X., & Thomas, M. K. (2005). Toward a model of development for instructional design expertise. *Educational Technology, 45*(1), 53–57.

Indar, G. K. (2018). An equity-based evolution of universal design for learning: Participatory design for intentional inclusivity. In *UDL-IRB international summit*, Orlando Florida.

Kenny, R., Zhang, Z., Schwier, R., & Campbell, K. (2005). A review of what instructional designers do: Questions answered and questions not asked. *Canadian Journal of Learning and Technology/La revue canadienne de l'apprentissage et de la technologie, 31*(1).

Kline, J., Kumar, S., & Ritzhaupt, A. D. (2020). Project management competencies of educational technology professionals in higher education. *The Journal of Applied Instructional Design, 9*(3). doi:10.51869/93jkskadr

Koszalka, T., Russ-Eft, D., & Reiser, R. (2013). *Instructional design competencies: The standards* (4th ed.). Information Age Publishing.

Kowch, E. G. (2019). Introduction to systems thinking and change. In M. J. Spector, B. B. Lockee, & M. D. Childress (Eds.), *Learning, design, and technology: An international compendium of theory, practice, and policy* (pp. 1–14). Springer.

Kwak, J. (2020, November). *How equity-centered design supports anti-racism in the classroom.* Retrieved July 2021, from http://everylearnereverywhere.org/blog/how-equity-centered-design-supports-anti-racism-in-the-classroom/

Larson, M. B., & Lockee, B. B. (2020). *Streamlined ID: A practical guide to instructional design* (2nd ed.). Routledge.

Martin, F., Chen, Y., Oyarzun, B., & Lee, M. (2021). Learning and development roles and competency domains in higher education: A content analysis of job announcements. *Journal of Computing in Higher Education*, 1–24. doi:10.1007/s12528-021-09290-2

Martin, F., & Ritzhaupt, A. D. (2021). Standards and competencies for instructional design and technology professionals. In J. K. McDonald & R. E. West (Eds.), *Design for learning: Principles, processes, and praxis.* EdTech Books. Retrieved from https://edtechbooks.org/id/standards_and_competencies

Morrison, G. R., Ross, S. M., Kalman, H. K., & Kemp, J. E. (2013). *Designing effective instruction* (7th ed.). Wiley.

Nelson, H. G. (2020). The promise of systemic designing: Giving form to water. In M. J. Spector, B. B. Lockee, & M. D. Childress (Eds.), *Learning, design, and technology: An international compendium of theory, practice, and policy* (pp. 1–49). Springer.

Oliveri, M. E., Nastal, J., & Slomp, D. (2020). Reflections on equity-centered design. *ETS Research Report Series, 2020*(1), 1–11.

Perez, R. S., & Emery, C. D. (1995). Designer thinking: How novices and experts think about instructional design. *Performance Improvement Quarterly, 8*(3), 80–95.

Poe, M., Inoue, A. B., & Elliot, N. (Eds.). (2018). *Writing assessment, social justice, and the advancement of opportunity.* WAC Clearinghouse.

Quinn, J. (1994). Connecting education and practice in an instructional design graduate program. *Educational Technology Research and Development, 42*(3), 71–82. doi:10.1007/BF02298096

Quinn, J. (1995). The education of instructional designers: Reflections on the Tripp paper. *Performance Improvement Quarterly, 8*(3), 111–117. doi:10.1111/j.1937-8327.1995.tb00690.x

Richey, R. C., Klein, J. D., & Tracey, M. W. (2011). *The instructional design knowledge base: Theory, research, and practice.* Routledge.

Ritzhaupt, A. D., & Kumar, S. (2015). Knowledge and skills needed by instructional designers in higher education. *Performance Improvement Quarterly, 28*(3), 51–69. doi:10.1002/piq.21196

Ritzhaupt, A. D., & Martin, F. (2014). Development and validation of the educational technologist multimedia competency survey. *Educational Technology Research and Development, 62*(1), 13–33. doi:10.1007/s11423-013-9325-2

Rowland, G. (1992). What do instructional designers actually do? An initial investigation of expert practice. *Performance Improvement Quarterly, 5*(2), 65–86. doi:10.1111/j.1937-8327.1992.tb00546.x

Rozitis, C. P. (2017). Instructional design competencies for online high school teachers modifying their own courses. *TechTrends, 61*(5), 428–437. doi:10.1007/s11528-017-0204-2

Seels, B., & Richey, R. (1994). *Instructional technology: The definition and domains of the field.* Association for Educational Communications and Technology.

Smith, P. L., & Ragan, T. J. (2005). *Instructional design* (3rd ed.). Jossey-Bass.

Stefaniak, J. (2020). The utility of design thinking to promote systemic instructional design practices in the workplace. *TechTrends, 64*(2), 202–210. doi:10.1007/s11528-019-00453-8

Stefaniak, J., Luo, T., & Xu, M. (2021). Fostering pedagogical reasoning and dynamic decision-making practices: a conceptual framework to support learning design in a digital age. *Educational Technology Research and Development, 69*(4), 2225–2241. doi:10.1007/s11423-021-09964-9

Stefaniak, J. E., Reese, R. M., & McDonald, J. K. (2020). Design considerations for bridging the gap between instructional design pedagogy and practice. *Journal of Applied Instructional Design, 9*(3). doi:10.51869/93jsrmrjkmd

Sugar, W., Brown, A., Cafeteria, O., & Daniels, L. (2007). Media production curriculum and competencies: Identifying entry-level multimedia production competencies and skills of instructional design and technology professionals: Results from a biennial survey. Paper presented at the *Association of Educational Communications and Technology.*

Sugar, W., Hoard, B., Brown, A., & Daniels, L. (2012). Identifying multimedia production competencies and skills of instructional design and technology professionals: An analysis of recent job postings. *Journal of Educational Technology Systems, 40*(3), 227–249. doi:10.2190/ET.40.3.b

Sugar, W., & Moore, R. L. (2015). Documenting current instructional design practices: Towards a typology of instructional designer activities, roles, and collaboration. *The Journal of Applied Instructional Design, 5*(1).

Tessmer, M., & Wedman, J. F. (1990). A layers-of-necessity instructional development model. *Educational Technology Research and Development, 38*(2), 77–85. doi:10.1007/BF02298271

Tracey, M. W., & Boling, E. (2014). Preparing instructional designers: Traditional and emerging perspectives. In J. M. Spector, M. D. Merrill, J. Elen, & M. J. Bishop (Eds.), *Handbook of research on educational communications and technology* (4th ed., pp. 653–660). Springer.

Villachica, S. W., Marker, A., & Taylor, K. (2010). But what do they really expect? Employer perceptions of the skills of entry-level instructional designers. *Performance Improvement Quarterly, 22*(4), 33–51. doi:10.1002/piq.20067

Visscher-Voerman, I. (2017). Necessary ingredients for the education of designers. In A. A. Carr-Chellman & G. Rowland (Eds.), *Issues in technology, learning, and instructional design: Classic and contemporary dialogues* (pp. 73–80). Routledge.

Visscher-Voerman, I. (2019). Necessary ingredients for the education of designers. In A.A. Carr-Chellman & G. Rowland (Eds.), *Issues in technology, learning, and instructional design: Classic and contemporary dialogues* (pp. 73–79). Routledge.

Wang, X., Chen, Y., Ritzhaupt, A. D., & Martin, F. (2021). Examining competencies for the instructional design professional: An exploratory job announcement analysis. *International Journal of Training and Development, 25*(2), 95–123. doi:10.1111/ijtd.12209

Williamss van Rooij, S. W. (2010). Project management in instructional design: ADDIE is not enough. *British Journal of Educational Technology, 41*(5), 852–864. doi:10.1111/j.1467-8535.2009.00982.x

Williams van Rooij, S. W. (2011). Instructional design and project management: Complementary or divergent? *Educational Technology Research and Development, 59*(1), 139–158. doi:10.1007/s11423-010-9176-z

Yalçın, Y., Ursavaş, Ö. F., & Klein, J. D. (2021). Measuring instructional design competencies of future professionals: Construct validity of the ibstpi® standards. *Educational Technology Research and Development,* 1–27. doi:10.1007/s11423-021-10006-7

York, C. S., & Ertmer, P. A. (2011). Towards an understanding of instructional design heuristics: An exploratory Delphi study. *Educational Technology Research and Development, 59*(6), 841–863. doi:10.1007/s11423-011-9209-2

2 An Overview of the Competencies and Career Outcomes in Educational Technology

Florence Martin, Swapna Kumar, and Albert D. Ritzhaupt

Chapter Overview

Competencies are defined as knowledge, skills, and abilities that professionals need to perform various roles and functions within their organizational settings (Richey et al., 2001). Graduate programs aiming to prepare educational technology professionals develop competencies for their students drawing from professional experiences, research, standards, and professional organizations. This chapter identifies both foundational and specialized educational technology competencies for graduates in this field based on an analysis of 12 educational technology graduate programs in the United States (U.S.). The alignment between the educational technology competencies of graduate programs and recent job announcements of educational technology professionals is analyzed and discussed.

Career outcomes are the roles professionals fulfill within an organization upon graduation. Career outcomes for educational technology graduate students are diverse and educational technology graduates fulfill jobs in different sectors of the economy, including, K-12 education, higher education, corporate, healthcare, non-profit, government, or military settings. Based on a review of the research and the different program websites, career outcomes for the various sectors are discussed in this chapter.

Guiding Questions

1. What are the competencies and career outcomes addressed in educational technology degree programs?
2. How are competencies identified by educators and professionals in the field of educational technology?
3. What are the competencies needed by educational technology professionals?

Educational Technology Definition

The term educational technology in this chapter encompasses other terms such as instructional design, instructional systems design, instructional technology, instructional systems technology, learning technologies, learning design, learning design technology, etc. The field of educational technology includes several professional associations such as Association of Educational and Communication Technology (AECT), Association for the Advancement of Computing in Education (AACE), International Board of Standards for Training and Instruction (ibstpi), International Society for Performance Improvement (ISPI), American Talent Development (ATD), and International Society for Technology in Education (ISTE). All of these professional organizations provide guidance and standards for professionals in the field of educational technology. AECT provides a definition for the field which is used in this chapter as the grounding definition for educational technology.

DOI: 10.4324/9781003109938-2

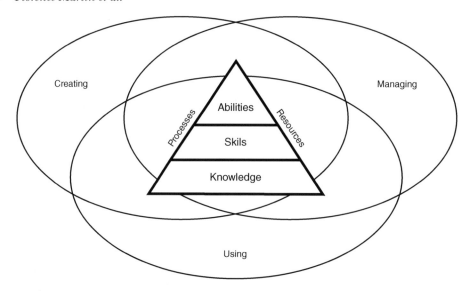

Figure 2.1 Educational technology conceptual framework.

Educational technology is "the study and ethical practice of facilitating learning and improving performance by creating, using, and managing appropriate technological processes and resources" (Januszewski, & Molenda, 2008, p. 1). Based on this definition, the emphasis is on both "facilitating learning" and "improving performance." In addition, there is focus on creating, using, and managing technological processes, and resources. Creating refers to the "research, theory, and practice involved in the generation of learning environments" (Januszewski, & Molenda, 2008, p. 6). Using refers to "the theories and practices related to bringing learners into contact with learning conditions and resources" (Januszewski & Molenda, 2008, p. 6). Managing refers to the intentional organization of processes and resources. Ritzhaupt et al. (2010) developed a framework aligned to this definition of educational technology and included knowledge, skills and abilities (competencies) requirement for an educational technology professional (see Figure 2.1). Focusing on creating, using, and managing, educational technology professionals employ a wide range of knowledge, skills, and abilities to carry out their work (Ritzhaupt et al., 2010).

Educational Technology Competencies in Graduate Programs

A content analysis of the top 12 master's programs in educational technology, based on U.S. News (https://www.usnews.com/) rankings, was conducted. The rankings and thus, this chapter focus only on master's programs within the U.S., and not in other countries. The websites of the 12 programs were reviewed and information about the content of the program and courses was collected and analyzed. The analysis resulted in the following foundational and specialized competencies. Figure 2.2 provides an overview of the foundational and specialized competencies. Foundational competencies are those that are gained from core courses in the graduate program, and specialized competencies are those that students have choices to learn from various elective courses.

Foundational Competencies

From the analysis of the curriculum of the top 12 master's programs in educational technology, the foundational competencies included, 1) Foundations of Instructional and Performance Technologies, 2) Design and Development of Instruction, 3) Learning

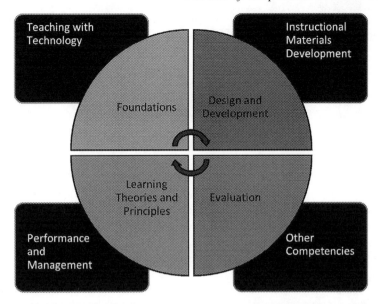

Figure 2.2 Foundational and specialized competencies for educational technology degree programs.

Theories and Principles and 4) Evaluation. One competency that was not explicitly included in course titles or descriptions but was emphasized in the AECT educational technology definition was the focus on ethical practice. It is possible that this competency is addressed within master's courses, but was not identified as a competency domain in this chapter because it was not listed among the courses. It is nevertheless an essential foundational competency that should be addressed in master's programs in educational technology.

Foundations of Instructional and Performance Technologies

Usually taught in an introductory course or course sequence, a foundations course is common among educational technology programs as the means to provide students general knowledge of instructional design and technology. Often, this course (or courses) provide(s) entry-level students with their first exposure to both historical and recent developments in the field (Klein et al., 2002; Reiser & Dempsey, 2012). The open-source textbook "Foundations of Learning and Instructional Design Technology" (West, 2020) includes chapters on definitions and history, learning and instruction, design, technology, and media, and on becoming an instructional design and technology professional. The foundational topics focus on contemporary issues and historical development of educational technology and also provide an overview of learning theory, instructional systems analysis and design, instructional design models, technology innovations, and factors affecting the use of technology for learning. Reiser and Dempsey's (2012) trends and issues in instructional design and technology and Spector's (2015) Foundations of Educational technology are commonly used books in foundational courses.

Design and Development of Instruction

Usually as a second course in the sequence, an instructional design course is a staple of educational technology programs. A course on instructional design could include topics such as instructional analysis, design, and evaluation principles and practices.

12   *Florence Martin et al.*

It provides an opportunity for students to apply theory and instructional design principles and processes such as goal and task analysis, learner and context analysis, instructional strategies, selection and development of instructional materials, and formative, and summative evaluation. Morrison et al.'s (2019) process on designing effective instruction and Dick et al.'s (2001) systematic instructional design is commonly used instructional design models to teach instructional design competencies. The open-source textbook "Design for Learning" (McDonald & West, 2020) includes chapters focusing on instructional design knowledge and practice.

Learning Theories and Principles

There is usually a specific course focusing on learning theories and learning principles in educational technology programs. This course usually focuses on how people learn in a variety of instructional settings and encompasses the characteristics of different learners. It is common practice to perform a learner analysis as part of the instructional design process and students investigate several learning theories to inform better instructional design decisions. Tennyson (2002) discusses that by linking theories, instructional design can improve learning outcomes. Behavioral, cognitive, and constructivist theories of learning are the ones most commonly used. In addition, Gagne's (1962) sequencing of content, Merrill's (2002) first principles of instruction, Reigeluth's (1992) elaboration theory (1983) focusing on how to teach are important theories and principles for educational technologists. Knowles (2012) learning principles focusing on adult learner characteristics to assist adults learn are also covered.

Evaluation

Evaluation is an important aspect of instructional design, and it is common to see a course on assessment and evaluation included in graduate programs. Evaluation is considered as an important competency for educational technologists as they examine the effectiveness of instructional solutions (Dick & Johnson, 2002). Weston et al. (1995) developed a model for understanding formative evaluation in instructional design. Kirkpatrick's (1996) four-level model focused on measuring reactions, learning, behavior, and results on investment is commonly used in evaluating training. Another influential model is the CIPP model proposed by Stufflebeam (1971) which focuses on Context, Input, Process, and Product. Russ-eft and Preskill (2009) focus on defining evaluation, designing an evaluation plan including instruments, analyzing data, and communication, and reporting evaluation activities.

Specialized Competencies

From the analysis of the curriculum of the top 12 master's programs in educational technology, in addition to the foundational competencies, the following specialized course competencies were identified. These specialized competencies are categorized into the following 1) Instructional materials development 2) Teaching with technology 3) Performance and Management, and 4) other competencies based on context and specialization.

Instructional Materials Development

Educational Technologists are expected to be prepared to use the latest software or multimedia tools to design and develop instructional materials that can be used in various learning environments. Web design, graphic design, courseware development, video production, mobile application development, educational game design, videogame design, are included as specialized courses in graduate programs. Ritzhaupt et al. (2010) examined multimedia competencies through a job announcement analysis and found that knowledge of multimedia software tools was essential for educational technologists. Martin and Winzeler (2008) examined multimedia competencies for instructional technologists through a survey focusing on multimedia knowledge, skills, and tools.

Teaching with Technology

In addition to courses focused on the development of materials, a) the design of instructional activities and teaching strategies across various delivery methods, and b) the different ways in which technologies can be integrated into teaching are important competencies for educational technologists. Courses focused on applying foundational competencies (design and development and learning theories) but acquiring specialized competencies related to design, teaching, and assessment in online environments or blended environments. Additionally, courses focused on the integration of various popular and emerging technologies ranging from social networks to games, simulations, mobile technologies, robotics, augmented reality, and virtual reality in educational environments.

Performance and Management

Educational technologists must be prepared to lead, manage, and participate in technology-related projects of various sizes; manage course development and improvement projects; coordinate and manage professional development and training, student and staff support; and also coordinate and manage technology-based environments (Kline et al., 2020). Courses that address these specialized competencies such as project management, human performance technology, technology leadership, and technology coordination are taught in graduate programs in educational technology.

Other Competencies

Additional competencies focusing on needs in various specializations in K-12, corporate, higher education are also included as courses in graduate programs in educational technology (Table 2.1). Some of these include human computer interaction, learning and

Table 2.1 Specialized Competencies

Instructional Materials Development	Teaching with Technology	Performance and Management	Other Competencies
• Instructional Web design • Graphic Design • Interactive Courseware development • Video production • Mobile application design • Educational, computer, and video game design	• E-learning • Online Learning • Blended Learning • Games and Simulations • Mobile Technologies • Robotics for Teaching and Learning • Social Network Learning • Augmented/Virtual Reality • Makerspaces	• Human Performance Technology • Project Management • Technology Integration and Management • Technology and Leadership	• Human Computer Interaction • Creative Thinking • Computational Thinking • Programming Concepts • Learning and Cognition • Learning Analytics

14   *Florence Martin et al.*

cognition, creative thinking, computational thinking, programming concepts, effective communication, and learning analytics.

Research on Educational Technology Competencies and Alignment with Curriculum

Wang et al. (2021) examined 185 professional competencies for instructional designers by reviewing 1,030 unique job announcements. Their analysis revealed that soft skills, the ability to work with diverse stakeholders, and technical competencies like knowledge of video and audio authoring were critical competencies. They analyzed competencies based on knowledge, skills, and abilities required. Instructional design models and principles, e-learning development, and online teaching, and learning were top three knowledge competencies. Collaboration skills, content development skills, oral, and written communication skills were the top three skill competencies. The ability to develop course materials, ability to create effective instructional products, and ability to advise and consult with Subject Matter Expert (SMEs) were the top three ability competencies.

Klein and Kelly (2018) examined 393 job announcements and interviewed 20 instructional design project managers. The top five competencies in their job announcement analysis from the employers' perspective were 1) collaborate effectively with stakeholders, SMEs, teammates, and others, 2) utilize ADDIE (Analysis, Design, Development, Implementation, and Evaluation) procedures to create learning solutions, 3) have knowledge and experience with e-learning authoring software such as Captivate, Presenter, Storyline, or Lectora, 4) apply knowledge of learning theories and principles and 5) communicate effectively in visual, oral, and written form. The top five competencies from the interview data were 1) collaborate effectively with stakeholders, SMEs, teammates, and others, 2) use analysis techniques for determining content and tasks, 3) have strong client-relationship skills, 4) have knowledge and experience with e-learning authoring software and 5) have project management knowledge and experience. These competencies were in the categories of communication/interpersonal, instructional design, instructional technology, and management.

Ritzhaupt and Kumar (2015) examined competencies for instructional designers in higher education by interviewing eight instructional designers. Their interviews revealed that a solid foundation in instructional design and learning theory, soft skills and technical skills, and a willingness to learn on the job were required competencies. They also found that it was important for instructional designers to stay up to date with multiple emerging information and communication technologies. While instructional design and learning theory were identified as foundational competencies in the curriculum analysis, emerging information, and communication technologies were identified in specialized competencies. Soft skills were identified in the Ritzhaupt and Kumar (2015) study as important competencies.

Kang and Ritzhaupt (2015) analyzed 450 job announcements for educational technology professionals and derived 150 knowledge, skill, and ability competencies. Knowledge of instructional design models and principles, word processing software, presentation software were the top three knowledge competencies. Oral and written communication skills, collaboration skills, and interpersonal communication skills were the top three skill competencies. Collaborate with different team members, work well with others, and deliver training to learners were the top three ability competencies.

Using the categorization proposed by Klein and Kelly (2018), we have tabulated the top-rated or frequently occurring competencies from these studies in Table 2.2.

Table 2.2 Top-rated or Frequently Occurring Educational Technology Competencies from Research

Category	Wang et al. (2021)	Klein and Kelly (2018)	Ritzhaupt and Kumar (2015)	Kang and Ritzhaupt (2015)
Instructional design	Instructional design models and principles	Instructional design	Instructional design and learning theory	Instructional design models and principles
Instructional technology	Knowledge of e-learning development Knowledge of online teaching and learning	e-learning authoring software	Technical skills, keep abreast of multiple emerging information and communication technologies	Word processing software, presentation software
Communication/ interpersonal	Collaboration skills, content development skills, oral, and written communication skills Ability to develop course materials, ability to create effective instructional products Ability to advise and consult with Subject Matter Expert	Collaboration with stakeholders	Soft skills, oral and written communication skills	Oral and written communication skills, collaboration skills, and interpersonal communication skills Collaborate with different team members, work well with others, and deliver training to learners
Management	Ability to work on multiple projects	Management	Project management	Project management
Personal	Use of feedback		Willingness to learn	

- Instructional design;
- Instructional technology;
- Communication/interpersonal;
- Management;
- Personal.

Career Outcomes

Graduate students in educational technology programs are prepared for varied positions including instructional design, technology integration, performance improvement, distance learning, and more (Table 2.3). More importantly, the graduates of these programs work across different settings such as K-12, higher education, and business/industry. From the 12 programs that were reviewed in this case, the following job titles were identified on the program websites as possible career outcomes.

Table 2.4 includes titles for educational technologists from a review of research and job postings. These are categorized into design and development focused positions, consulting, and specialist positions, leadership positions, and other. The other category includes some unique titles that have recently emerged including learning engineers. This category also includes support positions.

16 *Florence Martin et al.*

Table 2.3 Career Outcomes for Educational Technologists

K-12	Business/Industry	Higher Ed
Technology Coordinator	E-learning Developer	Instructional Designer
Technology Integration Specialist	Multimedia Designer	Instructional Technologist
Media Specialist	Instructional Designer	Online Learning Specialist
Technology Teacher	Corporate Trainer	Evaluator
Technology Facilitator	Education Content Developer	Director of Online Learning
Curriculum Designer	Learning Consultant	
Curriculum Specialist	Project Manager	
	Evaluator	
	Training and Development Specialist	

Table 2.4 More Career Outcomes for Educational Technologists

Designer and Developer	Consultant & Specialist	Leadership Positions	Other Positions
Instructional Developer	Training and Development Consultant	Training Manager	Learning Engineer
Training Developer	Learning and development Consultant	Learning and Development Manager	Learning Architect
Learning Developer	Talent Development Consultant	Chief Learning Officer	Facilitator
Instructional Systems Designer	Instructional Design Consultant	Training Project Manager	Training Administrator
Multimedia Designer	Performance Improvement Consultant	Learning Project Manager	Training Professional
Instructional Technology Designer	Instructional Design Specialist	Instructional Project Manager	Training Coordinator
E-learning Designer	E-learning Specialist	Talent Development Manager	Learning Management System Administrator
Online Learning Developer	Multimedia Specialist	Talent Development Leader	Instructional Support Assistant
Multimedia Designer	Talent Development Specialist	Training Director	Instructional Support Associate
Learning Experience Designer			Training Program Administrator
E-learning Developer			Performance Technologist

Depending on their interests, graduate students are able to pursue positions. For the leadership positions, graduates are expected to have years of experience and some positions require doctoral degrees.

Connecting Process to Practice

1. What competencies are essential for educational technology graduates?
2. What courses are essential to be included in an educational technology graduate program?
3. What career outcomes are available for educational technology graduates?

References

Dick, W., Carey, L., & Carey, J. O. (2001). *The systematic design of instruction* (5th ed.). Longmann.

Dick, W., & Johnson, R. B. (2002). Evaluation in instructional design: The impact of Kirkpatrick's four-level model. In R. A. Reiser & J. V. Dempsey (Eds.), *Trends and issues in instructional design and technology* (pp. 145–153). Upper Saddle River.

Gagne, R. M. (1962). The acquisition of knowledge. *Psychological Review, 69*(4), 355.

Januszewski, A., & Molenda, M. (2008). Definition. In A. Januszewski & M. Molenda (Eds.), *Educational technology: A definition with commentary* (pp. 1–14). Routledge.

Kang, Y., & Ritzhaupt, A. D. (2015). A job announcement analysis of educational technology professional positions: Knowledge, skills, and abilities. *Journal of Educational Technology Systems, 43*(3), 231–256.

Kirkpatrick, D. (1996). Great ideas revisited. *Training & Development, 50*(1), 54–60.

Klein, J. D., Brinkerhoff, J., Koroghlanian, C., Brewer, S., Ku, H., & MacPherson-Coy, A. (2002). The foundations of educational technology: A needs assessment. *TechTrends, 44*(6), 32–36. doi:10.1007/BF02763314

Klein, J. D., & Kelly, W. Q. (2018). Competencies for instructional designers: A view from employers. *Performance Improvement Quarterly, 31*(3), 225–247. doi:10.1002/piq.21257

Kline, J., Kumar, S., & Ritzhaupt, A. D. (2020). Project management competencies of educational technology professionals in higher education. *The Journal of Applied Instructional Design, 9*(3). https://dx.doi.org/10.51869/93jkskadr

Knowles, M. (2012). Andragogy: An emerging technology for adult learning. In M. Tight (Ed.), *Education for adults: Adult learning and education* (pp. 53–70). Routledge.

Martin, F., & Winzeler, B. (2008). Multimedia competencies for instructional technologists. In *Proceeding of the UNC teaching and learning with technology conference*. Raleigh, NC.

McDonald, J. K., & West, R. E. (2020). *Design for learning: Principles, processes, and praxis*. EdTech Books. Retrieved from https://edtechbooks.org/id

Merrill, M. D. (2002). First principles of instruction. *Educational Technology Research and Development, 50*(3), 43–59. doi:10.1007/BF02505024

Morrison, G. R., Ross, S. J., Morrison, J. R., & Kalman, H. K. (2019). *Designing effective instruction* (8th ed.). John Wiley & Sons.

Reigeluth, C. M. (1992). Elaborating the elaboration theory. *Educational Technology Research and Development, 40*(3), 80–86. doi:10.1007/BF02296844

Reiser, R. A., & Dempsey, J. V. (Eds.). (2012). *Trends and issues in instructional design and technology*. Pearson.

Richey, R. C., Fields, D. C., & Foxon, M. (2001). *Instructional design competencies: The standards* (3rd ed.). Eric Clearinghouse on Information Technology.

Ritzhaupt, A., Martin, F., & Daniels, K. (2010). Multimedia competencies for an educational technologist: A survey of professionals and job announcement analysis. *Journal of Educational Multimedia and Hypermedia, 19*(4), 421–449.

Ritzhaupt, A. D., & Kumar, S. (2015). Knowledge and skills needed by instructional designers in higher education. *Performance Improvement Quarterly, 28*(3), 51–69. doi:10.1002/piq.21196

Russ-Eft, D., & Preskill, H. (2009). *Evaluation in organizations: A systematic approach to enhancing learning, performance, and change*. Basic Books.

Spector, J. M. (2015). *Foundations of educational technology: Integrative approaches and interdisciplinary perspectives*. Routledge.

Stufflebeam, D. L. (Ed.). (1971). *Educational evaluation & decision making*. Wadsworth.

Tennyson, R. D. (2002). Linking learning theories to instructional design. *Educational Technology, 42*(3), 51–55.

Wang, X., Chen, Y., Ritzhaupt, A., & Martin, F. (2021). Examining competencies for the instructional design professional: An exploratory job announcement analysis. *International Journal of Training and Development, 25*(2), 95–123.

West, R. E. (2020). *Foundations of learning and instructional design technology*. EdTech Books. Retrieved from https://edtechbooks.org/lidtfoundations

Weston, C., McAlpine, L., & Bordonaro, T. (1995). A model for understanding formative evaluation in instructional design. *Educational Technology Research and Development, 43*(3), 29–48. doi:10.1007/BF02300454

3 Inscribing a Designer Mindset to Instructional Design Students

Elizabeth Boling, Colin M. Gray, and Ahmed Lachheb

Chapter Overview

In this chapter, we focus on building a designer's mindset among instructional design (ID) students by using frame experiments as an instructional method. We provide the theoretical foundation of frame experiments with a sample scenario of their use and conclude by sharing specific instructional activities that instructors may use to build design judgment.

Guiding Questions

1. What is the core of design thinking?
2. How is a designer's mindset different from other professional mindsets?
3. How can we best teach ID students to design?
4. How do designerly tools like frame experiments support students in developing design judgment and developing awareness of ethics, including their responsibilities as designers?

Case Study

Kim is teaching Instructional Design Practice – an introductory ID course for master's students. Her students are working in groups, each of which completes an instructional design project. Kim teaches from a design thinking perspective, and she is speaking with one group just starting their work.

TEAM MEMBER A: "We've talked about it, and we plan to start with an analysis. Like the model in our textbook."

KIM: "OK, what kind of analysis do you think is appropriate?"

TEAM MEMBER A: "Well ... we're not sure. We're developing a lesson on fractions for 9-year-olds in an after-school program, so, maybe – talk to a teacher?"

KIM: "Yes, sure." [nods approvingly] "And what kinds of ideas do you have for the lesson itself?"

The students look at each other, hesitating.

TEAM MEMBER B: "Uhm. Should we really be doing that before the analysis? Before we have all the facts? I mean – we might design the wrong thing and then it would be our fault for skipping a step in the process. If we stick to the process, it will come out right."

DOI: 10.4324/9781003109938-3

Kim had half expected the pushback, but she hopes they will go along with her for a minute.

KIM: "Let's try ... Have you pictured anything about what the lesson might be like?"

After a second....

TEAM MEMBER B: "I thought ... maybe ... it could be a workbook? I used a lot of math workbooks in school!"

All team members nod.

TEAM MEMBER C: "I've seen a cute math workbook online – we could use that; it looked so fun!"

KIM: "Well ... let's think about a workbook just as a possibility. Who is using it – and where did they get it?"

Silence. Then...

TEAM MEMBER A: "The kids are using it, obviously. And they get it from the program – person."

KIM: "Makes sense. They work on it alone?"

TEAM MEMBER B: "They might need help. I wonder if the people at the program know how to help them?"

The team begins to speculate on who works at the after-school program, whether they are prepared to teach fractions, and how much nine-year-old can learn independently. They establish that none of them have been teachers, and only one has a child of his own, still just a baby.

TEAM MEMBER D: "I think we need to visit an after-school program instead of a school-teacher."

Kim has been listening and now interjects.

KIM: "Maybe also ask them where they get materials for the kids? Do they have a budget? A photocopier?"

A team member interrupts.

TEAM MEMBER A: "Oh! Maybe we should create an app? Then it's kind of free. And it could be customized for each kid. We could use a strategy of individualized learning because we don't know if each kid is starting at the same place."

TEAM MEMBER B "I thought they went to after-school programs because they are behind in school."

KIM: "The public program here in town includes academics, but the kids actually choose their own activities based on their interests."

TEAM MEMBER D: "Will they even choose math?"

This student slaps her forehead with her palm.

TEAM MEMBER D: "This project is going to be harder than I thought!"

TEAM MEMBER A: "Well, we don't know ... We totally have to start with a context analysis!"

20 *Elizabeth Boling et al.*

Theory and Processes

Design Thinking as a Distinct Form of Reasoning

The designer's mindset is arguably a capacity that every human has, and it represents "the oldest human tradition" (Nelson and Stolterman, 2012, p. 11), although a scientific mode of thought is often privileged in instructional design practice (Smith & Boling, 2009). Dorst (2011) offers a clear explanation of how design thinking is distinguishable from other forms of reasoning. These are *Deduction, Induction, Abduction-1*, and *Abduction-2*.

Deduction Form of Reasoning

Deduction is a form of reasoning in which we know the "players in a situation we need to attend to [WHAT]" and the rules that will govern HOW they operate together (Dorst, 2011, p. 523). This reasoning allows for a safe prediction of results, like predicting the movement of planets. Dorst represents this as a formula (Figure 3.1):

Induction Form of Reasoning

Induction is a form of reasoning where we know the "what" and the "results," but we lack the knowledge of the "how" (working principles). This reasoning is used to generate hypotheses or theories, subjected to falsification or confirmation – the core act of science:

> [...] in the sciences, inductive reasoning informs 'discovery,' while deductive reasoning informs 'justification.' These two forms of analytical reasoning help us to predict and explain phenomena in the world.
>
> (Dorst, 2011, p. 523)

This form of reasoning could be displayed using this formula (Figure 3.2), as suggested by Dorst (2011):

Abduction-1 Form of Reasoning

Abduction-1 is a form of reasoning where we know the aspired value (rather than a specific result) and the "how" (working principles) that will help us achieve that value. However, we do not know the "what" – it could be a device, a service, an experience, or a whole system. This form of reasoning is used for conventional problem-solving where outcomes solve a particular problem in a given context, and the working principles are known. Examples include software designers who rely on computer science principles to create computer applications or engineers who rely on the laws of physics to design bridges. Dorst's (2011) formula represents this reasoning as shown (Figure 3.3):

WHAT	+	**HOW**	*leads to*	**???**
(thing)		(working principles)		(observed result)

Figure 3.1 Formula for deductive reasoning.

WHAT	+	**???**	*leads to*	**RESULT**
(thing)		(working principles)		(observed result)

Figure 3.2 Formula for inductive reasoning.

???	**+**	**HOW**	*leads to*	**VALUE**
(thing)		(working principles)		(aspired)

Figure 3.3 Formula for Dorst's form Abduction-1 reasoning.

???	**+**	**???**	*leads to*	**VALUE**
(thing)		(working principles)		(aspired)

Figure 3.4 Formula for Dorst's form Abduction-2 reasoning.

Abduction-2 Form of Reasoning

Abduction-2 is the most complex form of reasoning because we do not know the "what" *or* the "how"; we only know the value to which we aspire. Abduction-2 is a challenging form of reasoning since one has to figure out what to create (the "what") without a working principle (the "how") that can be trusted to lead to the aspired value. The "what" and the "how" must be created simultaneously. Open and complex problems in design require this form of reasoning. As an example, designers, scientists, and engineers involved in space exploration programs created space vehicles (the "what") in parallel with discovering the working principles of low-orbit maneuvers (the "how") through experimentations and several design failures. Dorst's (2011) formula for Abduction-2 is this (Figure 3.4):

Framing Form of Reasoning

To manage the complexity of the Abduction-2 form of reasoning, Dorst (2011) argues that experienced designers rely on a well-known strategy called *framing*, placed in the formula as shown (Figure 3.5):

Schön (1983) explains that framing is the creation of a new perspective from which a problematic situation can be approached. In framing, statements or metaphors are used to describe the problem at hand and, simultaneously, to suggest a working principle (the "how") that can lead to the solution (the "aspired value"). A framing statement includes a presumption: "IF we look at the problem situation from this viewpoint, and adopt the working principle associated with that position, THEN we will create the value we are striving for" (Dorst, 2011, p. 525). An instructional designer might approach the problem of increased injuries on the job framed by clients as a lack of safety knowledge and skills among employees. Reframed as a lack of space/time management in the factory, the designer can consider several solutions, which may not include safety training.

Compared to disciplines/professions predominantly based on analysis (i.e., deduction and induction) and conventional problem solving (i.e., Abduction-1), Dorst's typology clearly differentiates design thinking from other types (1997, 2006). In practice, though, this distinction is not as clear-cut as in theory:

> [...] design is not one way of thinking: it is a mix of different kinds of thinking, building as it does on induction and problem solving. It also inherently contains quite a bit of strict analytical reasoning, as rigorous deduction is needed to check if design solutions will work.
>
> (Dorst, 2011, p. 525)

WHAT	**+**	**HOW**	*leads to*	*VALUE*
(thing)		(working principles)	*frame*	(aspired)

Figure 3.5 Formula for frame form of reasoning.

The Designer Mindset

The *designer mindset* refers to the knowledge designers use *and* the ways in which they use that knowledge (Nelson & Stolterman, 2012). Both are evident in the designerly activity termed the "frame experiment" (Schōn, 1983). A frame experiment is a form of *thought experiment* in which designers imagine and consider, in more or less detail, different ways of viewing a problem, thus, generating multiple statements/frames, as noted earlier. During a frame experiment, particular constraints are brought to the foreground while others move to the background. Such an experiment can reveal both new information about a problem and gaps in designers' knowledge about that problem. Frames can also be used to suggest where design effort needs to be focused on at a given point in a project.

The frame experiment is a distinct feature of designing but may not be familiar to those who have been asked to approach primarily problems that are well-structured or solvable. "Solvable" problems are situations where (a) the answer to a problem may be discovered via sufficient analysis (Dorst, 2011; Goel, 1995), (b) the answer is embedded within the components of the problem (Archer, 1979), and (c) where one best solution to a problem exists (Petroski, 1992). None of these is true for design. Design problems are not solvable; they are only addressable and shapeable.

We will address several important aspects of designerly behavior by examining the frame experiment and demonstrating its utility in teaching design: 1) the use of *designerly tools*; 2) engagement in *design judgments* (distinct from decision making); 3) *awareness of ethical concerns* as a part of designing; and 4) use of *in-process design failure* as a means of exploring and methodologically moving through the design space, as well as iterating on one's understanding of the design process.

The Frame Experiment as a Designerly Tool

Designers do not solve problems, as we have noted. They engage with a design space, and in that space, they use *tools*, which could include methods, techniques, approaches, technological means, and theories (Stolterman et al., 2008). Tools are used to navigate, raise awareness, work through challenging tensions, and negotiate the form and structure of design outcomes. Much like a woodworker with a range of tools to shape wood in different ways, or a chef who carries a fully stocked knife roll, the designer builds a collection of external and internal tools to structure and support their design work. These tools are termed *designerly* because they afford, but do not dictate, design actions (Stolterman et al., 2008) as, for example, specific process models may do (e.g., 4C/ID model, Reigeluth & An, 2020).

As an example, Boling and Gray (2015) describe sketching as one such designerly tool that can support ID activity. Many other designerly tools exist – from evocative methods to structured toolkits; from a conceptual vocabulary that highlights the indeterminate and creative nature of design work (Yanchar et al., 2010) to means of building a shared vocabulary to communicate with diverse stakeholders (Spector, 2002). While many of these tools enjoy more currency in fields of design outside of ID, Lachheb and Boling (2018) have found empirical evidence for a designerly approach to tools and their use among instructional designers in diverse contexts.

The frame experiment is a *designerly* tool. It facilitates exploration and moving through or shaping a design space, actions more appropriate to design than fully goal-directed and stepwise problem-solving. The frame experiment supports the designer's work without guiding it, can be appreciated by the designer in multiple ways, and is not used exclusively for one specific design activity.

Building Design Judgment through Frame Experiments

Designers' activities encompass more than simple decision making. For example, multiple complicating constraints and needs within a design space have to be considered, evaluated, and prioritized, for determining possible paths forward. This requires complex and overlapping judgments to be made, which are not easily reduced to "making a decision." Nelson and Stolterman (2012) have identified 12 design judgments as "[…] essential to design. [They do] not replicate decision making but [they are] necessary" (p. 139) for doing so. In this sense, design judgments are different from design decision-making: Judgments are the means to achieve "wise action" (p. 139), or – in other words – good design decisions. The range of different judgments – studied in more detail during everyday ID practices by Gray et al. (2015) – demonstrates that the designer's engagement in judgment is continuous and layered, with non-deterministic links between judgments and decisions. Additionally, guidance for developing design judgments among ID students is discussed in Lachheb and Boling (2020).

Building Ethical Awareness through Frame Experiments

While engaging in a frame experiment, designers implicitly privilege, or foreground, certain kinds of design knowledge and constraints over others, calling into play critical and ethical concerns. In considering design alternatives, the designer must both consider their own character and values and the emergent values and constraints that are discovered throughout the frame experiment (Gray & Boling, 2016). Designers are responsible for recognizing and responding to the concerns surfaced during frame experiments; in fact, several design scholars have argued that designers must be the guarantors of their design (e.g., Cross, 2001; Lawson, 2005; Nelson & Stolterman, 2012; Petroski, 1992; Schön, 1983). The responsibility for design success or failure, and for how the design privileges certain stakeholders over others, cannot be placed elsewhere–say in a prescriptive model – than the designer.

> Designers must accept responsibility for all they design. This accountability must be an integral part of their character. Designers should be relied on to fulfill obligations, not only to their clients, but also to a higher authority, one that is concerned for the sake of others and the environment in which we all live.
>
> (Nelson & Stolterman, 2012, p. 211)

In this sense, the frame experiment allows for a safe space where questions of ethics, values, power, and privilege can be brought to the foreground and addressed early on in the design process. This not only promotes the idea that designers are the guarantors of their designs, but also brings a sense of rigor to the work that design students are about to do and for their future work once they become designers in practice, as Campbell et al. (2005) argued.

Using In-Process Design Failure (Petit Failure) in Frame Experiments

Finally, as the designer works through the frame experiment in a dialogic manner, their exploration is not always solely goal directed. In contrast, the frame experiment allows the designer to actively move about the design space as a means of understanding both the coherence of the design frame and the possibilities that may exist within that space. Thus, this movement – sometimes viewed through the lens of *ideation* or *iteration* – reveals the potential, or even the likelihood of, in-process design failure. This failure can be seen as productive and future-oriented rather than conclusive or final. We refer to this form of

24   *Elizabeth Boling et al.*

failure as *petit* failure in that it is not indicative of a damning indictment on design choices that leads to inevitable summative failure, but rather a small and often generative failure that points toward other more salient design possibilities.

Schön (1983) described design students experimenting with different design solutions so they can reframe the design problem and/or test the adequacy of their hypotheses (i.e., the working principles; the "how") of a design problem at hand. Schön did not use the term 'failure' per se. However, it does appear that such a process lends itself to the concept of design failure; design students experience *petit* in-process design failure that plays a generative role in their design process as a reflection-in-action. As Schön (1983) stated:

> The experimentation [that the design student referred to earlier in the text] has conducted prior to the design review has made him aware of a conflict of appreciations. But he does not yet perceive it as a fundamental dilemma demanding for its resolution a significant change in one or both sets of values. In order for this to happen, he would have to carry out another sort of inquiry, one that would reveal both the intractability of his dilemma and an alternative approach to overall organization of the building [he is designing].
>
> (p. 136)

Design tools – such as the frame experiment – as well as movement within the frame, design judgment, and ethical awareness, can be used to promote this form of early failure. The ultimate goal of the petit failure is understanding the broader coherence of the design space and the most productive framings of that space. This view privileges a subjective and emergent sense of design value and opportunity, rather than a rationalist vision of design that is primarily reductive and could result in the wrong type of logical reasoning.

Professional Practice Revisited

The case of Kim and her design students illustrates the frame experiment (Schön, 1983), in which we create a new view of the problem in order to move forward.

The Frame Experiment as a Designerly Tool

As one of Kim's students noted: "We plan to start with an analysis. Like the model says." The students perceive this frame experiment as unsystematic, messy, and unorganized compared to the design model they know, but the frame experiment allows them to discover facets of the design project that they had not considered – one says: "This project is going to be harder than I thought!" Engagement with the frame experiment centers the designer, not the process or a model, as responsible for a design's probable success or failure.

The Frame Experiment and Design Judgments

Design judgments are formed continuously as a means of understanding the design space – sensemaking – and design judgments support subsequent actions. The student's statements revealed their implicit design judgments. For example, when a student says, "I thought ... maybe ... it could be a workbook? I used a lot of math workbooks in school!" they evoke a deliberated off-hand design judgment, bringing previous designs to mind to match current circumstances. Another student says, "I think we need to visit an after-school program instead of a schoolteacher," a navigational design judgment – choosing an intentional path intended to move toward satisfying the design problem. Note that these judgments are shaped by core design judgments – values or thoughts that are buried deep within each individual in the form of personal beliefs (Boling et al., 2017).

The Frame Experiment and Design Ethics

One student suggested reproducing a math workbook they had seen online, without carefully regarding the context. Another is creating an app. While these ideas seem legitimate during a brainstorming activity, they highlight different levels of ethical awareness regarding potential social impacts, like budgets and accessibility. Without inspection via framing, design ideas can sound good without activating critical empathy with a target audience. Rather than rejecting these ideas, Kim treated them as frame experiments. Prompting to question feasibility in practical terms encouraged the team to consider an ethical dimension of their design ideas.

The Frame Experiment and Design Failure

Through framing, the student team speculates on who works at the after-school program, whether they are prepared to teach fractions, and how much a nine-year-old can learn independently. Such realizations prompted them to visit an after-school rather than talk to a schoolteacher. This was a petit design failure, a productive form of design failure, which opens new possibilities for design action.

Connecting Process to Practice

Implementing a Frame Experiment as a Designerly Tool

- ID instructors can plan frame experiments into design cycles as an instructional activity;
- Repeating the frame experiment multiple times is crucial to:
  a) inscribe a designer mindset;
  b) emphasize a different focus/lens each time a frame experiment is conducted.

As noted in the case study earlier, Kim is emphasizing in this frame experiment "how to get started" and "what are the preliminary ideas" students had before they get started on their project. In a future frame experiment, the focus can be on:

- The knowledge that the students acquire about the project's context (i.e., the working principle; the "how");
- How such knowledge can afford sound decisions that lead to the aspired value.

Resources Needed and Tactics to Use. Instructors should carefully allocate time and resources for this activity to be repeated throughout the term, through:

26 *Elizabeth Boling et al.*

- Constant check-ins with the students;
- Team debrief sessions;
- If a traditional textbook is used, helping students reconcile their classroom experiences with an approach prescribed by prescriptive models (for example, the team in our example did decide to conduct an analysis as a model might have prescribed but they were the owners of their decision on which form of analysis to use and more disciplined in their goal for this design action than they would have otherwise been).

Implementing Frame Experiments to Teach Design Judgments

Engaging design students in frame experiment affords them:

- The opportunity to evoke and reveal the design judgments that precede their design decisions;
- To be conscious of their design judgments.

Such design judgments, regardless of their perceived "quality," drive the design process and impact the design outcomes, even when designers claim an "objective," data-driven approach.

Discussions of design constraints during frame experiment should not be dominated by one voice, either the instructor's or any single student.

Resources Needed and Tactics to Use. One possible instructional activity to accompany the frame experiment is the design reflection:

- Such reflections will be *reflections-on-action* (Schön, 1983), where design students look back at what they experienced in the classroom with their teammates, "to make sense of what happened, what worked well, what did not work well, why taking one design approach seemed to be better than the other, etc." (Lachheb & Boling, 2020);
- In these reflections, they focus on the design judgments they heard from each other or expressed themselves.

Implementing Frame Experiments to Promote Design Ethics

One possible instructional activity that accompanies the frame experiment is asking students to respond to scenarios or context cues and ask, in an explicit manner, questions about the presented scenarios related to ethics, values, power, and privilege.

Resources Needed and Tactics to Use. Questions raised to students could be:

- Similar to what Kim asked: *"Do they have a budget? A photocopier?"*
- Additional questions: "Who will benefit from this design the most and who will be disadvantaged?" "What if there are students with learning disabilities and/or special needs?" "What if this design ends up 'on the shelf' since teachers will not buy-in into it?"

These questions can be addressed through collective and individual reflections, as they bring to the foreground ethical concerns early in the design process.

Implementing Frame Experiments to Engage in Petit Design Failure

One possible instructional activity that accompanies the frame experiment is to plan sessions when students share their early design proposals proactively, and the instructor engages with them through questions that point to "holes in their thinking."

Resources Needed and Tactics to Use. Instructors can:

- Use "What if [this] happens?" type of questions;
- Plan to share new details about the design project during the frame experiment discussion.

New details should prompt students to diverge from a certain path, come to a stop, and spend time thinking about the new path that ought to be taken. This is similar to when Kim said, "The public program here in town includes academics, but the kids actually choose their own activities based on their interests." These new details revealed to the students a new design constraint and pointed to a "hole in their thinking" when they proposed designing a math workbook, not an open-ended solution for kids' interests.

This instructional activity is best when planned and executed in early design critique sessions, where initial plans, ideas, thoughts, and processes are still being drafted and not have not been committed to. This way, design students experience petit and productive failure, not a kind of a massive failure that evokes anxiety and stress about their class performance. After all, learning experiences need to be ethically driven and motivated.

Reflections and Accounting for Project Timelines

Frequently ID classes center on one project that lasts over a term (often 16 weeks). This provides students and the instructor with ample time to practice, reflect, iterate, and, most importantly, traverse a design space in a disciplined manner. The key considerations in planning a course are:

- Providing students with the opportunity to reflect on their design work;
- Constantly visiting their design judgments, ethical awareness, and what they learned from their *petit* design failure;
- Not presenting reflections to students with the simple instruction to "think about it" or offering reflection as an arbitrary activity at one point in class;
- Carefully considering the role of the reflection as a driving force that allows students to navigate through their design project a reflection opportunity after a major design milestone is completed – for instance, when a design draft is formalized or after presenting beta testing their prototypes.

It might also be beneficial to consider a course in which:

- Reflections are crucial milestones in themselves, each following a rapid design sprint;
- Each project spans four weeks – three weeks of design work and one week of presentations/critique and reflections;
- Smaller-scale design projects, with tighter timelines, emphasizing the mastery of different design competencies in chunks, with design reflections framed as the last milestone in the design process and the beginning of the next design project. Such a design would also emphasize opportunities to practice frequent frame experiments.

References

Archer, B. (1979). Design as a discipline. *Design Studies, 1*(1), 17–20. doi:10.1016/0142-694X(79)90023-1

Boling, E., Alangari, H., Hajdu, I. M., Guo, M., Gyabak, K., Khlaif, Z., … Techawitthayachinda, R. (2017). Core judgments of instructional designers in practice. *Performance Improvement Quarterly, 30*(3), 199–219. doi:10.1002/piq.21250

Boling, E., & Gray, C. M. (2015). Designerly tools, sketching, and instructional designers and the guarantors of design. In *The design of learning experience* (pp. 109–126). Springer.

28 *Elizabeth Boling et al.*

Campbell, K., Schwier, R. A., & Kenny, R. F. (2005). Agency of the instructional designer: Moral coherence and transformative social practice. *Australasian Journal of Educational Technology, 21*(2). doi:10.14742/ajet.1337

Cross, N. (2001). Designerly ways of knowing: Design discipline versus design science. *Design Issues, 17*(3), 49–55. Retrieved from https://www.jstor.org/stable/1511801

Dorst, K. (1997). *Describing design: A comparison of paradigms.* Technische Universiteit Delft.

Dorst, K. (2006). Design problems and design paradoxes. *Design Issues, 22*(3), 4–17. doi:10.1162/desi.2006.22.3.4

Dorst, K. (2011). The core of 'design thinking' and its application. *Design Studies, 32*(6), 521–532. doi:10.1016/j.destud.2011.07.006

Goel, V. (1995). *Sketches of thought.* MIT Press.

Gray, C. M., & Boling, E. (2016). Inscribing ethics and values in designs for learning: A problematic. *Educational Technology Research and Development: ETR & D, 64*(5), 969–1001. doi:10.1007/s11423-016-9478-x

Gray, C. M., Dagli, C., Demiral-Uzan, M., Ergulec, F., Tan, V., Altuwaijri, A. A., … Boling, E. (2015). Judgment and instructional design: How ID practitioners work in practice. *Performance Improvement Quarterly, 28*(3), 25–49. doi:10.1002/piq.21198

Lachheb, A., & Boling, E. (2018). Design tools in practice: Instructional designers report which tools they use and why. *Journal of Computing in Higher Education, 30*(1), 34–54. doi:10.1007/s12528-017-9165-x

Lachheb, A., & Boling, E. (2020). The role of design judgment and reflection in instructional design. In J. K. McDonald & R. E. West (Eds.), *Design for learning: Principles processes, and praxis.* EdTech Books. Retrieved from https://edtechbooks.org/id/design_judgment

Lawson, B. (2005). *How designers think.* Routledge.

Nelson, H. G., & Stolterman, E. (2012). *The design way: Intentional change in an unpredictable world* (2nd ed.). MIT Press.

Petroski, H. (1992). *The pencil: A history of design and circumstance.* Alfred a Knopf Incorporated.

Reigeluth, C. M., & An, Y. (2020). *Merging the instructional design process with learner-centered theory: The holistic 4D model.* Routledge.

Schön, D. A. (1983). *The reflective practitioner: How professionals think in action.* Basic Books.

Smith, K. M., & Boling, E. (2009). What do we make of design? Design as a concept in educational technology. *Educational Technology,* 3–17. Retrieved from https://www.jstor.org/stable/44429817

Spector, J. M. (2002). Knowledge management tools for instructional design. *Educational Technology Research and Development, 50*(4), 37–46. Retrieved from https://www.jstor.org/stable/30220349

Stolterman, E., McAtee, J., Royer, D., & Thandapani, S. (2008). Designerly tools. *Undisciplined! Design Research Society Conference 2008, 116,* 1–14.

Yanchar, S. C., South, J. B., Williams, D. D., Allen, S., & Wilson, B. G. (2010). Struggling with theory? A qualitative investigation of conceptual tool use in instructional design. *Educational Technology Research and Development, 58*(1), 39–60. doi:10.1007/s11423-009-9129-6

4 Preparing Instructional Design Students for Reflective Practice

Jason K. McDonald

Chapter Overview

Typically, the formal processes, frameworks, and theories that characterize the field of instructional design and technology provide only a starting point in the work of expert practitioners (Ertmer et al., 2009). Professional designers tend to base decisions on reservoirs of prior experience and practical judgment that are flexible and adaptable, and that allow them to cope with the variability, nuance, and paradoxes that characterize authentic working conditions. In the literature this is known as reflective practice, or being a reflective practitioner (Schön, 1983). Reflective practitioners are "active ... agents of innovation" (Tracey et al., 2014, p. 316). They can be found "responding to complex and dynamic forces, thinking multi-dimensionally, and continually monitoring the relationship between one's goals and actions" (Rowland et al., 1992, p. 37). They solve problems and contribute toward important aims not because of their proficiency in following generalized processes, but through their sensitivity to local needs and ability to respond in whatever manner their circumstances dictate. Given the importance of these capacities in instructional design, especially when solving the difficult problems that designers often face, helping students develop into reflective practitioners should be a key outcome of instructional design education (Tracey et al., 2014). My purpose in this chapter is to provide guidance to instructional design educators in pursuit of this goal. I do this by reviewing the importance of reflective practice within professional contexts, and by describing strategies educators can use to help their students nurture the dispositions associated with reflective practice. But first, I turn to a situation that may be familiar to many readers.

Guiding Questions

1. What is reflective practice? What is a reflective practitioner?
2. Why is it important to help instructional design students become reflective practitioners?
3. What is knowing-in-action?
4. What is the difference between reflection-on-action, reflection-in-action, and reflection-for-action?
5. How can instructional design educators help their students nurture the dispositions of reflective practice?

DOI: 10.4324/9781003109938-4

30   *Jason K. McDonald*

Case Study

Not for the first time, Professor Sandra Rushton questioned whether she should be a teacher at all.

Today, it was because of what happened in her advanced ID class. These were some of the most innovative and capable students she had ever taught, but somehow, they kept disappointing their clients. Despite their excellent learner and needs analyses, and their inventive designs for learning environments, they fumbled whenever their clients responded in unexpected ways. For one group it was a sudden addition to the learner population. For another it was a client who insisted they use her favorite instructional strategy. But whatever happened, Professor Rushton could count on one of two reactions. Some students panicked and expected her solve the problem. Others tried to push through as if nothing had gone wrong at all.

Walking to her office she brooded over an email that one group, Erika and Travis, had received from their very irate client. They were designing a module to train his to process insurance claims. He had reviewed their latest prototype, and, to put it mildly, was disappointed. Erika and Travis had followed a basic, "nine events" structure: they started with a funny story to gain the learners' attention, presented the three objectives of the module, and so on. The client found this uninspiring, and even condescending. He thought the story was childish. He questioned why they made the objectives so explicit. And the criticisms went on, for three more pages. At the end, he said that if his staff used the current module, they would not learn anything at all. In fact, unless he required it, he doubted any of them would move past the first screen.

Erika and Travis were part of the "push through" crowd. They argued the client had approved their outline (and after reviewing their documentation, Professor Rushton agreed they were correct), so what right did he have to change anything now? They also maintained that they were the experts in learning, and they understood the theory, so how could he claim that their module would not produce learning? So, they were just going to deliver what they had already completed. Changing the module would require them to come up with new ideas, rewrite the content, and reshoot videos that had already been edited. And the term was almost over.

Professor Rushton was uncomfortable with their rigidity, but also recognized they were in a hard position having this feedback given at such a late stage. She did not want to endorse walking away from the problem, but also did not have any better ideas herself.

Reflective Practice – Theory and Strategy

What Professor Rushton experienced (students who have difficulty coping with the dilemmas of practice) is typical of situations encountered by educators in many fields, including design (Findeli, 2001), teacher preparation (Russell, 2005), and healthcare (Fragkos, 2016). In these fields, practitioners commonly address complex problems that not only have more than one acceptable solution, but can also be framed (defined) in multiple ways. Many problems are also novel, and resist being reduced to previously encountered forms. Stakeholders frequently expect that practitioners will be able to respond to this complexity and novelty with little time to formally analyze or evaluate alternative courses of action. In response to needs such as these, all of these disciplines (along with many others) have developed theories of reflective practice, along with strategies for helping students become more reflective practitioners.

The Theory of Reflective Practice

Contemporary discourse on reflective practice – especially in design fields – is often traced back to the work of Donald Schön (1983, 1987), with important antecedents found in the work of other 20th century scholars such as John Dewey (1933). However, more fundamentally the notion of reflective practice can be traced back to Aristotle's writings on practical judgment, where situationally appropriate actions are not defined in advance by a system of rules, but are based on the principled acumen of wise actors (Dunne, 1997). This is not to minimize Schön's impact; in particular, Schön's arguments were important at a time (the 1970s and 1980s) when many professional fields – including instructional design – were attempting to define themselves as sciences that were as technically precise as the physical sciences. Many researchers had the goal of creating dependable bodies of knowledge that practitioners could apply to achieve consistent and uniform results. Much like a chemical reaction could be depended on to always work under the proper conditions, so, too, did researchers assume they could discover the processes (such as those governing learning) that could be depended on to always produce the results they were aiming toward (such as certain types of learning outcomes). Yet, while many of those studying professional fields often viewed this goal as not only possible, but also inevitable, Schön argued that their historical failure to achieve the desired results was not due to their sciences still being in the process of maturation. Instead, he argued that the problems professionals were attempting to solve required a different type of knowledge than that produced by scientific inquiry.

What was needed, Schön (1983) argued, was for practitioners to develop an ability for "knowing-in-action" (p. 50). Knowing-in-action is a practical know-how that cannot be separated from the actual performance an activity, such as how "a tightrope walker's know-how ... lies in, and is revealed by, the way he takes his trip across the wire," or, "a big-league pitcher's know-how is in his way of pitching to a batter's weaknesses, changing his pace, or distributing his energies over the course of a game" (pp. 50–51). Schön's definition was intentionally in contrast to how practical knowledge is sometimes defined, as the translation of the intellectual content of a theoretical discipline into forms that can be used to solve practical problems (e.g., engineering as the practical application of physics, or instructional design as the practical application of the learning sciences). As Schön defined knowing-in-action, it was a type of knowledge that was somewhat independent of the technical facts, rules, or systems of a domain. One's know-how should certainly be *informed* by academic bodies of knowledge, but the know-how needed for skillful practice cannot be *reduced* to only the application of academic knowledge. Examples from instructional design might include the sense designers develop for how prepared a student population is for a particular learning activity, how open clients will be to an innovative instructional strategy, or whether the potential returns of taking a chance on an unproven approach are worth the possible risk.

Schön also argued that knowledge-in-action was developed as practitioners were *reflective* about the circumstances they encountered. In the context of professional practices, reflection can connote two, somewhat different, ways that practitioners might approach a situation. First, reflection is sometimes defined as "thinking about your own work"

32   *Jason K. McDonald*

(Lousberg et al., 2019, p. 3). The value of this definition lies in its sensibility; when someone encounters a difficult or unfamiliar situation, it seems reasonable to suggest they should pause and examine (or reflect) on their options for moving forward. This form of reflection might be analogous to someone finding her way around an unfamiliar city during her first trip away from home. It would not be out of the ordinary to find a tourist stopping at a street corner, consulting a map, looking for landmarks, or carefully checking street numbers on the side of a building, before making a decision about what direction to follow next.

But while at times reflective practitioners are certainly found stopping in their tracks and explicitly considering various options, more often reflective practice suggests a more seamless approach to finding one's way around. In this sense, reflective practice is comprised of the countless moments of adjustment that professionals continuously make in response to small saliences they notice in their situation – details of which they may only have the slightest conscious awareness. Schön (1983) described this as "finding the groove" (p. 54), such as what happens "when good jazz musicians improvise together" (p. 55). Such musicians "manifest a 'feel for' their material and they make on-the-spot adjustments to the sounds they hear. Listening to one another and to themselves, they feel where the music is going and adjust their playing accordingly" (p. 55). Describing a musician as reflective does not mean they stop and think about what note to play next. It means they are in tune with the situation, reflecting back through their music the opportunities their collaborators offer. Similarly, an experienced tourist might find her way around by noticing environmental cues – street signs, patterns of traffic, and so on – using them to make reasoned judgments about the next stage of her route, and hardly pausing at all before turning a corner to continue her journey. Being a reflective practitioner is often found in this space, a type of improvisation where one recognizes possibilities as they arise, but where action is rarely preceded by rational, conscious decision making (Mortier & Anderson, 2017). Reflective practice is therefore frequently a stance that relies on a refined sensitivity for detail so one can discriminate more carefully, more than it is about deliberate, studied contemplation (Parrish, 2012).

Both types of reflection, however, are important in generating one's knowing-in-action. Frequently at first, but even after people develop more expertise, their knowing-in-action breaks down when they encounter unexpected, unusual, or particularly difficult situations. Either immediately, or at some convenient time afterwards, they can pause to "[think] back on what [they] have done in order to discover how [their] knowing-in-action may have contributed to [the] unexpected outcome" (Schön, 1987, p. 26). This type of reflection (often called reflection-on-action) has a parallel to the more contemplative type of reflective practice described above; practitioners consciously weigh alternative courses of action and explicitly decide what they might have done differently to better cope with what happened. Additionally, people might reflect on what they are experiencing while they are still acting ("reflection-in-action," according to Schön, p. 26). Their reflections might be deliberative, similar to when they reflect-on-action. But often they will not so much take time to frame a problem and search for a solution, but use the unusual circumstance to sharpen their abilities for noticing possibilities already available, adjusting their own activities to better align with what's available, and sensing whether the result is more desirable.

Building upon Schön's framing, other scholars have also proposed that one can also develop practical know-how through still another form of reflection, "reflection-for-action." In this form of reflection, people "[analyze] events and [draw] conclusions that give [them] insight into future decision points" (Killion & Todnem, 1991, p. 15).

Strategies that Nurture Reflective Practice

Instructional design educators can draw upon a body of techniques from a number of professional fields to help their students develop these reflective dispositions. Common strategies include:

- Modeling: Demonstrating how a designer might approach problems in a reflective way. Modeling for reflection also includes a think-aloud aspect where the instructor/model articulates why certain actions are, or are not, being considered, as well as their initial judgments of the efficacy of their choices (Schön, 1987). Level of difficulty: Simple;
- Reflective writing (or other forms of expression): Providing students formal prompts or other guidelines as scaffolds to guide their personal reflection process. As students articulate challenges and how they responded, they come to see themselves as legitimate, reflective practitioners (Tracey et al., 2014; Tracey & Hutchinson, 2016). Level of difficulty: Simple;
- Critique: The evaluation of students' design process and product. Critiques can be formative or summative; they can also range from informal conversations to formal events at the conclusion of a project or achievement of a milestone. Critics can be instructors, other students (also called peer critiques), or outside experts (Hokanson, 2012). Level of difficulty: Simple to get started; more formal critiques may introduce additional planning and complexity;
- Precedent: Drawing upon the design knowledge provided by studying concrete examples of prior designs. Precedent informs reflection by highlighting aspects of problems, solutions, or processes that designers might not see when only contemplating a situation (Boling, 2020). Level of difficulty: Simple to moderate;
- Project-based assignments: The complex and open-ended character of projects mimics the situations in which reflective practice authentically occurs (Ayas & Zeniuk, 2001). Level of difficulty: Moderate to complex; good project-based assignments require planning and iterative evaluation;
- Studio-based learning: An educational pattern found in many design and artistic fields, that relies on particular combinations of the strategies described above to form a culture of learning that encourages reflective practice (Cennamo, 2016; McDonald, 2018). Level of difficulty: Complex; requires more intense planning, and often includes the use of dedicated or specialized facilities.

To a certain extent, all of these strategies rely on more explicit, deliberative reflection than is often found in authentic reflective practice. So, educators should also be mindful that their goal is to support students' practice to the point that they (the students) can fluidly discriminate and respond without the need to stop and determine which rules or principles to apply next. This happens as students are given many opportunities to practice, that differ in both significant and minute details, so they can learn to distinguish between situationally unique saliences, and as well as the emotions or other embodied reactions that accompany various performances and associated outcomes (Dreyfus, 2014).

Whatever techniques are used, however, they should be integrated into a curriculum in a meaningful way, not merely provided as an add-on or supplement. As Russell (2005) noted, "fostering reflective practice requires far more than telling people to reflect and then simply hoping for the best" (p. 203). Relying on Schön's theoretical framing, Russell further suggested that teaching reflective practice could include four phases:

34   *Jason K. McDonald*

- Encountering a puzzling event;
- Reframing the event to develop a novel course of action;
- Exploring the new perspective in action;
- Assessing the impact of the reframed approach.

(see pp. 200–202)

Combining Russell's phases with the three forms of reflection (on, in, and for-action) results in a 4×3 matrix, as illustrated in Figure 4.1. This matrix can be used for planning how to meaningfully integrate strategies of reflective practice into an educational setting.

An example of how the matrix can be used might start with an instructor designing a project-based assignment to include a twist or an unexpected challenge (a puzzling event). She can plan a reflection-in-action scaffold to accompany the twist, perhaps in the form of being prepared to model various saliences she sees in the situation if a student has a difficult time coping with the challenge. She can also include a reflection-on-action activity to help students reframe the event, in the form of a peer critique guided by questions that allow them to see the challenge from different perspectives. Students' growing capacity for reflection-in-action is further nurtured as they explore the new possibilities opened up by the challenge. The activity then concludes as students reflect-for-action, perhaps in the form of a writing assignment where they assess the impact of the design decisions they made in response to the twist (see Figure 4.2). For purposes of illustration this example includes all of the rows and columns in the matrix; however, there is no need for instructors to be this comprehensive in their own planning. When starting out they may choose to begin with only one or two of the phases. They can then add more complexity as they gain more experience.

Professional Practice Revisited

It took a few days to figure out a plan, but Professor Rushton thought it would work. It was based on her fundamental goal that by completing her course students became more independent, reflective practitioners. So whatever Ericka and Travis did, Professor Rushton's priority was that they meaningfully reflected on the experience. The core of her plan was to help them break out of their instinct to charge ahead, and be more thoughtful about what they might learn for their future practice.

Because Professor Rushton was teaching a studio course she had freedom to adjust the daily schedule as new needs arose. As students arrived, she told them it would be a project workday. Then she sought out Erika and Travis. She critiqued their design process using the concept of knowing-in-action as a foundational standard, and pointed out how they were assuming their academic knowledge of instructional design was all that was necessary to produce a high-quality product. While their current dilemma was certainly related to the design problem they were attempting to solve, their explicit knowledge would not be enough to help them navigate the challenge successfully. They also needed to recognize situational cues concerning how to apply what they knew. Professor Rushton asked Erika and Travis to consider how successful they would be as instructional designers if they produced theoretically sound courses that their clients refused to use.

Professor Rushton next asked Erika and Travis to reframe the event they had experienced. Rather than blaming their client, she asked them to reflect. Were there any clues in their client's emails that could have helped them predict that something like this might have happened? She modeled clues they could look for by telling a story of one of her own client relationships that had fallen apart early in her career. She described how when she reviewed her project, she could see that while her client had been telling her yes, at the same time he had also been asking lots of questions that indicated he did not fully understand the proposed solution. Maybe Erika and Travis were experiencing something similar?

Professor Rushton also asked the students to explore new possibilities for moving forward in a manner that did not demand they get their own way. It was true the term was coming to an end, so they might not have time to respond to all the feedback from their client. But was there anything they could do? Might they could find a way to turn the problem into an opportunity? Could they think of a simple, yet valuable, idea that could be developed in the time they had left?

Finally, Professor Rushton offered to change the way she would grade Erika's and Travis's project. Originally, she had planned that the client's assessment would determine one-third of their grade. But Professor Rushton offered to temper this. She still wanted the client's input. But if each student completed a reflection assignment that assessed the impact of the new ideas they developed, she would decrease the weight of his evaluation. She emphasized this could be a learning experience. If Erika and Travis could find something that would help them be better designers in the future, that was more important than the actual outcomes of the project. They were students, after all, and she wanted her class to be a place that allowed them to turn their failures into something productive.

	Reflection-on-action	Reflection-on-action	Reflection-on-action
Encountering puzzling events			
Reframing events			
Exploring new perspectives			
Assessing impact			

Figure 4.1 A matrix for planning reflective strategies.

36 Jason K. McDonald

	Reflection-on-action	Reflection-on-action	Reflection-on-action
Encountering puzzling events		Project-based assignment with a twist, accompanied by instructor modeling of how to cope	
Reframing events	Peer-critique based on questions to see project challenge from different prespectives		
Exploring new perspectives		Student exploration of paths opened up by project challenge	
Assessing impact			Writing assignment where students reflect on the impact of their design decisions

Figure 4.2 A completed matrix for an example course.

Connecting Process to Practice

1. Consider the three types of reflection (on, in, and for-action). How have each of them played a role in your own practice as a teacher? As a designer?
2. How can your experiences as a reflective practitioner inform how you teach reflective practice to your students?
3. Observe an expert in a performance-based field (perhaps another teacher, or maybe an athlete, musician, or craftsperson). Take note of moments where they seem to be explicitly making decisions, or implicitly moving down one possible path instead of another;
4. After your observation, ask them to reflect on how conscious their deliberations were in those moments. Would you characterize what they told you as reflection-on-action, reflection-in-action, or reflection-for-action?
5. How can what you learned from this exercise inform how you teach reflective practice to your students?

References

Ayas, K., & Zeniuk, N. (2001). Project-based learning: Building communities of reflective practitioners. *Management Learning, 32*(1), 61–76.

Boling, E. (2020). The nature and use of precedent in designing. In J. K. McDonald & R. E. West (Eds.), *Design for learning: Principles, processes, and praxis.* EdTech Books. Retrieved from https://edtechbooks.org/id/precedent

Cennamo, K. (2016). What is studio? In E. Boling, R. A. Schwier, C. M. Gray, K. M. Smith, & K. Campbell (Eds.), *Studio teaching in higher education: Selected design dases* (pp. 248–259). Routledge.

Dewey, J. (1933). *How we think: A restatement of the relation of reflective thinking to the educative process.* D. C. Heath.

Dreyfus, H. L. (2014). *Skillful coping: Essays on the phenomenology of everyday perception and action* (Ed. M. A. Wrathall). Oxford University Press.

Dunne, J. (1997). *Back to the rough ground: Practical judgment and the lure of technique.* University of Notre Dame Press.

Ertmer, P. A., York, C. S., & Gedik, N. (2009). Learning from the pros: How experienced designers translate instructional design models into practice. *Educational Technology, 49*(1), 19–27.

Findeli, A. (2001). Rethinking design education for the 21st century: Theoretical, methodological, and ethical discussion. *Design Issues, 17*(1), 5–17.

Fragkos, K. C. (2016). Reflective practice in healthcare education: An umbrella review. *Education Sciences, 6*(3). doi:10.3390/educsci6030027

Hokanson, B. (2012). The design critique as a model for distributed learning. In L. Moller & J. Huett (Eds.), *The next generation of distance education: Unconstrained learning* (pp. 71–83). Springer-Verlag.

Killion, J. P., & Todnem, G. R. (1991). A process for personal theory building. *Educational Leadership, 48*(6), 14–16.

Lousberg, L., Rooij, R., Jansen, S., van Dooren, E., Heintz, J., & van der Zaag, E. (2019). Reflection in design education. *International Journal of Technology and Design Education.* doi:10.1007/s10798-019-09532-6

McDonald, J. K. (2018). The instructional design studio as an example of model-centered instruction. *Journal of Applied Instructional Design, 7*(2), 5–16. doi:10.28990/jaid2018.072003

Mortier, T., & Anderson, D. (2017). Understanding tacit knowledge in decision making. In D. Jaziri-Bouagina & G. L. Jamil (Eds.), *Handbook of research on tacit knowledge management for organizational success* (pp. 418–435). IGI Global. doi:10.4018/978-1-5225-2394-9.ch016

Parrish, P. (2012). What does a connoisseur connaît? Lessons for appreciating learning experiences. In S. B. Fee & B. R. Belland (Eds.), *The role of criticism in understanding problem solving: Honoring the work of John C. Belland* (pp. 43–53). Springer.

Rowland, G., Fixl, A., & Yung, K. (1992). Educating the reflective designer. *Educational Technology, 32*(12), 36–44.

Russell, T. (2005). Can reflective practice be taught? *Reflective Practice, 6*(2), 199–204. doi:10.1080/14623940500105833

Schön, D. A. (1983). *The reflective practitioner: How professionals think in action.* Basic Books, Inc.

Schön, D. A. (1987). *Educating the reflective practitioner: Toward a new design for teaching and learning in the professions.* Jossey-Bass.

Tracey, M. W., & Hutchinson, A. (2016). Uncertainty, reflection, and designer identity development. *Design Studies, 42*, 86–109. doi:10.1016/j.destud.2015.10.004

Tracey, M. W., Hutchinson, A., & Grzebyk, T. Q. (2014). Instructional designers as reflective practitioners: Developing professional identity through reflection. *Educational Technology Research and Development, 62*(3), 315–334. https://doi.org/10.1007/s11423-014-9334-9

5 Creativity and Design Thinking
Crucial Mindsets in Instructional Design Education

William Cain and Danah Henriksen

Chapter Overview

This chapter examines the role of creativity and design thinking in instructional design, and how these concepts can be enacted and fostered in instructional design programs and training.

Guiding Questions

1. What are the defining characteristics of creativity and design thinking?
2. What roles do creativity and design thinking play in instructional design?
3. How can they be fostered in instructional design education?

Case Study

In this case, we discuss changes to an EdD course on Instructional Design Application in a College of Education at a research university. The course was scheduled for revising and updating to reflect a shift in program focus from Instructional Technologies to Learning, Design, & Technology. EdD students who enrolled in the course were typically in-service teachers and professionals in educational contexts familiar with basic principles of instructional design. The faculty member in charge of revising and teaching the course was interested in design and incorporating new opportunities for student creativity, collaboration, and design thinking.

The instructor identified several major course elements he wanted to change. For example, he wanted to avoid having students engage in semester-long ID projects that can feel tedious or repetitive over time. He felt having the students engage in several smaller ID projects over the semester would provide them with greater variety in addressing different instructional design contexts. He also wanted to avoid complications that seemed to arise with the use of outside "clients," individuals outside the class who were meant to provide ID projects and supervision for the students. Conversations with students who took part in past iterations of the course found that while some had positive experiences, many of them were dissatisfied because they felt too much time was spent trying to communicate with the outside clients to get necessary project information and guidance. Too often, the students reported, the outside

DOI: 10.4324/9781003109938-5

clients were slow to provide the information or provided incomplete information that would cause anxiety due to delays, miscommunication, and missed deadlines.

The instructor felt that the types of ID projects the students worked on and the variations between the students' learning experiences needed to be addressed in a new course design. For example, he wanted to give the students more opportunities to think creatively about the different projects they would work on, to become more fluent in different ID contexts, and to practice flexibility and adaptability when designing their solutions. He also wanted to incorporate elements of social constructivism by providing the students opportunities for collaboration, negotiation, and empathy in safe and constructive design environments.

So, what course design strategies could help him achieve all of that? Better yet, how could he employ his own creativity and design thinking to bring out those same qualities in his students?

Creativity – often defined as an ability to devise ideas, products, artifacts, or solutions that are relatively new and effective – is a valuable commodity (Runco & Jaeger, 2012). The value of this creative thinking is present across a range of disciplines, but most notably design-related fields, such as instructional design (Clinton & Hokanson, 2012). For most people, thinking back to any instructional experience they have had in their life, there is often a sense of being inspired, impressed, and even amazed at the creativity on the part of the instructor. Yet, even a brief review of existing research and practitioner articles on the state of instructional design programs reveal concerns about the lack of training in creativity as part of the curriculum (Yocum, 2015). With so many instructional designers creating innovative learning experiences, in a wide variety of educational contexts, how can creativity not be a part of the instructional design curriculum?

Part of the answer lies in a long running tension between two major aspects of instructional design: Analyzing and planning for the needs of learners, and designing and developing instructional solutions to meet those needs. The analysis and planning aspect of instructional design tends to be process oriented. Indeed, design models or strategies like ADDIE (Analysis, Design, Development, Implementation, and Evaluation) emphasize a staged, methodical (process) approach and are meant to help designers break down projects into manageable steps or stages. Formal activities like front-end analysis are meant to break things up even further to give designers the means to comprehensively examine the many contextual factors that can and/or should be taken into account in the design. Given the exacting, sometimes formulaic, and somewhat scientific nature of the analysis and planning aspect of instructional design, it is not surprising that creativity often slips into the background of the work of instructional designers.

The debate between the use of specified processes and development of creativity has been a running theme in instructional design (ID) education and training for many years (see Rowland, 1992). Embedded in this debate is the concern that a strictly process-oriented approach to instructional design education can lead to gaps in what ID students learn in training and their activities, responsibilities, and experiences in real-world practice (Carr-Chellman & Rowland, 2016). In fact, in a seminal study on the practices of working instructional designers, Rowland (1992) found that many ID professionals use formal design models sporadically and often only certain parts of a model. In other words, the real-world work experiences of an instructional designer may not involve the use of formal design models as instructional design programs might have us believe (York & Ertmer, 2016). This theme has similarly played out in other research over the years, in advocating for a case-based approach to helping designers balance theoretical knowledge with practice-based flexibility (McDonald & Yanchar, 2020). Many instructional design programs now recognize they should pay as much attention to fostering creative ID mindsets when educating their students as they do reviewing traditional ID models and processes. While sometimes fruitful, a strictly process-oriented approach to instructional design education often simulates only part of the overall responsibilities instructional designers take on in real-world situations (Stefaniak et al., 2020).

We argue that while process models have their value and can provide useful foundational knowledge for ID students, they are also restrictive and limiting if not paired with a mindset for creative flexibility and openness, as well as a 'designerly' approach to ID processes. Such process models can provide ID learners with a sense of the building blocks of the field of instructional design. Yet, real-world learning or course design situations are complex and contextual. Thus, they require creativity to know how to craft novel and effective learning experiences or course designs, or work with different faculty needs, concerns, or challenges. In essence, the models can provide those building blocks, but a designer must be comfortable in knowing how to build different creations with them, how to rearrange or rethink them, and what blocks to use or not, depending on situational needs.

We will discuss theoretical background on creativity to offer an understanding of the mindset that undergirds creative thinking. We later connect this to the creative fluency that would support the training of instructional designers who are prepared for the complexity of real-world educational design tasks and instantiate this in the case setting noted above.

On Creativity: Characteristics and Research Perspectives

The value of creativity in education is inarguably central to developing learning experiences that are engaging and effective (Henriksen & Mishra, 2015), and this has obvious relevance to instructional design. Creativity is a vast area of research though, even within education. So, it is useful to understand what we mean in focusing on a mindset for creativity.

Although creativity is often thought of as subjective, most research defines it through a few key components. First, creativity involves the production of something that is novel – it generates something that either did not exist before or is relatively (even slightly in some cases) new for its context. This is often the case in a new or revised course design situation. Cropley (2001) asserts, however, that a novel idea with no potential use cannot be taken as "creative" because novelty does not guarantee that something will be effective. So creative outcomes (e.g., ideas, processes, or products – in this case course designs or presentations of learning experiences) should be "effective" – or useful, logical, understandable, or of some value to others.

Existing creativity research describes traits or characteristics that are associated with a creative mindset (Runco, 2014). For example, a tendency toward openness is important in order to support adaptability and the ability to see new possibilities. Similarly, flexibility and fluency are traits or habits of mind that describe how creative people can adapt to change, and come up with ideas and solutions (Karakelle, 2009). Extant research has identified habits of mind (or orientations) that reliably correlate with creativity, including flexibility, open-mindedness, tolerance for ambiguity, intellectual risk-taking and willingness to "play" with ideas or details, or tinker with plans and designs (Prabhu et al., 2008). Many scholars note that adopting or practicing habits of mind like flexibility and openness can influence creative skill growth and performance (Karwowski, 2014). Thus, creativity need not be seen as a fixed trait, but rather it is a mental orientation to the new, to flexible and adaptable thinking and an openness to possibilities as well as a willingness to rethink existing ideas.

While there may be other traits or habits of a creative mindset, some of the most critical ones are also those which students can learn and improve on, such as flexibility, open-mindedness, willingness to try new things and intellectual play or risk-taking. Therefore, we also note the utility of design thinking skills as a possible frame for enacting creativity.

On Design Thinking: A 'Designerly' Perspective

Instructional design projects and contexts often require flexibility and openness on the part of designers and stakeholders because they often deal with contexts, artifacts, and objectives that initially may be only loosely defined. As Stefaniak, Reese, & McDonald (2020) note, "A key skill for new Instructional Designers (IDs) is the ability to embrace project constraints, working among changing project expectations, and interacting with multiple stakeholders on a variety of projects" (Stefaniak, Reese, & McDonald, 2020).

To consider why and how design mindsets are valuable to instructional design practices, it is useful to understand the utility of design as a method and way of thinking, as well as its own creative nature. Design is neither purely an art nor a science – rather it embodies its own space, blending the two in its own ways of knowing. It is not art because designers must not only consider aesthetics but also practical goals such as utility, influence, communication, or social significance (Frascara, 1988). And design is not science because its goal is not to discover generalizable knowledge, but to work in ultimate particulars (Stolterman, 2008, p. 59). Thus, it is an integrative discipline, as Buchanan (1992) argues that designers select and integrate relevant knowledge as needed in complex problems, contexts, or situations. Because of this integration, Buchanan described design as the "new liberal arts of technological culture." And in this, a design focused mindset sits well with the complex problem-solving or goal-oriented real-world learning design tasks that instructional designers use.

Defining a design mindset is a complex endeavor and involves more than we could cover in this chapter. Rather, we would advocate for developing a sense of what Cross (2001) termed as 'designerly thinking' which aligns with many of the characteristics of creativity that we have already noted. However, it also suggests a kind of design-minded orientation to the world that emphasizes empathy, visualization, problem framing (and re-framing) skills, and a willingness to create and try prototypes and move forward from what is learned through these (Dorst, 2011, 2015).

Therefore, we assert that in pairing the development of creativity with a design mindset, instructional design faculty are well positioned to prepare new instructional designers for the complex and variable range of learning design situations that they face. We return to the case outlined at the beginning of this chapter, to help instantiate these ideas within an exemplar.

Professional Practice Revisited

Having covered the characteristics of creativity and design thinking, let's return to the case of designing for a graduate course on applied instructional design.

Base Course Elements

In his initial needs analysis of the course, the instructor (first author) already identified a number of pedagogical elements he wanted in his new course design. These elements were chosen based on the affordances they provided to support and foster creativity and design thinking opportunities and interactions. They include:

- Basis in social constructivism;
- Collaboration between students;
- Closed communication (no 3rd party "clients");
- Real-world examples (not text-book case studies);
- Multiple small ID projects (as opposed to one semester-long project).

Given those elements as starting points, the instructor began to imagine a course structure that would allow students to engage with real-world design cases that were relevant to their own professional practice without the need to work with people outside the course. It seemed logical that these cases should come from the students themselves, since many of them already worked as teachers and/or instructional designers in their professional lives. The instructor also wanted elements and opportunities for the social construction of new knowledge and growth, as well as collaboration among students, so it seemed logical to break the students into teams and have them work on several projects over the course of the semester.

Intra-teamwork Dynamics: Adopting Instructional Design Roles

The instructor noted that the course had 12 students enrolled that semester, which accommodated 4 teams of 3 students each. To provide a sense of structure, the instructor decided to designate roles within the teams that correspond with traditional roles in instructional design work: Stakeholder Leaders, Design Leaders, and Support Leaders. During the course, students would be asked to engage in extended role-playing exercises with their peers and the instructor by assuming each of these 3 roles during the semester. This notion of role playing is essential to the design-centered notion of empathy or perspective taking – e.g., that instructors and teams must try on different perspectives in order to see beyond their own and identify new possibilities. The instructor then imagined how the students would interact with one another in their teams – Figure 5.1 illustrates the intended team dynamics and responsibilities.

Inter-team Interactions: Negotiating ID Proposals and Solutions

Seeing the balance of teams, the instructor then imagined how the course design could be enhanced to allow for student interactions not just within teams but between teams as well. He decided that for each project period, each team would assume the role

Creativity and Design Thinking 43

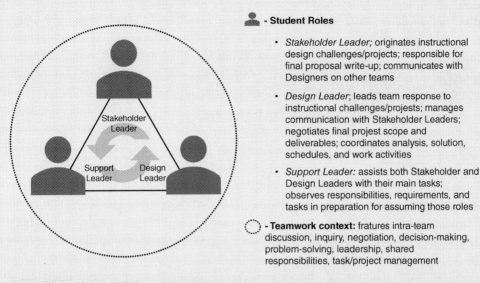

Figure 5.1 Intra-team structure and dynamics for Stakeholder, Design, and Support Roles.

of a Stakeholder Team that was responsible for developing and proposing an instructional design project/challenge for which another team would design a response or solution. At the same time, each team also assumed the role of a Design Team that would address an instructional design project/challenge proposed by another team (see Figure 5.2 for a visualization of the inter-team roles and interactions).

The instructor saw many opportunities for student creativity and design thinking embedded in this new course design. For example, when acting in the Stakeholder role, students would need to keep in mind project constraints, such as the time required for completion (4 weeks) and the type of expertise available to the receiving Design Team. This meant learning to create and craft Stakeholder proposals that

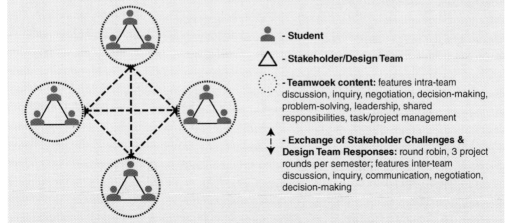

Figure 5.2 Inter-team interactions during design challenge/project rounds.

were more focused on specific design issues, more detailed in their descriptions, and hence more likely to meet with successful completion.

To provide additional opportunities for open-ended problem solving, open-mindedness, and flexibility, the instructor would instruct both Stakeholders and Design Teams to negotiate on both the scope of the proposals and the types of deliverables that would satisfy the proposal requirements. As Kim (2015) notes, "Instructional design practice in the real world, however, is largely about negotiation – that is, addressing emerging design constraints. The process is likely to be externalized via dialogues between instructional designers and stakeholders" (Kim, 2015, p. 27). By requiring students to role-play in simulated negotiations between Stakeholders and Design Teams, the new course design could better reflect the back-and-forth that often arises in the early phases of instructional design planning and development.

Concluding negotiations, project periods would end with Design Teams submitting their final products to the Stakeholder Teams for review. Stakeholders would be required to write a brief evaluation of the final product, gauging its effectiveness in meeting the proposal objectives and offering constructive insights and lessons learned for future projects. By the end of all 3 project periods and over the course of the semester, students and their teams would have:

- Created and refined 3 Stakeholder project proposals (1 per student);
- Created and designed 3 Design Team responses/solutions (again, 1 per student);
- Supported the creation of other team members' proposals and design solutions;
- Created a shared team Design Journal that chronicles their discussions, negotiations, brainstorming sessions, designs, decision-making, and problem-solving activities;
- Written 3 self-reflections on their learning experiences and insights from each project period;
- And written a final reflection on their overall growth and development as instructional designers.

Outcomes and Lessons Learned

Final student reflections from this course design were highly informative. They indicated that students found changing their leadership roles (Stakeholder, Design Team, Support) for each design challenge round helped them develop a heightened understanding and appreciation for the different responsibilities and actions required for each role. By assuming the different leadership roles, a number of students claimed they developed greater empathy for different perspectives in the ID process. This aligns with existing research which has found that building empathy through perspective taking is a useful approach to expanding creativity (Wang et al., 2017). In particular, students expressed a greater appreciation for the complexities and ambiguities that often characterize initial Stakeholder conceptualizations and proposals. Having to craft their own proposals and then negotiate their final product outcomes seem to help these students cultivate more open-mindedness, flexibility, and adaptability in finding creative and effective solutions – all essential skills in developing their professional creativity.

The student reflections also indicated students found the act of negotiation to be a helpful format for discussing Stakeholders needs and goals while keeping in mind the strengths and limitations of Design Teams. From a social constructivist perspective, the different teams were able to engage in constructing mutual understanding of particular ID challenges, and then apply this understanding to the creation of new and effective strategies related to those challenges. Negotiation also provided the different teams and their respective leaders opportunities to think objectively about not just their capabilities as instructional designers, but also their responsibilities as stakeholders and project managers. Likewise, a number of students said as Design Team leaders, they had become more insightful in probing and getting to understand the exact needs and aspirations of different Stakeholders. Negotiations often involved extensive back-and-forth communication marked by knowledgeable discussions of course concepts and theories, a developing sense of comradery, empathy, open-mindedness, and adaptability on both sides of the ID process. All of these elements should be considered essential to fostering greater creativity and learner autonomy among ID students seeking a better understanding of ID craft from multiple perspectives (Matthews et al., 2017).

Connecting Process to Practice

The case in this chapter describes a course structure that would foster interactions and opportunities for creativity and designerly thinking among student instructional designers. The design emphasizes the use of student teams, intra- and inter-team dynamics, role playing, working within design constraints, and negotiations to foster creativity and shared sense-making. The following questions and activity are meant to help further the discussion and help us explore how creativity and designerly thinking can inform learning and growth in instructional design programs.

1. In the case described in this chapter, negotiation played an important part in the design interactions among students. What are some other forms of interaction that could be substituted for negotiation? How would these interactions support creativity and design thinking at the individual student level? At the team level?
2. Further, mindsets and skills for creativity and design thinking are central to the notions that we advance for professional practice in instructional design. What other types of approaches or activities might be appropriate in this course context to foster creativity and design thinking among instructional design students?
3. In having students assume different leadership roles (i.e., Stakeholder Leader, Design Team Leader, Support Leader) throughout the course, the instructor sought to create a balanced structure for exploring and engaging in different perspectives. How do you think adopting different roles might help students to think creatively about process and performance in ID contexts?
4. This chapter takes note of the tension between using structured models and working to develop the flexibility and creativity of ID students as needed in their professional roles and futures. What are some ways that we might manage or address this tension

46 *William Cain and Danah Henriksen*

in courses which need to both use or apply models and address the ability to move beyond them when exercising creativity?

5. Wilson and Thompson (2014) describe a classic problem-solving scenario in which two sisters are vying for possession of a single orange. When asked to devise a solution to accommodate both sisters, many students will propose cutting the orange in half without investigating the different reasons why the sisters want the orange (one wants only the peel, the other wants just the juice) and how a negotiated solution might become a win-win for both parties. The "2 Sisters and an Orange" scenario is used to help students better understand how investigation, empathetic outlook, problem framing, ideating on solutions, and negotiation can lead to creative solutions that achieve higher satisfaction levels than more obvious approaches. As a creative exercise, try designing your own scenario that requires students to investigate competing objectives, gather information, and come up with solutions that satisfy all parties involved.

References

Buchanan, R. (1992). Wicked problems in design thinking. *Design Issues, 8*(2), 5–21. doi:10.2307/1511637

Carr-Chellman, A. A., & Rowland, G. (Eds.). (2016). *Issues in technology, learning, and instructional design: Classic and contemporary dialogues.* Taylor & Francis.

Clinton, G., & Hokanson, B. (2012). Creativity in the training and practice of instructional designers: The design/creativity loops model. *Educational Technology Research and Development, 60*(1), 111–130.

Cropley, A. J. (2001). *Creativity in education & learning: A guide for teachers and educators.* Psychology Press.

Cross, N. (2001). Designerly ways of knowing: Design discipline versus design science. *Design Issues, 17*(3), 49–55.

Dorst, K. (2011). The core of 'design thinking' and its application. *Design Studies, 32*(6), 521–532. doi:10.1016/j.destud.2011.07.006

Dorst, K. (2015). Frame creation and design in the expanded field. *She Ji: The Journal of Design, Economics, and Innovation, 1*(1), 22–33. doi:10.1016/j.sheji.2015.07.003

Frascara, J. (1988). Graphic design: Fine art or social science? *Design Issues, 5*(1), 18–29.

Henriksen, D., & Mishra, P. (2015). We teach who we are. *Teachers College Record, 117*(7), 1–46.

Karakelle, S. (2009). Enhancing fluent and flexible thinking through the creative drama process. *Thinking Skills and Creativity, 4*(2), 124–129.

Karwowski, M. (2014). Creative mindsets: Measurement, correlates, consequences. *Psychology of Aesthetics, Creativity, and the Arts, 8*(1), 62.

Kim, S. M. (2015). How do we train instructional designers? Instructional design as negotiation. *Educational Technology, 55*(4), 26–30.

Matthews, M. T., Williams, G. S., Yanchar, S. C., & McDonald, J. K. (2017). Empathy in distance learning design practice. *TechTrends, 61*(5), 486–493.

McDonald, J. K., & Yanchar, S. C. (2020). Towards a view of originary theory in instructional design. *Educational Technology Research and Development*, 1–19.

Prabhu, V., Sutton, C., & Sauser, W. (2008). Creativity and certain personality traits: Understanding the mediating effect of intrinsic motivation. *Creativity Research Journal, 20*(1), 53–66.

Rowland, G. (1992). What do instructional designers actually do? An initial investigation of expert practice. *Performance Improvement Quarterly, 5*(2), 65–86. doi:10.1111/j.1937-8327.1992.tb00546.x

Runco, M. A. (2014). *Creativity: Theories and themes: Research, development, and practice.* Elsevier.

Runco, M. A., & Jaeger, G. J. (2012). The standard definition of creativity. *Creativity Research Journal, 24*(1), 92–96.

Stefaniak, J., Reese, R. M., & McDonald, J. K. (2020). Design considerations for bridging the gap between instructional design pedagogy and practice. *The Journal of Applied Instructional Design, 9*(3). doi:10.51869/93jsrmrjkmd

Stolterman, E. (2008). The nature of design practice and implications for interaction design research. *International Journal of Design, 2*(1), 55–65.

Wang, J., Zhang, Z., & Jia, M. (2017). Understanding how leader humility enhances employee creativity: The roles of perspective taking and cognitive reappraisal. *The Journal of Applied Behavioral Science, 53*(1), 5–31.

Wilson, E., & Thompson, L. (2014). Creativity and negotiation research: The integrative potential. *International Journal of Conflict Management, 25*(4), 359–386. doi:10.1108/IJCMA-05-2014-0033

Yocum, K. A. (2015). *Design creativity: Using Agile principles in instructional design for online learning* (Ph.D. dissertation). ProQuest Dissertations & Theses Global Database.

York, C. S., & Ertmer, P. A. (2016). Examining instructional design principles applied by experienced designers in practice. *Performance Improvement Quarterly, 29*(2), 169–192.

6 Learning Experience Design in Practice
"Theoretically, We Did Everything Right"

Matthew Schmidt

Chapter Overview

This chapter explores the emerging focus area of learning experience design (LXD) in the field of learning/instructional design and technology (LIDT) and how associated methods and processes might be applied in practice. Specifically, I highlight how a learning design team engaged in a successful redesign process using a range of human-centered methods and processes that are commonly applied in traditions outside of LIDT such as human–computer interaction (HCI) and user-centered design (UCD), but are less common in our field. I present a brief case study in which a team of learning designers were confronted with unsatisfactory learning outcomes after learners had used an online learning environment to help them solve a sales management problem. The case highlights how the design team first identified design flaws and then applied LXD methods to remedy these flaws, with a specific focus on the design processes that guided this work. I detail how we applied in our own practice a variety of methods associated with LXD, including iterative design, rapid prototyping, analytics, and usability testing. I then briefly present outcomes reported in previously published papers (Schmidt & Tawfik, 2018; Tawfik et al., 2020). The chapter concludes with questions to guide discussion and application of the terms, methods, and theoretical framing presented. Recommendations for further readings are provided.

Guiding Questions

1. How does the case presented in this chapter exemplify learning experience design?
2. How did instructional theory inform understanding and guide learning experience design practice in the case presented in this chapter?
3. How did the process of learning experience design unfold in the context of the real-world learning design project presented in this chapter?
4. How might learning experience design inform your own design practice?

Case Study

This case focuses on a university course with a unit that did not engage students. To address this, a case library was developed that consisted of multiple sales management hiring cases. These were used to provide context for sales management course concepts and to support students in solving a broader, overarching problem. The general objective was for students to engage in critical thinking while solving

---

DOI: 10.4324/9781003109938-6

the decision-making problem. Specific learning objectives included students: (1) increasing their understanding of the different areas of the hiring process; (2) enhancing their awareness of the complexities of the hiring process; and (3) justifying hiring recommendations within a dilemma-type problem. The case library was designed to support problem-based learning using the theoretical construct of case-based reasoning (CBR). In CBR, students engage in problem solving and are supported with relevant cases that are presented as stories. Essentially, these cases provide a form of vicarious experience for novice learners that serve to shore up gaps in prior knowledge.

Our case library design had students read through an overarching problem and supporting cases and then complete a concept map to demonstrate understanding. These were later coded to determine their quality, after which they were statistically compared with those of a control group to determine what impact the online learning environment might have had on students' learning. Quality of concept maps ranged from minimal development of the concept all the way to expert representation of the concept. Based on CBR theory, we anticipated fairly robust understanding of concepts demonstrated in the concept maps; however, students' concept maps were predominantly of low quality and minimally developed. Furthermore, we did not find any statistically significant differences between the students who had used the online learning environment and the control group.

Theoretically, we had done everything right. We had ensured that the case library incorporated all elements of CBR theory during the design process. Students who used the online learning environment should have developed a more robust understanding of the overarching problem. Except they hadn't. The question became: Why?

This decision to look more deeply into students' usage behavior led our design team to uncover a number of design flaws, better understand how students were engaging with Nick's Dilemma, and subsequently redesign the case library. To this end, the design team engaged in an iterative, learner-centered design process using user experience design (UXD) methods (Schmidt, Tawfik, Jahnke, & Earnshaw, 2020), which I present here as learning experience design (LXD). In the following sections, I introduce the key terms and concepts related to LXD and present provisional work toward characterizing this phenomenon. Following this, I detail how the design team applied LXD in the redesign of Nick's Dilemma.

Central to this chapter is the concept of LXD and the associated notion of learner experience (LX). I present working definitions for both in this section; however, the definition of these terms remains the subject of debate. LXD draws influences from multiple disciplines, including human–computer interaction (HCI), interaction design, human-centered computing, etc. Providing context and definitions across such a broad and diverse conceptual landscape would be outside the scope of this chapter. Therefore, I present below terms and concepts that are arguably most central to LXD.

1. **Learning Experience Design (LXD):** An umbrella concept that describes LIDT design practice as a human-centric, theoretically-grounded, and socio-culturally sensitive approach to learning design that is informed by user experience design (UXD) methods (Schmidt & Huang, in press; Tawfik et al., 2021);
2. **Learner experience (LX):** The user experience (UX) of learners during technology mediated learning; an emergent quality predicated by all aspects of the individual learner's interaction with a given learning technology (Schmidt & Huang, in press);
3. **User-Centered Design (UCD):** An umbrella term used to describe iterative design practice that actively seeks user validation across all phases of design and recognizes users' needs, abilities, and desires as central drivers across all stages of the design process (Abras et al., 2004);
4. **User Experience Design (UXD):** Design practice rooted in ergonomics, human factors, and HCI that seeks to consider all aspects of the individual experience of a user (including usability, accessibility, appearance, branding, context of use, etc.) in the design of products, systems, etc. (Law et al., 2009; Marcus, 2002; Norman & Draper, 1986);
5. **Learning Design:** The currently preferred term used to describe a field of scholarship and practice with historical roots in instructional systems design that aligns closely with instructional design, but with attention focused more on learning activities than instructional processes. Importantly, this is not to be confused with formally established definitions of learning design as put forward, for example, in the Lanarca Declaration or the IMSG specification (Dalziel, 2015; Dalziel et al., 2016; Koper & Olivier, 2004).

Theory and Processes

Although the term *instructional* design is still regularly used to describe design practice in the field of learning/instructional design and technology, the concept of *learning* design is increasingly preferred (Mor & Craft, 2012). Concurrently, practitioners have begun adopting the title *learning experience designer*, and are applying user-centered design (UCD) and UXD methods and processes to design the *learning experience* (Gray, 2020). When encountered by learners, their perceptions of these learning experiences contribute to their overall *learner experience.* LX is currently a hot topic. A quick web search at one of the many job search engines (i.e., LinkedIn, monster.com), will yield thousands of hits from companies looking to hire learning experience designers. However, exactly what a learning experience designer is, and what the job skills required of an LX designer are, are currently not well defined.

Defining terms in the field of LIDT is a tricky business. Terms and concepts in our field often can overlap substantially, differ in nuanced ways, and be contextually dependent. For example, the term *learning design* can refer to many things, including the process of design, design products (Cameron, 2009), and even a formally defined markup language (IMS Global Learning Consortium, 2006). This challenge of defining terms and concepts extends to the concept of LXD. Terms and concepts associated with LXD have emerged rapidly in our field and have been readily accepted by practitioners and researchers alike; however, these terms frequently are used in relaxed, imprecise, and sometimes contradictory ways. The colloquial manner in which LXD terminology is used complicates efforts to differentiate it from related phenomena (e.g., learning design, learning experience, learner experience). I speak to this in an open-access book (Schmidt et al., 2020) on LX and UX research in the field of learning/instructional design and technology (LIDT). To begin to approach the issue of clarifying LXD, and based on the content of the chapters in that book, I and my colleagues characterize it as a phenomenon that rests on three principles: (1) transdisciplinarity; (2) complexity; and (3) multiple literacies (Schmidt et al., 2020). I briefly discuss these three principles in the following paragraph.

LXD is transdisciplinary, complex, and requires multiple literacies. It is transdisciplinary in that it draws from multiple fields such as educational technology, informatics, HCI, information technology, education, instructional design, and psychology. We can see the individual contributions of these fields in LXD; however, the sum of their parts when applied in an LXD context is distinct. The complexity of LXD is apparent in that it is based not only on a purely technological perspective as in UX usability studies, but is also concerned with pedagogy and the socio-cultural contexts in which learners are situated. The socio-cultural context considers things like the quality of different forms of communication, collaboration, sociality, social presence, and social interactivity. Pedagogical considerations include things like the interaction with the course type, learning goals, learning activities, forms of assessment, and learner control. These three things – technology, pedagogy, and socio-cultural context – all play an interconnected and interdependent role in LXD, leading to substantial design complexity. Finally, LXD practice requires multiple literacies such as interface design, UX design, interaction design, graphic design, etc. This is not to imply that instructional and learning designers must master all of these areas, but they do need to have solid foundational knowledge. This allows LX designers to productively collaborate with professionals from other fields (e.g., HCI experts, UX designers, interface designers). The prospect of learning designers collaborating with professionals from other fields (for example using participatory or co-design methods) presents exciting opportunities for powerful synergies that can drive outstanding learner experiences.

Based on content analysis of the book chapters in the previously mentioned edited volume (Schmidt & Huang, in press), we have identified the following characteristics of LXD:

1. **Human-centric**. LXD focuses centrally on human experience from the perspective of the learner, as well as other learning technology users (e.g., teacher, LMS administrator);
2. **Theoretically grounded**. Theory is foundational to LXD, which is principally inspired and guided by theoretical perspectives that have found resonance in the field of LDT (but also draws from theories rooted in outside traditions such as HCI and UX);
3. **Informed by UXD methods**. LXD is informed by UXD methods, but these methods are adapted and extended in LXD so as to be more appropriate and effective within a learning design context;
4. **Socio-culturally sensitive**. LXD seeks to promote empathetic understanding of the learner, their socio-cultural context, as well as the context in which they engage in socially mediated meaning making.

These characteristics have implications for both theory and process. Learning designers interested in UXD or LXD methods will be hard-pressed to find guidance within the field of learning/instructional design and technology and, as a consequence, likely will seek guidance from outside our field (e.g., in the HCI or interaction design literature). Undeniably, the methods and processes that guide those disciplines overlap with our field in terms of both application and theory. However, theories and processes are representative of their associated disciplines. In this case, they are informed by and advanced through the conventional perspectives of traditions that do not necessarily have a fundamental focus on learning. Conversely, LX designers draw principal insight from theories that focus on the process of learning (e.g., constructivism, behaviorism: Ertmer & Newby, 2013; Schuch & Barab, 2008) and instantiate these theories in their designs.

52 *Matthew Schmidt*

While theories of human perception and attention are often referenced to guide LX design (Blythe et al., 2006; Kuutti, 2010), such theories must be considered from the perspective of learning when applied in an LX design context (Schmidt & Huang, in press). In the current case, the design team referenced theories relevant to the HCI community such as interaction design theories (e.g., Coiera, 2003; Waern & Back, 2017) and theories of attention relative to web design (e.g., Grier et al., 2007; Nielsen, 2006; Pernice, 2017). However, most central to our design were constructivist theories of learning in general, and specifically theories related to ill-structured problem solving (Jonassen, 2002) and case-based reasoning (Jonassen & Hernandez-Serrano, 2002; Kolodner, 1993). The confluence of multiple theoretical perspectives in our LXD processes is what led to discovery of interface and usability flaws, which allowed us to identify and incorporate improvements, and subsequently led to improved learning outcomes.

Why is LXD Important for Instructional Designers?

Having provided some background and definitions, the question becomes how LXD fits into the broader ecosystem of instructional design. LXD is not distinct or separate from ID, but instead sits alongside ID as a complementary approach to design for learning. As opposed to designing instruction or activities, LXD focuses on designing highly engaging, meaningful, and interactive learning experiences. To this end, LXD places the learner centrally in the design process and continually references the learner across all phases of design. It further differentiates itself in how instruction and activities are designed, being more methods-focused than the historically process or procedural focus of ID (e.g., ADDIE). In addition, LXD explicitly considers the perceptive qualities of individual learners while they are engaged in digitally enabled learning and how this can influence effectiveness, performance, etc. Given the iterative nature of LXD, it can be particularly useful within Agile teams or to inform design-based research. Positioning the learner centrally in the design process and continually referencing the learner across all phases of learning design can lead to designs that are pleasing and easy to use, intuitive and engaging, and that effectively and efficiently propel learners toward their learning goals. I illustrate this in the following section.

Professional Practice Revisited

The following case highlights how LXD methods allowed the design team to redesign a learning intervention in a learner-centered manner in response to how learners actually used the intervention as opposed to the designers' intent. We began by analyzing Google Analytics data, which uncovered learners' usage patterns. Learners tended to move between just two web pages and then exit the site. Learners almost never accessed supporting cases. This went against our design intent and suggested learners were not reading the materials. Indeed, learners only spent 11 minutes on average using the case library – far too little time to read the cases or solve the overarching problem. Analytics data analysis unveiled three key design flaws: (1) supporting case design did not support web-based reading patterns; (2) learners were not sufficiently cued that supporting cases were important to access; and (3) case presentation may have lacked appeal. Although CBR theory was incorporated throughout our design, the way the case library was used was divergent from our design intent. On this basis, we pivoted for our redesign. We adopted iterative, learner-centered methods, beginning with rapid prototyping and usability testing.

Our assumption that if students were presented with a collection of cases, they would use them as intended proved false. Our redesign efforts, therefore, focused on improving on case presentation and understanding how learners perceived them. Since learners were not reading text-heavy cases, we drew design inspiration from comic books and video games and iteratively designed and developed a gamified case library using Twine (http://twinery.org). Learners could choose responses from a list of decisions and see the outcome of their decisions. We segmented cases across multiple screens to promote fast reading, and designed the visual display of text to accommodate web-based reading patterns. This redesign was a departure from our original design. Learners could not simply go back-and-forth between screens and ignore supporting cases. The new system required learners to access cases in order to unlock the next stage of the game. An example of the redesigned learning environment is provided in Figure 6.1.

Findings from iterative usability testing with five participants suggested that this redesign supported decision-making, perspective-taking, retention of cases, and retrieval/reuse. However, findings also revealed that problem representation was insufficient to provide ownership of the problem. The system did not support making a final decision about how to solve the overarching problem or to see the outcome of decisions. We therefore made refinements to the online learning environment based on what we had learned from usability testing and then performed a pilot study to

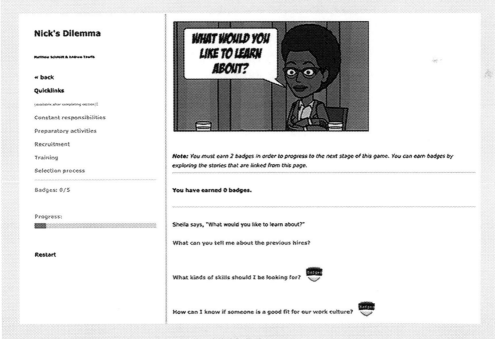

Figure 6.1 Redesigned case library for Nick's Dilemma.

determine the effectiveness of the changes we had made on student performance. Specifically, we added a new decision structure requiring learners to make a final decision based on what they had learned from the cases, after which they were presented with an outcome that varied from better to worse (Figure 6.2).

In a subsequent study, learners (n = 64) developed a causal map that articulated their solutions. We investigated whether learners used the new design differently and whether causal maps demonstrated improvements compared to the previous version of the case library. Analytics data revealed that the new design promoted interaction across all pages, suggesting that the new design was more effective at leading learners to view supporting cases. Students also tended to spend more time in the new version. Comparison of differences between students' maps from the previous version and the new version of the learning environment suggested substantial improvements. Students who used the gamified version were more likely to generate maps that demonstrated complex and fluid expertise. Taken together, the outcomes of our learning experience design processes had improved both learner experience and learning outcomes.

Connecting Process to Practice

1. How would you characterize the relationship between theory and design presented in the case of Nick's Dilemma?
2. How are the methods and processes presented in this chapter similar to more traditional learning/instructional design approaches? How do they differ?
3. This chapter characterizes learning experience design as being (1) human centric; (2) theoretically grounded; (3) informed by UXD methods; and (4) socio-culturally sensitive. To what extent are these characteristics present and/or absent in the case of Nick's Dilemma? What are the implications?
4. How might considerations of learners' experiences promote theorized learning outcomes when designing learning technologies?
5. If you were to design your own learning technology, how might you apply LXD methods? Why?

Activity

Create a Learner Persona

A common approach to understanding learners is to develop personas. A persona is a made-up example that provides a detailed description of a learner/user with characteristics that are representative of the kinds of learners/users you anticipate will use a given educational or learning technology. Learner personas provide a human-centered lens for designers to reference while devising learning technologies. When you are developing a persona, you will typically include demographics, goals, needs, descriptions of a typical day, and experiences that are germane to the design focus. Personas should not be developed based on assumptions, but instead on data. For example, interviews or observations allow the designer to gather information from or about individual learners and to extrapolate from these specifics into more general information. To borrow from the Nick's Dilemma case, the designers referenced analytics data to explore usage patterns and, on

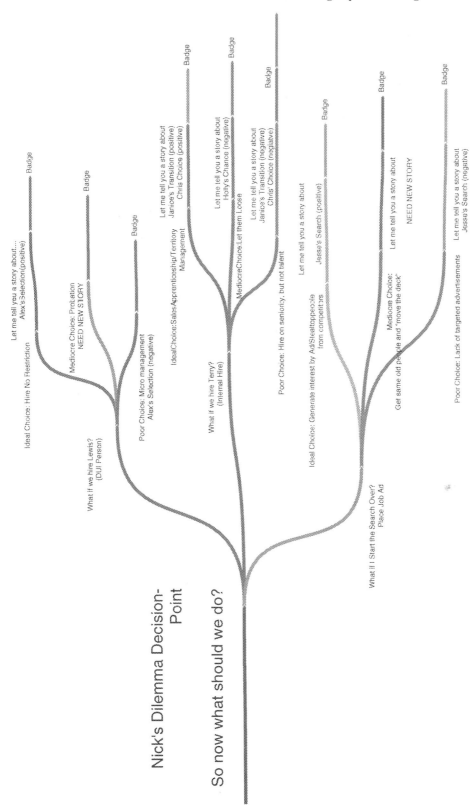

Figure 6.2 Rapid prototype decision tree for students' final decision and related consequences in solving the overarching problem.

56 *Matthew Schmidt*

this basis, were able to generate a profile that fit most of the learners. In order to develop a learner persona, follow the below steps:

1. Perform an Internet search to identify examples of user and learner personas;
2. Study the presentation, form, and content of these personas;
3. What information seems most critical or useful in the personas? What information seems superfluous? Does any information seem to be stereotypical or biased?
4. In the personas you found, was sufficient information provided to inform the design of learning technologies?
5. How would you use personas in your own design practice? What challenges would you anticipate?
6. Individual activity: Create your own template for a learner persona. Include all information you feel is necessary;
7. Group activity: Discuss the template you developed with your group. How is your template similar? How is it different? What might you change? How do these templates help guide design?

References

Abras, C., Maloney-Krichmar, D., & Preece, J. (2004). User-centered design. In W. Bainbridge (Ed.), *Encyclopedia of human–computer interaction*. Thousand Oaks, CA: Sage Publications.

Blythe, M., Wright, P., McCarthy, J., & Bertelsen, O. W. (2006). Theory and method for experience centered design. In *CHI'06 extended abstracts on human factors in computing systems* (pp. 1691–1694). doi:10.1145/1125451.1125764

Cameron, L. (2009, December 10). *How learning design can illuminate teaching practice*. Retrieved from https://ro.uow.edu.au/fld/09/Program/3

Coiera, E. (2003). Interaction design theory. *International Journal of Medical Informatics, 69*(2), 205–222. doi:10.1016/s1386-5056(02)00106-5

Dalziel, J. (2015). *Learning design: Conceptualizing a framework for teaching and learning online*. Routledge.

Dalziel, J., Conole, G., Wills, S., Walker, S., Bennett, S., Dobozy, E., … Bower, M. (2016). The Larnaca declaration on learning design. *Journal of Interactive Media in Education, 1*(7), 1–24. doi:10.5334/jime.407

Ertmer, P. A., & Newby, T. J. (2013). Behaviorism, cognitivism, constructivism: Comparing critical features from an instructional design perspective. *Performance Improvement Quarterly, 26*(2), 43–71. doi:10.1002/piq.21143

Gray, C. M. (2020). Paradigms of knowledge production in human–computer interaction: Toward a framing for learner experience (LX) design. In *Learner and user experience research*. EdTech Books. Retrieved from https://edtechbooks.org/ux/paradigms_in_hci

Grier, R., Kortum, P., & Miller, J. (2007). How users view web pages: An exploration of cognitive and perceptual mechanisms. In P. Zaphiris (Ed.), *Human–computer interaction research in Web design and evaluation* (pp. 22–41). IGI Global.

IMS Global Learning Consortium. (2006). *Learning design specification*. Retrieved from http://www.imsglobal.org/learningdesign/index.html

Jonassen, D. H. (2002). Toward a design theory of problem solving. *Educational Technology Research and Development, 48*(4), 63–85.

Jonassen, D. H., & Hernandez-Serrano, J. (2002). Case-based reasoning and instructional design: Using stories to support problem solving. *Educational Technology Research and Development, 50*(2), 65–77.

Kolodner, J. (1993). *Case-based reasoning*. San Francisco, CA: Morgan Kaufmann Publishers Inc.

Koper, R., & Olivier, B. (2004). Representing the learning design of units of learning. *Educational Technology & Society, 7*(3), 97–111.

Kuutti, K. (2010). Where are the Ionians of user experience research? In *Proceedings of the 6th Nordic conference on human–computer interaction: Extending boundaries* (pp. 715–718). doi:10.1145/1868914.1869012

Law, E., Roto, V., Hassenzahl, M., Vermeeren, A., Kort, J. (2009). Understanding, scoping and defining user experience: a survey approach. In: *27th International Conference on Human Factors in Computing Systems*, pp. 719–728. Boston, MA.

Marcus, A. (2002). Dare we define user-interface design? *Interactions, 9*(5), 19–24. doi:https://doi.org/10.3402/rlt.v20i0.19196

Mor, Y., & Craft, B. (2012). Learning design: Reflections upon the current landscape. *Research in Learning Technology, 20*(Suppl. 1), 19196. doi:10.3402/rlt.v20i0.19196

Nielsen, J. (2006). *F-shaped pattern for reading web content* [Original eyetracking research]. Nielsen Norman Group. Retrieved from https://www.nngroup.com/articles/f-shaped-pattern-reading-web-content-discovered/

Norman, D. A., & Draper, S. W. (1986). *User centered system design: New perspectives on human–computer interaction.* CRC Press.

Pernice, K. (2017). *F-shaped pattern of reading on the web: Misunderstood, but still relevant* [Even on mobile]. Nielsen Norman Group. Retrieved from https://www.nngroup.com/articles/f-shaped-pattern-reading-web-content/

Schmidt, M., & Huang, R. (in press). Defining learning experience design: Voices from the field of learning design & technology. *TechTrends.*

Schmidt, M., & Tawfik, A. A. (2018). Using analytics to transform a problem-based case library: An educational design research approach. *Interdisciplinary Journal of Problem-Based Learning, 12*(1). doi:10.7771/1541-5015.1635

Schmidt, M., Tawfik, A. A., Jahnke, I., & Earnshaw, Y. (Eds.). (2020). *Learner and user experience research: An introduction for the field of learning design & technology.* EdTech Books. Retrieved from https://edtechbooks.org/ux

Schmidt, M., Tawfik, A. A., Jahnke, I., Earnshaw, Y., & Huang, R. (2020). Introduction to the edited volume. In *Learner and user experience research.* EdTech Books. Retrieved from https://edtech-books.org/ux/introduction_to_ux_lx_in_lidt

Schuch, K.L., & Barab, S.A. (2008). Philosophical perspectives. In J.M. Spector, M.D. Merrill, J. van Merrienboer, & M. Driscoll (Eds), *Handbook of research on educational communications and technology* (3rd ed., pp. 667–682). Routledge.

Tawfik, A. A., Gatewood, J., Gish-Lieberman, J. J., & Hampton, A. J. (2021). Toward a definition of learning experience design. *Technology, Knowledge and Learning.* doi:10.1007/s10758-020-09482-2

Tawfik, A. A., Schmidt, M., & Hooper, C. P. (2020). Role of conjecture mapping in applying a game-based strategy toward a case library: A view from educational design research. *Journal of Computing in Higher Education, 32*(3), 655–681.

Waern, A., & Back, J. (2017). Activity as the ultimate particular of interaction design. In *Proceedings of the 2017 CHI conference on human factors in computing systems* (pp. 3390–3402). doi:10.1145/3025453.3025990

7 Empathy for Action in Instructional Design

John Baaki and Monica W. Tracey

Chapter Overview

Empathy is the ability to identify with other people's thoughts and feelings. Empathic design is the attempt to get closer to the lives and experiences of the audience of focus (Baaki & Tracey, 2019, 2020). As instructional design instructors and practitioners, we teach empathy as a means for instructional design students to act by producing meaningful design deliverables. We guide design students to embrace empathic design and engage empathically with the audience of focus. Empathy drives action for design and is a means to an end. The end is a meaningful design deliverable that meets the audience of focus where the audience is (Tracey et al., 2021). A meaningful design deliverable is designed to a localized context of use which emphasizes scaling context to what is needed in a situation.

We present *A Journey Through Ratios* where one of our instructional design graduate student teams designed a meaningful lesson on understanding ratios for adult learners preparing for a high school equivalency exam. The client was a non-profit who focused on developing educational interventions customized to the needs of adults with literacy-related knowledge skill gaps. Keeping adult learners at the forefront of the design and student designers' minds, an empathic design approach required student designers to tap into their sensitivity toward the adult learners, the design process, and the collaborative nature of design practice. We discuss empathy and empathic design processes. We then return to the *Understanding Ratios* case and discuss the professional practice implications of empathy and empathic design processes. We conclude with *The Power of Observation* activity where instructors provide students a direct observation experience, and we share recommended readings.

Guiding Questions

1. When guiding design students, how do instructors present the role empathy plays in students' design process?
2. When guiding design students, how can instructors help students make design decisions to move their design forward?
3. When guiding design students, how can instructors assist designers in designing meaningful design products that are focused on learners' learning and performance context?

Key Terms

Empathy
Empathetic design

DOI: 10.4324/9781003109938-7

Empathy for action
Localized context of use
Meaningful design deliverable

Case Study

Rick, Sara, Kate, and Paula, the Understanding Ratio team, were tasked with creating a course to teach math ratio concepts to adult learners preparing to take their high school equivalency exam. Rick and Sara were thrilled with this instructional design project as they are both high school math teachers. Kate and Paula however, identified themselves as math haters.

Empathic Design Approach

The team learned that empathic design is getting closer to the lives and experiences of the audience (Kouprie & Visser, 2009). The team used Kouprie and Visser's (2009) 4-phase Framework of Empathy for Design to support their empathic design practice, beginning with (1) discovery, where they entered the learner's world. The team interviewed math tutors and volunteer workers who worked with adults studying for the high school equivalency exam, and a non-profit executive director with expertise in instructional design and the adult learners. Team members analyzed math content for adults with literacy gaps and read articles on high school equivalency exam preparation (Patterson & Song, 2018). The team then constructed end learner personas (Dotan et al., 2009) and learner empathy maps to better understand the adult learners.

During the second phase of the 4-phase framework, (2) immersion, the design team mentally lived in the adult learner's world. The team learned about the learners while remaining open minded, refraining from any judgment. Team members began designing the Understanding Ratio course starting with course goals, outcomes, and assessments. Rick and Sara identified 'must have' course content along with activities, test questions, and assessments. Kate and Paula focused on getting to know the learners in a deeper way, looking at learner challenges working with ratios. They talked about relatives who studied for their equivalency exam and their difficulties relating to the material. The team was assigned to present a pilot of an instructional activity to their graduate class. The team fell into dissention as Rick and Sara had a ratio formula they wanted to teach while Kate and Paula designed a ratio activity using illustrations of a cup of coffee, black, with milk, and with milk and sugar. This activity made sense to Kate and Paula, teaching ratios, 1/3, 2/3, and whole; although Rick and Sara argued that it was too simple. The team presented both activities to their classmates.

After both activities, the class overwhelmingly identified with the coffee cup activity. The pilot experience triggered the third phase in the 4-phase framework, (3) connection. The design team connected emotionally with learners, witnessing how the coffee cup activity helped classmates understand ratios. The team was united, which was a critical moment in moving the course forward.

Understanding Adult Learners

The team noted, "In this unit we identify the most essential and practical components of ratios and present them in an easy to follow and engaging manner." Furthermore, "The goal for this unit is to provide learners with a working knowledge of ratios that they can apply to their everyday lives, education, or occupation."

Course context is simple, ratios are used all the time. The course design enables adult learners to choose the context they want to learn ratios in; Fourbucks Coffee, Rita's Café, Joe's Auto shop, or Cindy's Home Improvement Garden. Adult learners realize that they deal with ratios in different contexts every day. Learners can be a coffee shop worker and the ratios apply to what they could see on the job. As the course unfolds, the math activities become more challenging.

Finally, the team entered the final phase, (4) detachment. Designers left the learner's world, detaching the emotional connection with the learner, stepping back into a designer's role. Keeping adult learners at the forefront, the team tapped into their sensitivity toward the adult learners, the design process, and design's collaborative nature. Regarding sensitivity toward the learner, a team member explained, "We had a heart for the learner who would be trying to improve their understanding of ratios."

Reflecting on sensitivity toward the design process, a team member stated, "We tried to have empathy for one another. Rick and I had to work at keeping it simple, but Kate and Paula helped remind us when we would get too math-focused."

Empathy and the Empathic Design Process

We address empathy and the empathic design process by discussing how the Understanding Ratio team embraced an empathic design approach when making design decisions that resulted in a meaningful lesson. The Understanding Ratio team engaged in three key elements of empathy and the empathic design process: (a) be empathic toward the audience of focus; (b) design with empathy for action; and (c) produce a meaningful design deliverable.

Be Empathic Toward the Audience of Focus

In order to understand what empathy is, it is helpful to realize what empathy is not.

Empathy is not sympathy. In a study of terminal cancer patients receiving palliative care regarding their experiences with sympathy and empathy, sympathy was perceived as self-serving while empathy was perceived as genuine (Sinclair et al., 2017). Empathy is not self-serving. In design, it is the ability to 'be' as the other, while remaining your whole self, or the ability to stand in someone else's place while standing in your own. Batson (2009) describes staying in your own shoes as designers opening themselves in a responsive way to their audience's experiences and feelings without losing awareness that the designer, "…is a distinct other self," (p. 7). Batson (2009) suggests that the concern is not so much what one knows about the audience's feelings and concerns but one's sensitivity to the way the audience is affected by the situation. In empathic design, designers must be willing to engage with the audience of focus (Batson, 2009, 2011; Bloom, 2016; Kouprie & Visser, 2009). Humans were born with the capacity for empathy, but it is learned behavior that grows over time from self-awareness. When designers have empathy in design, they have a heightened understanding of the learner.

Empathic design complements an instructional design approach. Empathic design is not a box to check during the learner analysis phase. Empathic design occurs during all elements of the instructional design process. Being sensitive to the way the audience of focus is affected by a situation is at the forefront of the key elements of an instructional design approach such as:

- Identifying the design problem or opportunity;
- Express sensitivity toward the audience of focus;
- Identify outcomes;
- Verify content;
- Design interventions (instructional strategies and activities); and
- Determine an evaluation plan.

The Understanding Ratios team followed Kouprie and Visser's (2009) 4-phase Framework of Empathy for Design to keep adult learners at the forefront of the design and student designers' minds. The 4-phase framework of discover, immerse, connect, and detach is not a linear approach. Through collaboration and at times dissention, the *Understanding Ratios Team* found itself engaging and then re-engaging with the phases as the team constructed personas and an empathy map; identified course goals, outcomes, and assessments; presented initial activities to peers; reflected on peer feedback; and then agreed on final design decisions. As an approach that is not linear, the 4-phase framework complements well an instructional design approach that is nonlinear in practice.

Design for Empathy in Action

Designers make design decisions keeping in mind empathy for the audience of focus, empathy for oneself regarding one's biases and designer precedents (Boling, 2021), and empathy for a learning context and performance context. Dorst (2003) suggests, "A design can be seen as a tightly knitted web of decisions which are not independent from one another," (p. 29). Keeping track of the design story (in research notes, annotated sketches, reflective feedback sessions, key decision points, etc.) can keep a designer from getting tangled in their own design (Dorst, 2003). Empathy drives action for design.

Empathy for the Audience of Focus

Batson (2009) describes eight distinct concepts of empathy that we might experience in an interchange with another person. In our experience and research (Baaki & Tracey, 2020; Tracey et al., 2021) working with graduate instructional design students, we find students most often experience what Batson (2009) refers to imagine-self and imagine-other. In imagine-self, a designer imagines how they would think and feel in another person's situation. As noted above, in imagine-other, a designer opens themself in a responsive way to the feelings and experiences of another person without losing awareness that the designer is their own person. Reflecting on the *Understanding Ratio team's* design journey, we feel that imagine-other best aligns with an empathic instructional design approach.

Empathy for Oneself

A designer's perception and understanding of a design situation are influenced by a designer's experiences (Fraquelli, 2015). A designer comes to a design with biases, inspiration and a repertoire of precedents (Boling, 2021; Cross, 2011; Dorst, 2003). Cross

62 *John Baaki and Monica W. Tracey*

describes designers drawing from a repertoire of precedents as, "...remembered images and recollection of other objects that helped him [designer] give a more coherent, predictable, and attractive form to the concept," (p. 19).

Dorst (2003) explains that a designer is part of a design process where the designer is free to design according to their preferences, style, and abilities. A designer proposes interventions that include their interpretation of the design problem and possible interventions to the problems. A designer becomes empathic as they match their freedom to follow their preferences to the design challenge's requirements.

Empathy for a Learning and Performance Context

Design is a complex and iterative process where designers need to tolerate and work with uncertainty (Cross, 2011; Dorst, 2003). Even though instructional designers continue to use models, instructional designers, for years, have admitted that the instructional design process is anything but a linear process. As an author of one of the most used instructional design models (Dick, Carey, and Carey model), Walter Dick (1995) clearly noted, "My response to this observation (ISD models are too linear) is that the model that appears in the Dick and Carey (1990) text was *never* intended to reflect how instruction is designed in 'real life'" (p. 9).

Reflecting on Dick's poignant and timeless statement, we substitute context for real life. As a complement to an instructional design process, a designer embracing empathic design makes design decisions that impact both the learning and performance contexts. Context is hard to precisely define and is better defined by how context is used (Baaki & Tracey, 2019; Duranti & Goodwin, 1997; Meloncon, 2017). For example, the *Understanding Ratios Team* participated in three different learning context layers: instructor to team, team to peers, and team to adult learners with math-related knowledge skill gaps. First, the team participated in our empathic approach to introducing empathic design and the 4-phase framework of Empathy for Design. Second, the *Understanding Ratio team* presented the ratio formula and coffee activities to the team's peers to gain feedback and direction. Finally, the team designed a course with a straightforward context – ratios are used all the time.

A challenge to dealing with performance context is we tend to scale context as large and complex (Meloncon, 2017). Meloncon calls for scaling back the size of context to localized contexts of use. A localized context of use emphasizes specific moments where context is scaled back to what is needed in a situation (Baaki & Tracey, 2019). When designing to a localized context of use, designers meet the learner where they are and not where they should be. Although Rick and Sara, the math teachers, first proposed designing a ratio formula activity much like one found in an Algebra textbook, Kate and Paula helped the team meet the adult learners at their current situation: learn a working knowledge of ratios that can be applied to a job and everyday life. When instructional designers produce meaningful design deliverables, a learner has what they need to perform in a specific situation or moment.

Produce Meaningful Design Deliverables

When a design team produces a meaningful design deliverable, a learner has what they need to perform in a situation, their localized context of use. A localized context of use stresses a personal side of context (Meloncon, 2017). Both instructional designer and learner weave together a dynamic context that is about interpretation, filling spaces, meaning-making, and creating meaning to move forward (Baaki & Tracey, 2019).

Empathy for Action in Instructional Design 63

Learner and Designer Contexts are Dynamic

Adult learners with math-related knowledge skill gaps actively connect ratio information to the world where the adult learners find themselves be it Fourbucks Coffee or Cindy's Home Improvement Garden. Context is woven together contingently, and not deterministically (MacPhail, 2014). The *Understanding Ratios Team* designed with uncertainty as they learned about the design challenge and worked toward an intervention. The more the team learned about adult learners with math-related knowledge skill gaps the more the team gained insight into the design's nature and boundaries (Dorst & Cross, 2001). As the team reduced its uncertainty, the team altered its design space context.

Learner and Designer Contexts are about Interpretation

MacPhail (2014) suggests that interpretation and context are synonymous. Adult learners with math-related knowledge skill gaps interpret how the *Understanding Ratios* lesson meet their goals. Successfully completing a high school equivalency exam may mean a better paying job and higher education opportunities. Rick and Sara, the math teachers, drew on their experience as teachers and their perceptions on how to prepare adult learners for a high equivalency exam. Kate and Paula interpreted the design challenge by reflecting on how we use ratios in our daily life. The team's interpretation of their own values, prior experiences, and knowledge played a part in design decisions.

Learner and Designer Contexts are about Filling Spaces

Adult learners with math-related knowledge skill gaps weave together their current situation and preparing for a high school equivalency exam to fill in spaces that create ratio knowledge that adult learners can use. What is important is not necessarily what the ratio information is but how ratio information fills spaces in the adult learners' situation (MacPhail, 2014). The *Understanding Ratios Team* employed an empathic design approach to fill in the spaces of the adult learners and their experiences.

Learner and Designer Contexts are about Meaning-Making

Meaning-making is very sensitive to context (Bruner, 1990) where adult learners with math-related knowledge skill gaps participate in a context of practice which is the creative synthesis of personal knowledge (using ratios each day) and impersonal data (memorizing a ratio formula) (MacPhail, 2014). The Understanding Ratios Team's combined personal, educational, and professional experiences as instructional designers created meaning for the *Understanding Ratios* design. The team envisioned how adult learners will use ratios at Fourbucks Coffee or Joe's Auto Shop.

Learner and Designer Context are about Creating Meaning and Moving Forward

Csikszentmihalyi & Rochberg-Halton (1981) discussed meaning-making and survival in that people keep experiences, situations, and information that have helped in the past. Adult learners with math-related knowledge skill gaps free themselves of their past and current situation and discover the opportunities of moving forward toward a better job or a college education. The *Understanding Ratio team's* biases, inspirations, experiences, and repertoire of precedents along with empathy for adult learners weaved together a context that produced a memorable *Understanding Ratios* lesson.

Professional Practice Revisited

An empathic design journey is engaging and difficult. We embrace empathy as a means to a successful design deliverable. Empathy drives action. The team tapped into their sensitivity toward the adult learners, the design process, and design's collaborative nature.

Audience of Focus – Engagement Required

A team member reflected, "We had a heart for the learner who would be trying to improve their understanding of ratios." A designer must be willing to engage with the audience of focus (Batson, 2009, 2011; Bloom, 2016; Kouprie & Visser, 2009). Batson (2009) argued that empathic feelings produce motivation to address the needs of another person. Engaged in the adult learners' lives and experiences, the team designed a course that enables adult learners to choose the context they want to learn ratios in (e.g., Fourbucks Coffee).

Design Process – Difficulty Accepted

A team member confessed, "Developing content that would be considered relatable was challenging." Empathic design is difficult. The second author provided guidance as the team designed the Understanding Ratios course. She aided the team because design students tend to do what they already know (Woodcock et al., 2019). Taking the initial lead, math teachers Rick and Sara did what they know; identify ratio formula course content and align it with traditional math activities.

Mentoring design teams helps designers step back from a pre-occupation with important, but routine design methods. By regularly meeting, the instructor championed an empathic attitude, and more importantly allowed the team to deliberately practice empathic design (Battarbee et al., 2014).

Design's Collaborative Nature: Social Process Embraced

Sara explained, "Rick and I had to work to make it simple, but Kate and Paula helped remind us when we would get too math-focused." After the pilot, the team connected with the learners, witnessing how the coffee cup activity helped classmates better understand ratios. United, the team achieved a shared understanding with their classmates and the audience of focus.

Designers bring their own knowledge, viewpoints, expectations, and ambitions to a design process (Cross, 2011; Dorst, 2003). The team disagreed, argued, united, and consented. Because each designer brings their own background to the design, teams struggle understanding one another (Dorst, 2003). Empathic design, therefore, becomes a process of negotiating a consensus among the team.

Connecting Process to Practice

The purpose of this activity is to have students experience opening themselves in a responsive way to the feelings and experiences of others through direct observation. In week two or three an instructional design course, have students spend 60 minutes during their week to observe people. In a following class, have each student present what they observed. Encourage students to be creative. Do students tell a story, show visuals, bring something for other students to see, smell, touch, and/or hear? Discuss how students showed empathy for others, the situation, and themselves.

The Power of Observation prompts are as follows:

- Think of something you do on a regular basis that you can observe others doing (e.g., ordering a coffee and Starbucks);
- Go to the place where you do this (e.g., your local Starbucks);
- Sit for 60 minutes and observe others performing the task you do (e.g., ordering coffee);
- Observe the people's actions, the environment they are in (their own personal environment and the larger environmental space), the interactions they have with others and with objects, and who they are;
- Observe how individuals do it differently from how you do it (e.g., pay cash instead of using their phone);
- What do you want to know about them?
- Open yourself in a responsive way while observing them by tapping into your sight, touch, smell, and hearing. For example, why do you think they used cash? What do you observe to help you answer your questions? Write it down;
- Observe yourself during this activity. Be mindful of your own personal reactions and as you observe others write it down. Are you bored? Excited? Angry? Impatient? Why?
- What details did you notice watching someone else perform a task that you have performed many times yourself?
- How did you think your own experience colored your observations?
- Spend 60 minutes observing others and yourself and document whatever you feel, see, hear, touch, and smell.

Adapted from Neck et al. (2014)

References

Baaki, J. & Tracey, M. J. (2019). Weaving a localized context of use: What it means for instructional design. *Journal of Applied Instructional Design, 8*(1), 2–13. doi:10.28990/jaid2011.00100

Baaki, J. & Tracey, M. J. (2020). Graduate instructional design students using empathy as a means to an end. Manuscript submitted for publication.

Batson, C. D. (2009). These things called empathy: Eight related by distinct phenomena. In J. Decety & W. Ickes (Eds.), *The social neuroscience of empathy* (pp. 2–15). MIT Press. doi:10.7551/mitpress/9780262012973.003.0002

Batson, C. D. (2011). *Altruism in humans.* Oxford University Press. doi:10.1093/acprof:oso/9780195341065.001.0001

Battarbee, K., Suri, J. F., & Howard, S. G. (2014). Empathy on the edge: Scaling and sustaining a human-centered approach in the evolving practice of design. *IDEO.* Retrieved from http://www.ideo.com/images/uploads/news/pdfs/Empathy_on_the_Edge.pdf

Bloom, P. (2016). *Against empathy: The case for rational compassion.* HarperCollins Publishers.

Boling, E. (2021). The nature and use of precedent in designing, In J.K. McDonald & R.E. West (Eds.), *Design for learning: Principles, processes, and praxis.* EdTech Books. https://edtechbooks.org/id/precedent

Bruner, J. (1990). *Acts of meaning.* Harvard University Press. doi:10.1017/s0033291700030555

Cross, N. (2011). *Design thinking: Understanding how designers think and work.* Berg. doi:10.5040/9781474293884

Csikszentmihalyi, M., & Rochberg-Halton, E. (1981). *The meaning of things: Domestic symbols and self.* Cambridge University Press. doi:10.1017/cbo9781139167611

Dick, W. (1995). Instructional design and creativity: A response to the critics. *Educational Technology,* 35(4), 5–11.

Dorst, K., & Cross, N. (2001). Creativity in the design process: Co-evolution of problem–solution. *Design Studies,* 22(5), 425–437. doi:10.1016/s0142-694x(01)00009-6

Dorst, K. (2003). *Understanding design: 150 reflections on being a designer.* BIS Publishers.

Dotan, A., Maiden, N., Lichtner, V., & Germanovich, L. (2009, August). *Designing with only four people in mind? –A case study of using personas to redesign a work-integrated learning support system.* In *IFIP conference on human-computer interaction* (pp. 497–509). Springer. doi:10.1007/978-3-642-03658-3_54

Duranti, A., & Goodwin, C. (1997). The notion of context. In A. Duranti & C. Goodwin (Eds.) *Rethinking context: Language as an interactive phenomenon* (pp. 2–10). Cambridge University Press.

Fraquelli, R. (2015). Deep empathic design. *Journal of Industrial Design and Engineering Graphics,* (10)2, 89–94.

Kouprie, M., & Visser, F. S. (2009). A framework for empathy in design: Stepping into and out of the user's life. *Journal of Engineering Design,* 20(5), 437–448. doi:10.1080/09544820902875033

MacPhail, T. (2014). *The viral network: A pathology of the H1N1 influenza pandemic.* Cornell University Press. https://doi.org/10.7591/9780801454899

Meloncon, L. K. (2017). Patient experience design: Expanding usability methodologies for healthcare. *Communication Design Quarterly,* (5)2, 20–28. https://doi.org/10.1145/3131201.3131203

Neck, H. M., Greene, P. G., & Brush, C. G. (2014). *Teaching entrepreneurship: A practice-based approach.* Edgar Elgar Publishing Limited. https://doi.org/10.4337/9781782540564

Patterson, M. B., & Song, W. (2018). *Critiquing adult participation in education, report 1: Deterrents and solutions* [Online]. Retrieved August 31, 2018, from http://www.valueusa.org/projects

Sinclair, S., Beamer, K., Hack, T. F., McClement, S., Raffin Bouchal, S., Chochinov, H. M., & Hagen, N. A. (2017). Sympathy, empathy, and compassion: A grounded theory study of palliative care patients' understandings, experiences, and preferences. *Palliative Medicine,* 31(5), 437–447. doi:10.1177/0269216316663499

Tracey, M. W., Baaki, J., & Hutchinson, A. (2021). *Empathy and empathic design for action in design.* Manuscript submitted for publication.

Woodcock, A., McDonagh, D., Magee, P., Ball, T., & Iqbal, S. (2019). Expanding horizons: Engaging students with empathic thinking. In *DS 95: Proceedings of the 21st international conference on engineering and product design education (E&PDE 2019),* University of Strathclyde, Glasgow, September 12–13, 2019. doi:10.35199/epde2019.49

8 Designed Failure in Instructional Design and Technology

T. Logan Arrington and Andrew A. Tawfik

Chapter Overview

Recent literature in the instructional design field has noted that the field usually focuses heavily on leading learners toward success (Tawfik et al., 2015). However, learners' failure experiences can be just as beneficial if not more beneficial than the traditional methods (Tawfik et al., 2015; Darabi et al., 2018). Other literature suggests that repeated instances of failure can lead to issues of self-efficacy and negatively impact engagement. The purpose of this chapter is to provide instructional design and educational technology students with a broad, yet practical, overview of failure-based instructional strategies, more broadly referred to as learning from failure. We want to make an important distinction here at the onset of this chapter. In many instances, failure is considered a natural part of the learning process (i.e., at some point, a group of learners can be unsuccessful or encounter great struggle). We do not dispute this point! The purpose of this chapter is to instead focus on instructional strategies and approaches that presume failure will occur and discuss how to utilize that failure to lead to more meaningful learning.

Guiding Questions

1. Why is it important to design learning experiences where learners encounter failure or struggle?
2. When should intentional failure be leveraged for the learning process?
3. What are some of the most effective ways of leveraging that failure?

Case Study

Within a comprehensive regional university in the Southeastern United States, an instructor and instructional designers were exploring ways to improve a survey chemistry course taught to non-STEM majors. The primary intent of the course was to provide students with a conceptual understanding of chemistry.

Design of the Course

With this being a course for non-STEM majors, the instructor and designers looked for various ways to engage the students. The first method was to implement a thematic focus. When possible, the instructor focused on how the chemical concepts the students were learning played a role in the creation and maintenance of artwork.

DOI: 10.4324/9781003109938-8

The intent of doing this was to help the students anchor the chemical concepts to another domain.

One area of interest to the team was failure-based instructional strategies. The team decided to integrate a strategy that would task students with solving complex, ill-structured problems prior to instruction on the topic. Thus, their problem-solving efforts became the introductory aspect of the material.

Implementation of the Failure-based Component – Recreating the "Entombment of Christ"

The implementation of this approach included three episodes. In the first episode, students were tasked with creating a specific shade of blue, known as Prussian blue, which would be used to restore a painting, "The Entombment of Christ." Students attempted to recreate this shade of blue through two separate chemical reactions and later provide the equation of the reaction. Students not only generated the specific shade, but they were required to explain the differences between the reactions. They attempted to recreate the chemical reaction described to them given a scenario prompt. They had to provide a written explanation on how the two reactions differed, including an identification of the formula for each reaction and the reaction type. Within their problem-solving attempts, students struggled with finding the solution to the problem. No student was able to successfully solve the problem during this phase. Students were encouraged to spend the entire time problem solving; however, the majority of students ended their problem-solving attempts early. Additionally, the students were encouraged to make multiple attempts at the problem and look for a variety of solutions. On average, the students made three attempts at solving the problem. At the conclusion of the problem-solving process, students were frustrated and noted their dissatisfaction with the instructional approach.

In the second episode, the instructor delivered an interactive lecture focused on the types of chemical reactions and how a chemical equation represents a chemical change. Within the instruction, common misconceptions or mistakes in chemical reactions were highlighted. To conclude, the instructor returned to the problem and pointed out the correct solutions.

In the final episode, the students completed an exam covering their conceptual understanding of chemical reactions. The questions were focused on students explaining the reaction occurring in a chemical equation rather than balancing the equation itself. The instructor also gathered feedback from the students on their satisfaction after completing the exam.

Outcomes and Modifications

The instructor found that the students performed better than in previous semesters on the exam. That said, this change could not definitively be attributed to the new instructional strategy alone. In addition to the higher exam scores, the students reported satisfaction with the instructional approach after the exam. Interestingly, some made comments that they were initially frustrated but their reflection on the instruction played a key role in their perceived understanding of the concepts The instructor also felt that the level of student engagement after problem solving was higher than a traditional lecture, such as asking better questions.

For future iterations of this approach, the team made a few minor adjustments to the design. First, they would introduce the strategy in a less intensive experience. Additionally, the team noted that providing some scaffolding and introduction to failure response would be beneficial. Lastly, they wanted to spend more time focusing on the problem itself and its contrasting solutions. Specifically, they denoted the importance of highlighting the common mistakes that students may have made in their initial problem-solving attempt as part of their instruction.

Theory and Processes

"I have not failed. I've just found 10,000 ways that won't work"

– Thomas Edison

The quote above by Thomas Edison speaks volumes to the idea of failure and learning from that experience. However, the idea that Edison is speaking to is the natural occurrence of failure during the learning process. Oftentimes, failure will be encountered through the learning process. Various theories address this aspect. Within self-regulation, learners should recognize deficiencies in their various learning experiences through metacognitive awareness (Zimmerman, 1990). Within expertise literature, the concept of deliberate practice notes that learners need to receive feedback, especially when they encounter failure (Ericsson et al., 1993). Additionally, ideas such as impasse-driven learning and negative knowledge address what to do with failure when it happens or how to leverage it after it has happened. While all of these concepts address failure as an expected outcome (i.e., it will happen sometime), they do not treat it as a planned occurrence.

The Interaction of Performance and Learning

Kapur (2016) discussed the different types of outcomes that can occur in any learning situation. A dichotomous breakdown of performance (i.e., short-term or initial attempt at a task) and learning (meaningful long-term changes in knowledge or behavior) creates these outcomes. These outcomes are productive failure, productive success, unproductive failure, and unproductive success (see Table 8.1). Performance is typically thought of through the initial foray into a topic, whereas learning is the knowledge or skills gained through instruction. Failure or success refers to short-term outcomes, usually through a learner's initial performance. Whether an item is productive or unproductive is based on whether meaningful long-term learning occurs after the performance. The important distinction is made between productive success and productive failure in this case. Kapur (2016) argued that there was a key benefit to allow learners to encounter failure in their short-term performance, as long as it was remedied quickly through some type of instructional experience or feedback. Essentially, this initial failure in short-term performance better prepares learners for future learning (Schwartz & Martin, 2004).

When you consider the idea behind productive failure outcomes, it is no surprise that learners need to be receptive to struggle and failure. Within their performance, they are going to face those challenges. Dweck's (2016) work on growth mindset aligns well with

70   *T. Logan Arrington and Andrew A. Tawfik*

Table 8.1 Overview of Outcomes between Performance (Short-term) and Learning (Long-term) based on Kapur (2016)

Long-term Learning	Short-term Performance	
	Failure	*Success*
Productive	Failure in the short-term, after instruction or consolidation, leads to meaningful long-term learning.	Success in the short-term leads to meaningful long-term learning.
Unproductive	Failure in the short-term does not result in meaningful long-term learning.	Success in the short-term does not lead to meaningful learning.

addressing failure. Learners need to be able to see their failure in the initial performance as a "stepping stone" to their future learning. Much of Dweck's work is based on goal orientation; thus, it is important for learners in this approach to be more mastery focused (i.e., interested in learning the content and mastering it) than performance focused (i.e., interested in being successful). Additionally, students should have some capacity to persevere in their problem-solving efforts. Duckworth et al.'s (2007) work on grit is a characteristic that would be beneficial for students within these outcomes as their response to failure would not necessarily be aversive. While elements like mindset and grit might not be considered *teachable* by some, it is important that designers and instructors create an environment that considers elements of these (e.g., stresses long-term outcomes over short-term performance, focuses on students mastering the content).

There are a variety of methods that can be used to elicit productive failure outcomes. Confusingly, the most common instructional approach is also referred to as productive failure as well. Additionally, there have been a variety of investigations that have looked at using failure experiences of others in lieu of those learners attempting to solve a problem or failing on their own. These two types of strategies will be discussed below.

Productive Failure

Productive failure is an instructional approach that asks students to solve complex and ill-structured problems prior to gaining knowledge of those problems' underlying conceptual framework (Kapur, 2008). As an instructional strategy, productive failure is broken down into two phases, exploration and consolidation (Kapur & Bielaczyc, 2012). Exploration refers to the phase where learners examine the problem and create multiple solutions (i.e., problem-solving phase). The design of this phase should aim to create a problem that is complex and ill-structured, but not overtly frustrating to the learners. One of the most crucial factors from these types of problems is the ability to generate multiple solution methods (Kapur & Bielaczyc, 2012; Kapur, 2016). In a sense, the concepts being covered are not ill-structured; instead, they should be placed in a scenario that elicits these types of factors. Within the exploration phase, learners can solve the problem individually or collaboratively (Mazziotti et al., 2014). The final consideration in designing this phase is creating a conducive environment for failure (Kapur & Bielaczyc, 2012). The social surroundings of this phase must allow and encourage failure (i.e., not being able to create an appropriate solution).

Following exploration, students must consolidate the knowledge generated when creating multiple solutions. Typically, direct instruction of some form is used. This consolidation should address elements of solutions generated by students in the previous phase (Kapur & Bielaczyc, 2012). Some have argued that the type of instruction should focus on comparing solutions to the problem (Loibl & Rummel, 2014). Instruction focusing on contrasting solutions typically leads to a much higher conceptual understanding than instruction focusing on the procedural and conceptual factors. While direct instruction may be a common method, there should be opportunities for learners to engage with the material during the instruction as well; thus, this process needs to be interactive. Lastly, a similar atmosphere introduced in the exploration phase should carry over to the consolidation phase. The emphasis is not on the students' errors during the previous stage but on how the generated solutions relate to the most appropriate solution (Kapur & Bielaczyc, 2012). These two phases combine to create productive failure learning experiences. The design of each of these phases must complement one another, as each holds import in productive failure.

As an instructional strategy, productive failure has been compared against learners solving well-structured problems prior to instruction and facilitated or guided problem solving. Studies have also compared the approach versus direct instruction before problem solving. Lastly, the approach has been compared with other preparation for future learning activities, vicarious failure (i.e., students evaluating solutions to problems before instruction), problem posing, and examining worked examples prior to the instructional experience. Typically, this instructional approach has been applied in science, technology, engineering, and mathematics (STEM) domains. There has been some debate about whether this type of approach is effective in non-STEM disciplines (Nachtigall et al., 2020). While this strategy's efficacy is still under investigation in other fields, it has been shown to have a vast impact on specific types of learning outcomes.

Within productive failure, a variety of types of learning outcomes have been investigated. The most commonly examined learning outcome is conceptual knowledge, as contrasted to procedural knowledge. When the learner understands or can use a procedure to solve a problem, they are considered to have procedural knowledge; conceptual knowledge represents the case of a learner understanding how the components involved in a procedure relate to one another (Rittle-Johnson & Alibali, 1999). Across studies, productive failure as a strategy has had the greatest impacts on conceptual knowledge. Using this approach will lead to learners having a better understanding of the underlying concepts that are part of the targeted knowledge within the problem. Unsurprisingly, when comparing learners' problem-solving abilities, productive failure has more of an impact than other instructional strategies on students' complex problem-solving skills. Besides learning outcomes, this process could affect other skills, such as those discussed surrounding productive failure as an outcome.

While this approach does lead to improved knowledge gains, it is not without its detriments to learners. This approach can impact learners' self-efficacy and confidence, especially following the generation phase (Glogger-frey et al., 2015). Depending on the state of the learning environment, this impact on learners' beliefs could negate some of the benefits of productive failure, though research on this topic is inconclusive (Kapur, 2011). Additionally, this approach has been criticized for increasing the learners' cognitive load, especially during the exploration phase. Learners exert extensive mental effort in attempting to solve the problem; however, Kapur (2016) countered the notion that this higher load negatively impacted the learners' ability to learn. To mitigate this factor, designers can use other failure experiences in the exploration phase. These can include having learners evaluate solutions or using cases instead of learners attempting to solve the problem.

Using Cases of Failure for Learning

In addition to solving the existing problem, another important aspect of learning through failure is how one reasons through and later references that experience. The proclivity to reason through complex cases is founded on case-based reasoning (CBR) theory.

Case-based reasoning theory contends that individuals naturally reason through previous problem-solving experiences situated within authentic contexts (Tawfik, Gill et al., 2019). As analogous cases are encountered within the domain, the learners reference an individual case memory in order to help solve the extant problem (Kolodner, 1992). Thus, new problems are resolved by remembering analogous situations and reusing problem-solving knowledge embedded within previous cases (Aamodt & Plaza, 1996).

The foundation of CBR is the ability to remember relevant cases situated within an authentic context to better facilitate knowledge acquisition and subsequent transfer (Jonassen & Hernandez-Serrano, 2002). Experts generate scripts as problem-solving expertise is accumulated throughout one's life. As homogenous cases are reencountered, it is possible that the script is not updated over time (Schank, 1999). As such, Schank's (1999) theory of failure-driven memory suggests that cases of failure are a powerful force to instigate the learning process. Failure plays a central role in learning because it serves as a *mental warning* (Gartmeier et al., 2008) to modify one's mental model (Ellis et al., 2006). Whereas scripts are a form of automated activity that allows an individual to engage in thinking without deep processing, episodes of failure act as the impetus for prediction, self-explanation, and causal reasoning about why an experience may have resulted in the breakdown of a goal (Schank, 1999; Tawfik & Kolodner, 2016). Failure cases may also engender opportunities for creativity of new solutions and techniques not afforded by cases of successful problem solving (Hoeve & Nieuwenhuis, 2006; Parviainen & Eriksson, 2006). As such, "dynamic memory is always changing as each processing failure causes learning to take place" (Schank, 1999, p. 47).

A powerful way to employ CBR in pedagogy is by reminding learners of relevant problem-solving experiences by using case libraries. Case-based reasoning suggests that case libraries provide an essential role in learning by providing experiential knowledge of practitioners where novices may lack experience (Jonassen, 2011). Case libraries thus serve as a proxy for the experience the novices do not yet possess. Research has shown that exposure to experiences of successful problem-solving experiences positively influences problem-solving skills such as prediction, inferences, and explanations (Hernandez-Serrano & Jonassen, 2003; Tawfik, Kim et al., 2019). Additionally, using items such as these cases in lieu of learners' problem solving in initial performance (i.e., a review of cases or a critique of solutions) can lower learners' reported cognitive load (Kapur, 2013).

Professional Practice Revisited

Productive Failure as an Outcome

There was a clear productive failure outcome. In their initial performance, the students were unable to solve the problem; that is, they failed in their initial performance. However, the failure experience prepared them for the interactive lecture. Based on the instructor's observations and the exam scores, the team felt that this productive failure indeed supported problem-solving. However, the team cannot be certain that meaningful long-term learning occurred.

Productive Failure Applied

Within each episode, the tenets of productive failure were somewhat adhered to. Within exploration, the students were encouraged to make multiple attempts to solve the problem and explore the problem space. Within the consolidation phase, the instructor presented direct instruction that focused on the problem's conceptual facets. As noted by the team, there were intended modifications to the approach that would improve this experience and align it to the best practices discussed in the literature. There are additional improvements that can be considered. One change would be to provide more time for students to debrief before learning the correct solution to the problem, which could allow for improved acquisition of knowledge during the consolidation phase. An additional modification could be to scaffold the exploration phase to also allow learners to arrive at the correct solution at the conclusion of that phase.

The instructor wanted learners to grasp the conceptual underpinnings of chemical reactions than directly know the procedure for creating the reactions. This goal was supported by productive failure. It also had a potential impact on the students' engagement and learning by better positioning them to ask more pointed questions during the consolidation phase. Their struggle provided them with the opportunity to uncover potential relationships between the constructs of interests that they may have never considered. The students also were more engaged during the interactive lecture. Also, this strategy was impactful as it can produce secondary effects, such as enhancing learners' persistence or self-efficacy if implemented correctly.

Using Failure Cases

There are multiple ways to interpret this learning activity from a CBR and failure-driven memory perspective. At the core of CBR is how to examine an experience in a way that develops robust episodic memories; that is, cases. These cases include the details of the experience, lessons learned, and other important contextual material. Therefore, it is critical that learners engage in extensive and critical reflection of the experience to repair misconceptions as they label the case. In the context of this case, facilitators could spend less time on the *right answer* and instead reflect on the micro-failures that occurred during the problem-solving failures. For example, facilitators could ask what chemical combinations were tried and did not work, and then discuss the reasons as to why they yielded unfavorable results. Theorists of CBR and failure-driven memory argue that learners are then able to engage in additional inquiry as to why the error occurred, which identifies latent causal processes they may have otherwise missed. As learners refine the indices associated with the case, they are able to better label their memory for future retrieval and subsequent transfer.

Another strategy could be used during the problem-solving experience. Because novices lack the episodic memory that is important for problem solving, learners could have access to a set of related cases that serve as *vicarious memory* in a case library. This database of germane experiences could depict how other practitioners tried to solve similar cases, yet failed. For example, there could be a case about how another museum used specific chemical reactions, along with their outcomes. These narratives could be diverse enough in context, but similar in their underlying structure and indices. Alternatively, learners could use a shared space (e.g., a wiki) to develop their own cases and share them with their peers. Learners could then use these narrative formats to foresee how their proposed solutions might work as they solve the main problem, which supports analogical transfer. As the activity progressed, learners may identify patterns and indices across cases, abstract principles about the chemical reactions, combine solutions from different cases, and reason about how they relate to the solution. Whereas productive failure may lead to frustration, a more CBR and failure-driven approach uses the narratives to support analogical transfer and other high-order reasoning skills.

Connecting Process to Practice

1. What are some scenarios or situations where you believe failure-based instructional strategies would be beneficial? Consider each of these settings: K-12, Higher Education, Business/Industry, Government/Military, or Healthcare;
2. What do you believe are some beneficial methods for enhancing learners' responses to failures, both designed and unintentional?
3. What types of factors should you consider about learners prior to attempting to integrate a failure-based instructional strategy?
4. How do these two approaches (i.e., productive failure and using failure cases) complement each other? Describe a scenario where they are applied in tandem;
5. What are some methods of peer support that can be added into these failure approaches to improve them? Consider both the exploration and consolidation phases.

Debate Activity

Given the presentation of these two complementary strategies, allow students to take a perspective on which of these approaches would be the most effective strategy to implement within the initial case study environment. Should it remain the same (productive failure), or should a case-based approach be implemented? Consider the following three components at least to frame the debate: the intended outcomes, the time of the course that the strategy was introduced, and its short- and long-term impact on students.

Design Activity

Task students in teams or individually with creating a brief learning activity that utilizes a failure-based strategy for a given content and context. Encourage the students to consider the following in their design:

- To what extent is failure to be encountered (i.e., what type of strategy will you use)?
- What methods of support are going to be used as students encounter failure either directly or vicariously?
- What methods of support are going to be used to help students consolidate the information?

Upon completion of the design, have the students implement their activities with the other members of the class. Students then would provide feedback on what worked well and what could be improved within the activity.

References

Aamodt, A., & Plaza, E. (1996). Case-based reasoning: Foundational issues, methodological variations, and systems approaches. *Artificial Intelligence Communications, 7*(1), 39–59. doi:10.3233/aic-1994-7104

Darabi, A., Arrington, T. L., & Sayilir, E. (2018). Learning from failure: A meta-analysis of the empirical studies. *Educational Technology Research and Development, 66*(5), 1101–1118. doi:10.1007/s11423-018-9579-9

Duckworth, A. L., Peterson, C., Matthews, M. D., & Kelly, D. R. (2007). Grit: Perseverance and passion for long-term goals. *Journal of Personality and Social Psychology, 92,* 1087–1101. doi:10.1037/0022-3514.92.6.1087

Dweck, C. (2016). *Mindset: The new psychology of success.* Penguin Random House.

Ellis, S., Mendel, R., & Davidi, I. (2006). Learning from successful and failed experience: The moderating role of kind of after-event review. *The Journal of Applied Psychology, 91*(3), 669–680. doi:10.1037/0021-9010.91.3.669

Ericsson, K. A., Krampe, R. T., & Tesch-Römer, C. (1993). The role of deliberate practice in the acquisition of expert performance. *Psychological Review, 100*(3), 363–406. doi:10.1037/0033-295x.100.3.363

Gartmeier, M., Bauer, J., Gruber, H., & Heid, H. (2008). Negative knowledge: Understanding professional learning and expertise. *Vocations and Learning, 1*(2), 87–103. doi:10.1007/s12186-008-9006-1

Glogger-Frey, I., Fleischer, C., Grüny, L., Kappich, J., & Renkl, A. (2015). Inventing a solution and studying a worked solution prepare differently for learning from direct instruction. *Learning and Instruction, 39,* 72–87. doi:10.1016/j.learninstruc.2015.05.001

Hernandez-Serrano, J., & Jonassen, D. H. (2003). The effects of case libraries on problem solving. *Journal of Computer Assisted Learning, 19*(1), 103–114. doi:10.1046/j.0266-4909.2002.00010.x

Hoeve, A., & Nieuwenhuis, L. F. M. (2006). Learning routines in innovation processes. *Journal of Workplace Learning, 18*(3), 171–185. doi:10.1108/13665620610654595

Jonassen, D. H. (2011). *Learning to solve problems: A handbook for designing problem-solving learning environments* (1st ed.). Routledge.

Jonassen, D. H., & Hernandez-Serrano, J. (2002). Case-based reasoning and instructional design: Using stories to support problem solving. *Educational Technology, Research, and Development, 50*(2), 65–77. doi:10.1007/bf02504994

Kapur, M. (2008). Productive failure. *Cognition and Instruction, 26*(3), 379–424. doi:10.1080/07370000802212669

Kapur, M. (2011). A further study of productive failure in mathematical problem solving: Unpacking the design components. *Instructional Science, 39*(4), 561–579. doi:10.1007/s11251-010-9144-3

Kapur, M. (2013). Comparing learning from productive failure and vicarious failure. *Journal of the Learning Sciences, 23*(4), 651–677. doi:10.1080/10508406.2013.819000

Kapur, M. (2016). Examining productive failure, productive success, unproductive failure, and unproductive success in learning. *Educational Psychologist, 51*(2), 289–299. doi:10.1080/004615 20.2016.1155457

Kapur, M., & Bielaczyc, K. (2012). Designing for productive failure. *Journal of the Learning Sciences, 21*(1), 45–83. doi:10.1080/10508406.2011.591717

Kolodner, J. (1992). An introduction to case-based reasoning. *Artificial Intelligence Review, 6*(1), 3–34. doi:10.1007/bf00155578

Loibl, K., & Rummel, N. (2014). Knowing what you don't know makes failure productive. *Learning and Instruction, 34,* 74–85. doi:10.1016/j.learninstruc.2014.08.004

Mazziotti, C., Loibl, K., & Rummel, N. (2014). Does collaboration affect learning in a productive failure setting? In J.L. Polman, E.A. Kyza, D.K. O'Neill, I. Tabak, W.R. Penuel, A.S. Ju-Row, K. O'Connor, T. Lee, & L. D'Amico (Eds.), *Proceedings of the 11th international conference of the learning sciences (ICLS 2014),* Vol. 3 (pp. 1184–1185). International Society of the Learning Sciences, Inc.

Nachtigall, V., Serova, K., & Rummel, N. (2020). When failure fails to be productive: Probing the effectiveness of productive failure for learning beyond STEM domains. *Instructional Science, 48*(6), 651–697. doi:10.1007/s11251-020-09525-2

Parviainen, J., & Eriksson, M. (2006). Negative knowledge, expertise and organizations. *International Journal of Management Concepts and Philosophy, 2*(2), 140–153. doi:10.1504/ijmcp.2006.010265

Rittle-Johnson, B., & Alibali, M. W. (1999). Conceptual and procedural knowledge of mathematics: Does one lead to the other? *Journal of Educational Psychology, 91*(1), 175–189. doi:10.1037/0022-0663.91.1.175

Schank, R. (1999). *Dynamic memory revisited* (2nd ed.). Cambridge University Press.

Schwartz, D. L., & Martin, T. (2004). Inventing to prepare for future learning: The hidden efficiency of encouraging original student production in statistics instruction. *Cognition and Instruction, 22*(2), 129–184. doi:10.1207/s1532690xci2202_1

Tawfik, A. A., Gill, A., Hogan, M., York, C. S., & Keene, C. W. (2019). How novices use expert case libraries for problem solving. *Technology, Knowledge and Learning, 24*(1), 23–40. doi:10.1007/s10758-017-9324-1

Tawfik, A. A., Kim, K., Hogan, M., & Msilu, F. (2019). How success versus failure cases support knowledge construction in collaborative problem-solving. *Journal of Educational Computing Research, 57*(6), 1376–1399. doi:10.1177/0735633118799750

Tawfik, A. A., & Kolodner, J. (2016). Systematizing scaffolding for problem-based learning: A view from case-based reasoning. *Interdisciplinary Journal of Problem-Based Learning, 10*(1). doi:10.7771/1541-5015.1608

Tawfik, A. A., Rong, H., & Choi, I. (2015). Failing to learn: Toward a unified design approach for failure-based learning. *Educational Technology Research and Development, 63*(6), 975–994. doi:10.1007/s11423-015-9399-0

Zimmerman, B. J. (1990). Self-regulated learning and academic achievement: An overview. *Educational Psychologist, 25*(1), 3–17. doi:10.1207/s15326985ep2501_2

9 Instructional Design from the Lens of Self-Regulated Ill-Structured Problem Solving

Research and Practical Applications

Xun Ge, Ali Ceyhun Muftuoglu, and Spencer Brickell

Chapter Overview

The purpose of this chapter is to demonstrate that instructional design is an ill-structured problem-solving process involving iterative processes guided by self-regulation from problem representation to generating solutions. It is argued that instructional designers must focus on the process of iterative problem representation and generating solutions, and as instructional design educators or trainers, we must engage students in complex instructional design problem solving activities. Through an ID case, we intend to illustrate the interrelationship between various concepts, including instructional design, ill-structured problem solving, self-regulation, and problem-based learning. We follow up the case by illustrating how the instructional design process is an ill-structured problem-solving process, and why it is important for us to assume the problem-solving mindset when approaching instructional design. Through a case study, this chapter also showcases how to develop students' problem-solving mindset and guide them through ill-structured problem solving, which consists of iterative processes and multiple cycles of planning, execution, and reflection.

Guiding Questions

1. What is instructional design? What is the primary goal of instruction design?
2. Recall your own instructional design experience, how do you identify problems and define goals and processes? How do you develop solutions to address an instructional problem?
3. From your experience, is instructional design a systematic and linear process or a dynamic, iterative, and complex process? Why? Please provide your rationale;
4. What is the role of planning and reflection in developing effective instructional design projects?

Case Study

Sarah was an instructional designer for a small eLearning company. Recently, she and her team had been awarded a contract to work on a new design project for One United, a global insurance company. The purpose of this project was to develop a course to help new employees gain an understanding of the processes of the company and pass the state licensing examination. Sarah's team was given a year and a half to complete the contract with a $566,000 budget.

DOI: 10.4324/9781003109938-9

Sarah's team consisted of the following members: Two instructional designers, two multimedia artists, two software engineers, and a graphic artist. Sarah's role was to lead the design team and manage the project. Her responsibilities included overseeing the project, planning and managing the budget, communicating with the clients and fellow team members, and helping the team make executive decisions in different phases of the project. The two instructional designers worked with a subject matter expert (SMEs), developed content, and collaborated with the graphic and multimedia artists to create multimedia assets. The two multimedia artists also worked closely with the software engineers to develop the content for the course. Below is a brief description of some issues Sarah's team had encountered in the instructional design process.

During the analysis phase, One United requested that the course meet the purposes of (1) onboarding new employees to the company's benefits and processes, and (2) preparing the new employees to take their state licensing examination. Sarah's team decided to divide the instruction into two main parts according to the project goals provided by the client. They only conducted a preliminary task analysis, but they failed to conduct a thorough analysis, including learning objectives, subordinate skills, and entry-level behaviors because the company pressured the team to complete the analysis phase in two months with $67,000, when it was originally planned to last three months with a budget of $100,000.

During the content development period, the instructional designers realized that the failure to conduct a thorough task analysis had made it difficult for the team to select and develop instructional materials and learning activities from the hundreds of pages of content and materials provided by the client. Sarah had to pause the content development and return to the analysis phase, working with the SMEs again to reconduct the task analysis, which enabled them to select the course materials, instructional strategies, and develop learning activities and assessments that were aligned with learning goals and objectives.

Revisiting the content analysis allowed the team to move forward to the development phase, but also forced Sarah and her team to reevaluate the milestone schedule and budget. It cost additional time and resources, which would have gone toward the development phase needed to be reallocated. Consequently, Sarah had to write a contract amendment proposal to reopen the task analysis phase for a period of two weeks. The contract amendment included a $16,000 price tag and a two-week extension of the contract.

Going back to the previous phase, although costly, was necessary and essential to develop effective instructional materials, learning activities, and assessments. As a result, in working with the multimedia team and the software engineers, the design team were successful in developing scenario-based instruction to emphasize the real-world application.

Theory and Practice

In this section, we present the key concepts related to problem solving and illustrate why instructional design is an ill-structured problem-solving process and how instructional designers should approach ID problems and solutions guided by the perspective of ill-structured problem solving. We first present some key concepts related to problem solving, particularly ill-structured problem solving; then we explain what instructional design is and why instructional design is to be considered an ill-structured process.

Problem Solving – Key Concepts

Problem solving is a process of searching for solutions in a *problem space*, which consists of various states of problems that eventually transforms a problem from the initial state to the goal state. The initial state is the start state of a problem, and the goal state is when a problem is solved (Anderson, 2020). Between the initial state and the goal state, there are a series of consecutive states. With each transaction, the problem state is transformed to be closer to the goal state through problem-solving operators. Problem-solving operators generate a space of possible states through which a problem solver must search to find a path to attain the goal. Therefore, determining problem space and selecting appropriate paths to solutions are the two key variables in solving a problem. The process of creating a problem space is referred to as *problem representation.*

Problem representation is schema driven, which guides problem solvers in the process of solution generation. Problem representation depends on "the problem solver's understanding and the representation of the type of the problem, including an understanding of the problem state and the goal state" (Jonassen, 1997). Problem solvers store applicable strategies and procedures for problem solving based on their previous experiences (Gick, 1986; Jonassen, 1997). Problem solvers must first activate their schema to represent the problem, and then they identify paths to problem solutions. If a clear solution path is not identified, the problem solvers will continue to search for solutions through the problem space by applying a different problem-solving strategy until a satisfactory solution is generated (Gick, 1986). This is known as search-based problem representation.

A successful problem solver applies various strategies (e.g., planning, analogy, means-end analysis, information gathering, decomposition or side-angle-side) to generate *problem solutions. Problem solving strategies* are techniques that direct problem solvers to reach the best possible solutions (Mayer, 1987; Gick, 1986). The early research on problem-solving focused more on general problem-solving strategies. The later research shifted its focus to schema-based, domain-specific problem representation (Gick, 1986). Some strategies are more appropriate for multiple domains (e.g., planning), while others are more appropriate for specific domains (e.g., means-end analysis for physics) (Gick, 1986; Jonassen, 1997; Anderson, 2015).

The problem-solving process requires not only domain knowledge (e.g., propositional information, concepts, rules and principles), but also structural knowledge (e.g., information networking, semantic mapping, and mental models), ampliative skills (e.g., constructing/applying arguments, analogizing, and inferencing), and most importantly, the metacognitive skills (Jonassen, 1997). Problem solvers develop problem representations in an attempt to better understand the gap between the initial state and the goal state (Jonassen, 1997). Different representations determine different paths to solutions and outcomes and affect the quality of solutions. The overall process of problem solving is an iterative process, where problem solvers constantly move back and forth between problem representation and solution stages in the problem space until the best fitting solution can be applied (Gick, 1986). The solutions reached by the problem solver can be divergent (i.e., single solution) or convergent (i.e., multiple solutions) (Jonassen, 1997). Expert problem solvers generally have a large number of schemas for the problems (Jonassen, 1997). Through practice and experiences overtime, they develop automaticity in problem solving (Anderson, 2020; Bransford et al., 1999; Jonassen, 1997).

Ill-Structured Problem Solving: Iteration and Self-Regulation

Problem solving can be viewed as a continuum from well-structured to ill-structured problems. Ill-structured problems have fuzzy goal states (Glaser et al., 1985), while well-defined problems have more clearly defined goals and paths to solutions (Dörner & Funke, 2017). In addition, well-structured problems are convergent in nature, engaging learners with a limited number of variables and confined within a defined scope of problem spaces. Therefore, the solutions are already prescribed. Meanwhile, in ill-structured problems there are multiple variables while some are unknown, such problem spaces are open to a variety of possible solutions (Jonassen, 1997). For example, deciding on the best form of instruction based on a needs analysis of a target audience may yield multiple paths and solutions and be regarded as an ill-structured problem. Compared to well-structured problem solving, ill-structured problem solving often starts with a fuzzy goal state and involves searching for solutions in multiple problem spaces with many unknown factors or uncertain situations that compel a problem solver to seek needed information and resources (Ge & Land, 2004).

Ill-structured problems may lead to multiple paths for solutions, or there may be no feasible solutions at all. Therefore, a problem solver is often compelled to select a solution that is most plausible and viable given a specific context or problem situation. In such a case, selecting the most feasible solution is left to the problem solvers' representation of the problem and their value judgment for the appropriateness of the solution (Kitchner, 1983). Ill-structured problem solving requires various types of knowledge, which includes ampliative skills (e.g., constructing convincing arguments for problem representation and selecting or generating solutions) and metacognitive skills (e.g., planning, monitoring, evaluation, and reflection) (Ge & Land, 2003, 2004; Jonassen, 1997).

Synthesizing the seminal works of Sinnott (1989), Voss and Post (1988), and Voss et al. (1991), Ge and Land (2004) identified a comprehensive scaffolding framework for ill-structured problem solving, including (a) problem representation; (b) generating and selecting solutions; (c) making justifications; and (d) monitoring and evaluating goals and solutions (Ge & Land, 2004). In this process, problem solvers need to engage in both cognitive and metacognitive processes (Schraw et al., 1995). Although ill-structured problem solving and well-structured problem solving share similarities (Ge & Land, 2004), problem solvers need to rely more on metacognitive skills in solving ill-structured problems, especially in interpreting the state or essence of the problem, defining the goals of a problem, comparing and selecting solutions, and generating defensible arguments (Ge & Land, 2004). In addition, solving ill-structured problems takes more iterations between various processes in comparison to solving well-structured problems (Ge, 2013).

Building on earlier work (Ge & Land, 2004; Jonassen, 1997; Sinnott, 1989; Voss & Post, 1988), Ge et al. (2016) developed a theoretical framework that clarifies the role of self-regulation in the ill-structured problem-solving processes. Ge et al.'s (2016) work integrates self-regulation theories (Pintrich, 2000; Zimmerman, 2002) and motivation and affective factors (e.g., beliefs). According to Ge et al. (2016), the ill-structured problem-solving process is a self-regulation process of constantly planning, monitoring, evaluating, and reflecting until a plausible, viable, and defensible solution is identified. In the context of problem solving, a self-regulation process is a constructive process in which problem solvers set goals first and then actively work to monitor, regulate, and control their problem-solving processes. Self-regulation, in the form of planning, monitoring, reflection, and evaluation, enables problem solvers to navigate through a problem space that has uncertain problem states, fuzzy situations, and unclear goals to represent problems and construct mental models. Problem representation facilitates the generation of solutions to the problems and the identified goals (Ge et al., 2016). In addition, a problem solver also evaluates the problem-solving process as part of the self-regulation process, determining if the information is adequate for problem solving or if it is necessary to weigh on the importance of some selected goals given the situation of the problem. They must also evaluate multiple views and perspectives to make sure that selected solutions are sound, valid, and unbiased.

Instructional Design Process

Traditionally, *instructional design* has been defined and recognized as a systematic process employed to develop educational and training programs in a consistent and reliable fashion (Reiser & Dempsey, 2007). This process consists of a number of identifiable and related subprocesses (Gagné et al., 2005), such as needs analysis, design, development, implementation, and evaluation. The conventional definitions of instructional design generally emphasize a systematic approach toward instructional design, which includes identifying, developing, and evaluating a set of strategies aimed at attaining a particular instructional goal (Morrison et al., 2011). Although many scholars recognize the complexity, reflectiveness, and iteration involved in instructional design (Gagné et al., 2005; Reiser & Dempsey, 2007; Smith & Ragan, 2005), instructional design has generally been misinterpreted by many as a linear process, where one subprocess is built upon the previous and leads to the next (Jonassen, 2008).

A closer examination of the instructional design process contends that it is an ill-structured problem-solving process. The purpose of instructional design is to address a complex learning process that is affected by various issues concerning learners, learning outcomes, and specific contexts, and to develop solutions to the identified instructional problems, including instructional environment, learning materials, instructional strategies, and activities, tools and resources. Throughout the instructional design process, instructional designers seek answers to the *where, how*, and *when* questions in their instructional decision making (Smith & Ragan, 2005). They have to provide justifications to support their decisions and solutions (Jonassen, 2008). Due to the complexity of instructional design, Young (1993) argued that instructional design is a problem-solving process reflective of the abilities of the problem solver and the unique characteristics of the context.

Professional Practice Revisited

The case study is an example of ill-structured problem solving in instructional design that has been discussed in the Theory and Practice section. It demonstrates how problem representation in the analysis phase can affect problem solutions in the subsequent instructional design phases. Instructional design often does not have clearly defined problems or goal states to begin with, so evaluation should have occurred constantly throughout the entire instructional design process before moving forward to the next phase to minimize the cost of time and resources.

The team's decision to move forward without conducting a thorough task analysis did not lead to successful problem solving and effective instructional design outcomes. Sarah and her team were given a fuzzy, ill-defined initial state that lacked clear goals. They should have engaged in the problem representation process characterized by learner analysis, contextual analysis, and task analysis, involving many variables or decisions which could affect one another and the following phases, such as design and development. In a rush to move into the design and development phases, Sarah's team skipped performing a thorough task analysis. It may seem easier and faster to take such a shortcut, but as Sarah's team discovered, it led to serious problems later in the instructional design process. By failing to complete the task analysis, Sarah's teams did not have proper objectives to begin for designing the content materials and learning activities. As a result, they had to propose an extension to the project, which subsequently pushed back the development phase. This lesson demonstrates that when a problem is not adequately represented in the previous phase, the subsequent phase suffers.

Sarah's case shows that instructional design is a complex problem-solving process, involving the interaction of numerous variables and multiple phases. If certain variables are not adequately considered during problem representation in the analysis phase, it can affect the development or generation of solutions in the next stage or phase. Therefore, it is necessary for instructional designers to return to the previous phase and reanalyze the problem situation until the problem is adequately represented before moving to the next phase.

Iterative Problem Solving in Instructional Design Process: Conceptual Framework

With the understanding that instructional design is an ill-structured problem solving process, we argue that instructional design should be approached as an iterative complex problem solving activity (Young, 1993; Smith & Ragan, 2005; Merrill, 2002; Jonassen, 2008; Morrison et al., 2011). Therefore, instructional designers should adopt the mindset of problem solvers and be reflective of their design experience as an ill-structured problem-solving process. To help instructional designers understand this perspective, we propose a conceptual framework demonstrating the iterative nature of ill-structured problem solving in the context of instructional design. This work is an extension of the self-regulated problem-solving framework developed by Ge et al. (2016). It is hoped that this framework will help instructional designers to develop the mental model of reflective problem solving in their design practice.

Designing an instructional project is working on an instructional design problem space, which consists of multiple sub-problem spaces with iterative processes of problem representation and problem solution over an overarching process that spans across analysis, design, development, implementation, and evaluation. This process is best illustrated with a bird's eye view in Figure 9.1.

As is stated, the instructional design process is conceptualized as a process of searching in a problem space for solutions to an instructional problem. This process consists of two layers of iterative processes between problem representation and solution generation. The outer layer is viewed from the overarching instructional design process that consists of various phases, such as analysis, design, development, implementation, and evaluation. The phase of analysis can be viewed as the problem representation stage while the other phases – design, development, implementation, evaluation, can be viewed as the solution development stage. Over these two stages, the two problem solving processes (i.e., problem representation and solution generation) are viewed as an iterative process until a plausible and viable solution is developed successfully. At the same time, the inner

Research and Practical Applications   83

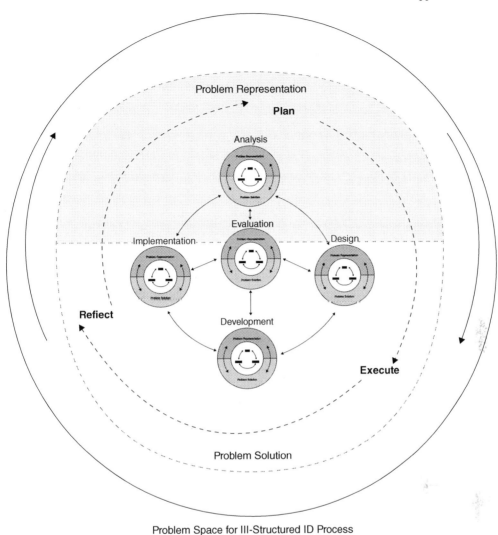

Figure 9.1 Iterative problem-solving process in instructional design.

layer shows each of the instructional design phases, from analysis, design, development, implementation, to evaluation. Within each of the instructional design phases, instructional designers go through an iterative cycle from problem representation to solution generation and then back to problem representation and solution generation until a satisfactory solution has been reached. In addition, we conceptualize that each phase (e.g., analysis) has its own iteration cycle and that each task within a specific phase (e.g., contextual analysis) also goes through the problem representation and solution cycle at another but deeper level. Figure 9.2 illustrates how iterative problem solving is conceptualized from the outer layer, that is, the overall instructional design layer, to the inner layer of the analysis phase, and how iteration occurs for each of the goals for various levels and specific tasks within the analysis phase.

As is visualized in Figure 9.1, each problem-solving iteration between problem representation and solution generation, in either overarching instructional design processes (outer layer) or each of the instructional design phases (inner layer), is accomplished and driven by the self-regulated process of planning, monitoring, and

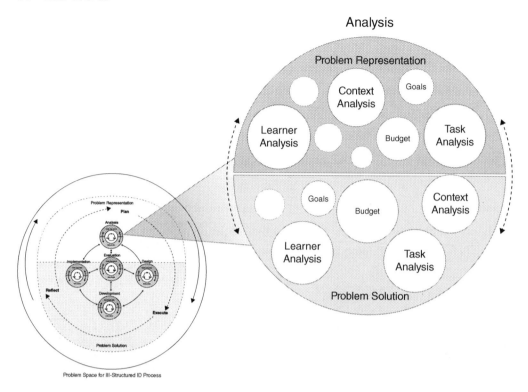

Figure 9.2 The analysis phases of the instructional design process in the inner layer.

reflection (Ge et al., 2016). The iterative problem-solving process is informed by continuous planning, execution, and reflection components of the self-regulation cycle.

In the case study, Sarah and her team went through multiple stages of iterative problem-solving processes while working on the design project for One United. The project team conducted analysis activities which allowed them to create a representation of the design problem. In view of the overarching goals for the instructional design, the analysis stage is a problem representation stage. Based on the information gathered and the analysis outcome, the team moved forward to the following instructional design stages to solve problems in designing, development, and implementation. However, reflecting on the inadequate problem representation in the analysis phase (e.g., lack of detailed context analysis and failure to conduct a task analysis), Sarah's team decided to go back to perform further analysis, which led to an expanded or alternative problem representation. The team's insufficient commitment to performing iterative and reflective analysis triggered a butterfly effect, which prevented the design team from moving forward successfully.

Connecting Process to Practice

Guided by the instructional design problem solving framework represented by Figure 9.1 and Figure 9.2, we propose a matrix of iterative instructional design process in Table 9.1 as a scaffolding tool to support instructional design students while they are engaged in the iterative processes of problem representation and solution and the self-regulation processes of planning, execution, and reflection.

Table 9.1 illustrates an overview of the instructional design processes and the iterative nature of instructional design activities. It shows both iterations between various ADDIE

Table 9.1 Iterative Instructional Design Process Matrix

			Iteration within ID Stages		
			Problem Representation ↔ Problem Solution ↔ Evaluation *(↔Problem Representation......)		
			Planning ↔ Execution ↔ Reflection *(↔ Planning ......)		
Iterative ID Process			Planning	Execution	Reflection
Problem Representation of ID Process ↕	*Planning* ↕ *Execution*	Analysis	Identify project goals and what analysis needed for representing the project problem	Conduct analysis (e.g., context, task analysis)	Does the analysis represent an investigable problem?
Problem Solution of the ID Process ↕	*Reflection* ↕ *Planning*	Design	Gather preliminary information to create the design plan	Develop instruction (e.g., organization and sequencing, delivery format, instructional strategies, learning activities)	Is formative evaluations of the solution or project effective?
Project Evaluation ↕	*(Planning......).*	Development	Identify and assign tasks	Develop or integrate technologies. Test design products Test procedures with facilitators	How well does the design product provide a solution?
(Problem Representation of ID Process....).		Implementation	Draft procedure for learners		How functional the product works?
		Evaluation	Schedule piloting (e.g., alpha, beta, gamma testing)	Collect data for further evaluation and validation	Did this iterative process yield an effective product?

* An Instructional Designer may jump back to any earlier stage in this iterative process.

86 *Xun Ge et al.*

phases and iterations within each of the phases. Horizontally, each row in the table represents the iterative problem solving in each of the ADDIE phases, which is monitored and regulated by iterative activities of *planning, execution,* and *reflection.* For example, starting from the row of the *analysis* phase, instructional designers represent problems so that they can generate solutions for instructional problems in the subsequent design phases. In the meantime, the *analysis* phase consists of activities that foster a deeper level of iteration and self-regulation within the problem space of the *analysis* phase. In other words, specific tasks performed within the *analysis* phase, such as *identifying project goals* and *identifying types of analysis required* are parts of the problem representation. This table helps to promote reflective thinking in instructional design practice so that informed decisions can be made. Using the case of Sarah and her team, we demonstrate how to apply the iterative design matrix to develop instructional design skills in the following section.

Activity 1: Identify Project Goals and Develop a Plan for the Analysis Phase

We may ask students such questions during the *analysis* phase:

- What have Sarah and her team done successfully?
- What did they fail to do that had affected their design phase?
- What would you have done differently to ensure that the analysis is adequately performed?

At this point, it is important to make sure that learners go through careful planning, execution, and reflection processes. The problem space in the analysis phase should include, but not limited to learner analysis, task and content analysis, and other factors, such as the timeline and budget. With the information provided by One United, such as content, identified objectives, needs analysis and considering timeline and budget, ask the questions:

- Does Sarah's team have sufficient information to move forward?
- Is there some unknown information that is critical for moving forward to make instructional decisions?

Asking such questions engages students to work on the iterative problem representation process to understand the problem, identify goals, and develop a plan for needs analysis. Planning instructional activities such as *identifying authentic project goals, mapping out a plan for the analysis activities (i.e., what type of analysis needed for the project)* or *using collaborative brainstorming activities* can help to engage students in answering these questions.

After completing the analysis activities, it is important to engage learners in reflection activities. Active reflection supports decision making regarding if instructional designers are ready to move forward to the next phase or if they need to go through another round of iteration in seeking better solutions.

Learners should be encouraged to critically think if the analysis phase represents an investigable problem. If not, why? Learners should be guided to ask the question at the beginning of the project what additional information they need to seek for conducting needs analysis and task analysis. After the execution, learners can be guided to answer reflection questions, such as "How does your plan represent a better investigable problem than Sarah's team?" This reflection question directs learners to think of multiple perspectives, multiple representations, and alternative solutions for a problem. In addition, the instructor can use the following strategies to support learners' reflections: *reflecting on individual or group learning experiences, negotiating a common understanding of the problem with collaboration or matching the project goals with the negotiated problem.*

Furthermore, it is critically important that instructional design students should develop argumentation skills to justify their reasoning and design decisions, so prompting them with "why" questions will help them to articulate their reasoning and formulate an argument in defense of their choices and decisions.

Activity 2: Engage in Reflections during the Design and Development Phases

As instructional design is not a linear process, there is not a clear-cut distinction for transitions between different phases. Sometimes the instructional design activities of different phases may overlap or be conducted simultaneously based on specific conditions of the design team, such as time and budget. Considering the design and development phases, we may ask students such questions:

- How did moving forward before conducting a task analysis affect the design and development phases?
- Would careful planning and reflection prevent this from happening?
- Why did Sarah's team not realize the problem before designing and developing the learning materials? What lesson do you learn from Sarah's case?

The problem space of the design and development phases include decisions for developing instruction (e.g., organization and sequencing, delivery format, schedule, instructional package, learning activities, assignments, and self-assessments for the students), storyboarding, multimedia development, software development, and more. Encouraging students to make inquiries into these phases would foster their understanding of the ill-structured nature of instructional design problems. Students can be supported to think critically about decisions made by Sarah and her team in the crucial periods of design and development. To contextualize, Sarah decided to pause all design and development activities when she realized that they had to go back and reconducted the task analysis. Faced with such a problem, Sarah decided to write a contract amendment asking for a two-week extension, which would allow her team to go back to the analysis while keeping the development active. Such problems may lead to multiple problem representations and alternative solutions. Learners should be guided to think about the following questions:

88 *Xun Ge et al.*

- How would Sarah's decision to keep the development active while returning to the analysis phase affect the project goals?
- What would be the alternative solutions in this case?
- How would you apply the iterative and metacognitive processes of planning, execution, and reflection to effectively solve problems occurring during the design and development phases?

References

Anderson, J. R. (2015). *Cognitive psychology and its implications* (8th ed.). Worth.

Anderson, J. R. (2020). *Cognitive psychology and its implications* (9th ed.). Worth.

Bransford, J., Bransford, J. D., Brown, A. L., & Cocking, R. R. (1999). *How people learn: Brain, mind, experience, and school.* National Academies Press.

Dörner, D., & Funke, J. (2017). Complex problem solving: What it is and what it is not. *Frontiers in Psychology, 8,* 1153. doi:10.3389/fpsyg.2017.01153

Gagné, R. M., Wager, W. W., Golas, K. C., Keller, J. M., & Russell, J. D. (2005). Principles of instructional design. *Performance Improvement Quarterly, 44*(2), 44–46. doi:10.1002/pfi.4140440211

Ge, X. (2013). Designing learning technology to support self-monitoring and self-regulation during ill-structured problem-solving tasks. In R. Azevedo & V. Aleven (Eds.), *International handbook of metacognition and learning technologies* (pp. 213–228). Springer.

Ge, X., & Land, S. M. (2003). Scaffolding students' problem-solving processes in an ill-structured task using question prompts and peer interactions. *Educational Technology Research and Development, 51*(1), 21–38. doi:10.1007/BF02504515

Ge, X., & Land, S. M. (2004). A conceptual framework for scaffolding Ill-structured problem-solving processes using question prompts and peer interactions. *Educational Technology Research and Development, 52*(2), 5–22. doi:10.1007/BF02504836

Ge, X., Law, V., & Huang, K. (2016). Detangling the interrelationships between self-regulation and ill-structured problem solving in problem-based learning. *Interdisciplinary Journal of Problem-Based Learning, 10*(2), 11. doi:10.7771/1541-5015.1622

Gick, M. L. (1986). Problem-solving strategies. *Educational Psychologist, 21*(1–2), 99–120. doi:10.1080/00461520.1986.9653026

Glaser, R., Chi, M. T. H., & Farr, M. J. (1985). *The nature of expertise* (p. 26). Columbus, OH: National Center for Research in Vocational Education, The Ohio State University. doi:10.4324/9781315799681

Jonassen, D. H. (1997). Instructional design models for well-structured and Ill-structured problem-solving learning outcomes. *Educational Technology Research and Development, 45*(1), 65–94. doi:10.1007/BF02299613

Jonassen, D. H. (2008). Instructional design as design problem solving: An iterative process. *Educational Technology, 48*(3), 21–26.

Kitchner, K. S. (1983). Cognition, metacognition, and epistemic cognition. *Human Development, 26*(4), 222–232. doi:10.1159/000272885

Mayer, R. E. (1987). Learnable aspects of problem solving: Some examples. In D. E. Berger, K. Pezdek, & W. P. Banks (Eds.), *Applications of cognitive psychology: Problem solving, education, and computing* (pp. 109–122). Routledge.

Merrill, M. D. (2002). First principles of instruction. *Educational Technology Research and Development, 50*(3), 43–59. doi:10.1007/BF02505024

Morrison, G. R., Ross, S. J., Morrison, J. R., & Kalman, H. K. (2011). *Designing effective instruction* (6th ed.). John Wiley & Sons.

Pintrich, P. R. (2000). The role of goal orientation in self-regulated learning. In M. Boekaerts, M. Zeidner, & P. R. Pintrich (Eds.), *Handbook of self-regulation* (pp. 451–502). Academic Press.

Reiser, R. A., & Dempsey, J. V. (2007). *Trends and issues in instructional design and technology* (2nd ed.). Pearson/Merrill Prentice Hall.

Schraw, G., Dunkle, M. E., & Bendixen, L. D. (1995). Cognitive processes in well-defined and ill-defined problem solving. *Applied Cognitive Psychology, 9*(6), 523–538. doi:10.1002/acp.2350090605

Sinnott, J. D. (1989). A model for solution of ill-structured problems: Implications for everyday and abstract problem solving. In J. D. Sinnott (Ed.), *Everyday problem solving: Theory and applications* (pp. 72–99). Praeger Publishers.

Smith, P. L., & Ragan, T. J. (2005). *Instructional design.* John Wiley & Sons.

Voss, J. F., & Post, T. A. (1988). On the solving of ill-structured problems. In M. H. Chi, R. Glaser, & M. J. Farr (Eds.), *The nature of expertise* (pp. 261–285). Erlbaum Associates.

Voss, J. F., Wolfe, C. R., Lawrence, J. A., & Engle, R. A. (1991). From representation to decision: An analysis of problem solving in international relations. In R. J. Sternberg & P. A. Frensch (Eds.), *Complex problem solving: Principles and mechanisms* (pp. 119–158). Lawrence Erlbaum Associates.

Young, M. F. (1993). Instructional design for situated learning. *Educational Technology Research and Development, 41*(1), 43–58. doi:10.1007/BF02297091

Zimmerman, B. J. (2002). Becoming a self-regulated learner: An overview. *Theory into Practice, 41*(2), 64–70. doi:10.1207/s15430421tip4102_2

10 Designing for Service-Learning Experiences

LuAnn Batson-Magnuson, Beth Sockman, Laurene Clossey, and Olivia Carducci

Chapter Overview

Service-Learning (SL) is considered a high-impact practice because of its great potential to create deep learning experiences and to transfer in class learning to the real world (Kuh, 2008). The authentic problems often consist of dynamic features, emerging concerns, and multiple stakeholders. Each of these components need to be considered in the instructional design of a course (Darby & Newman, 2014). This chapter will show ways an instructional designer can leverage the frameworks in instructional design to plan, implement, and evaluate SL projects. First, the reader is presented with a case in which two courses collaborate with the same community partner to implement a SL project. The theory and process section describe the value of SL, the supportive theories, and the instructional design emphasis for designing and implementing this pedagogy. Lastly, the professional practice synthesizes the theory with the case study.

Guiding Questions

1. Why should service-learning be considered when designing instruction?
2. How can the lens of instructional design and technology help design for service-learning?
3. What instructional design processes are amplified when designing service-learning experiences?
4. Why is student-reflection important in a service-learning experiences?

Case Study

Meals on Wheels (MoW), a USA national non-profit, freely delivers meals to seniors experiencing food insecurity. They typically purchase and distribute food. The director of MoW in Monroe County (MoW-MC) was interested in building a kitchen to make meals themselves and build a community kitchen for food production by local entrepreneurs, job-training and cooking classes. The MoW-MC board of directors was concerned about the cost of the community kitchen. Two courses at the university collaborated with MoW-MC to help solve their problem: Introduction to Mathematical Modeling and Social Work with Communities.

As a capstone course, Introduction to Mathematical Modeling for math majors provides real-world situations to student while making assumptions and build

DOI: 10.4324/9781003109938-10

mathematical systems to predict outcomes. In the MoW-MC project, the students built an Excel spreadsheet to estimate the cost of the community kitchen under specific scenarios (buying/renting a building, appliances, etc.) and a separate program that used the results of the Excel model to estimate the return on investment and years needed until profitability.

The Social Work with Communities students applied their community social work skills by organizing a community forum. Students obtained stakeholders list who could benefit, and then prepared a presentation for community to secure interest and mobilize funding grants.

What and Why Service-Learning

SL pedagogy supplies a clear sense of purpose and a belief that education exists for the benefit of society. Increased student motivation (Celio et al., 2011; Mahendra et al., 2013), improved student confidence (Butler, 2013; Mahendra et al., 2013), renewed energy in the classroom along with the development of enhanced problem-solving skills are realized (Bringle & Hatcher, 2006; Sockman et al., 2018). When instructors and designers embark on creating SL experiences, they are often dedicated to real-life experiences, transformational processes, and a learner-centered approach to instruction.

SL experiences acknowledge that real life problems are messy which contrasts with the problems that we often give to students. Therefore, designing for SL is challenging due to the dynamic features that come with an open-ended context, and is complicated by multiple stakeholder goals that need to be taken into consideration during feedback points of the instructional design process (Darby & Newman, 2014).

Designing for Service-Learning

In order to craft a compelling and impactful service-learning experience, course instructional design is essential (Maddrell, 2014). Usually, the instructor wants the students to work on a real-world problem provided by a partner organization. Either the instructor or the designer pairs the course or a part of the course with a partner organization. The problem is agreed upon by the instructor of the course and the partner organization. In solving the problem, the students are applying the theoretical learning from their course to the problem thereby creating a mutually beneficial partnership.

There are various types of SL projects that can be incorporated into learning. They can be short- or long-term projects and each produces a variety of deliverables. See Table 10.1 for types of projects, description of those types and some examples.

Purpose – Stakeholders – Implementation

There are elements of the instructional design process that are essential to ensure alignment between the course goals, design, project development, and project implementation when conducting a SL experience. The acronym PSI is often remembered as "pounds of force per square inch," as units to measure force. Here, PSI is used to help remember principles that require emphasis or "force" throughout the successful SL design processes.

92 *LuAnn Batson-Magnuson et al.*

Table 10.1 Types of Service-Learning Projects

Type of Project	Descriptions	Examples
DIRECT to Individuals	Person-to-person, face-to-face projects in which service impacts clients who receive direct service	tutoring, working with the elderly, oral histories, peer mediation, counseling, mentoring
INDIRECT	Projects with benefits to a community as opposed to specific individuals	developing cost estimates, educational materials, advertising, marketing campaigns
ADVOCACY	Working, acting, speaking, writing, teaching, presenting, informing, etc., on projects that encourage action or create awareness on issues of public interest	public campaigns, public service announcements, promoting reading, safety, care for the environment, local history, violence and drug prevention, disaster preparedness
RESEARCH	Gathers information through extant data, or current through surveys, studies, evaluations, experiments, interviewing, etc., to find, compile, and report information on topics in the public interest	research, action research, energy audits of homes or public buildings, water testing, flora and fauna studies, conducting surveys

"P" – Purpose

The first principle represents purpose or "P." As noted in the section above there must be a clear sense of purpose from the standpoints of the instructor, designer, and the partner organization. Purpose provides the momentum to keep the process moving forward. This purpose is addressed in the front-end analysis of instructional design, where the problem is developed.

There is an understanding that the course is part of the larger societal system in which it is wanting to interact (Sockman et al., 2019). The instructional designer considers four systems levels. On the micro-level, the designer contemplates the individual student and community partner contact person's needs. On the meso level, the designer thinks about the educational environment and the entire community partner organization. On an even larger level, the macro level, it is necessary to consider how this project ties the educational institution and the larger community together. Finally, it can be helpful to consider how the project might affect the larger society on the supra level. Instructional designers must look at how all these systems intersect when planning the service-learning project.

Finding a suitable community partner can take time. Carducci (2014) recommends that the instructor locate a partner and sell that potential collaborator on what the class can offer. This takes an understanding of how the course knowledge can be skillfully applied to a real-world problem.

Purposes need to be explicitly stated in the front-end analysis. The designers and professors identify the purpose of the collaboration including the instructional goals and objectives. There are usually two stakeholder groups, the course and partner organization. Both have issues that need to be resolved: course objectives and the partner organization's problem. Partners need to agree upon the product or final deliverable provided by the students (Carducci, 2014) to create a mutually beneficial relationship.

"S" – Stakeholders

The second principle stands for stakeholders or "**S**." Traditionally a course front-end analysis includes the learner analysis, but with SL there are other stakeholders in addition to the course learners. The partner organization becomes a stakeholder that the students

Designing for Service-Learning Experiences 93

want to please. If the course takes place within a university or school, an affiliation agreement may be needed to operate with another partner. Organizations care about their reputation. If the SL project fails, it could be problematic to the school's reputation, but if the SL project succeeds, the school reaps the reward of a positive community impact.

During the front-end analysis it is helpful if the designers and the community partners designate logistical constraints such as timelines and determine the communication mediums (Carducci, 2014). Courses operate within a set timeline and community partners often operate on a different timeline, so time needs to be negotiated. It is helpful when preferred communication methods are negotiated ahead of time such as email, phone, or video conferencing. Deliverable mediums should be determined. Would a common cloud drive be helpful to share deliverables? SL projects are often fluid in nature. Deciding how often and how sharing will occur can make the partners feel more secure about the process. See Figure 10.1 as a guide to assist with planning.

"I" – Implementation with Feedback

Solving society's problems means that SL experiences are often open-ended problems that may be difficult to solve. In striving to resolve these complex problems, students will gain transferable skills by applying classroom knowledge to actual practice dilemmas. Most SL projects require an emergent design during the implementation stage. SL is a practical pedagogy. The instructor guides the students to act on something that needs resolution. Thus, the teaching and learning is constantly in motion, as students act on the problem, take in feedback, and adapt their methods in response. The learning design must take into account this type of pedagogical process. Flexible design is necessary to allow the SL experience to meet the demands of real-life problems. Designers and instructors have to be able to respond to unanticipated feedback to create the scaffolding that supports students during this fluid process.

A model can help visualize the movement of an SL project. The movement of solving an actionable or practical problem considers course input, transformation process, and the output that will likely produce feedback from the community partner (Meadows, 2008). That feedback will then provide new input for the next iteration of problem resolution (Meadows, 2008). This emergent instructional design is often referred to as the motion-picture model (Banathy, 1973), which parses implementation into processes so the instructional designers can examine the components within the system by experiences according to the progressing needs (see Figure 10.2).

The classroom that will implement the SL project provides the skills and curriculum that the community partner needs. The organization that is the partner has the expectation of problem resolution. Skills, course curriculum, community partner problems, and expectations for resolution are the input/inflows that provide the raw material for the SL project. When implementing SL, the professor must first identify the inputs. Inputs include the people, items, and pressures that are continually added to the system. Because the students are attacking an organization's real problems some inputs are unanticipated.

Once the problem is known, the transformation process begins. In the classroom, there are many teachings and learning facilitation strategies used which include ongoing collaboration, communication, and scaffolding students throughout the problem. For larger projects, often students drive the learning with a student acting as the project manager and other class member fulfilling various roles. The instructor may use emergent design to shift strategies based on student's experience to resolve the problems that arise.

94 *LuAnn Batson-Magnuson et al.*

SL Project Name

Purpose

Short description of the project: Include how the project meets the learning goals and the community partner's goals. Think about the different levels of the system.

Goal(s): What **course goals** should be accomplished?
Goal(s): What are the **community partner's goals?**

Objective(s): What are the objectives to accomplish this goal(s)?

Stakeholders

Course Stakeholders

Partner Organization and Contacts

Timeline: How much time is needed to complete the SL project? Create a calendar with a start and end date for your project. List dates when important "milestones" or activities that must be completed.

Implementation

Inflows

Curriculum Resources: What is needed to complete the project? (<u>materials,</u> expertise needed from others, funding, etc.).

Communcation with the community partner: How ofter and how to communicate with the community partner?

Transformation

Instructional Strategies: What strategies and processes will be used to facilitate the student learning?

Reflection: How will stakeholders (learners and partner) reflect on the process? This is a crucial for larger projects to sure that the students are meeting the goals.

Outflows

Presentations and Reflection: How will stakeholders (learners and partner) reflect on the deliverable? This is a crucial step to gain a deeper understanding of what it meant by personal growth, learning, and service.

Sharing Your Project: What method(s) will be used to share the results of the SL project and with whom.

Figure 10.1 Basic service-learning project guide.

After specific points during the instructional process, some output/outflows will be produced. These outputs are dependent of the type of SL project. For direct-service projects the result could be tutoring or mentoring. The outcome could be research, a report, or a model with other types of service projects. Significantly, if learners get periodic feedback from the community partner throughout the process, they can revise the outputs. This is especially true for lengthy projects. At a minimum, the community partner and students exchange expectations and processes about the deliverable at least once before

Designing for Service-Learning Experiences 95

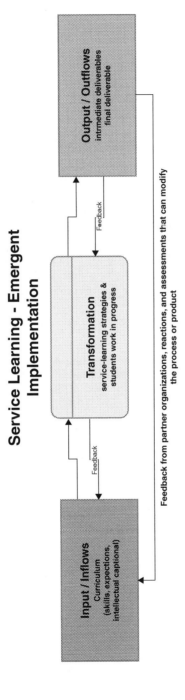

Figure 10.2 Service-learning: emergent design.

completion. Virtual and face-to-face communication provides a stimulus for the students, increasing student investment in the problem when they discover if they are solving the problem in a way that the community partner values.

Lastly, the students will produce the final deliverable for the partner organization. Open feedback at the end is extremely beneficial for both the partner organizations and students. Often, this instigates a feeling of student pride, and helps them to feel the value of their learning. If the final output or deliverable is beneficial for both partners (the classroom and their community partner organization), the community is made stronger through the interdependent relationships.

Assessment and Student Reflection

In an SL project, evaluation must include student reflection on their learning and process (Hullender et al., 2015). Students need to connect their work to the course content. They need to think about how they put the classroom theory into practice, and how they changed. The work can lead to student frustration or an overwhelmed feeling, yet working through this productive struggle with guidance can lead to strong learning gains (Hullender et al., 2015). Well-developed reflection, including faculty/student dialog, can maximize the potential for transformative learning.

Journaling reflections have been found to expand student understanding of diversity and greater awareness of their own perceptions and biases (Carrington & Selva, 2010) and increased community self-efficacy. However, structured reflections have been found to yield higher levels of personal growth and personal self-efficacy (Sanders et al., 2016).

For a large project, pre-reflection, in-process reflection, and a final reflection are recommended (Sanders et al., 2016). In this way, reflections can act as a feedback loop for transforming the teaching and learning experiences. Their feedback will allow the community partner, instructor, and designer to scaffold students' needs. The final reflection on the SL experiences encourages students to make sense of the process in hindsight and addresses the self-evaluation of the final product. This reflection could be conducted by individuals or in groups, verbal or in writing. Students can self-assess or peer-assess. It is often beneficial for students to reflect on the objectives of the product.

Well-developed reflection should be scaffolded and supported by course content and readings. Instructors and designers can use specific models of reflective practices including Bain's 5 Rs (Bain et al., 2002), the ABC123 Method (Welch, 1999) or the DEAL model (Ash & Clayton, 2004) to develop a reflective process that moves students from a basic description of their role into a deeper analysis of the experiences. This can be done through the development of rubrics and models designed to assess the development of critical thinking (Molee et al., 2010). Combining online discussions with faculty and written reflections may result in more critical reflection on culture and clarification of values (Smit & Tremethick, 2017).

Conclusion

Service-Learning embraces authentic problems where students make a meaningful societal impact in the here and now (Batson et al., 2020). Since the process models real life work where the product is the result of multiple revisions, this critical pedagogy stimulates students and encourage deep learning (Kuh, 2008; Molely & Ilustre, 2014) with thoughtful emergent design to support the process.

Professional Practice Revisited

Purpose

Both the Math Modeling and Social Work with Communities classes had professors dedicated to using SL with purpose. The math professor with the MoW-MC Director who wanted to open the community kitchen. Food insecurity is a pressing problem in the United States (Ramadurai & Sharkey, 2012) in a and estimated 12% households (USDA.gov) with an increase to 38% during the COVID 19 pandemic (Wolfson & Leung, 2020). Studies support the positive effects hunger assistance programs have on nutritional status (Price, 2017). Community kitchens are one positive approach that decreases food insecurity (Iacovu et al., 2020).

Stakeholders

The math professor, director and a volunteer discussed the issues MoW-MC discussed accounting and sustainability concerns, and the volunteer collaborated with the math professor to design a project that would also meet the course objectives.

The MoW-MC Director discussed plans to write a grant for the kitchen and find committed renters to maintain a revenue stream with the sociology professor for Social Work with Communities. Both the math and sociology professors were responsible for logistical course planning.

Math Modeling

Inputs

To begin the project a representative from MoW-MC visited the class through video conferencing to describe the situation and to request the needed support and sent the class a layout of a kitchen that they were considering.

Transformation

The professor ran the class election for student project leaders and monitored student progress throughout the project. Students researched community kitchens and model developments. For example, some researched the fee structure to decide how to incorporate income from the community kitchen into the model.

Output

In the final output, student created two models. The first was a detailed Excel model that estimated the kitchen costs and allowed the user to vary the number of cooktops, etc. The second used the cost/revenue outcomes from the first model to estimate the return on investment and potential profitability timeline. One student proposed adding a greenhouse to grow food and save money. She developed a complete model for the costs/benefits of a greenhouse similar to that for the community kitchen. The executive directors and other MoW-MC representatives attended the student's final (virtual)

98 *LuAnn Batson-Magnuson et al.*

presentation during the class' regularly scheduled final exam time and provided feedback to the students.

Student Evaluation and Reflection

The overall all grade on the SL project was worth 30% of the final course grade. The student groups gave progress reports in class. The instructor monitored student interactions and each student prepared a written reflection on the project. See Figure 10.3.

As a class, you have been working on to develop a tool for Meals on Wheels of Monroe County to use to determine the economic viability of running their own kitchen. This project falls under the category of service-learning. Please reflect on what you've learned from this project and iths effect on you and the community. Some questions to help you get started appear below.

Learning:
1. What mathematica ideas have you learned from this project?
2. What nonmathematical ideas have you learned form this project?
3. What was your greatest contribution to this project? Who else made significant contributions to this aspect of the project?
4. How, if at all, has working on this project changed your view of mathematics and its role in the world?

Service:
1. How will the tool the class developed support Meals on Wheels?
2. What impact will the tool the class developed have on Meals on Wheels of Monroe County and the community?

After careful consideration of the role of this project, please write a brief essay about your experience. Please do not feel compelled to answer each question nor to limit youself to the question I've posted.

Figure 10.3 Math modeling final student reflection.

The students learned to together on a large project. They learned about researching costs and potential revenue. They became much more adept at using Excel, and realized the value of mathematics in explaining and evaluating complicated situations.

Social Work with Communities

Inputs

The sociology professor and MoW-MC agreed that a community forum to educate stakeholders, assess, and maintain their support and commitment to kitchen. To establish logistics, the professor attended two onsite meetings. She arranged the community partner – class meeting to discuss the kitchen.

Transformation

The professor organized student groups to plan out sections of the community forum. Five student groups researched different aspects of community kitchens: what are they; what are the benefits; how can they be structured; how can renters use them,

Designing for Service-Learning Experiences 99

how kitchens increase social capital and ameliorate food insecurity. The students had to manage the group work such as work allocation and develop norms.

Next, students planned a community forum to engage the stakeholders in discussion about community kitchens with training to educate about the benefits. As a large group the class spent days discussing and developing questions to facilitate rich dialog. When they were done, students discussed their feelings about resolving this problem and their passions about amelioration of food insecurity. Unfortunately, due to Covid 19, Spring 2020, the forum was canceled. The class created a slide presentation and with guiding questions for the community forum, and a guide for focus groups after the presentation.

Student Evaluation and Reflection

The overall all grade on the SL project was worth 20% of the final course grade. Since the forum was interrupted by Covid 19, students wrote about how these tasks tied into the course's content. Regardless of the change, the students became excited about a real problem in their own community. They learned about the power of communities to solve serious problems, food insecurity, and could actually engage in community social work.

Connecting Process to Practice

1. Reread the case study in the beginning and professional practice at the end the chapter. There were two courses that collaborated with the same community partner. Compare the way the courses collaborated with the community partner, analyzing the difference in purpose and implementation. What other courses could have collaborated with a community partner that assisted with food insecurity?
2. Pick a course that you help design or teach. Based on the goals of the course, brainstorm three different types of service-learning projects and potential community partner(s). See Table 10.1 to help with ideas;
3. Review your ideas from number 2. Choose one and build it out. Identify a potential community partner and how the service-learning project could supply a purpose in the class beyond the course and help the community partner. Complete the Service-Learning Project Learning Guide in Figure 10.1 and plan through how implementation would occur;
4. What are the best ways to design a course to encourage communication between stakeholders in SL projects?
5. How can the course provide the opportunities for regular, in-depth reflection for faculty-to-student, peer-to-peer, and community partner –students feedback for emergent design of the SL project?
6. What instructional and learning strategies can facilitate and scaffold knowledge and skill development to increase student independence?
7. In a course with SL, reflection is expected. When creating the final assignment, what is the appropriate weighting of reflection in the student's final grade?

References

Ash, S. L., & Clayton, P. H. (2004). The articulated learning: An approach to guided reflection and assessment. _Innovative Higher Education, 29_, 137–154.

Bain, J. D., Ballantyne, R., Mills, C., & Lester, N. C. (2002). _Reflecting on practice: Student teachers' perspectives_. Flaxton, Queensland, Australia: Post Pressed.

Banathy, B. H. (1973). *Developing a systems view of education: The systems model approach.* Fearon Publishers.

Batson-Magnuson, L., Carducci, O., & Clossey, L. (2020). Service learning: Use your learning to make a difference. In P. Prium & M. Ball (Eds.), *University matters for your success* (pp. 195–208). Cognella Publishing.

Bringle, R. G., & Hatcher, J. A. (2006). Implementing service-learning in higher education. *The Journal of Higher Education, 67,* 221–239.

Carducci, O. M. (2014). Engaging students in mathematical modeling through service=learning. *PRIMUS: Problems, Resources, and Issues in Mathematics Undergraduate Studies, 24*(4), 354–360. doi:10.1080/10511970.2014.880862

Carrington, S., & Selva, G. (2010). Critical social theory and transformative learning: Evidence in pre-service teachers' service-learning reflection logs. *Higher Education Research and Development, 29*(1), 45–57.

Celio, C. I., Durlak, J., & Dymnicki, A. (2011). A meta-analysis of the impact of service-learning on students. *Journal of Experiential Education, 34*(2), 164–181. doi:10.5193/JEE34.2.16

Darby, A., & Newman, G. (2014). Exploring faculty members' motivation and persistence in academic service learning pedagogy. *Journal of Higher Education Outreach & Engagement,* 18(2), 91–119.

Hullender, R., Hinck, S., Wood-Nartker, J., Burton, T., & Bowlby, S. (2015). Evidences of transformative learning in service-learning reflections. *Journal of the Scholarship of Teaching and Learning, 15*(4), 58–82. doi:10.14434/josotl.v15i4.13432

Iacovu, M., Pattieson, D. C., Truby, H., & Palermo, C. (2020). Social health and nutrition impacts of community kitchens: A systematic review. *Public Health Nutrition, 16,* 535–543.

Kuh, G. D. (2008). *High impact educational practices: What they are, who has access to them, and why they matter.* Association of American College.

Maddrell, J. (2014). Service-learning instructional design considerations. *Journal of Computing in Higher Education, 26*(3), 213–226.

Mahendra, N., Fremont, K., & Dionne, E. (2013). Teaching future providers about dementia: The impact of service-learning. *Seminars in Speech and Language, 34*(1), 5–17. doi:10.1055/s-0033-1337390

Meadows, D. (2008). *Thinking in systems.* Chelsea Green Publishing.

Molee, L. M., Henry, M. E., Sessa, V. I., & McKinney-Prupis, E. R. (2010). Assessing learning in service-learning courses through critical reflection. *Journal of Experiential Education, 33,* 239–257.

Molely, B., & Ilustre, V. (2014). The impact of service-learning course characteristics on university students' learning outcomes. *Michigan Journal of Community Service Learning, 21*(1), 5–16.

Price, T. (2017, July 7). Hunger in America. *CQ Researcher, 27,* 557–580. Retrieved from http://library.cqpress.com/

Sanders, M. J., Van Oss, T., & McGeary. S. (2016). Analyzing reflections in service learning to promote personal growth and community self-efficacy. *Journal of Experiential Education, 39,* 73–88.

Smit, E. M., & Tremethick, M. J. (2017). Value of online group reflection after international service-learning experiences: I never thought of that. *Nurse Educator, 42*(6), 286–289.

Sockman, B., Clossey, L., Carducci, O., Batson-Magnuson, L., Mazure, D., White, G., ... Wells, H. (2019). Systems thinking as a heuristic for the implementation of service-learning in a university. In M. J. Spector, B. B. Lockee, & M. D. Childress (Eds.), *Learning, design, and technology* (pp. 1–26). Springer Publications.

Sockman, B. R., Carducci, O. M., Clossey, L., Batson-Magnuson, L., White, G., Wehmeyer, A., ... Rauch, G. (2018). Service-learning experiences promote the university strategic mission regardless of discipline or matriculation level. *Journal on Excellence in College Teaching, 29*(1), 75–117.

Welch, M. (1999). The ABCs of reflection: A template for students and instructors to implement written reflection in service-learning. *NSEE Quarterly,* 16. Retrieved from https://digitalcommons.unomaha.edu/slceeval/16.

Wolfson, J. A., & Leung, C. W. (2020). Food insecurity during COVID-19: An acute crisis with long-term health implications. *American Journal of Public Health.* doi:10.2105/AJPH.2020.305953

11 Inclusive Online Courses

Universal Design for Learning Strategies that Impact Faculty Buy-In

Amy Lomellini and Patrick R. Lowenthal

Chapter Overview

Record numbers of diverse students are enrolling in online higher education. As a result, institutions find themselves challenged to meet the needs of students with disabilities, English language learners, non-traditional learners, and those without consistent access to the technology required for online learning. Instructional designers have the potential to support institutions to meet this challenge by helping faculty implement inclusive course design strategies, such as Universal Design for Learning (UDL), in the online courses that they develop. Unfortunately, most graduate programs lack courses in designing accessible instruction in general or more specifically on effective ways to address common misconceptions surrounding accessibility. This chapter explores the historical approach to accessibility and proposes a shift to a social model of disability focusing on shared responsibility for inclusive course design. The chapter analyzes common faculty misconceptions about accessibility and presents effective ways to connect process to practice by providing strategies for instructional designers to have difficult conversations that can ultimately garner increased faculty buy-in for UDL-based initiatives.

Guiding Questions

1. What do instructional designers need to know about accessibility and Universal Design for Learning?
2. How can instructional designers start conversations about accessibility at their institutions?
3. What strategies can instructional designers take to address misconceptions about accessible course design?
4. How can educational technology and instructional design graduate programs help prepare instructional designers to address diverse student needs and design inclusively?

Case Study

Jamie recently graduated with a Master of Educational Technology degree and landed a job as an instructional designer. Jamie has the basic technical knowledge to create accessible instructional materials; however, Jamie is unfamiliar with managing difficult conversations about accessible course design. Faculty often express feeling overwhelmed with the thought of accessibility, the perceived extra work, and

DOI: 10.4324/9781003109938-11

confusion over their responsibility when working with students with disabilities. While Jamie can fix some of the accessibility issues, Jamie thinks a better solution is to create a culture where everyone is invested in designing accessible online courses. But where should Jamie begin?

Jamie's story is common among instructional designers. In this chapter, we will explore accessibility-related scenarios that instructional designers like Jamie may face and provide evidence-based strategies on how instructional designers might respond in similar situations.

Higher education has a diverse student body than ever before (Hartsoe & Barclay, 2017; Izzo et al., 2008; LaRocco & Wilken, 2013). As such, faculty increasingly find themselves, as Izzo et al. (2008) explain, "challenged to recognize the impact of multiculturalism in the classroom, embrace a broad age range of students, and address the needs of students with disabilities" (p. 60). This challenge is daunting because most faculty are subject matter experts who were never taught how to teach, and even those with some background in teaching have little to no experience with supporting a diverse student body or designing accessible instruction (Linder et al., 2015; Izzo et al., 2008). Further, as content experts who are traditionally rewarded and promoted for scholarship, many faculty report that they simply do not have the time to attend training and/or to develop expertise in accessible course design (Trinkowsky, 2015).

Increasingly institutions of higher education employ instructional designers (IDs) to help faculty design and develop blended and online courses (Decherney & Levander, 2020; Kim, 2015). These instructional designers not only play critical roles in the design of online courses, but also as resources uniquely poised to collaborate with faculty to create online courses that are accessible and usable by the most possible students. However, we contend that few graduate programs in educational technology/instructional design adequately prepare students on how to design accessible online courses or how to have difficult conversations with faculty about the importance of designing accessible courses. Developing expertise like this is critical for instructional designers because many faculty have misconceptions about the importance of designing accessible online courses (Tobin & Behling, 2018). Thus, the purpose of this chapter is to explore some common misconceptions about accessible online course design in higher education and to provide potential strategies IDs can use the next time they find themselves working with a faculty member who may be unfamiliar with inclusive design strategies.

Background

Historical Approach to Accessibility in Higher Education

Most faculty tend to think of issues about accessibility as the responsibility of the office of disability services found on most campuses (Tobin & Behling, 2018). Centers like these began to emerge on campuses during the late 1940s and early 1950s (Madaus, 2011). These centers developed a process of supporting students with disabilities that was rooted in the medical model of disability where students have to provide medical documentation to apply for accommodations (Singleton et al., 2019). The medical model argues that disability is a problem that needs to be fixed within a person's body (Thornton & Downs, 2010, p. 72). With this type of model, students are required to initiate requests by self-disclosing details about their disabilities to faculty and disability services professionals every semester. In many ways, this process has remained unchanged for decades. However, COVID-19 has further complicated this process with the majority of courses being moved into some type of remote or online format (Legon et al., 2020). Students in need of accommodations on most campuses have found it harder than ever to make medical visits to obtain the proper medical documentation sometimes needed to request the accommodations they need.

This medical model, which essentially views a disability as an individual student's problem, we posit is simply ineffective and outdated. The model's reliance on requesting accommodations is problematic because most students with disabilities choose not to self-identify that they have a disability or need an accommodation for a myriad of reasons (Izzo et al., 2008; Roberts et al., 2011). Further, according to the World Health Organization (2020), disability is now thought to stem from the interaction between a person's health and any number of environmental factors, thus aligning more with a social model of disability that shifts the onus of accessibility from any individual onto the environment. In the social model, disability becomes another part of a person's diversity and not something negative that needs to be fixed (Thornton & Downs, 2010). Given this perspective, supporting all learners and designing accessible online courses requires shared responsibility among students, faculty, disability support professionals, instructional designers, and higher-level administrators (Singleton et al., 2019; Tobin & Behling, 2018).

Modern Approach to Accessibility in Higher Education

One popular framework that can assist in designing more accessible online courses is Universal Design for Learning (UDL). UDL is a conceptual framework developed in the 1990s by the Center for Applied Special Technology (CAST) intended to optimize teaching and learning for all (CAST, 2020). In the following section, we provide a brief overview of UDL.

Universal Design

UDL stemmed from the architectural concept of Universal Design that emphasized how certain designs such as curb cuts can benefit not only people who use wheelchairs but also others (e.g., people on bicycles, or using shopping carts, and rolling luggage) (Tobin & Behling, 2018). Universal Design gained popularity because it coincided with major historical events in the United States such as deinstitutionalizing people with disabilities, the U.S. civil rights movement, and subsequently Section 504 of the Rehabilitation Act of 1973, and the Americans with Disability Act (ADA) of 1990. In fact, Tobin and Behling (2018) argue that today, 25 years since the ADA, "we seldom think twice about the universal design that surrounds us" (p. 2).

Universal Design for Learning (UDL)

The creators of UDL posited that curriculum is the problem that needs to be addressed, not a person's body (Tobin & Behling, 2018). Thus, they strived to apply the principles of Universal Design to learning. Aware that no two students learn the same, they were interested in providing students with choices that could improve their learning. They built on the idea of planning for variability and created what we know today as the UDL guidelines.

UDL consists of three main guidelines that "offer a set of concrete suggestions that can be applied to any discipline or domain to ensure that all learners can access and participate in meaningful, challenging learning opportunities" (CAST, 2020, para. 3). The three main guidelines are multiple means of engagement, representation, and action and expression. UDL moves beyond merely ensuring access to content like many accommodations. Instead, UDL emphasizes both supporting and challenging learners (Gronseth, 2018). When learning is designed with variability in mind from the start, UDL can reduce the need for individual accommodation and improve learning for all students including those with and without disabilities (Tobin & Behling, 2018).

UDL was adopted faster in K-12 than in higher education (Tobin & Behling, 2018). This could be in part because of the lack of enforcement of accessibility laws and procedures compared to K-12 education (Seok et al., 2018). In addition, K-12 teachers have been trained on how to make accommodations and modifications for students with disabilities, while most higher education faculty have not been similarly trained (Seok et al., 2018). Instructional designers in higher education, thus, find themselves in a unique position to be able to address this gap and find ways to implement UDL in online course design and improve the accessibility of the online courses colleges and universities offer. But to make this a reality, graduate programs need a stronger focus on training future instructional designers in UDL, accessible course design, and strategies for working with faculty and administrators.

Instructional Designers and Accessible Instruction

The field of instructional design began in the twentieth century and gained popularity during World War II with training designed for the military (Larson & Lockee, 2014). Since that time, the field of instructional design and specifically the role of instructional designers has changed and grown. Instructional designers today do not simply design instruction. Instead, they often take on a variety of roles, including "facilitators, mentors, trainers, collaborators, reviewers, and mediators, and more likely some combination of those" (Miller & Stein, 2016, para. 6). However, despite taking on these different roles, the job of an instructional designer still centers around designing instruction – instruction that since the COVID-19 pandemic, is more often than not offered in a blended, remote, and/or online learning format.

Designing instruction in a blended, remote, and/or online learning format requires instructional designers, more so than in the past, to have different competencies, including skills in making content and courses accessible to students (Park & Luo, 2017). In fact, common quality assurance frameworks such as Quality Matters, the Open SUNY Course Quality Review Rubric (OSCQR), and California State University Quality Online Learning and Teaching (QOLT) all focus to some degree on accessibility and UDL (Baldwin et al., 2018; Baldwin & Ching, 2019). However, despite this increased focus on accessible course design, we have found that many instructional designers are not prepared to address the kinds of questions and misconceptions surrounding accessibility that they may face when working with faculty and administrators. The following sections of this chapter will explore some of these common misconceptions and provide evidence-based strategies instructional designers can use as they continue to support faculty, administrators, and their institutions as a whole design accessible blended, remote, and online courses for all students. However, we will first start with a case to help ground our discussion in practice.

Professional Practice Revisited

No One in my Course has a Disability

When working with a faculty member, Jamie stressed the need to make all content accessible to students with disabilities. The faculty member, though, questioned the need for this. The faculty member claimed that they would know if a student was disabled and added that students cannot have a disability in this field.

The number of students reporting a disability in higher education has risen from 11% in 2010 to 19% in 2015 (National Center for Education Statistics, 2019). The most reported category of disability in higher education is learning disability (Gladhart, 2010). Learning disabilities along with many other disabilities – such as psychological, attention deficit hyperactivity disorder (ADHD), and deafness – are largely invisible. This suggests that faculty cannot rely on seeing or knowing which students have a disability, even when teaching face-to-face.

Research has shown that students with disabilities are taking online courses (Roberts et al., 2011) and most faculty have been notified of a student accommodation request at least once (Gladhart, 2010). Some suspect that more than half of all students are facing other types of invisible barriers to the successful completion of courses – such as having family commitments, grieving a loss, demanding work schedules, and mental health challenges (Tobin & Behling, 2018). English learners and students relying on mobile devices face additional barriers to online learning (Bergey et al., 2018; Magda & Aslanian, 2018). The effects of COVID-19 have likewise exposed inequalities in internet access, technology availability, and home environments conducive to effective learning (Basham et al., 2020). In other words, it is almost impossible to know who may have a disability or any other factors affecting student success. Therefore, faculty need to assume that some of their students will have a disability or other barriers to success and therefore should design accessible online courses from the start.

Instead of focusing on students' disabilities, instructional designers like Jamie could focus on the inherent variability in all students' background knowledge, experiences, and current situations. UDL principles are based on improving course design for all learners, including those who may not have disabilities or those who are ineligible for accommodations. For example, optimizing relevance by designing authentic learning can make it more engaging and motivating for all students (CAST, 2020; Quality Matters, 2018). Any strategy to reduce barriers in the online environment will benefit all learners, regardless of their situations.

There is Nothing I Can Do If Students Don't Disclose a Disability

While working with Jamie, a professor expressed a desire to ensure their content is accessible but felt they needed to wait until a student discloses a disability to act. This perspective equates accessibility with retroactive accommodations, or "making one change, one time, to help one person" (Tobin & Behling, 2018, p. 5) and is very common in higher education.

Research suggests that most students with disabilities choose not to disclose their disability (McAndrew et al., 2012; Schelly et al., 2011). Potential reasons include a lack of understanding of the processes, convoluted requirements including extensive medical documentation, feeling uncomfortable interacting with faculty or disability services professionals, fear of being stigmatized by faculty and peers, and a desire to start college without labels experienced in earlier educational settings (Roberts et al., 2011). It is likely that some students are struggling to be successful and not necessarily seeking support.

Faculty often become frustrated trying to meet the "needs of an increasingly diverse and technologically expectant student demographic" (Izzo et al., 2008). Instructional designers like Jamie should weave UDL and accessibility into all phases of course design and faculty consultations so that it becomes ingrained in the process rather than something addressed retroactively at the request of a student with a disability (Linder et al., 2015). For example, Jamie could focus on how representing content in multiple ways, such as providing short videos with captions and the accompanying slides could benefit all learners. Research suggests that students today use slides to take notes, enable captions to improve their focus in noisy environments, and listen to the audio while driving to work or school (Kumar & Wideman, 2014; Morris et al., 2016; Tobin & Behling, 2018). Using this strategy, Jamie can illustrate how planning for variability can support diverse students including those with and without disabilities.

Accessibility is Not my Job

While working with Jamie, an instructor reported feeling overwhelmed by their teaching responsibilities on top of their full-time job. The instructor viewed accessibility as beyond the scope of their teaching responsibilities and something that should be addressed by the Office of Disability Services.

Ensuring that all students can effectively use instructional content and achieve learning objectives is the purpose of teaching. It is everyone's responsibility to ensure online learning strategies are beneficial and sustainable for students with all types of disability (Fichten et al., 2009). Building in accessibility from the start can serve a wide range of students, even beyond those eligible for accommodations. Designing multiple ways for students to perceive materials, engage with content, and express knowledge aligns with good teaching practices that support all learners. Linder et al. (2015) recommended positioning accessibility as pedagogy instead of something extra for individual students.

Connecting Process to Practice

Now more than ever, faculty are being asked to forget how they were previously taught and to transform their teaching strategies to better align with best practices for designing online courses. They are being asked to learn new technologies, incorporate new instructional strategies, be sensitive to copyright issues, and address accreditation concerns in addition to thinking about UDL (Singleton et al., 2019). In addition, many faculty teaching online courses are adjuncts with other full-time commitments, lower compensation, and less time to design quality online courses (Singleton et al., 2019). These concerns make the relationship between faculty and instructional designers like Jamie of utmost importance in the design of quality online education. When faculty and instructional designers work together, it creates "an optimal environment for developing rich, dynamic, and interactive online courses" (Puzziferro & Shelton, 2008, p. 119). This collaborative relationship relies on faculty to provide subject matter expertise and instructional designers to provide design and pedagogical expertise (Halupa, 2019). With faculty members looking to instructional designers for support and guidance, what can IDs do to encourage the integration of UDL guidelines in online courses?

Reframe Accessibility and UDL

The negative association with accommodations can often turn faculty off to incorporate UDL principles. Shifting the focus away from disabilities removes the stigma and avoids the misconception that no one in their class has a disability or that they need to wait for student requests for accommodations before acting. Instead, UDL can be reframed in a more positive way. For instance, Tobin and Behling (2018) suggest reframing UDL as a mobile-friendly strategy that can improve student engagement through "anytime, anywhere interactions" (p. 9). Similarly, Singleton et al. (2019) found that avoiding terms like "accessibility" and "UDL" and replacing them with "improving student learning" or using "inclusive design choices" can be a more successful approach when working with faculty (pp. 223–224). Another strategy could involve focusing on best practices for quality course design. Most quality assurance frameworks (e.g., Quality Matters or the Online Learning Consortium's (OLC) Scorecard) emphasize multimodal and accessible instruction.

Start Small

After carefully considering the language used to discuss the topic, it is important to streamline the process by narrowing down the number of things faculty need to address in their courses (Singleton et al., 2019). Even with a positive reframing of UDL, the number of changes and possible ways of approaching the topic can lead to a sense of paralysis that results in no action (Linder et al., 2015). For example, captioning course videos is one of the most common requirements that faculty think of when contemplating accessibility. This is often a painstakingly time-consuming project, especially for long videos, and can reinforce faculty's misconceptions and negative views on the topic. Tobin and Behling (2018) suggested a "20, 20, and 20" approach in which strategies can be implemented in 20 minutes, 20 days, and 20 months (p. 108). Start small by identifying areas where students often have questions and content is presented in only one way. A common example would be when PowerPoint slides are posted to the learning management system (LMS). Tobin and Behling (2018) refer to this common practice as "both single-stream and also cryptically incomplete without the professor's explication of each bullet point" (p. 110). Adding a short video would not only present content in another way, but it could also be more engaging for all learners. Another example would be to review how students are expressing their knowledge. Could students submit an audio comment instead of a written response? Could they create a chart or diagram to compare and contrast perspectives on a topic? If writing a paper is essential, could the assignment be broken down into manageable parts such as an outline and/or a draft to receive additional feedback from peers and the instructor? Encouraging students to express themselves in a variety of ways often involves less effort from faculty and can be an easier starting point for incorporating UDL strategies. Eliciting student feedback after a UDL-based intervention can help encourage faculty that their efforts will result in positive student attitudes and outcomes in the course (Singleton et al., 2019). Embedding similar small steps throughout the course development process is more effective than addressing accessibility at the end of the process (Singleton et al., 2019).

Faculty Development Training

Working with faculty one-on-one is an initial step toward changing an institutional culture to one that prioritizes accessible course design. Once one faculty member has had a "UDL aha moment," it is often easier to get them on board and involved in spreading awareness across the institution (Tobin & Behling, 2018, p. 141). Developing a partnership with faculty who are successfully utilizing UDL strategies can be a way of inviting other faculty to share similar successes. Designing faculty development initiatives that involve UDL and accessibility throughout the process will allow instructional designers to reach a wider audience while modeling best practices. Keeping in mind the importance of reframing mentioned earlier, workshops and courses focused on diversity or quality online learning may draw more attention than ones with disability or accessibility in the title or description (Tobin & Behling, 2018). Research showed that faculty who received training had more confidence in their knowledge and ability to implement UDL strategies more often in their courses (Izzo et al., 2008; Schelly et al., 2011). Faculty often cite UDL as a topic they want to learn more about (Izzo et al., 2008). Integrating UDL into currently existing faculty development workshops, webinars, courses, and consultations can be a starting point to bring awareness and sensitivity to faculty who may be new to these types of strategies (Fichten et al., 2009). Administrative support and incentives for faculty who implement UDL and make their courses more accessible can further exemplify an institutional commitment to quality education for all learners (Gladhart, 2010; Singleton et al., 2019).

Shared Responsibility and Institutional Support

Leadership support for any initiative is essential for buy-in and allocation of resources. For example, Tobin and Behling (2018) suggest appealing to institutional leaders by emphasizing the potential impact UDL can have on "student retention, persistence, and satisfaction" (p. 11). All personnel involved with course design at an institution should receive training in UDL to increase adoption campus-wide (Tobin & Behling, 2018). For UDL initiatives and training to increase adoption, they need to be shared among a group of people from a variety of backgrounds at the institution. They should also focus on learner variability and not just on students with disabilities to gain a wider support base (Tobin & Behling, 2018). Typically, disability service providers spearhead UDL initiatives but these initiatives can and should also come from instructional designers, faculty, and students. Tobin and Behling (2018) even recommend taking a team approach with an action plan and realistic timelines (Tobin & Behling, 2018). Having clear guidelines and policies in place can reinforce an institution's commitment to supporting all learners through quality education (Gladhart, 2010).

Suggested Activities for Instructional Design Programs

Graduate programs in educational technology and instructional design often lack courses focused specifically on accessible course design and effective strategies for addressing accessibility-related misconceptions. To address that gap, we recommend for programs to include at least one course in their curriculum focused on accessibility as well as to integrate instructional activities focused on accessible course design as well as effectively collaborating with faculty in multiple courses. The following are a few examples of activities that could be integrated into any instructional design course:

- Employ accessible content principles (e.g., proper heading structure, logical hyperlinks, and sufficient color contrast) when creating instructional materials (e.g., when designing a syllabus or creating a presentation);
- Identify and discuss where accessibility should be addressed in popular instructional design models and processes;
- Role play collaborating with faculty and subject matter experts, with a specific focus on responding to common accessibility misconceptions;
- Develop a proposal for a faculty development initiative or training that utilizes a strategy for reframing accessibility and UDL;
- Conduct accessibility-related research.

Finally, faculty should strive to model accessible course design in the courses they design and teach.

Conclusion

Higher education continues to see an increase in diverse learners and a demand for high-quality online courses. To remain competitive, institutions need to find easy-to-implement strategies to meet the needs of most learners. It will take a cultural shift away from the medical model of disability that views students' bodies as the problem and toward a model that puts the focus on the online learning environment. While typically championed by disability service providers, we contend that instructional designers can further promote UDL and facilitate the shift to a more widely accepted focus on learner variability. Sharing responsibility and obtaining buy-in from leadership can make a seemingly large job more manageable. This new responsibility will lead to instructional designers like Jamie sometimes having difficult conversations with faculty who believe that students in their courses do not have disabilities, or that there is nothing they can do until a student self-identifies, or that accessibility is not their job. If appropriately trained for these topics in graduate programs, instructional designers can reframe UDL in positive terms and convince faculty to implement small, impactful changes. Instructional designers can start to make online learning more inclusive and equitable for all learners. Bringing awareness by modeling best practices in faculty development training and incorporating UDL throughout the course design process can result in further buy-in.

References

Baldwin, S., & Ching, Y. -H. (2019). Online course design: A review of the Canvas Course Evaluation Checklist. *International Review of Research in Open and Distributed Learning, 20*(3), 268–282. doi:10.19173/irrodl.v20i3.4283

Baldwin, S., Ching, Y. -H., & Hsu, Y. -H. (2018). Online course design in higher education: A review of national and statewide evaluation instruments. *TechTrends, 62*(1), 46–57. doi:10.1007/s11528-017-0215-z

Basham, J. D., Blackorby, J., & Marino, M. T. (2020). Opportunity in crisis: The role of Universal Design for Learning in educational redesign. *Learning Disabilities, 18*(1), 71–91.

Bergey, R., Movit, M., Simpson Baird, A., & Faria, A. -M. (2018). Serving English language learners in higher education unlocking the potential. *American Institutes for Research*. Retrieved from https://www.air.org/sites/default/files/downloads/report/Serving-English-Language-Learners-in-Higher-Education-2018.pdf

CAST. (2020). *Universal design for learning.* Retrieved from http://www.cast.org

Decherney, P., & Levander, C. (2020). The hottest job in higher education: Instructional designer. *Inside Higher Education*. Retrieved from https://www.insidehighered.com/digital-learning/blogs/education-time-corona/hottest-job-higher-education-instructional-designer

Fichten, C. S., Ferraro, V., Asuncion, J. V., Chwojka, C., Barile, M., Nguyen, M. N., ... Wolforth, J. (2009). Disabilities and e-learning problems and solutions: An exploratory study. *Educational Technology & Society, 12*(4), 241–256.

Gladhart, M. A. (2010). Determining faculty needs for delivering accessible electronically delivered instruction in higher education. *Journal of Postsecondary Education and Disability, 22*(3), 185–196.

Gronseth, S. (2018). Inclusive design for online and blended courses: Connecting web content accessibility guidelines and Universal Design for Learning. *Educational Renaissance, 7*, 1–9. https://edtechbooks.org/-fML

Halupa, C. (2019). Differentiation of roles: Instructional designers and faculty in the creation of online courses. *International Journal of Higher Education, 8*(1), 55–68. doi:10.5430/ijhe.v8n1p55

Hartsoe, J. K., & Barclay, S. R. (2017). Universal Design and disability: Assessing faculty beliefs, knowledge, and confidence in Universal Design for Instruction. *Journal of Postsecondary Education and Disability, 30*(3), 223–236.

Izzo, M. V., Murray, A., & Novak, J. (2008). The faculty perspective on Universal Design for Learning. *Journal of Postsecondary Education and Disability, 21*(2), 60–72.

Kim, J. (2015, March). Instructional designers by the numbers. *Inside Higher Education*. Retrieved from https://www.insidehighered.com/blogs/technology-and-learning/instructional-designers-numbers

Kumar, K. L., & Wideman, M. (2014). Accessible by design: Applying UDL principles in a first year undergraduate course. *Canadian Journal of Higher Education, 44*(1), 125–147.

LaRocco, D. J., & Wilken, D. S. (2013). Universal design for learning: University faculty stages of concerns and levels of use. *Current Issues in Education, 16*(1), 1–15.

Larson, M. B., & Lockee, B. B. (2014). *Streamlined ID: A practical guide to instructional design.* Routledge.

Legon, R., Garrett, R., Fredericksen, E. E., & Simunich, B. (2020). CHLOE 5: The pivot to remote teaching in spring 2020 and its impact. *Quality Matters & Encoura.*

Linder, K. E., Fontaine-Rainen, D. L., & Behling, K. (2015). Whose job is it? Key challenges and future directions for online accessibility in US Institutions of Higher Education. *Open Learning, 30*(1), 21–34.

Madaus, J. W. (2011). The history of disability services in higher education. *New Directions for Higher Education, 154*(1), 5–15.

Magda, A. J., & Aslanian, C. B. (2018). *Online college students 2018: Comprehensive data on demands and preferences* [The learning house]. Retrieved from https://49hk843qjpwu3gfmw73ngy1k-wpengine.netdna-ssl.com/wp-content/uploads/2018/06/OCS-2018-Report-FINAL.pdf

McAndrew, P., Farrow, R., & Cooper, M. (2012). Adapting online learning resources for all: Planning for professionalism in accessibility. *Research in Learning Technology, 20*(4), 345–361. doi:10.3402/rlt.v20i0.18699

Miller, S., & Stein. G. (2016, February). Finding our voice: Instructional designers in higher education. *Educause Review*. Retrieved from http://er.educause.edu/articles/2016/2/finding-our-voice-instructional-designers-in-higher-education

Morris, K. K., Frechette, C., Dukes, L., III, Stowell, N., Topping, N. E., & Brodosi, D. (2016). Closed captioning matters: Examining the value of closed captions for "all" students. *Journal of Postsecondary Education and Disability, 29*(3), 231–238.

National Center for Education Statistics (NCES). (2019). *Fast facts: Students with disabilities.* Retrieved from https://nces.ed.gov/fastfacts/display.asp?id=60

Park, J.-Y., & Luo, H. (2017). Refining a competency model for instructional designers in the context of online higher education. *International Education Studies, 10*(9), 87–98. doi:10.5539/ies.v10n9p87

Puzziferro, M., & Shelton, K. (2008). A model for developing high-quality online courses: Integrating a systems approach with learning theory. *Journal of Asynchronous Learning Networks, 12*(3–4), 119–136. doi:10.24059olj.v12i3.58

Quality Matters. (2018). *Specific review standards from the QM higher education rubric* (6th ed.). Retrieved from http://www.qualitymatters.org/sites/default/files/PDFs/Standardsfromthe-QMHigherEducationRubric.pdf

Roberts, J. B., Crittenden, L. A., & Crittenden, J. C. (2011). Students with disabilities and online learning: A cross-institutional study of perceived satisfaction with accessibility compliance and services. *Internet and Higher Education, 14*(4), 242–250. doi:10.1016/j.iheduc.2011.05.004

Schelly, C. L., Davies, P. L., & Spooner, C. L. (2011). Student perceptions of faculty implementation of Universal Design for Learning. *Journal of Postsecondary Education and Disability,* 24(1), 17–30.

Seok, S., DaCosta, B., & Hodges, R. (2018). A systematic review of empirically based Universal Design for Learning: Implementation and effectiveness of Universal Design in education for students with and without disabilities at the postsecondary level. *Open Journal of Social Sciences, 6,* 171–189. doi:10.4236/jss.2018.65014

Singleton, K., Evmenova, A., Jerome, M. K., & Clark, K. (2019). Integrating UDL strategies into the online course development process: Instructional designers' perspectives. *Online Learning, 23*(1), 206–235. doi:10.24059/olj.v23i1.1407

Thornton, M., & Downs, S. (2010). Walking the walk: Modeling social model and Universal Design in the disabilities office. *Journal of Postsecondary Education and Disability, 23*(1), 72–78.

Tobin, T. J., & Behling, K. T. (2018). *Reach everyone, teach everyone: Universal Design for Learning in higher education.* West Virginia University Press.

Trinkowsky, S. (2015). *Interpretative phenomenological analysis of accessibility awareness among faculty in online learning environments* (Doctoral dissertation). ProQuest Dissertations Publishing (3717916).

World Health Organization (WHO). (2020). *Disability.* Retrieved from https://www.who.int/health-topics/disability#tab=tab_1

12 Systems Thinking in Instructional Design

Angela Doucet Rand

Chapter Overview

This chapter is an introduction to systems thinking and becoming a systems thinker. The chapter provides a background and definitions of systems and systems thinking, tools and frameworks as well as a short case for considering how you might use the tools to analyze problems from a systems thinking mindset.

Guiding Questions

1. What are the systems that you experience every day?
2. What are the personal mental schemas you hold (your beliefs and values) influencing your expectations of the systems?
3. Why is systems thinking a better way of solving problems?
4. How can feedback loops help you analyze systems interactions that are out of control?
5. How can stories and archetypes assist in systems thinking problem solving?

Case Study

University Library is the campus library for a midsized regional university and is responsible for providing electronic and print materials, reference services, and instruction for students and faculty. Each year the library adds 25,000 books to the shelves and has over 50,000 patron visits to the building, provides instruction to 6,500 students, and answers 8,000 reference questions. The library has been an important part of the university's accreditation and educational expectations from the beginning, easily meeting the strategic plan expected outcomes outlined by the university for accreditation purposes. Over time the library began to experience problems. Gate counts were steadily decreasing, and a library user survey revealed low satisfaction levels. The number of reference questions and instruction sessions dropped and the number of student complaints about library services increased. The library was in danger of not meeting accreditation standards that could impact the entire university's standing.

A consulting firm was contracted to assist with determining the why the library is experiencing problems. Among top issues were employee satisfaction, professional development activities, and patron awareness of library's resources.

DOI: 10.4324/9781003109938-12

Employees rated professional development opportunities, interdepartmental communication, and pay scales as unsatisfactory. A student and faculty survey indicated low awareness of available library resources such as building hours, physical materials such as books and maps, and instruction and research services. Further investigation using systems thinking strategies revealed underlying issues contributing to the problem.

South University has grown from a small educational program that was an extension of the state's higher education system, into its own rights as a regional, R2, doctoral granting university. The university has come a long way in furthering access to education for residents of the southern part of the state. However, in many ways its culture retains that of the original educational program it began as. Some library employees were hired by the original university president. These long-term employees know a lot about library processes and their institutional knowledge put them in a privileged position. The library operates in a culture where local, tacit knowledge of processes was acceptable. Another pressure on the library is the university's newly implemented modern online learning system and the increased offering of online courses and fully online degree programs.

From a systems perspective how might the library solve the problem of diminishing use of its services? The answer lies in systems thinking wherein processes, mechanisms, and systems facilitate the continuous learning and knowledge management processes included in a shared creative culture fostered by teamwork. What variables can be best used to leverage change that will improve library usage in the long term?

What is a System? What are the Parts of the System?

The father of general systems thinking, Ludwig Von Bertanlanfly, a biologist, proposed a unified way of thinking about life systems. General systems theory proposed that even within its complexities systems can be characterized generally as having parts and relationships that make up the whole system and changes in any part of the system affect the whole system.

We encounter systems in our everyday lives all day long. Think of the water system that allows you to extract water from a faucet into a glass and the actions you take to start the water flowing and stop the water when the glass gets full. This is a simple system with inflow and outflow and a defined parameter for how much water the system can hold.

We can adjust these simple systems in a couple of ways: we can alter the inflow, increase the outflow, or get a bigger glass to facilitate more inflow. In other words, we can influence the system through interactions with one or more of the elements. By adjusting the elements of the system, we can achieve a balanced effect. Systems change over time in response in response to environmental and stakeholder pressures, and this often introduces problems to our balanced system. The systems thinker must examine what changes occurred to unbalance the system. Technology, time, politics, and employee turnover are examples of pressures that influence systems.

A simple system you likely encounter every day is the air conditioning system in your home or automobile. You may jump into your car and adjust the air temp and flow for maximum cooling and continue to adjust the airflow and temp until you achieved a comfort level. You could mitigate this system in a few ways. You could put a sunshield in the window to keep the sun from heating up the interior of the car. You could also leave windows slightly open for airflow; or if it's wintertime you may park in a sunny spot so the interior will be warmer when you get in. This is an example of ways in which we deal with systems and make adjustments to systems in our everyday life.

An example of economic policy change influencing a large customer supply system is a challenge to asset reporting procedures in bookstores where bookstores were penalized on the number of items unsold on the shelves (Wikipedia: https://en.wikipedia.org/wiki/Thor_Power_Tool_Co._v._Commissioner). Prior to 1979, bookstores could keep unsold books on the shelves without tax penalties for the number of assets they owned. Tax law changes resulted in unfavorable economic practices for keeping large inventories of books. Bookstores now return unsold boxes of books to the publishers rather than keeping them on the shelf and getting penalized for overstock. Agents in the system (bookstore owners and publishers) worked out a way adjust inflows and outflows and still meet the demands of readers to have books, while lowering bookstore overhead costs. The system was adjusted to benefit profitability for all stakeholders.

What is "Systems Thinking"?

Systems thinking is a mindset for approaching problem solving from a systemic level. In systems thinking everything is connected, but not always in an obvious way. The role of the systems thinker to is discover parts, processes, and purposes or functions of a system and strive to provide long-term solutions. A well-known metaphor states that to give a person a fish feeds them for a day; but to teach them to fish feeds them for a lifetime. This is the systems thinking mindset. Systems thinking makes use of stories and metaphors to characterize problems, and other tools to gain access to non-obvious information affecting the system. Archetypes, simple causal loop diagrams, and computer software can all be used the assist the systems thinker in seeing the entire problem. This mindset and systems thinking tools are important to instructional designers.

Instructional Design and Systems Thinking

Instructional designers and human performance improvement professionals are primarily focused on human systems such as organizations and institutions but may also be involved in combinations of systems at the micro and macro levels (Haines, 2000). In human systems it is important to consider the whole environment. Mental models held by humans, their beliefs and values, evoke complexity in systems. In IDD and HPT we approach systems with the goal of discovering adjustments to inputs, outputs, and renewing or revising how people think about the system. Human systems tend to be open systems (Haines, 2000) which are those having the capacity for change through adjustments to inputs, outputs, or mental schemas. From this perspective we can see how change in one part of the system affects change in other parts of the system. System variables include inputs, outputs, and interactions, and they are interdependent in working to support the system. Instructional designers may be acquainted with education systems and the influence of administrative and record keeping processes, professional development of faculty and staff, classrooms, technology, online learning systems, and even transport and traffic rules and procedures. All of these components and their interactions make up a functioning education system.

Discovering the interdependencies of the whole system is necessary to troubleshooting issues. Key to working from a systems thinking perspective is recognition of mental models or schemas that are a part of the whole system. Unlike an electronic or telecom system, humans hold values and beliefs that are invisible when analyzing systems issues

(Reigeluth, 1999). Accessing or recognizing mental models contributes to the ability to explain why a system operates the way it does.

Consider again the system of filling a container with water. Incoming water fills the glass and outputs (drinking or pouring the water) both change the level of water in the container. The desired outcome may be to fill the container completely or to only measure out the amount required for a recipe. The schema for satisfactorily filling the container matters! The wrong amount of input will either leave your thirst unslaked or ruin the recipe. In this example the mental model of the system matters deeply to its success as a system.

Theory and Processes

Systems Thinking

Why acquire a systems thinking mindset? In an ever increasingly connected world, we can expect to encounter large scale, complex problems in our social and work lives. Systems thinking is a widely recognized 21st century skill for solving complex problems in society, work, and home life. It requires a certain mindset that looks not at just the parts of a problem, but at the whole, while discovering or recognizing how the parts interrelate and influence each other. Systems thinking is a mindset and a process (Senge, 2006). The practice of systems thinking relies on seeing the dynamic changes in interconnected parts and observing their impact on the whole. Systems thinking principles are derived from multiple fields such as social sciences, engineering, and cybernetics. Systems thinking practitioners strive to understand these interconnected parts in order to achieve a purpose by redirecting efforts based on feedback loops (Stroh, 2015). Systems thinking is about helping people discover what they see, feel, think, and do, and by empowering them to recognize and take responsibility for creating new interconnections to achieve an emergent or discovered purpose.

To be a systems thinker means to view the world as an interconnected group of elements whose dynamic efforts constitute a system that satisfies a function or purpose (Mella, 2012). The systems exist as a result of the interconnections demonstrated through feedback and reinforcing and balancing loops. Systems thinking explores the purpose or function of the system, the various elements of the system, and the interrelated actions on the system that contribute to its function or purpose. Furthermore, systems thinking takes on multiple perspectives from contributing elements. For example, a problem with book sales and supply takes into consideration the authors, publishers, bookstore owners, readers, and book formats. Bookstore customers expect on demand supplies of books to read. Publishers want to print and sell books, and bookstores want to drive customer usage to ensure future business. Each of these foci are interrelated and interruptions in one element impacts, or unbalances, the system leading to a failure of purpose or function.

The interconnected parts of the system include the elements, sometimes called variables. Variables might be the buildings in a neighborhood, public transportation vehicles in a city, or elements can be nonphysical items such as motivation levels, cognitive aptitudes, or organizational pride (Meadows, 2008). The variables of systems are usually easy to discover and we are generally comfortable with discovering these variables that make up systems. However, systems are not random groups of items. The magic of systems is in the interconnections between the elements. These interconnections carry information about the elements to other parts of the system and over time a systematic pattern can be observed. In systems thinking we consider interconnections, or flows, to be an important function of the system as they express and achieve the function or purpose for the system. In nonhuman systems, such as transportation or computer systems, flows support

116 *Angela Doucet Rand*

functions. In human systems flows support purposes. Examples of human system purpose are levels of affection or respect in family relationships, or school pride in an educational institution.

Variables, interconnections, and purposes or functions make up systems and systems may have multiples of these parts. Changing demands that occur over time on the parts has an impact on the system. It is often easier to identify and change variables, however this usually does not lead to a lasting solution. A systems thinking perspective focuses on seeing the relationships in the system to develop solutions that change the interconnections to achieve more long-term solutions.

Systems thinking is a mindset and a process (Senge, 2006). The practice of systems thinking relies on seeing the dynamic changes in interconnected parts and observing their impact on the whole. Systems thinking principles are derived from multiple fields such as social sciences, engineering, and cybernetics. Systems thinking practitioners strive to understand these interconnected parts in order to achieve a purpose by redirecting efforts based on feedback loops (Stroh, 2015). Systems thinking is about helping people discover what they see, feel, think, and do, and by empowering them to recognize and take responsibility for creating new interconnections to achieve an emergent or discovered purpose.

The complexity of systems and applying systems thinking can be demonstrated through the use of stories to explain the how, who, and what of systems problems. Archetypes represent recurring systems problems and can be used to describe interactions between systems elements.

In systems thinking, professionals agree on the use of archetypes to represent recurring systems situations and to help in thinking about and analyzing problems from a systems perspective (Senge, 2006; Stroh, 2015; Meadows, 2008). The archetypes are good tools to use when approaching problems from a systems thinking perspective. Systems thinking practitioners have identified recurring patterns of events in systems as archetypes (Meadows, 2008). Nine popular archetypes are used to describe these systems' patterns, but others occur throughout our vast and complex world. Knowing about the archetypes provides systems thinkers with tools for approaching problems (Stroh, 2015). The nine archetypes are shown in Table 12.1 with a short description, example, and action toward solution.

Professional Practice Revisited

Systems thinking research and the development of models for application are often based in higher education, medical professions, and business organizations (Senge, 2006). Systems thinking differs from explorations of stakeholders' organizational evaluations and restructuring, all often highlighted steps in the analysis and evaluation phases of ISD. In systems thinking, stakeholders are certainly considered at every phase of the project in all three arenas, however a systems thinking approach embraces active consideration of the effects of change in one area and how it might influence change in another part of the organization. Some factors to think about in systems thinking include the pressures on resources, skills, knowledge, and abilities of employees, time, world events, other organizational demands from within the system.

Using a Systems Thinking Mindset to Address Problems

Academic libraries operate as systems themselves with multiple departments taking a role in providing access to information. Librarians assigned to various disciplines teach information literacy skills, notify faculty of new publications and materials relevant to their research, and conduct outreach activities to keep faculty informed of program updates the acquisition of new library materials. Technical services is responsible for acquiring, licensing, managing, organizing, cataloging, and developing a balanced library collection according to the needs of current and new academic programs. Public services is responsible for access to a safe and secure building and for assisting with patrons' foundational information seeking efforts. Student engagement is a responsibility shared by public services and discipline librarians. Administration and leadership handle budgets and respond to accreditation and academic expectations for building access and services such as internet connections, proctoring software, and meeting rooms for student events, associations, and committees. Furthermore, libraries operate within the university system and must align its operations, management, and processes to the university's strategic plan.

Table 12.1 Systems Archetypes

Archetype	*Description*	*Example*	*Action*
Addiction/Shifting the Burden	Past fixes hide the real problem without really solving the issue causing perpetual dependence on the fix.	Addictive drugs are used to treat pain, and the original ailment is replaced with behavior that weakens the system.	Avoid or alleviate short term fixes. Look for long-term solutions.
Drifting Goals	Goals set to increase performance are adjusted downward due to budget issues instead of finding resources to facilitate goal achievement.	A student vows to write 1,000 words a day for an assignment, but due to a course overload only writes 100.	Increase motivation with the promise or reward, reduce the course load, give up another activity, or set more realistic goals.
Fixes that Fail	An easy fix in the moment solves a problem but in the long run, allows the original issue to grow.	A company accommodates demands for a custom product to keep a customer and cannot sustain production when other customers demand a similar product.	Map out the company's resources used to meet demands to see if increasing that resource (time, people, equipment) would alleviate the problem.
Escalation	Two parties are locked into a system of aggression to achieve a hold over their competitors.	An escalation of scarcity is created when one employee is allowed to work a special schedule. Other employees also demand special schedules leading to a lack of staffing during regular business hours.	Try to get the competitors to agree to more reasonable actions. Avoid setting up situations that can lead to escalation.

(*Continued*)

118   *Angela Doucet Rand*

Table 12.1 (Continued)

Archetype	Description	Example	Action
Tragedy of the Commons	A shared resource available for use by everyone becomes depleted due to overuse.	Unrestrained use of fossil fuels to the detriment of the global climate.	Regulation to control use; Education and persuasion to inform users of the consequences of overuse.
Success to the Successful	Top performers in a system are routinely rewarded facilitating future wins to the detriment of others benefit.	The availability of high-quality education to those in higher socio-economic systems at the cost of benefit to those in need.	End the competitive cycle and restart the system to allow diversification of competition.
Limits to Success	Professional development and availability of resources afford improvements to a point, after which growth tops out no matter how much effort is made.	A company experiences rapid growth, but successes are soon diminishing because of a lack of personnel, space, or inventory.	Early intervention is key; try to predict future pressures on the system and plan for ways to address those pressures.
Growth and Underinvestment	A period of growth or success is experienced but eventually delays in capacity and ability occur. Goals are adjusted down to accommodate demand on the system.	A parcel delivery service fails to provide updated navigation systems in delivery vehicles resulting in delayed packages. The company puts limits on its delivery radius thereby limiting growth.	Examine industry trends for expected growth and plan for future investment in equipment and employees. Make expansion a part of the business plan.
Accidental Adversaries	A collective endeavor starts off with colleagues sharing costs, workload, resources equally, and for the good of the company. One partner starts to gain more clients and markets themselves instead of sharing the client load.	Colleagues start a consulting business and one of the partners' special skill results in greater demand for their business and thus income.	Improve communication between the parties involved. Be specific about goals and intentions. Define unacceptable behaviors.

Doing Systems Thinking

Although systems thinking requires a whole system, non-linear mindset, there are some steps to take to ensure better success when approaching systems problems. Working from a systems thinking mindset we can begin to look at systems issues. Stroh (2015) refers to this as telling systems stories, asserting that, "the root causes of chronic, complex problems can be found in it underlying system structure – the many circular, interdependent, and sometimes time-delayed relationships among its parts" (p. 38). Senge (2014) recommends getting the big picture and taking a long-term view. This can be thought of as "interviewing the system." Keep a few questions in mind as you begin the interview and think about reinforcing and feedback loops and delays in response over time (Haines, 2000).

- What behaviors are a part of the system?
- What are environment or condition barriers and promoters in the system?
- What can be changed or eliminated in the system?
- What works well now?
- What works well over time?
- How will environmental changes affect the system over time?

Draw or Sketch the System

Gather information about the system using the questions. Collect stakeholder information and create a list that include names, roles, purposes and hidden agendas (Stroh, 2015). Use the iceberg tool (https://thinkingtoolsstudio.org/resources/) as a model to gain insight into underlying or tacit relationships and interactions. This model seeks information about patterns of behavior, events that have occurred, system structures, and mental schemas in the systems.

Next, sketch out or use a computer program to graphically represent system components. The sketch should include main components including the main issue or concern, two to three variables and consequences with arrows indicating relationships or pressures.

Draw a Feedback Loop (see Figure 12.1)

1. In the center of a blank page draw a square and inside it write the greatest issue or performance concern.
2. Next, brainstorm and list two to three variables, or inputs, and write each of them in boxes to the left of the center square.
3. Brainstorm and list two to three consequences, or outcomes, and write each of them in boxes to the right of the center square.
4. Draw links between the components to indicate interrelationships and influences on the system.
5. Now it's time to start asking the interview questions and think about the best leverage points for making change in the system to correct the issue. At this time, it will be helpful to refer to the archetypes to understand what kind of issue is happening with the system.

Figure 12.1 Main variable feedback loop.

Connecting Process to Practice

1. Consider the University Library's issues and document them in a feedback loop. Do as many feedback loops as you like then interview the system. Which archetype(s) best fit the system problem? Why? How can implicit knowledge from the various departments be made explicit?
2. What are some barriers and affordances to think about for updating processes in large complex systems?
3. Design an intervention for key stakeholders to collect roles and responsibilities and to promote the development of a team dialogue for solving the problem.
4. Reflect on restaurant and food services impacted by the COVID-19 pandemic and select archetypes that could characterize different aspects of restaurant and grocery operations. Remember to list all elements of the system and create a feedback loop. Note that a macro view of the restaurant business that considers economic growth might be different from a micro view that considers meeting customer needs. Which archetype or archetypes best fit the scenarios?
5. Systems exist all around us at work, home, and play. Reflect on the system in which you work or live. Take a macro perspective and think about the elements, forces, and feedback loops that are part of the system and keep the system working. Think about recommendations you would make. Now take a micro perspective and think about your own personal productivity system. Name the elements, interactions, and feedback loops and influencing forces. What archetype might you apply to problems in your own system? What can you do to keep a balance in this personal system?

Conclusion

Here are some final thoughts about adopting a systems thinking approach. Consider the overall desired outcome and the kinds of feedback in the system and where it comes from in the system? Is the system embedded in a larger system or group of systems? Remember that in systems causes and effects are circular and responsive to each other and there may be time delays that exacerbate problems. Finally, quick fixes don't stay fixed. Look for long-term solutions that balance the system.

The usefulness of systems thinking has potential to solve global and individual problems. You can practice a systems thinking mindset using one of the many systems you encounter every day. Stroh (2015) recounts the story of famed systems thinker, Donna Meadows, and her habit of applying systems thinking archetypes to news stories. Learning to be a systems thinker takes effort, but it is a skill that you can grow through practice.

References

Haines, S. G. (2000). *The complete guide to systems thinking and learning.* HRD Press.

Meadows, D. H. (2008). *Thinking in systems: A primer.* Chelsea Green Publishing.

Mella, P. (2012). *Systems thinking: Intelligence in action* (Vol. 2). Springer Science & Business Media.

Reigeluth, C. M. (Ed.). (1999). *Instructional-design theories and models: A new paradigm of instructional theory* (Vol. 2). Routledge.

Senge, P. M. (2006). *The fifth discipline: The art and practice of the learning organization.* Doubleday.

Senge, P. M. (2014). *The fifth discipline fieldbook: Strategies and tools for building a learning organization.* Currency.

Stroh, P. (2015). *Systems thinking for social change.* Chelsea Green.

13 Integrating Ethics into the Curriculum
A Design-Based Approach for Preparing Professionals to Address Complex Problem Spaces

Stephanie L. Moore and Gabrielle Griffin

Chapter Overview

In this chapter, we will explore an approach for teaching ethics for instructional design and educational technology that is not a class on moral philosophy but rather approaches it as a process of identifying and evaluating complex decisions and problems in the field that have an ethical dimension. The primary objective is to inform instructional design practices more deeply and support complex decision making around educational technologies. Specifically, this design is anchored in the principles of the reflective practitioner (Schön, 1983; Tracey & Baaki, 2014), with reflection-in-action as a key objective and quality of professional practice with scaffolding in developing more reflective questioning of technologies in learning then translating that form of analysis into either a decision-making or design process. We posit that a design-based approach anchored in reflection-in-action rather than a compliance-oriented approach better prepares future professionals for the complex problem spaces they encounter on the job.

Guiding Questions

1. How can we help future instructional design and educational technology practitioners frame learning problems to include ethical considerations?
2. How can we help future professional practitioners integrate ethical analysis and critical reflection into the design and decision-making processes they are learning about?
3. How can we design learning opportunities for students in this space that are engaging, creative, and generative, and that afford both opportunities for critical analysis and reflection as well as opportunities to devise practical solutions to ethical problems?

Case Study

An increasing number of cyberbullying incidents at your school combined with media reports of escalating school violence have put students, parents, staff, and the local community on edge. Many stakeholders fear the school will suffer an unexpected attack without safeguards to detect threats before they are carried out.

Responding to these fears, your principal has formed a committee to identify the most viable and cost-effective methods to expose and neutralize online threats. As the faculty advisor to your school's student council, you have been appointed to represent the students' voice on the committee.

DOI: 10.4324/9781003109938-13

> During the first meeting, a few colleagues spoke in favor of contracting with a third-party company to monitor students' social media, with comments such as, "We need to fight fire with fire!" and, "If technology can make us safer, we must use it!"
>
> At first glance, you agree that third-party monitoring appears to be the best and easiest solution. Still, you also have a sense of discomfort that you can't quite articulate yet, nor do you know exactly what to recommend as a course of action. As the representative for the students, you decide to evaluate social media monitoring by first asking questions about the ethics of this particular technology and gathering different stakeholder perspectives so you can then present your recommendations at the next meeting.

Early authors in the field argued that technology is not a collection of gadgets, hardware, and instrumentation but instead is "a way of thinking about certain classes of problems and their solutions" (Finn, 1996, p. 48, reprinted from 1953), arguing that as a result the question of "what is desirable and why" should be subjects of continual attention by the profession. Finn's recommendation to develop and maintain a code of ethics was realized through the code of ethics developed and maintained over the years by the Association for Educational Communication and Technology. However, his calls for continual reflection and questioning have received far less attention. Codes of ethics tend to be treated as compliance-oriented guardrails rather than opportunities for critical reflection and creative opportunities for design applied to complex learning problems that are also moral in nature (Berenbeim, 1987; Dean, 1992, 1999; Weaver & Treviño, 1999). For a long time, the literature and curricula in the ethics of educational technology have been under-developed (Moore, 2005) with these gaps persisting (Moore & Ellsworth, 2014; Kimmons, 2020) despite increasing public attention on significant ethical issues raised by new developments in this space – such as data rights and privacy around learning analytics and remote exam proctoring, the OER (Open Education Resources) movement's focus on making education more affordable, and racial and economic gaps magnified by educational technology divides during COVID-19. Even after Yeaman et al. (1994) sought to shift the focus from the behavior of individuals to the social responsibility of the profession, the main outcome was a revision of the codes of ethics to incorporate statements about social responsibility (Watkins et al., 2000; Yeaman, 2004a) with no discernible impact on curricula or research. Most of the literature to date has focused on the professional codes of ethics and topics like accessibility or copyright with treatments that at times wax more about legal obligations than ethical examination (Moore & Ellsworth, 2014).

Similarly, the current models in our field do not readily prompt designers to identify or address ethical issues in the design and decision-making process. This is despite the fact that when practitioners are confronted with authentic projects and tasks, they are often trying to work on complex problem sets that either are moral in nature or have a moral dimension that has to be considered (Whitbeck, 1996). For example, the instructional designer or educational technologist who is asked about proctoring software is being asked to address a learning problem that has significant ethical aspects. In addition to considerations about student learning and assessment of learning, proctoring raises questions about student data rights and privacy, and a professional in our field will need to incorporate ethical considerations along with the instructional considerations. Similarly, instructional designers often design online learning courses and environments, which include a range of additional ethical considerations such as accessibility and inclusion. In interviews with 20 professional practitioners, Lin (2007) identified copyright, learner privacy, and accessibility as three ethical concerns that commonly arise in practice, along with diversity, conflicts of interest, and professionalism/confidence also arising but with less frequency. Learning analytics, for example, may have some real benefits in supporting learners or identifying struggling learners earlier on so they can be provided better support. But there are additional significant ethical or moral considerations such as data rights and privacy and how students are engaged as stakeholders who have agency over their own data (Ifenthaler & Tracey, 2016).

A nascent body of work around various aspects of ethics has started to emerge: Rieber and Estes (2017) on reframing accessibility; Gray and Boling (2016) on inscribing ethics and values in designs for learning; Bradshaw (2018) on critical pedagogy and educational technology; Moore (2013, in press) on rethinking ethics as part of the design domain; and Benson, Joseph, and Moore (2017) on research and practice at the intersection of culture, learning, and technology. We also are seeing "hot spots" emerge around various dimensions of ethics in the field. For example, members of the professional research association, the Association for Educational Communications and Technology (AECT), formed a new division on Culture, Learning and Technology, and there is a growing body of work around this intersection (Amiel et al., 2009; Benson et al., 2017; Dickson-Deane et al., 2018; Gunawardena et al., 2018; Hornik & Tupchiy, 2006; Igoche & Branch, 2009). Researchers on learning analytics are also addressing ethical considerations both as a primary focus and secondary considerations (cf. the 2016 special issue of *Educational Technology Research & Development*, Ifenthaler & Tracey, 2016; Daniel, 2015; Klein et al., 2019; Pardo & Siemens, 2014; Rubel & Jones, 2016). However, even as a community of scholars may be emerging, the curricular elements still lag behind, with very few programs in our field offering courses on ethics generally or providing students with the necessary opportunities to learn how to address ethical considerations such as accessibility and inclusion, diversity and equity, data rights and privacy, and others directly in and through our design activities.

What is exciting about this collection of work – on top of preceding work by those like Kaufman (2000), whose strategic planning for performance improvement starts with societal impact, and Yeaman (2004a, 2004b), whose work focuses us on the social responsibility of our profession – is its implications for professional practice. Often, ethics are viewed (and treated) as esoteric – a discourse requiring specialized knowledge and vocabulary to be able to engage with it – and this results in a high degree of discomfort among faculty and students alike who may recognize the importance of these topics but not feel this is their area of expertise (nor desire to develop it as a particular expertise). But Whitbeck (1996), writing about ethics as design in engineering, argues that moral problems are practical problems because there is a need for a response – and this response is not simplistically choosing between "good" or "bad" (or "right/wrong") but rather being able to *evaluate* complex problems and *devise* solutions. By placing an emphasis on ethics as a form of critical analysis and problem solving where the design process can be engaged to help devise solutions, Whitbeck offers a framing for how ethics can be integrated into practice, thus also informing how we can teach ethics as we prepare future professionals.

Anchoring Content and Theory

When you hear the term ethics, you may start to think about codes of ethics or a philosophy class you once took and somewhere in the back of your mind something about Kant and Aristotle is bumping around. This often proves a daunting barrier for most in thinking about ethics, as most of us are not philosophy majors and may feel we don't have the time to stop and read such texts to brush up on moral reasoning. Ethics are also often misunderstood as a form of summative evaluation that happens after-the-fact, through declarations such as "that was unethical" or declaring something to be "right" or "wrong." However, ethicists have defined ethics in a different way that may be more approachable and practical. For example, in explaining the difference between ethics and morals, Pauline Shanks Kaurin (2018) describes ethics as the *process* of "reflection, critical questioning, justification, argumentation, and application of moral beliefs, ideas, and systems" (para. 4). By shifting from a set of philosophies to be covered to a process of reflection and critical questioning, we can better connect ethics to practice specifically through our design models and methods.

Ethical Issues and Considerations

Part of incorporating ethics into design and decision making includes developing the ability to identify ethical issues and considerations. In the class this chapter is based on, students read about ethical issues related to technology and educational technology generally as well as articles about specific issues in the field. The references at the end of the chapter include many of the readings used in class, both from inside and outside the field. The major themes from these readings are accessibility, inclusion, and equity; data privacy and cybersecurity; data rights and learning analytics; cultural considerations; digital equity/digital divide; and social justice. In addition, students are provided "An Ethics Primer" (Chowning & Fraser, 2007) that is a digestible summary of different ethical perspectives and a discussion about how to engage in ethical analysis. These readings are spread across several weeks, focusing on a different topic each week along with readings on systems thinking (from *Thinking in Systems: A Primer* by Meadows), change, and design.

Reflective Practice for Ethical Analysis and Synthesis

Schön's work on the reflective practitioner provides a framework for how exactly ethical reflection and critical questioning can occur in and through the design process and is strongly complementary to the sort of habitual reflection and interrogation that others have called for but never fleshed out with specificity. Two key ideas from Schön that are essential: problem setting (or problem framing) and reflection-in-action.

Problem Setting/Framing

Schön argued that most design problems we encounter are complex and have confused or conflicting ends. This requires designers to not just solve a problem but go through an initial process of problem setting. More recently, Svihla (2020) has focused specifically on "problem framing." She describes problem framing as a process by which the professional designer "take(s) ownership of and iteratively define(s) what the problem really is, decide(s) what should be included and excluded, and decide(s) how to proceed in solving it" (para. 2). In short, the implication for practice is that designers solve the problem as they have framed it, not merely as it exists. This in part explains why different designers can generate different solutions to the seemingly same problems: they have framed it differently. So, for example, one designer may frame a problem solely in terms of learning outcomes while another designer may frame the problem to include other types of impacts in addition to learning outcomes – such as accessibility, equity, etc. Ethics in design starts at the problem framing stage where the problem is framed to include

Integrating Ethics into the Curriculum   125

ethical considerations. Moore and Tillberg-Webb (in press) suggest questions to identify potential impacts on health and safety, the environment, self-sufficiency and wellbeing, discrimination, and access along with preliminary questions during front-end analysis.

While these questions as written may be helpful, we recommend that designers start by generating a set of questions more specific to the problem and context and continue to adapt and refine as you go and better understand the nature of the problem.

These questions also introduce the idea of "agency" in design: how much agency do designers feel they have, and how and where can they both exercise agency and share agency through involving stakeholders (Svihla, 2020). Being able to identify these opportunities requires designers to pull from a robust collection of ideas and options that includes not just carrying out tasks in the design process but also using change facilitation strategies like stakeholder involvement and thinking systemically, such as using the body of knowledge from performance improvement. For example, in the case study presented, the designer could collaborate with procurement to establish policies around student data rights and privacy and accessibility that all potential vendors must meet. They could engage students and other stakeholders in a process of defining desirable school policies that then inform class, procurement, and other policies. They could implement the technology only under opt-in conditions rather than opt-out, or they could recommend other strategies or technologies that better address the ethical issues.

Reflection-In-Action

Although reflection after action is important, Schön primarily emphasizes reflection-*in*-action, as occurring throughout the design process. Tracey and Baaki (2014) explain, "When a designer is presented with a complex problem or situation, the designer shows a series of questioning, making a decision, reflecting on the consequences of the decision, then making another move" (p. 4). Questioning and reflection are baked into the process, woven throughout every design action. As one participant in Lin's (2007) study noted, "Ethics prevails in all of our activities" (p. 431). But the questions we ask ourselves matter greatly. If the problem has been framed solely in terms of learning outcomes, then the questions may be limited to those that are learning-related. If the problem has been framed to include ethical considerations, then the designer should similarly be asking questions throughout that facilitate reflection and action on ethical aspects of the problem. Some of the questions in Table 13.1 relate specifically to learner analysis during the front-end, for example. One emerging example of this is a technology selection model developed by Beck and Warren (2020) through an iterative process of stakeholder involvement in which teachers identified questions to ask to facilitate the evaluation of learning technologies. The model starts with questions about the efficacy of the technology in supporting learning and then incorporates questions about different ethical considerations such as data rights and accessibility.

Rather than prescribing specific questions for designers to ask, we suggest the following themes from the ethics literature that designers can use to generate questions for reflection-in-action for different design decision points: equity, accessibility, privacy, security, sustainability, and efficacy. For example, at the point of materials creation and selection, designers could ask questions such as "How flexible and adaptable are the materials I'm choosing or creating for learners with accessibility needs?" or "Do the materials I've chosen reflect any forms of bias or discrimination, or could representations contribute to discrimination? If so, what adjustments can I make?" Figure 13.1 depicts integrating reflective questioning throughout the design process.

Table 13.1 Sampling of Questions for Ethics in Front-End Analysis. Used with permission from Moore and Tillberg-Webb (in press)

Stakeholders and Agency	Learner Characteristics	Needs	Context Analysis & Environmental Scan
Who are the relevant social groups (or stakeholders)? What are the potential benefits and the potential harms? What terms and conditions am I committing my learners (and perhaps their families) to? Am I giving them a say? Where and how can I ensure my students and other stakeholders have agency?	What are important personal and social characteristics I should take into account? How many learners are food – or housing – insecure? What accessibility barriers I can anticipate? What types of stress will my learners be experiencing, and how can I adjust plans and expectations accordingly?	What are the critical instructional needs? What learning gap(s) am I trying to address? What are critical non-instructional needs (e.g., health, safety, security)?	What are any major changes in learning context that are occurring, and what are some assumptions I should question? How many of my learners do and do not have reliable internet, phone/mobile service, or other means of connecting? What infrastructure am I assuming all students will have access to? What are the potential effects on our learning culture?

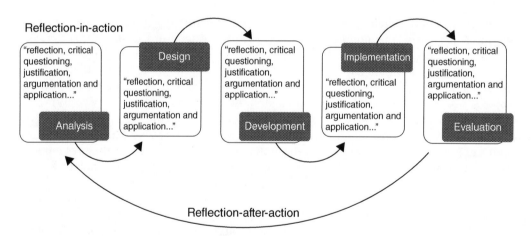

Figure 13.1 Integrating reflective questioning in the design process.

Ethics as Design

Caroline Whitbeck (1996) provides some foundational logic and examples that can help frame how we teach and integrate ethics. She argues that ethical problems are very similar to design problems and that most problems practitioners work on either are ethical or moral in nature or have an ethical component to them. As an engineer by training, she then explores how ethics are integrated in and through the design and development process using the example of designing a child seat for airline travel. Most students start with technical specifications, like what size and dimensions should the seat be to fit in a standard airplane seat and what materials fit the constraints and affordances of being light enough for parents to carry through an airport. But there are additional ethical and moral aspects of this design problem, in this case specifically safety of the child throughout the entire travel process and in the event of emergency. Addressing technical

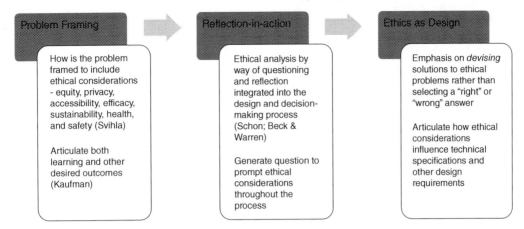

Figure 13.2 Integration and application for ethics as design.

specifications is insufficient and, in this case, would lead to a design that technically works but fails the most basic design requirement. Furthermore, the designers can't wait to address this until after they have worked on the technical specs. There is an interaction effect between ethical needs and specifications and the technical needs and specifications. For example, choosing the right material is both about weight and safety.

She argues that ethics and design inherently go hand-in-hand because most ethical or moral problems are *practical* problems in ways that make them very similar to design problems. Most often they are not problems requiring evaluative judgment; they are problems that require designers to devise a solution – to engage the design process. The design process helps us as designers to devise a range of solutions to complex problems that often have conflicting user or system needs and constraints. For example, addressing issues of accessibility or social justice that arise throughout design, development, and implementation of learning technologies, requires designers to generate solutions, not simply pick "option A" or "option B." Rarely are the potential harms and benefits so imbalanced. Rather, the designer has to think through the potential harms and benefits and devise options or solutions that navigate these icebergs in ways that minimize the harms and maximize the benefit. What may seem on the surface to be "only" a technology selection problem may in fact require an instructional designer or educational technologist to devise a more robust solution or engage in more systemic design thinking and problem solving.

Figure 13.2 summarizes how the three core ideas – problem framing, reflection-in-action, and ethics as design – provide students a process for integrating ethics with existing knowledge and applying ethical analysis in and through the design process.

Generative Learning Strategies

Engaging in the integration of ethical considerations into the design process is a more advanced competency for instructional designers, as it requires they draw from an existing body of foundational knowledge and integrate some new concepts and practices with existing knowledge. Generative learning theory posits that learning involves an active learning who constructs meaning from new information by reorganizing and integrating it existing knowledge (Fiorella & Mayer, 2016; Grabowski, 2004;). For generative learning to occur, learners must not only be presented with information for basic comprehension but also be provided opportunities to make sense of new content and integrate it into their existing schemas or mental models, so the information becomes usable. Grabowski (2004) identified a myriad of instructional strategies grounded in this theoretical approach and sorted them into two primary types of activities that are generative:

128 *Stephanie L. Moore and Gabrielle Griffin*

those in which learners generate organizational relationships and those in which learners integrate new learning with prior knowledge.

Both provide a useful way to frame instruction for a design-based approach to ethics. First, students must often develop a mental model or schema of not just ethical perspectives but a process for ethical analysis. This is often the daunting part, but some great resources exist, and a course does not necessarily have to devote a great deal of time to this aspect. For example, in our course, we used the ethics primer mentioned earlier and listed under Recommended Readings. Students then employed the ethical analysis process described in the primer through a paper that was scaffolded with a proposal, annotated bibliography, version 1.0 and version 2.0 process throughout the class.

After they have had some time to make sense of these perspectives and apply the analysis process, we then have activities focused on integration and translation. Specifically, students have an activity in which they select an existing design or decision-making model from the field and then generate a revised version of that model where they identify how and where to integrate in ethical analysis and questions. This provides learners an opportunity to connect the new knowledge around ethics and ethical analysis to existing knowledge of the instructional design process. The last third of class is primarily dedicated to a "Practical Project" wherein students have three choices for how to translate their analysis into a more applied approach: generate a case study, write an OpEd, or create a policy brief for your school or organization. They produce their practical projects while they are wrapping up their version 1.0 edits to their papers, so they are engaging in both analysis and application at the same time. Throughout the course, students also engage in reflection through on-going journaling, revision of their paper with instructor and peer feedback, and a summarizing activity in which they revise the integrative ethics-as-design models they generated earlier in the course.

Supporting the integration and generation is a foundation of prior and new knowledge, some of which are assumed prior knowledge a student would learn elsewhere and some which was presented at the beginning of class. Because of the curricular sequencing, students entered the ethics class with classes in instructional design and performance improvement, both of which are essential foundational knowledge for integrating ethical considerations into instructional design. Performance improvement proves critical for supporting more systemic design thinking and problem solving to help generate both more robust analysis and recommendations (explored in more detail below). Notably, the performance improvement class students completed prior used Kaufman's Organizational Elements Model, which emphasizes social impact as a part of the planning and evaluation process and provides a framework for organizing different types and levels of outcomes into a coherent plan. This particular prior content knowledge clearly showed up in how students conducted and organized their ethical analyses. In addition, at the start of the class, we introduced some new foundational concepts, framing ethics-as-design as an aspect of being a reflective practitioner and exploring literature on ethics and design cases that include ethical analysis, organized topically (e.g., accessibility, equity, privacy, social justice) to help students develop a schema for ethical considerations. Figure 13.3 is a summary of the design logic and sequencing for the instruction.

Figure 13.4 depicts how all of these ideas connect together to inform teaching ethics for instructional designers. Assuming a foundational knowledge of instructional design, systems theory and systems thinking, and performance improvement, we then build upon that knowledge by integrating in new knowledge on different approaches to ethics (using a basic primer) and developing knowledge about various ethical issues in the field. Generative learning strategies help learners integrate that new knowledge with the existing knowledge. Students also learn about problem framing, reflection-in-action, and ethics as design to revise their procedural knowledge (such as instructional design and performance improvement methods) and thus their practices.

Integrating Ethics into the Curriculum 129

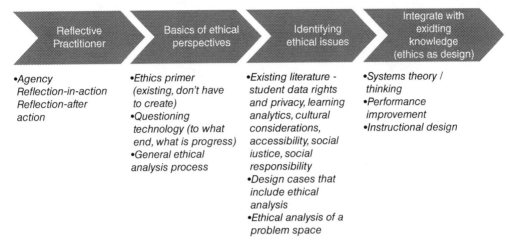

Figure 13.3 Instruction logic and sequencing.

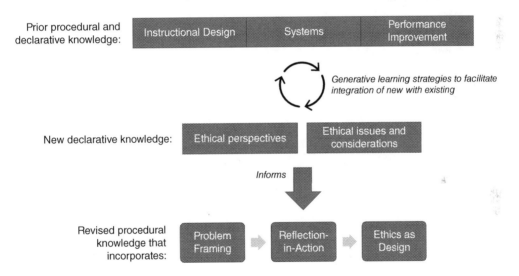

Figure 13.4 Relationship between theories.

Professional Practice Revisited

To explore how this worked in practice, one of the students from class, Gabrielle, provides her reflections below on how she tackled the case study presented earlier.

Student Reflections

As I digested the course readings and wrestled with the consequences of social media monitoring, my ethical framework began to emerge. By first evaluating and framing the problem of social media monitoring, I developed a holistic solution that addressed the root causes of threatening behavior and attended to the specific needs of each stakeholder group.

Evaluating the problem

From a systems standpoint, any solution would affect the entire school and the wider community. Therefore, I wanted to identify a solution that would bring the greatest good to the largest number of people. I reflected upon my school's mega-objective: Producing compassionate and self-sufficient citizens and preparing graduates for college and careers. I asked myself, would social media monitoring ultimately advance this outcome? Would it make students safer? Would it increase their compassion and self-sufficiency? Would it prepare them for life beyond high school in their college and careers?

Problem Framing

When considering social media monitoring's ethical implications, I framed the ethical problem. I questioned whether these threats were occurring because of the lack of online surveillance at the school. Once I concluded there was little connection between these behaviors and online surveillance, I decided to address the underlying causes of aggressive behavior.

As I began working through these issues, concerns about privacy, equity, security, and efficacy quickly emerged. In terms of privacy, monitoring students' social media is akin to surveilling their family and friends 24/7 – a troubling overstep of a school's authority. In terms of equity, research indicates that artificial intelligence (AI) monitoring platforms flag students of color at higher rates than white students and can lead to accidental or intentional discrimination. Finally, in terms of security and efficacy, research has failed to correlate social media surveillance with increased safety because students will post inappropriate or threatening messages in places beyond monitoring's reach.

Identifying stakeholders' needs

During my analysis, I discovered that each stakeholder group had specific and sometimes conflicting needs. Parents demanded a safe school environment but did not welcome intrusions into their privacy. Students wished to express themselves freely on social media without fear of repercussion from school officials. School administrators wanted to maintain order and discipline on the school campus. The community desired a peaceful school that developed self-sufficient and engaged citizens.

Devising recommendations

While developing recommendations to promote social media safety, I understood why many schools and districts opt for third-party surveillance. Monitoring companies market their services as a time and money-saving for overburdened school staff. Indeed, the digital age has conditioned many of us to embrace technology as the safest and most reliable way to solve problems. We entrust machines to apply logarithms – which we perceive to be infallible – while simultaneously losing faith in ourselves to address challenges with non-technical solutions.

The problem with fighting digital "fire with fire" is that surveillance fails to engage stakeholders in addressing the root causes of online threats. Instead, a more viable and effective plan would teach students digital citizenship and collective accountability. However, I knew that in most communities, any program without some form of online monitoring would be a non-starter. Therefore, to minimize the damage from surveillance, I recommended limiting it to school hours and school events. My overall recommendations centered upon anonymous reporting and the implementation of a digital safety curriculum:

- Create anonymous reporting platforms to advise of bullying and violent behavior,
- Prevent threats through education;
- Infuse soft skills and horizontal accountability into the digital citizenship curriculum;
- Make collaboration (both in-person and online) among student groups a routine instructional practice.

By first attending to ethics, I developed a plan that would cause minimal harm and benefit all stakeholders while advancing the school's mega-objective: Producing compassionate and self-sufficient citizens and preparing graduates for college and careers. These recommendations met the needs of each stakeholder group while also eliminating conflicting needs between groups.

Parents

By focusing on anonymous reporting programs and digital safety, surveillance would not inadvertently spy on families, friends, or anyone connected to the student's social media universe.

Student body

Students would be encouraged to join a community of accountability by being treated as partners in the digital safety process. A comprehensive curriculum would promote digital citizenship through personal responsibility for one's actions and reporting others' untoward actions.

School administrators

Integrating digital safety and responsibility into the curriculum is aligned with the school's mega-objective.

Community/society

Students trained in digital safety and responsibility will likely continue to practice appropriate behavior online and hold others accountable for their actions after they graduate.

132 *Stephanie L. Moore and Gabrielle Griffin*

Connecting Process to Practice

The following are a range of different questions and activities that can facilitate generative learning and application of the principles explored in this chapter. Moore and Tillberg-Webb (in press) provide a more extensive range of questions and activities you can use in class.

Discussion Questions/Generative Discussions

1. Often, the introduction of technology is considered "progress." But Marx reminds us that progress may be defined in a number of ways. Choose an example of a technology that you are considering using or implementing in your class, school, or organization. What would your definition of "progress" be in relation to the selection and implementation of that technology? What are potential learning benefits or harms? And what are other potential benefits or harms besides learning outcomes? How can you use that to construct a definition of "progress" that you could evaluate over time?
2. Select a design or decision-making model for educational technology and instructional design and modify it to how you would integrate ethical analysis and decision making into the process. See our prior readings from Gustafson and Branch for several options you can use/modify to develop more equitable and ethical design models. Expand upon what you already know about instructional design and think about what inclusive and ethical practices look like from the view of the learner and the consequences of developing and engaging in more responsive instruction. When posting your reply, please create a visual and write an explanation;
3. Identify design cases in the field, for example in the *Journal of Applied Instructional Design* or the *International Journal of Designs for Learning*, which include ethical considerations in their design case. Describe how and where designers integrated ethical decision making into their processes and practices. What ideas does this generate for you for your own practices?

Activities/Assignments

1. Conduct an ethical analysis of a learning technology and make recommendations to a set of stakeholders and/or decision makers. You may want to use performance improvement as a companion process to help you generate and organize recommendations;
2. Create a policy brief for your school, district, university, or organization that briefly explains the issues and makes policy recommendations to help your school or workplace navigate the complex issues and considerations of a learning technology procurement and/or implementation. This could include, for example, recommended requirements that are incorporated into the review and procurement process, governance committees, or other types of performance supports;
3. Write an OpEd on a recent issue that has been in the news where ethical issues around educational technologies have been raised by one or more stakeholders;
4. If lack of knowledge or skills is a gap you have identified through root cause analysis, develop an instructional intervention.

Conclusion

We conclude with noting that ethics are not actually organized under the cognitive or affective domain but under the under-studied conative domain (Kolbe, 1990). The conative domain includes will, volition, action, and doing. It makes sense that ethics would be situated here, as it is not merely a matter of understanding principles or different types of ethics but ultimately is a form of action, much like design itself. Like design, ethics is a form of envisioning "what should be" in contrast to "what is" and devising solutions to help bridge those gaps. It acknowledges that learning outcomes are not neatly discrete or separate from other types of outcomes, like social justice and accessibility, but rather are tied up with these "extra-instructional" considerations, and often to address learning we must also address moral and ethical aspects that are presented in the problems we are trying to solve. Problem framing and reflection-in-action that include ethical analysis provide a way for us to turn ethics into action. Ethics as design reminds us that perfection is not the aim of the endeavor, as pragmatic considerations will necessarily introduce constraints, but we can use our professional methods and processes to tackle complex problems in such a way that we have desired impacts on the people and social systems we serve.

References

Amiel, T., Squires, J., & Orey, M. (2009). Four strategies for designing instruction for diverse cultures: Context and localization of learning objects. *Educational Technology, 49*(6), 28–34.

Beck, D., & Warren, S. (2020). ECET: A proposed framework to guide ethical instructor choices with learning technologies. *TIL Inspired! (C)*. Retrieved from https://convention2.allacademic.com/one/aect/aect20/index.php?cmd=Online+Program+View+Session&selected_session_id=1697338&PHPSESSID=v2ehlnunjt2pgqr0p2sh9rq1nq

Benson, A., Joseph, R., & Moore, J. (Eds.). (2017). *Culture, learning, and technology: Research and practice*. Routledge. doi:10.4324/9781315681689

Berenbeim, R. (1987). *Corporate ethics*. Conference Board.

Bradshaw, A. (2018). Reconsidering the instructional design and technology timeline through a lens of social justice. *TechTrends, 62*, 336–344.

Chowning, J. T., & Fraser, P. (2007). *An ethics primer*. Northwest Association of Biomedical Research.

Daniel, B. (2015). Big data and analytics in higher education: Opportunities and challenges. *British Journal of Educational Technology, 46*(5), 904–920. doi:10.1111/bjet.12230

Dean, P. J. (1992). Making codes of ethics 'real.' *Journal of Business Ethics, 11*(4), 285–290. doi:10.1007/BF00872170

Dean, P. J. (1999). The relevance of standards and ethics for the human performance technology profession. In H. Stolovitch & E. Keeps (Eds.), *Handbook of human performance technology* (2nd ed., pp. 698–712). Jossey-Bass.

Dickson-Deane, C., Bradshaw, A. C., & Asino, T. I. (2018). Recognizing the inseparability of culture, learning, and technology. *TechTrends, 62*(4), 310–311. doi:10.1007/s11528-018-0296-3

Finn, J. D. (1996). A walk on the altered side. In D. Ely & T. Plomp (Eds.), *Classic writings on instructional technology* (pp. 47–56). Libraries Unlimited, Inc.

Fiorella, L., & Mayer, R. E. (2016). Eight ways to promote generative learning. *Educational Psychology Review, 28*(4), 717–741. doi:10.1007/s10648-015-9348-9

Grabowski, B. L. (2004). Generative learning contributions to the design of instruction and learning. In *Handbook of research on educational communications and technology* (2nd ed., pp. 719–743). Routledge.

Gray, C., & Boling, E. (2016). Inscribing ethics and values in designs for learning: A problematic. *Educational Technology Research and Development, 64*(1), 969–1001. doi:10.1007/s11423-016-9478-x

Gunawardena, C., Frechette, C., & Layne, L. (2018). *Culturally inclusive instructional design: A framework and guide for building online wisdom communities*. Routledge.

Hornik, S., & Tupchiy, A. (2006). Culture's impact on technology mediated learning: The role of horizontal and vertical individualism and collectivism. *Journal of Global Information Management, 14*(4), 31–56. doi:10.4018/jgim.2006100102

Ifenthaler, D., & Tracey, M. W. (2016). Exploring the relationship of ethics and privacy in learning analytics and design: Implications for the field of educational technology. *Educational Technology Research and Development, 64*(5), 877–880. doi:10.1007/s11423-016-9480-3

Igoche, D., & Branch, R. (2009). Incorporating cultural values into the ADDIE approach to instructional design. *Educational Technology, 49*(6), 4–8.

Kaufman, R. (2000). *Mega planning: Practical tools for organizational success*. Sage Publications.

Kaurin, P. S. (2018). Ethics: Starting at the beginning. *Wavell Room.* Retrieved from https://wavell-room.com/2018/08/23/ethics-starting-beginning/

Kimmons, R. (2020). Current trends (and missing links) in educational technology research and practice. *TechTrends, 64*(6), 803–809.

Klein, C., Lester, J., Rangwala, H., & Johri, A. (2019). Technological barriers and incentives to learning analytics adoption in higher education: Insights from users. *Journal of Computing in Higher Education, 31*(3), 604–625. doi:10.1007/s12528-019-09210-5

Kolbe, K. (1990). *The conative connection: Uncovering the link between who you are and how you perform.* Addison-Wesley Longman.

Lin, H. (2007). The ethics of instructional technology: Issues and coping strategies experienced by professional technologists in design and training situations in higher education. *Educational Technology Research and Development, 55*(5), 411–437. doi:10.1007/s11423-006-9029-y

Moore, S. L. (2005). *The social impact of a profession: An analysis of factors influencing ethics and the teaching of social responsibility in educational technology programs* [Publication No. 3183569] (Doctoral dissertation). University of Northern Colorado. ProQuest Dissertations Publishing.

Moore, S. L. (2013). Ethics as design: Rethinking professional ethics as part of the design domain. In B. Hokanson & A. Gibbons (Eds.), *Design in educational technology* (pp. 185–204). Springer. doi:10.1007/978-3-319-00927-8_11

Moore, S. L. (in press). The design models we have are not the design models we need. *Journal of Applied Instructional Design.*

Moore, S. L., & Ellsworth, J. B. (2014). Ethics of educational technology. In J. M. Spector, M. D. Merrill, J. Elen, & M. J. Bishop (Eds.), *Handbook of research on educational communications and technology* (pp. 113–127). Springer. doi:10.1007/978-1-4614-3185-5_10

Moore, S. L., & Tillberg-Webb, H. (in press). *Ethics and educational technology.* Routledge.

Pardo, A., & Siemens, G. (2014). Ethical and privacy principles for learning analytics. *British Journal of Educational Technology, 45*(3), 438–450. doi:10.1111/bjet.12152

Rieber, L., & Estes, M. (2017). Accessibility and instructional technology: Reframing the discussion. *Journal of Applied Instructional Design, 6*(1), 9–19. doi:10.28990/jaid2017.061001

Rubel, A., & Jones, K. M. L. (2016). Student privacy in learning analytics: An information ethics perspective. *The Information Society, 32*(2), 143–159. doi:10.1080/01972243.2016.1130502

Schön, D. A. (1983). *The reflective practitioner: How professionals think in action.* Basic Books.

Svihla, V. (2020). Problem framing. In J. K. McDonald & R. E. West (Eds.), *Design for learning: Principles, processes, and praxis.* EdTech Books.

Tracey, M. W., & Baaki, J. (2014). Design, designers, and reflection-in-action. In B. Hokanson & A. Gibbons (Eds.), *Design in educational technology* (pp. 1–13). Cham: Springer. doi:10.1007/978-3-319-00927-8_1

Watkins, R., Leigh, D., & Kaufman, R. (2000). A scientific dialogue: A performance accomplishment code of professional conduct. *Performance Improvement, 39*(4), 17–22. doi:10.1002/pfi.4140390408

Weaver, G., & Treviño, L. (1999). Compliance and values-oriented ethics programs: Influences on employee's attitudes and behavior. *Business Ethics Quarterly, 9*(2), 315–335. doi:10.2307/3857477

Whitbeck, C. (1996). Ethics as design: Doing justice to moral problems. *Hastings Center Report, 26*(3), 9–16. doi:10.2307/3527925

Yeaman, A. (2004a). Professional ethics for technology. *TechTrends, 48*(2), 11–15. doi:10.1007/BF02762537

Yeaman, A. (2004b). Professional ethics: The misuse of technology. *TechTrends, 48*(5), 14–16. doi:10.1007/BF02763524

Yeaman, A., Koetting, J., & Nichols, R. (1994). Critical theory, cultural analysis and the ethics of educational technology as social responsibility. *Educational Technology, 34*(2), 5–13.

14 Instructional Design Embedded in Culture

Beth Sockman and Laura Kieselbach

Chapter Overview

As gatekeepers to the student's learning experience, instructional designers have the opportunity to make learning environments an equitable space through our processes, accessibility, and expectations. This case study takes place in a higher education course where the instructor was mindful of her role as the gatekeeper, but with implementation, her biases were questioned. The readers consider the two concepts that influence instructional design: cultural systems that can lead to unexamined perspectives and depth levels of culture that can be parsed into the instructional design processes. Further extensions describe how to be deliberately mindful of cultural elements that could impact learners. Finally, looking back on the case, the higher education course design is analyzed in terms of the cultural conflict and resolution.

The concepts are sometimes written in first person because culture resides in a personal space nested within human identities and infiltrates all that we do. It is the hope that you build awareness of your own culture so that when you are a gatekeeper of knowledge and experience, you do so with wisdom.

Guiding Questions

1. What is important about examining the environment's dominant culture when designing a learning environment?
2. What are the systems influences that need to be taken into consideration with a culturally situated stance?
3. When looking at cultural depth levels (see Table 14.1), what are some examples of surface, shallow, and deep cultural elements for instructional design?
4. How can the processes of instructional design help to create culturally relevant learning environments?

Case Study

The Instructional Technology course was filled with 15 master's students that were enthusiastically anxious to create their upcoming assignment. They created their professional portfolio websites as a capstone project, displaying self-selected exemplary artifacts to showcase their skills. The class represented a cross section of the United States that included students that identified as White, Black, and Asian with international students from Ghana and Japan. The instructor enjoyed the class's diversity in perspectives and the creativity that imbued interactions.

DOI: 10.4324/9781003109938-14

There was an introduction to each module that had quotes from different cultures. Images were chosen based on their compositional representation of ethnic backgrounds and color pallets. Media was selected so that if genders were in stereotypical roles, the instructor helped the student question the assumptions. In the discussion boards, students were expected to question another's perspectives with netiquette laden examples. The class norm: the class was encouraged to analyze materials and state if something did not ring true for them.

Since this was an advanced course, the instructor did not expect any cultural dissonance. Up to now, the students had created projects in other classes and so were aggregating, aligning them to standards with justifications for the alignment. The professor created a portfolio rubric that included the criteria by which this culminating assignment would be scored, along with multiple examples for guidance.

There were two surprises to the professor in the final web portfolios. A student from an Asian country created a website with many small pictures in the corners with copious animated gifs. There was no single point of focus on the web page. In another project, a female student displayed a picture of herself pole dancing. In the self-evaluations, both students rated themselves very highly and did not note any discrepancies or concerns with their work, which was a distinctly different perspective than the instructor.

Table 14.1 Levels of Culture (Hammond, 2015, pp. 22–24) with Instructional Design Considerations

Cultural Depth Levels	Examples	Instructional Design Questions for Consideration
Surface	Observable and concrete elements, what we see, generally acknowledged	• Media: Does media represent various cultures, ethnicity, and race in equal status through position, dress, and intellect? • Greetings: Do opening messages welcome diverse perspectives? • Calendar: How do calendars and timelines acknowledge holidays of cultures other than the dominant or privileged culture?

Shallow	Unspoken rules around everyday social interactions & norms, non-verbal	• Social Interactions
		   • What is communication like with between genders and identities in different learning spaces (i.e., in-person, discussion boards, video conferencing)?
		   • What does communication with instructors look like (eye contact, questioning, and comfort)?
		 • Course Norms of time, sequence, and effort.
		   • How are assignment due dates viewed?
		   • What process is expected when learning the course content and how is that expectation conveyed?
		   • How much time and effort are learners expected to give assignments?

(Continued)

Table 14.1 (Continued)

Cultural Depth Levels	Examples	Instructional Design Questions for Consideration
Deep	Unconscious assumptions that govern the worldview view of good or bad that guides ethics, spirituality, health, and theories of group harmony	**Success**: What does success look like from the perspective of the learner and of the professor and why? Ethics • What are the ethical embodiments of communication (i.e., netiquette, speech)? • What are the expectations and enactments of Copyright, Creative Commons, and Plagiarism? Group Harmony – Individualistic or Collectivist • How are learners expected to generate thought in groups or individually and how do learners perceive the difference? • Is the course collaborative and/or competitive in its orientation? Exemplars • What is "good" and "exemplars"? Do they represent a diversity of perspectives with various cultures in equal position? Aesthetics • Is the course aesthetically pleasing for the content in its layout and design, to the beholder? • What is the basis for aesthetic preference that govern acceptable qualities?

Cultural Concepts Related to the Instructional Design Process

"Culture is at the heart of what we do in the name of education, whether that is curriculum, instruction, administration or performance assessment" (Gay, 2018, p. 8).

Researchers note that diversity enhances creativity in research, art, and even company profits (Phillips, 2014). With all the benefits, instructional designers should be harnessing the diverse cultural powers offered in learning environments, but often do not. Why? One explanation could be that culture is the "air" we breathe. It is hard to describe what air feels like daily, but if there is a breeze or a whiff of a flowery fragrance, then air is noticed. Similarly, often people are unconscious of their own culture until something noticeable happens – a difference.

We are all immersed within culture, each of us situated within an environment that we may or may not question. We are aware of some cultural elements, and blind to others. If we are working in a culture different than what we grew up with, we are lucky because we "see and feel" difference. If we are designing in a culture similar to our upbringing, we often unquestioningly work. The air never changed, so one may not fully understand what is influencing our instructional design.

Systems

Culture's multiplicity nests within systems that can be understood when parsed into multiple overlapping systems: supra, macro, meso, and micro systems. The dominant culture

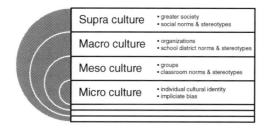

Figure 14.1 Simplified systems view of culture.

is part of the supra system, where a ruling culture – the privileged – overshadow the less prevalent but diverse cultural groups (Netting et al., 2017). Within the supra system, nests institutions of education, religion, geographic regions, etc. which create the macro-or institutionalized cultures. Inside the macro systems exist smaller groups, such as family, school, affinity groups – both virtual and physical spaces, constituting meso cultural systems. The systems of supra, macro and meso cultural levels exert influences over the individual level of people's identities, or the micro system of each person. Each system influences the other in which the sub systems nests. No system exists in isolation but overlaps the other (See Figure 14.1).

Often, we label behaviors as "normal" if the behavior matches our cultural paradigm or "not normal" if it is does not. Culture is mapped into us from birth. For example, when you eat, what hand is used to pick up your food or eating utensil? "Proper" ways to eat were mapped onto you from your initial family, but then modified some when you went to school. These could have been two similar or different meso cultures.

After years of programming, what happens if someone breaks the norm by "eating" differently than you? You take notice. You may consider the person inappropriate. Sometimes, we carry a superiority bias, "I am better than them" attitude. Then, the opposite may happen. Perhaps, you anticipated a meeting with a distinguished person, and to prepare, you research accepted etiquette for meals. In this situation, you determine what the supra system expectation dominates since you are concerned with making a "good" impression. Even how one eats becomes a cultural norm. There are millions of cultural norms (Wilkerson, 2020). Norms were established in our first home, then modified within each system we took part. We are socialized into systems with our brain telling us how the world is "supposed" to work. The cultural norms subconsciously spill over into every aspect of our lives.

These cultural norms influence our instruction design. Our awareness starts as a member of the supra, macro, meso cultures that influence a person and their identity (Kendi, 2019). When we become emersed in a particular organizational culture, we employ some or all of the cultural systems of that organization. Then, when a learning environment is created, it too reflects the cultural norms of that organization. The learning environment becomes part of the cultural examination: how the learning and the environment was designed; selection of content and resources; and the way learning reflects the values of the system.

If persons are part of the dominate cultural group, then they can find it difficult to tease out the norms since they are so comfortable. To help learning designers become more cognizant, next, explore the depth levels of culture and how they related to instructional design process.

Depth Levels of Culture

Not all culture elements are as apparent as others. Language and holidays are easily identified, but values and expectations are more challenging. To help "see" the various aspects, Hammond (2015) discusses depth levels of culture. She describes cultural levels in terms of surface, shallow and deep, metaphorically comparing culture to the depths of the ocean (see Table 14.1). The elements on the surface are easy to see, but plunging deeper, culture may be harder to discern.

The surface level is addressed with more observable traits. As designers, this may seem easier through images and holiday recognition, but even that can be a challenge. Image searches on the Internet often yields results that reflect the dominant supra system, marginalizing underrepresented groups are relegated to stereo typical roles unless the personal algorithm is used (Nobel, 2017).

On the shallow level, the overall design of instruction hinges on many unspoken rules around social interactions which may reflect cultural norms for the class. For example, it may be that all work is focused on the individual with very little interaction with peers. Or, the instructor assumes that students initiate questioning, when questioning is considered rude in some cultures.

Continuing the dive, deep culture delves into unconscious assumptions that govern worldview (Hammond, 2015). For example, student work may be assessed so only the top third succeed, utilizing the "bell – curve" philosophy that stigmatizing failure for $2^{nd}/3^{rd}$ of the class before they begin (Rose, 2015) rather than expecting mastery of all students. Or, there may be a mastery-based curriculum, but "good" exemplars only represent the dominant supra system culture's values.

Due to our differences, it is beneficial to become aware of one's own culture and the norms that influences us prior to designing instruction. Instructional design with cultural relevant pedagogy must be purposeful. Our norms are habitual, often going unnoticed by even by ourselves. These deep cultural elements easily lead to biases, marginalize learners, or emphasize inequalities within our learning environments. As we become more cognizant of our own norms, we can explicitly address our design-based assumptions and our learner's needs to help them succeed. Examine Table 14.1. Notice the different depth levels of culture with the coinciding instructional design questions, and then reflect on ways to make a course more inclusive.

Because of our unconscious bias and the wealth of diversity in our world, it is important that instructors practice cultural humility. As Nomikoudis and Starr write (2016), we need to "maintain a constant state as both learner and self-reflective practitioner" (p. 70) as we work to uncover ways to make our learning environments and content more accessible. This learning is messy. The act of learning anything implies failures before success. "Failing" in cultural aspects is not like failing how to write HTML. Cultural learning is related to our personal identities which can be hard for individual egos, and yet, a necessity for growth.

Cultural Inclusivity in Instructional Design and Technology Processes

Professional organizations have already established a foundational standard of instruction design and technology that explicitly value diversity in design, instruction, and professionalism. The Association for Educational Communications and Technology (AECT, 2012), espouse that instructional design candidate's examine diversity of learners and culture throughout the ID process. Similarly, the International Society for Technology in Education Instructional Technology Coach standards (ISTE, 2017) advocate that technology coaches support teachers culturally relevant technology use. See the Table 14.2 for a comparison.

Standards acknowledge the ethical imperative to embrace humanity's diversity, yet culture can be difficult to unteased in personal biases due to the subconscious nature of our individually programming. Fortunately, the ID processes process explicitly invites examination of culture in learning environments. The paragraphs below describe broad ID

Table 14.2 AECT Standards ID Standards (AECT, 2012), and ISTE Coach Standards (ISTE, 2017) Comparison Regarding Culturally Relevant Practices

Instructional Cultural Element	AECT Standards	ISTE Coach Standards
Designing for the Learning Environment	**Standard 2 Content Pedagogy – Ethics –** Candidates design and select media, technology, and processes that emphasize the **diversity of our society as a multicultural community.**	**Standard 3 – Collaborator** 3b. Partner with educators to identify **digital learning content** that is **culturally relevant,** developmentally appropriate and aligned to content standards.
Instruction	**Standard 3 Learning Environments – Diversity of Learners –** Candidates foster a learning community that empowers **learners with diverse backgrounds, characteristics, and abilities.**	**Standard 4 – Learning Designer** 4c Collaborate with educators to design accessible and active digital learning environments that accommodate **learner variability.**
Professionalism	**Standard 4 Professional Knowledge and Skills – Ethics-**Candidates demonstrate ethical behavior within the applicable cultural context during all aspects of their work and with **respect for the diversity of learners in each setting.**	**Standard 7b – Digital Citizen Advocate** Partner with educators, leaders, students and families to foster a **culture of respectful online interactions** and a **healthy balance in their use of technology.**

processes and explain how the process can propel designers to be more aware of culture. Each instructional design process can investigate the cultural depth implications that are interwoven throughout the process, starting with the front-end analysis.

Front-End Analysis

The first step in the ID process is front-end analysis. A thoughtful and thorough front-end analysis can save time throughout the entire process, and this is no different when thinking about culture. The front-end work often entails the learner and context analysis, articulation of actual and optimal conditions and identification of learning goals (Dick et al., 2014). The findings from this stage influence the design, development, implementation and evaluation so that learning can more easily honor our diversity which is emphasized in the standards (See Table 14.1).

To determine surface culture, various stakeholders could be interviewed when conducting the learner analysis. Surface level culture elements (see Table 14.2) can easily be identified such as the messaging that appeals diverse groups through images, appropriate greetings, and potential calendar conflicts. These surface cultural elements can be compared to the learners' background and with the organization's traditional means, and then the acceptance needs of greater society. A strong learner analysis does not stop with the surface level but moves into deeper characteristics.

Dipping into the shallow elements of culture, designers can determine students' expectations, clarify how due dates/times are perceived, how elders and genders are viewed, and how social interaction occurs. An example of interaction could include presumptions about questioning. In some cultures, student questions are considered rude, and yet, in other cultures, instructors depend on student's explicit inquisitiveness to guide instruction. Mismatches could be uncovered with the reasons for the feeling. Identifying these elements will help the instructor explicate expectations around interactions that need to be identified in the beginning of a course.

Diving into deep culture can be a little more challenging because questions and observations are not as obvious. Designer's probe into cultural relevancy. In the learner analysis the worldview can include what is perceived in qualitative statements such as aesthetics, motivations, collaboration and competition, group collaboration, and impacts of individualistic and collectivist cultures.

Deep culture is where designers are likely to find the implicit mismatches between groups of learners, the context, and even the subject matter experts. Interviews, observations, and surveys can be conducted with the various groups. Ask about importance, value, and what success. How do you know the class was successful? What is important in learning experiences? How should value be judged, and what inhibits success? The answers will expose discrepancies between potential participants.

There are limits to the front-end analysis. Planning for deep cultural understanding is imperative, but some elements will not be seen until implementation occurs. Another limitation lies with instructional environment. Most of K-12 education does not have time to conduct a thorough front-end analysis before engaging with students, so mismatches occur in the later stages of the instructional design process.

When time permits, a thorough front end analysis can provide data to inform the learning design. Multiple levels of culture can be uncovered so as the rest of the ID process unfolds, the learning environment compiles with standards, and importantly, makes the learning space meaningful for instructors and students.

Design and Development

When designing and developing learning experiences, instruction designers use their findings from the front-end analysis for the design and creation of the learning path that meets the ethical design standards and honors learners' diversity. On the surface, text and media should be chosen that represent the people equally and reviewed for unconscious bias. Images become a first impression landing point (Gay, 2018). Inclusive messages produce a welcoming and open environment while supporting learners. Though this seems simple, it will take time to find the images that do not have stereotypes of things like beauty and "good" and "bad" positioning, and clothing that represents different identities (Gay, 2018; Wilkerson, 2020). If doing an Internet search for images or resources, first results often yield representations of the dominate culture or finds are based on the personal algorithm. Plan on investing the extra time to find resources that represent people equally.

The norms of the course should be explicit with the expectations regarding discussion and questioning (Woodley et al., 2017). Consider asking students to share their preferred names and pronouns in the primary language used. Another norm includes responses to others. Courses commonly expect students to question one another in discussion boards. To assist, prompts could be provided for respectful ways. An example: "Please respond to two peers and help them to think more deeply about their statement." Here are some ideas for prompts: "I wonder...; From my experience.... Would you be able to explain what you mean by...." In addition, an open invitation to discuss culture norms could be provided in writing or in a video at the beginning. The explicit invitation to dialog establishes a welcoming climate so that intellectual work is not constrained.

When selecting the content, provide activities and readings representing or inviting different views. There are many benefits to this such as increasing critical thinking and creativity (Phillips, 2014), or acceptance of new processes. However, course goals and content purposes differ. Sometimes the learning goals seek to increase perspective, and sometimes the goal seeks to promulgate a best practice.

Content that represents informational knowledge may lends itself to a limited perspective such hygiene or solving a computational problem. In this case, imagery can represent different people providing a universal message. For example, if demonstrating the way to thoroughly wash hands before a surgery, there may be one way, but hands from people with different colors of skin or videos with different visible ethnicities all washing hands in similar ways, provides a universality message.

Assignments and assessments provide ways for students to access and demonstrate their understandings. Valid assessments need to reflect the student's actual ability to comprehend or perform the task goals of the course. To be valid, students need to have cognitive access to content work. The development of the course become most essential as designers offer options, many times through technology which affords a myriad of ways to make content accessible with opportunities through video, audio, and print media for both accessing and expressing what students know (Woodley et al., 2017).

Close ended assessment questions are often viewed as less bias but are not necessarily (Rose, 2015). Access to content can include the scenario that the problems are embedded in. Using examples such as sports, which is often seen as commonplace, assume that the learner has a background in sports. Even math "word problems" with context disadvantages some, because students cannot relate, and yet without context, math is merely computation. Instructional designers need to be mindful of the inherent conflict when they relate to the context of the problem (Gay, 2018) and work with diverse individuals to write examples that are inclusive.

Open ended assessments can easily encourage multiple perspectives. If paired with a rubric, the criteria can articulate different levels of justification. When learners justify their perspectives with resources, experience, and explicit observation, that aligns to the assessment, they can communicate their understandings, leading to increased validity (Wiggins & McTighe, 2005). Learners can express their knowledge in different ways based on their cultivated understandings. Similarly, to any assignments, it is helpful when different learner groups provided feedback to determine ways assessments could be strengthened by representing perspectives.

Instructors in K-12 environments experience unique challenges. They are often designing a few days before delivering the content. When this happens, routine learner feedback throughout the process will help teachers make modifications, which is true of any implementation. It is important that clear distinctions are made between the learner's feedback on design considerations and the classwork work. This can be tricky because learners may be inhibited, so anonymous surveys may afford more honest opinions. From the student feedback, instructors can make some real-time redesign demonstrating empathy – honoring the learners.

Implementation – Culturally Relevant Pedagogy

If the course is not self-automated, a live instructor greatly influences the delivery, perceptions, and sets the climate for the course. In their presentation, discussion, questioning, responses, and assessment teachers have the twin responsibilities of both pushing growth and accepting difference. In this push-pull challenge, instructors need to be mindful of the implications of the lasting effects of their actions.

To guide the work of how instructors approach their instruction, Gloria Ladson-Billings (1995) proposed the framework of culturally relevant pedagogy. Though her primary audience was PK-12 educators, the framework applies to all those who seek to create a more ethical world. The three components address student learning, cultural competence, and critical consciousness. Student learning focuses on intellectual, and moral development through problem solving and reasoning. The classroom should be a place that seeks to develop cultural competence through the appreciation of cultures of origin

Instructional Design Embedded in Culture 143

and fluency of another culture. In this posture, develop a deep critical consciousness through problem solving and analysis of authentic problems especially those nested in societal inequalities.

The issues of deep culture move into behaviors that may empower or threaten the individual. For example, one study demonstrated that instructors accept questions from some students but hold different expectations for other students. It has been observed that if students of color question, the teacher may become defensive but quickly accepts question from the culture that aligns with theirs (Fox, 2016). Instructors need cultural humility to become comfortable with unlearning these habits that are based on unchecked biases.

Cultural relevant pedagogy enactments lie with deep culture, externalizing the underpinnings that are often unconscious. When instruction is in action, instructor's biases emerge by the way the instructors interact and share expectations with students. For example, sometimes students find social norms confusing. To combat confusion, instructors can post written and verbal explanations, and invite students to meet. Open communication between the students and the instructors is affective when both parties are open to listening to the other, and if the student feels there will be with no repercussions on assessments. When in conversation, the instructor can ask the students, "What would make this course more valuable for you?" The instructor can also talk about their goals for the course and community. The open dialog can explicate the unspoken norms with humility.

Conclusion

The authors of this chapter do not feel that they have unpacked all the issues related to instructional design and culture, but rather provide a springboard for cultural considerations when designing instruction. The work begins with an awareness of the impacts of the systems on ourselves and our learning environments. In our wonderfully diverse world, many times there is a cultural mismatch between instructional design and the end learner's need. The gap needs to be bridged. First, self-examination is required to carry a personal disposition of cultural humility. Second, instructional designers acknowledge our designs are part of a larger system, and that we do not design in isolation. Our design is embedded in societal and cultural norms of the larger society, but also the organization we are designing for. Third, the instructor of the course can prepare for ethical implications by practicing culturally relevant pedagogy to discover differences that were unexpected. Rather than feeling threatened or resentful of a student's culture that may be different from their own, the instructor can maintain a sense of wonder in the unfolding of their personal learning. Therefore, it imperative that we become cognizant and question each piece of the instructional design to determine what aspects supports the norms, challenge the norms, and build toward equity.

Professional Practice Revisited

The instructor of the course used front-end analysis findings to addressed surface and shallow cultural elements. Designers considered students from various backgrounds. On the surface, the visual imagery included color schemes which varied for each module with images including marginalized cultures in power roles. Inspirational readings and quotes were used that represented leaders from different backgrounds. The syllabus was explicit with expectations and invited the students to ask questions if anything was unclear, including any timelines that would conflict with religious holidays that were not nationally recognized.

Shallow elements of culture were also addressed in the development through explicit examples of what "successful" social norms looked like. For example, on the discussion board, students were given prompt samples on the way respond to each other, and in conversation, some female students shared that they would not show their faces to men in the class, and wore a face-coverings, niqabs, when male students were present. The surface and shallow elements were easier identify when students shared their social norms with the instructor.

The challenge came with the deep cultural elements that also impacted the student's assessment and therefore, the student's success. Two situations will be addressed separately, first the portfolio design, and then, the image selection.

In the first situation, a student created a web page with multiple small images and gifs rather than having a signal point of focus. "Beauty is in the eyes of the beholder" is not just for love relationship, but the web too. In the USA, web design attempts to stay "clean" with a "single point of focus," yet website aesthetic differs across the world according to audience preference (Alexander et al., 2017). In other words, people are accustomed to seeing more movement at the same time, and there in not a need for a single point of focus. Preferred website design includes the layout, color scheme, and architecture which are all dominated by what a culture thinks is ideal for the visual display. Deep culture acknowledges aesthetic difference.

On the pre-made rubric, one criterion – aesthetics – layout/design included descriptions such as single point of focus, and aesthetically pleasing. Aware of the cultural aesthetic differences, the instructor had a conversation with student to learn about his rational (Alexander et al., 2017). From the instructor's perspective, the student from Asia created a "busy" web page, but from the student's perspective the aesthetics displayed the ideal, and USA websites were boring. The instructor altered the rubric to include flexibility for cultural differences to include aesthetically pleasing based on the cultural target with a student explanation. Both the teacher and students gained a more sophisticated understanding of aesthetic that could be articulated to others.

The second situation involved a recreational picture that a student chose for her portfolio website. It is common in the USA to list hobbies on a resume or portfolio to connect with others or show complementary disciplines. In this situation, the student displayed an image of herself pole-dancing. Pole-dancing has historically erotic origins, but recently has been recognized as a sport due to the required athleticism (Burke, 2019; Just & Muhr, 2020).

The image discrepancy represented a generational cultural regarding what is an appropriate skill to showcase. In conversation, the professor invited the student to "tell a little about the image and why it was selected." Born and raised in the USA but 20 years younger than the professor, the student felt the image represented her physical and mental discipline. The professor felt the image invited critique, misunderstanding, and at worst, a sexual stereotype. Both the instructor and the student identified as female and discussed the different perspectives. The instructor did not deduct assessment points for the image choice, and the graduate student chose what she felt was appropriate.

The college course case demonstrated how instructional design embeds culture from its inception, through implementation, and ultimately, the evaluation of the student and the validity of the course key assessment. Though the front-end analysis was able to unearth most surface and shallow cultural elements, it was the instructor-student mutually respectful dialog during implementation that resolved the deeper elements through intentional praxis of cultural relevant pedagogy.

Connecting Process to Practice

1. **Reflect on SELF:** Before you embark on designing for others think about your background and what may implicitly affect your instructional design. What are the cultural systems that influence your thinking? Consider the identity wheel (Hawkins et al., 2017) to examine the parts of you that are valued, oppressed, honored, or disregarded. What level of the system has influenced each part? Is it part of your individual identity? As Hammond notes, "if teachers want to be successful in their work with culturally diverse students, they must first and accept and understand themselves as cultural beings" (p. 56). Personal culture shapes our actions in ways that seem invisible and normal.
   a. Shallow culture: What is your religion, holidays celebrated, gender, sexual orientation, and how do they relate to the supra, macro, meso systems?
   b. Surface culture: What attributes were praised in your community, and which were you taught to avoid? How were you instructed to interact with authority?
   c. Deep culture: explore values related to communication, self-motivation, effort, behavior patterns, volume of interaction, importance of education, etc;
   d. Question: What do you think of as a person who is beautiful? Who should be feared? Who is successful? Who is intelligent?
   e. Take some of the Harvard Implicit Bias tests: https://implicit.harvard.edu/implicit/takeatest.html
   f. Reflection on ways that you would benefit from cultivating an understanding of another culture.
2. **Reflect on the PAST:** Complete an audit of a course already designed and implemented. It could be a course you designed or one that you have taken. To do this review the questions in Table 14.1 with a peer that is different from you. Your peer could be of a different culture, race, religion, ethnicity, belief system, etc. After the audit, determine how the course could have been more inclusive or equitable. Use intentional images, quotes, etc. to ignite student's imagination about what is possible.
3. **Reflectivity for the PRESENT & FUTURE:** Design a course using the full or part of the processes under the heading Cultural Inclusivity in Instructional Design and Technology. Compare the design to ways to designs that were traditionally done in the past. Encourage counternarratives to emphasize literary representation of culture in comparison to mainstream media representation. Develop a Growth Mindset using Hammond's design (p. 116), ultimately reaching ever-higher levels of achievement.

References

Alexander, R., Murray, D., & Thompson, N. (2017). Cross-cultural web design guidelines. In *Proceedings of the 14th international web for all conference*, Perth, Western Australia, Australia. doi:10.1145/3058555.3058574

Association for Educational Communications and Technology (AECT). (2012). AECT standards: 2012 version. *AECT*. Retrieved from https://www.aect.org/docs/AECTstandards2012.pdf

Burke, S. (2019, April 19). Pole dancing with the nudity and G-strings: Just express yourself. *New York Times*. Retrieved from https://www.nytimes.com/2019/04/19/arts/dance/pole-dancing-championship.html

Dick, W., Carey, L., & Carey, J. O. (2014). *The systematic design of instruction.* Pearson Education.

Fox, L. (2016). Seeing potential: The effects of student–teacher demographic congruence on teacher expectations and recommendations. *AERA Open.* doi:10.1177/2332858415623758

Gay, G. (2018). *Culturally responsive teaching: Theory, research, and practice.* Teachers College Press.

Hammond, Z. (2015). *Culturally responsive teaching & the brain: Promoting authentic engagement and rigor among culturally and linguistically diverse students.* Corwin Press.

Hawkins, B., Morris, M., Nguyen, T., Siegel, J., & Vardell, E. (2017). Advancing the conversation: Next steps for lesbian, gay, bisexual, trans, and queer (LGBTQ) health sciences librarianship. *Journal of the Medical Library Association: JMLA, 105*(4), 316–327. doi:10.5195/JMLA.2017.206

International Society for Technology in Education (ISTE). (2017). ISTE standards for coaches. *ISTE.* Retrieved from https://www.iste.org/standards/for-coaches

Just, S. N., & Muhr, S. L. (2020). Holding on to both ends of a pole: Empowering feminine sexuality and reclaiming feminist emancipation. *Gender Work Organ, 27*(6), 23. doi:10.1111/gwao.12339

Kendi, I. X. (2019). *How to be antiracist.* One World.

Ladson-Billings, G. (1995). Toward a theory of culturally relevant pedagogy. *American Educational Research Journal, 32*(3), 465–491. doi:10.3102/00028312032003465

Netting, E. F., Kettner, P. M., McMurty, S., & Thomas, M. L. (2017). *Social work macro practice* (6th ed.). Pearson Publishing.

Nobel, Safiya U. (2017). *Algorithms of oppression: How search engines reinforce racism.* NYU Press.

Nomikoudis, M., & Starr, M. (2016). Cultural humility in education and work: A valuable approach for teachers, learners and professionals. In J. Arvanitakis & D. J. Hornsby (Eds.), *Universities, the citizen scholar and the future of higher education* (pp. 69–84). Palgrave Macmillan UK.

Phillips, K. W. (2014). How diversity works. *Scientific American, 311*(4), 42–47. doi:10.1038/scientificamerican1014-42

Rose, T. (2015). *The end of average: How we succeed in a world that values sameness.* Harper One.

Wiggins, G., & McTighe, J. (2005). *Understanding by design* (2nd ed.). Association for Supervision and Curriculum Development.

Wilkerson, I. (2020). *Caste: The origins of our discontents.* Random House.

Woodley, X., Hernandez, C., Parra, J., & Negash, B. (2017). Celebrating difference: Best practices in culturally responsive teaching online. *TechTrends, 61*(5), 470–478. doi:10.1007/s11528-017-0207-z

15 Preparing Instructional Designers to Scale Needs Assessment

Jill E. Stefaniak, Lisa A. Giacumo, and Steve Villachica

Chapter Overview

This chapter emphasizes the importance of needs assessment in instructional design practice. It differentiates between needs assessment and needs analysis while providing strategies that can be employed by instructional designers to scale needs assessments to address project constraints and time limitations in real-world settings. Strategies for how needs assessment learning experiences can be integrated into instructional design coursework are provided as well as recommendations for the role instructors can serve while facilitating these types of activities.

Guiding Questions

1. What is a needs assessment?
2. Why should instructional designers learn to conduct needs assessments and needs analyses?
3. What role does needs assessment serve in schools and organizations?
4. What strategies can we use to teach an instructional designer how to adequately determine the needs of their project?
5. How can ID instructors and students qualify potential needs assessment projects?

Case Study

It's a late Tuesday night, and instructor Pat Patient has just read a frantic email from one of the students in her graduate-level capstone project course. Alexander has completed graduate-level instructional design coursework and works as an eLearning developer in a Fortune 100 company. He is a strong student who has consistently aced his courses. Alexander's capstone project involves conducting a needs assessment for a local nonprofit organization.

The message explains that Alexander's project has run into a brick wall. The client never seems to be available – except during regular business hours when Alexander is already working. Further, the client has yet to provide documents that she said she would deliver a week ago. While the client agreed to help the team arrange interviews with key stakeholders, she's now reported that most of the stakeholders are not available. She confides that other interview participants Alexander requested "may

DOI: 10.4324/9781003109938-15

148   Jill E. Stefaniak et al.

not be trustworthy." The client is now pushing back on distributing the online survey that Alexander had counted on to provide more generalizable information about
what is causing the discrepancy between existing and desired performance. The client has just requested a meeting to "repurpose the needs assessment effort." Pat is
an ID instructor by trade, not a consultant. How does Pat help Alexander chart a way
through this situation?

Have you ever been asked to design instruction and you were not sure it would fix the
problem? Have you ever wondered how your boss or client concluded that training was
necessary? When you engage in instructional design, do you want to develop and implement sustainable solutions? Too often, instructional designers are brought onto a project
after a decision has been made that training is needed. Your client or boss will tell that
you that training is needed, and you are left assuming that they have done their due dili-
gence to verify that training is the most viable solution.

An instructional designer's role in needs assessment will vary depending on the project
and where they work. Some instructional designers may be involved in the early stages
of a project where a large-scale needs assessment is conducted to identify a variety of
training and non-training solutions. Other times, they may be determining and assessing
the needs of their learning audience while they are engaging with them during class.
Regardless of these varying degrees of involvement and scale of needs assessment, it is
important for instructional designers to understand the importance of needs assessment
in instructional design practice.

What is Needs Assessment and Analysis?

Needs assessment is the process of identifying any discrepancies that may exist between a
current state of affairs and a desired state of affairs (Altschuld & Kumar, 2010). In order
to determine if any discrepancies (or gaps) exist, it is important that data is gathered from
multiple sources to provide those involved in the needs assessment with sufficient information to state with confidence where a gap may exist. You may not be responsible, but
you need to be a part of identifying causes and specifying solutions. If the causes of the
gaps remain unaddressed, the gap will remain, and training will typically take the blame.

Once a learning or performance gap has been identified, those involved in identifying
the gap should conduct further analysis to understand what is causing the gap. Needs
analysis involves developing a deep understanding of the context surrounding the gap
in performance. This may involve reviewing data that was initially collected during the
assessment to determine that a gap exists as well as gathering additional data to understand what is causing the problem and whether the problem can be fixed.

Instructional design is recognized as a process for creating detailed specifications for
the design, development, evaluation, and maintenance of situations that facilitate and
support learning (Richey et al., 2011). Minimizing, or excluding altogether, the role
that needs assessment plays in the instructional design process makes the instructional
designer's job impossible as they attempt to create detailed specifications and long-lasting
design solutions. Needs assessment and analysis not only serve as a mechanism to identify
and verify the needs of a learning audience, but it also identifies other non-instructional
needs that are essential in providing an infrastructure that supports learning.

While most instructional designers will recognize needs analysis as the "A" found in
the common instructional design process otherwise known as ADDIE (analysis, design,

Preparing Instructional Designers 149

Table 15.1 Needs Assessment Models

Model	Description
Harless' Front-End Analysis (Harless, 1970)	
Organizational Elements Model (Kaufman et al., 2003)	Provides a framework to examine multiple levels of an organization by identifying outputs, products, processes, and inputs. This framework includes four levels of needs assessment: mega, macro, micro, and quasi.
Performance Pipe Analysis Model (Mager & Pipe, 1997)	Presents a series of questions to help practitioners determine factors contributing to a problem and whether or not the problems can be solved.
9 Variable Framework (Rummler & Brache, 2013)	A framework that dissects organizational performance across three levels: (1) organizational, (2), process, and (3) performer. Each level examines goals, design, and management to identify gaps in workplace performance.
Performance Pyramid (Wedman, 2010)	This model provides a systemic view of an organization by exploring the following organizational components: (1) tools, environments, and processes; (2) expectations and feedback; (3) rewards, recognition, and incentives; (4) performance capability; (5) motivation, values, and self-concept; and (6) knowledge and skills.
Three-Phase Model (Witkin & Altschuld, 1995)	Approaches needs assessment in three phases: (1) pre-assessment; (2) assessment; and (3) post-assessment
Training Needs Assessment Model (Rossett, 1987)	Model places emphasis on identifying source of training problems and gathering data to bridge the ap between actual and desired performance.

develop, implement, and evaluate), it is often limited to examining the needs of a learning audience from a peripheral level when designing instruction. One of the goals for this chapter to convey the importance for instructional designers to engage in assessing the needs related to their projects.

A challenge inherent in the literature pertaining to needs assessment is the proliferation of models and varying interpretations and uses of terminology (Leigh et al., 2000). Terms such as needs assessment, needs analysis, performance analysis, and training needs assessment are often used interchangeably. For purposes of this chapter, we want to distinguish that needs assessment goes beyond the process of identifying a need for improved learning and performance exists and extends to determining the contributing factors.

There are a number of needs assessment models that an instructional designer may refer to while engaging in needs assessment. Table 15.1 provides an overview of common needs assessment models that have been recognized by the field. When identifying a needs assessment model to guide activities for a project, Stefaniak (2021) stresses the importance of "knowing enough about the problem to determine the purpose of the project" (p. 82). Each of the models outlined in Table 15.1 serve different purposes and should be aligned to properly guide the goals of a project.

Needs Assessment in the Field

Needs assessments are highly scalable and contextualized. That means they can look very different from client to client and project to project. In this section, we will review examples of needs assessment projects in different settings and at different scales and the kinds of decisions they can help you make. Also, we will share what often gets ignored, how to select scalable performance improvement strategies, and the common challenges IDs face when trying to advocate for needs assessment project support.

150 *Jill E. Stefaniak et al.*

Customized Needs Assessment Projects Range in Scale and by Context

A large-scale needs assessment project can span several weeks or months and include multiple extant data sources along with original data collection efforts. These projects tend to take place in larger organizations under executive sponsors such as in government agencies, international nongovernmental organizations, professional societies, military branches, or multinational businesses. Alternatively, one of the smallest needs assessment projects one could complete might include only one individual whose performance you observe over the course of some period of time. Teachers and department directors or managers often assess needs in this context, sometimes without knowing they've been doing performance-driven needs assessments. One of us has conducted pretty stealthy and what we call a 'back of the napkin needs assessment,' solely through gathering data by talking at the water cooler, in bi-monthly one-on-one meetings, observing others' projects, and while out to lunch with colleagues. Do any of these contexts sound familiar?

The first step to determining the scale of any needs assessment project is to determine if the cost of closing the gap is dearer than the cost of letting the performance gap exist. There are times when any given system, or redundancies in a system, budgets allow for specific rates of less-than-ideal performance. For example, in manufacturing, an acceptable number of widgets will come off of a production line that don't work, because the machines people make aren't perfect. However, after a certain amount of failure, the system is no longer viable, and the performance gap must be closed to stay in business. To make this a bit more concrete, let's assume you make $60,000 a year, or $90,000 a year with overheads. If a performance gap costs $25,000 in a year, you would not spend two quarters of your work year on closing the gap and identifying a solution that costs $300,000, because you wouldn't have enough return on your salary investment. In short, once you have a ballpark estimate of what the cost of the gap is, you know how to scale your needs assessment project.

There are many different contexts where needs assessments can take place, from educational settings such as a school district, an individual classroom, a university or college, a small business, a multinational organization, a military branch, a not-for-profit organization, or international nongovernmental organization. We have seen needs assessments completed in all types of organizations and all sizes, although they are planned and carried out differently.

What Often Gets Ignored in Needs Assessments?

These days, IDs and Learning and Development leaders tend to be well versed in training methods and sometimes even in instructional design. From their experience and career development, executive leaders often understand that training can help them to become more effective. It's no wonder why if everyone has experienced some success with upskilling through training, that training is sometimes a great answer to basic performance gaps.

However, it's only an answer when performance gaps are related to individuals' missing or underdeveloped knowledge and skills. Because performance improvement is such a new field and relatively unknown as compared with learning, training, and education, we find there is often a default assumption that learning or training will be the default solution for any gap between existing and desired performance. In reality, we know from evidence-based practice and some research that there are other environmental and individual causes of performance gaps. Sometimes even intuitively, this leads us to realize that there are other solutions that training will need to support. For example, if workplace training uses job aids, managers will need to support their use in the workplace. Or, if the organizational incentives or accountability measures don't reward the desired performance, managers and leaders may need to make changes to them. Or, if no one has the correct access to the software they need to use to record reports, strategic policy changes, and changed protocols, perhaps with subsequent dissemination, practice, and feedback, are really what is needed to obtain the desired performance.

Scaled Interventions are Best Identified in Partnership and Aligned with the Causes of the Performance Gap

We advocate for teaching IDs to select an appropriate model or framework for cause analysis. When we use a model or framework for a cause analysis as part of our top-down coding, it helps to find patterns that can be used to share a meaningful story with the client. The aggregated data collected over a specific timespan, and potentially even across triangulated sources, can also help clients to interpret the patterns and begin to point to potential interventions needed to close the performance gap.

Ideally, when we can show our clients what's happening in different levels and areas of a system, more defensible data-driven decisions can be made by a group of stakeholders working together with a consultant to help close a performance gap. From there, IDs can research and present clients and stakeholders with a potential set of industry-standard solutions grounded in evidence-based practice and aligned with the causes of the performance gap. IDs can then partner with the client to select specific interventions aligned to the performance gap, in order to ensure feasibility of solutions.

Challenges IDs Face Trying to Advocate for Needs Assessment

As Breman et al. (2019), mention a common challenge with needs assessment projects is gaining client buy-in and adequate resources. Far too often, clients and sponsors assume they know the causes of the performance gap and fail to obtain perspective from those at the pointy end of the problem before selecting appropriate intervention(s). This mindset can be a barrier to obtaining the budget support needed to accommodate IDs' access to extant data sources (i.e., someone often needs time to make the data available), original data collection (i.e., participants need time away from their primary responsibilities and IDs need time to collect the data), specialized data analysis software, and time for IDs to analyze the data, present the data in aggregated formats, meet with stakeholders to interpret the aggregated data, investigate potential solution sets, meet with stakeholders to prioritize a set of solutions, and create the final reporting documentation, and disseminate the results to all stakeholders.

Instructional Designers are Often Consultants

We advocate for teaching emerging and advancing practitioners to assume a consultant role in needs assessment projects. A consultant role means that we offer services. These services include professional communications competencies including project management competencies as well as technical competencies. As part of our professional communications skillsets, ID consultants should be able to ask relevant questions, listen closely so that we can speak in our clients' terms, share information early and often so as to avoid surprises, and establish relationships quickly with stakeholders, colleagues, and participants. We see our project management role to include the ability to plan for short-, mid-, and long term timeframes, shape expectations, dance the 'consultant's back-step shuffle when we learn new/more information, build projects that create success stories for our client organization, negotiate a shared and feasible project timeline, renegotiate for resources as a project unfolds, mitigate risk, and continue to confirm shared value

152 *Jill E. Stefaniak et al.*

throughout the project. Our technical knowledge should be strong enough to provide defensible analysis, professional advice, and make recommendations that are grounded in research, evidence-based practice, and our own experience.

Further, our contributions should be in support of specific clients' goals, feasible, aligned to the organization's strategic objectives, and the specific performance improvement needs. We need to take our clients' needs into consideration during all of our work and provide the input our clients need to make well informed and defensible decisions. These practices ensure our credibility, help us secure sponsorship, a seat at the table, and repeat business.

Internal Consultants

Internal consultants are those IDs who are employed by an organization. The benefit of working as an internal consultant is that as you gain experience working in an organization, you have more nuanced understanding of the politics, practices, history, and more access to or awareness of potential data sources. You may be able to complete or update a past organizational analysis and environmental analysis more efficiently. You may already be familiar with the organizational systems and processes that are contributing to the performance gap. Likewise, you will likely have some hunches about some of the factors that contribute to the causes of the performance gap. Finally, you might be more able to brainstorm feasible set of performance improvement interventions.

External Consultants

External consultants are those IDs who are independent contractors, self-employed, volunteers, or for some other reason, not affiliated with the organization that's sponsoring the needs assessment project. The benefit of working as an external consultant is that you will gain experience working in a wider variety of different organization types, organizational cultures, sponsors, and/or industries. While you will likely need more resources to complete an organizational analyses, environmental analyses, you will likely bring a very fresh perspective that is also highly valued. One caution is that as an external consultant it's even more important to negotiate a level of client sponsorship that will enable you to deliver a project that will deliver the desired results.

How Can ID Instructors and Students Qualify Potential Needs Assessment Projects?

For first time experience conducting needs assessment, best for students to work on qualified projects. IDs will not always have such sponsorship in the workplace. Students and instructors can approach potential needs assessment clients with good intentions. They would like to find projects that are authentic and align with the learning outcomes of the course. Likewise, potential clients typically would like to help students and instructors. They may even view a needs assessment project as a "favor" they can grant to students and instructors. Clients often have their own ideas about organizational performance they would like to achieve and the solutions that would deliver it. In a rush to find and start projects, students, instructors, and clients can start down a path that can quickly lead to mutual disappointment.

While there are no guarantees that any given needs assessment project will be successful, qualifying potential projects before anyone begins significant work on them can help. Successful project qualification turns initial needs assessment requests into potential projects worth doing and client agreement to meet their sponsorship responsibilities. In addition to aligning with the course's learning outcomes, qualified projects provide an

Preparing Instructional Designers 153

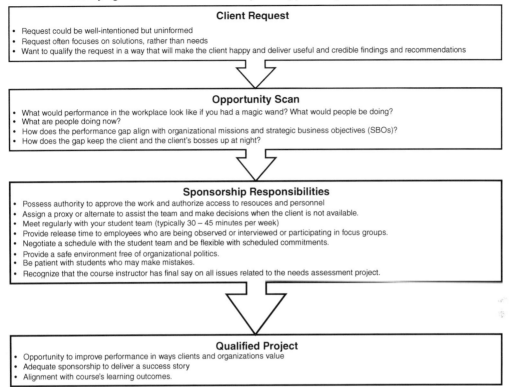

Figure 15.1 Qualifying a needs assessment project.

opportunity to improve organizational performance – along with the client sponsorship required to deliver a success story.

Figure 15.1 depicts the components of qualifying a needs assessment project as part of a university course. The first component recognizes that the request for a needs assessment project for a given course can be risky. Students, instructors, and clients may think they have agreed to what they think will be a great project, only to find otherwise. The first component of needs assessment qualification is about recognizing the potential for different parties to have their own perspectives on this effort. Client requests for needs assessments or training are often well intentioned but uninformed. Their requests often focus on solutions the client has already envisioned, rather than a focus on identifying needs, analyzing them, and then specifying solutions. Ultimately, successful project qualification requires a successful choreography that makes the client happy and delivers some sort of credible and useful findings and recommendations. Savvy performance consultants seek to change this initial conversation to obtain approval to conduct an initial quick scan of the overall needs assessment opportunity and the potential client's sponsorship responsibilities. To initiate this conversation, Harless (1970) used a phrase along the lines of, "We'd be happy to help. I'd like to ask a few questions to get some background information."

The initial opportunity scan consists of posing several questions to determine the broad outlines of the needs assessment. The first two questions begin framing the broad outlines of a performance gap between actual and desired performance. In answering these questions, it is important to focus on observable performance – the tasks that people perform in the workplace. Steer the client away from words like "understand," "appreciate," or "know" to focus on describing what people *do*. The second two questions help focus

154 *Jill E. Stefaniak et al.*

clients on needs assessment projects that are worth completing. Client responsibilities for sponsoring a needs assessment team are numerous and imposing. It is important to ensure that the potential needs assessment effort aligns with what the organization and the client care about. Formally, organizations care about meeting their missions and strategic business objectives. Informally and more importantly, clients and project stakeholders care about those performance gaps that keep them up at night. Unless the students and instructors are working on something that the organization and the client really care about, odds are the client will not provide adequate support throughout the project.

The next project qualification component consists of client responsibilities. At its heart, a needs assessment project is a dance with clients and students conducting the needs assessment. Without the active collaboration of clients, students cannot conduct their needs assessments. For a potential needs assessment project to qualify, a potential client must indicate that they are willing and able to meet all specified responsibilities throughout the needs assessment project.

Strategies to Support Needs Assessment Instruction

Enrolling in a needs assessment course and teaching a needs assessment course can be a very overwhelming experience for students and faculty. Most instructional design students are familiarized with needs assessment as a part of the ADDIE process. Most introductory instructional design courses will provide a very brief overview of needs assessment and focus instructional activities around learner and contextual analyses as they relate to designing a unit of instruction. While these types of activities are suitable for introductory courses, it is important that students are provided with opportunities to spend an extended amount of time learning about how to conduct a needs assessment and needs analysis. It is important for the instructor to embrace a coaching role in the class to provide guidance to students as they work on authentic needs assessment projects.

In this section, we outline several strategies to support instructors responsible for teaching needs assessment in their courses. Needs assessment may be a stand-alone course or it may be a topic that is covered in an introductory or advanced instructional design class.

Scaling Projects

The biggest challenge related to teaching needs assessment is being able to teach within the confines of a semester. With most semesters ranging from 12 to 15 weeks, instructors need to be mindful that their students need to be taught fundamental skills associated with needs assessment before they can engage in conducting a needs assessment.

It is important that the instructor works with their students to scale projects to a suitable experience that fits within the length of the semester. While learning how to collect data and analyze it is incredibly important when engaging in needs assessments, we encourage instructors to exert some flexibility when establishing standards for their assignments. We recommend that instructors consider the following when teaching needs assessment:

- How much time is needed at the beginning of the semester for students to learn essential skills before they can embark on a needs assessment project?
- How many needs are associated with the project?
  - Can one of two of these needs be explored independently?
- What experience do the students have regarding data collection?
- How many data collection tools can be developed during the semester?
- How much time has been allocated for students to collect data?
  - What happens if students are not provided with sufficient access to participants?

When students identify a project and present a proposal to their instructor for conducting a needs assessment, they may not be aware of the challenges that may arise due to the number of needs that have been identified and the amount of time they have to complete the project. Oftentimes, students may unknowingly experience scope creep where clients present multiple needs that could be broken down into several compartmentalized projects.

If there are multiple needs that are identified at the beginning of the project, we encourage the instructor to work with their students to determine how many of the needs are intertwined and whether certain needs could be stand-alone projects. If students can focus their time on a few needs that are related, the subsequent phases of the needs assessment project may be easier to manage.

We also recommend allocating some cushioning around assignment deadlines when teaching needs assessment classes. While an instructor may identify due dates for assignments throughout the semester, students may encounter challenges with gaining access to clients and subject-matter experts in time to complete assignments, issues with not gaining access to participants (i.e., employees, learners, teachers) when collecting data, or having clients that do not uphold their responsibilities for the project.

Working in Phases

One challenge with teaching needs assessment that has been noted in this chapter is that it takes time for students to gain access to an organization or school, develop data collection instruments, collect data, analyze the data, and make data-driven recommendations. The needs assessment process can be overwhelming for students who have had minimal experience conducting needs assessments, evaluations, and data collection activities.

Provide Templates and Examples

It can sometimes be difficult to ensure consistency with evaluating authentic projects in a course since the clients and topics will vary. This can be especially overwhelming for students if they are unsure of what the expectations are related to assignments. We have found that students often will question whether they have provided *enough* information for a project or whether they have collected *enough* data to suffice for a good grade on an assignment.

Providing students with templates can help with setting expectations for the types of information they should be providing for each phase of their project and helps to establish some degree of consistency when grading projects. Depending on the amount of time an instructor may allocate to teach needs assessment (i.e., a few weeks in an instructional design course or an entire semester dedicated to needs assessment), there are a variety of books that provide practical templates for students to complete (e.g., Altschuld & Kumar, 2010; Stefaniak, 2021; Watkins et al., 2012). These resources are provided in the *Recommended Readings* section at the end of this chapter.

Importance of Data-Driven Decisions

Good recommendations that are a result of a needs assessment are based on data. The importance of making data-driven decisions and recommendations should be a primary learning objective for a needs assessment course or activity. Instructional designers may find themselves making recommendations to clients and improving their own designs on projects. In order to make appropriate recommendations and design decisions, they

156 *Jill E. Stefaniak et al.*

must have evidence that supports their actions. Data-driven decisions are evidence-based, objective, defensible, and compelling.

Whether students are learning how to gather data to conduct a learner analysis or are involved in leading a large-scale needs assessment for an organization, it is important that they gain practice using data to make compelling arguments that support their recommendations and instructional design practices. We recommend that instructors allocate time in their courses to discuss and emphasize the importance of making data-driven decisions when engaged in needs assessment activities.

A common challenge that students encounter when conducting needs assessments for the first time is that the results of their data collection and analysis may differ from what their client assumed was an issue at the beginning of the project. Stefaniak (2021) forewarns that while needs may be identified at the beginning of the project in conversation with the client, it is the needs assessor's responsibility to collect evidence to verify that they are the actual needs.

We recommend that instructors consider the following when teaching students about making data-driven decisions:

- Discuss the importance of data-driven decisions throughout the various phases of a needs assessment class and activity;
- Work with students while they are developing data collection instruments to support their ability to make data-driven decisions upon completion of data collection and analysis;
- Provide examples for how students can organize data in a compelling manner when presenting findings to clients;
- Discuss strategies for how to engage in conversation with clients when the results of the needs assessment identify other challenges within an organization.

Prepare for the Unexpected

We mentioned earlier in this chapter the need for an instructor to be flexible when teaching needs assessment courses. Situations that may arise within projects that might not align with assignment deadlines and project expectations that are beyond the control of students. Needs assessments are often messy with several variables emerging throughout the project.

Students should be prepared at the beginning of the project that unexpected barriers may arise during the project. To alleviate their stress, instructors should explain how those barriers may be addressed as they relate to assignments and grades in a course. We recommend incorporating time for students to check in with the instructor through meetings, project logs, or journals at various times throughout the semester to help the instructor step in if additional assistance is needed.

Sometimes, students may feel that they are being put in a position where they have to put out performance deficiencies of learners or employees. The instructor should be mindful of this and discuss these possibilities with the students at the beginning of the course before their needs assessment projects have started. Strategies for how to handle these challenges tactfully can be aligned with discussions about making data-driven recommendations to clients.

Role of the Instructor in Needs Assessment Classes

In this setting, the primary responsibility of the instructor is to provide an authentic and safe learning environment where students can build and demonstrate needs assessment

Preparing Instructional Designers   157

skills. Further, the instructor needs to facilitate a set of authentic learning activities that lead to the creation of project deliverables that students can place in their academic and personal portfolios, such as project plans, final reports, and executive briefings. Additional responsibilities include:

- Building and maintaining a network of potential clients of needs assessment and other training/performance improvement projects;
- Working with potential clients to prequalify needs assessment projects before course-work begins;
- Working with students and potential clients to qualify needs assessment projects that students have scouted;
- Providing a mechanism students can use to select qualified needs assessment projects that they will complete;
- Providing feedback that students would otherwise receive from project managers and senior performance consultants in the workplace as they review project deliverables;
- Acting as a consultative resource to individual students and student teams providing coaching, encouragement, and troubleshooting support as they conduct their needs assessments;
- Providing students with project management support, including project scoping, team collaboration, client communication, and project tracking.

Novice practitioners face challenges understanding the overall nature of the project, where they are in completing it, and interpreting client instructions and feedback. It's easy for novices to reach a decision that project obstacles they face are personal in nature. In their eyes the problem lies with the client, with a stakeholder, with a team-mate who is choosing to be unresponsive, aggressive, or obtuse. As a rule of thumb, these project obstacles lie somewhere in the project environment – unspecified expecta-tions, unclear guidance, faulty feedback, inefficient processes and tools, or consequences that don't reinforce desired behavior. In other words, the environmental causes that appear in needs analysis models also affect the completion of needs assessment projects. Instructors can help students by facilitating conversations to apply needs assessment tech-niques to project work.

It is hard to be an expert in all aspects of needs assessment. Further, students may feel that academics in universities lack practical experience and perspective in conducting needs assessments "in the real world." It's good practice to reach out to needs assessment practitioners in professional organizations to ask them to host webinars for students in needs assessment courses. (See Boise State's OPWL webinar page in the recommended resources.) Instructors can record these webinars and collect presenters' slides, building a library of needs assessment practice that students can consult. Further, these practi-tioner experts typically say the same things as course instructors do. Because they conduct needs assessments outside the classroom, savvy instructors draw on their credibility.

Students Interacting with the Client

Conducting a successful needs assessment is more than merely applying abstract models in a way that completes the initial needs assessment, needs analysis (a.k.a. "cause anal-ysis"), and solution specification. Needs assessment projects also require students to interact with clients in ways that can shape a successful choreography for completing the projects. Much of this interaction requires consulting in ways that provide ongoing form-ative evaluative data about how the project is working in the client's eyes. During regular meetings, students can ask probing questions to the following ends:

Determine the Extent to Which the Client is Comfortable with Students Pushing Back on the Client's and Organization's Beliefs and Perceptions

To "do right by the client," students completing needs assessment projects may need to question or even argue against the client's or organization's take on a given situation. Ideally, project qualification would weed out clients who are uncomfortable with students pushing back. If this doesn't happen, students may need to conduct a more "guerilla" version of a needs assessment, doing what they can and noting any limiting factors beyond their control that may affect the findings and recommendations that appear in the final report.

Determine How the Client Feels about Progress on the Project

In just about any client contact, students can ask questions successful consultants use to choreograph needs assessment projects. Questions such as "How are we doing?", "Is this project working for you?", "To what extent are we meeting the needs of project stakeholders?" can provide an ongoing stream of data for shaping the project and client and organizational perceptions.

Preview Needs Assessment Findings and Recommendations

During a needs assessment project, students will be collecting data iteratively. With each round of data collection, students should share emerging findings and recommendations with their clients. From a consulting standpoint, sharing information keeps student practitioners from accidentally surprising their clients. From a pragmatic perspective, sharing findings and recommendations supports effective collaboration. While student practitioners may know what their data tell them, they typically do not possess the same organizational experience as their clients, who can help them contextualize findings and recommendations.

Professional Practice Revisited

The panicked email from Alexander to Pat indicates a needs assessment project that was not well qualified. It seems that the client may have agreed to sponsor a needs assessment project as a "favor" to the instructor and the students. The instructor may not have had an adequate pool of alternative needs assessment projects that may have been better candidates. It's clear that the client isn't meeting sponsorship responsibilities. The client may lack the organizational authority to provide access to existing organizational data or release time for needs assessment participants for observations, interviews, and surveys. In other words, the client may be unable to provide access to the resources and people Alexander has requested. The client isn't available or flexible to meet regularly – especially during the days and times when Alexander is available. Alexander may not have a good sense of what is really important to the client. The organizational environment seems rife with dysfunctional politics that could be too complex for a student to navigate.

The project scope seems to be in question. The client request for a "repurpose" risks a significant increase to project scope and the work Alexander needs to complete by the end of the semester. Alexander may not have the time and resources to conduct two different projects. This request also provides an opportunity for the instructor to provide coaching and guidance to help Alexander negotiate project scope and responsibilities in a way that could turn the project around. During the meeting, Alexander can ask about the organizational landscape and how this project fits into existing politics. Knowing more about the politics, Alexander and the client may be able to find a way to get access to the resources and personnel Alexander needs to collect and analyze data.

Alexander can also ask the client how the problem the needs assessment is addressing keeps the client and her bosses up at night. If the problem actually affects the client, then Alexander can feel emboldened to negotiate for what he will need to deliver a needs assessment report the client and organizational stakeholders will find credible and useful. If the problem doesn't affect the client and organizational stakeholders, Alexander can note any relevant limitations in the final report, as well as the extent to which they could affect the credibility and usefulness of the findings and recommendations in the final report.

Connecting Process to Practice

1. Based on the frantic email that Alexander sent Pat Patient in the case study, how would you advise Alexander to communicate with his client regarding the repurposing of the needs assessment?
2. After considering how much time you have to allocate to needs assessment in the course you are teaching, discuss strategies for scaling Alexander's needs assessment project;
3. Provide students with a case scenario where the project needs and sample data are provided. Assign students to work in groups and make recommendations based on the information. Discuss with the class whether the data collected does not align with the initial needs presented at the beginning of the project.

References

Altschuld, J. W., & Kumar, D. D. (2010). *Needs assessment: An overview.* Sage.

Breman, J., Giacumo, L. A., & Griffith-Boyes, R. (2019). A needs analysis to inform global humanitarian capacity building. *TechTrends, 63*(3), 294–303. doi:10.1007/s11528-019-00390-6

Harless, J. (1970). *An ounce of analysis is worth a pound of objectives.* Harless Performance Guild.

Kaufman, R., Oakley-Brown, H., Watkins, R., & Leigh, D. (2003). *Strategic planning for success: Aligning people, performance, and payoffs.* Jossey-Bass.

Leigh, D., Watkins, R., Platt, W. A., & Kaufman, R. (2000). Alternate models of needs assessment: Selecting the right one for your organization. *Human Resource Development Quarterly, 11*(1), 87–93. doi:10.1002/1532-1096

Mager, R. F., & Pipe, P. (1997). *Analyzing performance problems or You really oughta wanna* (3rd ed.). Center for Effective Performance.

Richey, R. C., Klein, J. D., & Tracey, M. W. (2011). *The instructional design knowledge base: Theory, research, and practice.* Routledge.

Rossett, A. (1987). *Training needs assessment.* Educational Technology Publishing Company.

Rummler, G. A., & Brache, A. P. (2013). *Improving performance: How to manage the white space on the organizational chart* (3rd ed.). Jossey-Bass.

Stefaniak, J. (2021). *Needs assessment for learning and performance: Theory, process, and practice.* Routledge.

Watkins, R., Meiers, M. W., & Visser, Y. L. (2012). *A guide to assessing needs: Essential tools for collecting information, making decisions, and achieving development results.* The World Bank.

Wedman, J. (2010). The performance pyramid. In R. Watkins & D. Leigh (Eds.), *Handbook of improving performance in the workplace: Selecting and implementing performance interventions* (Vol. 2, pp. 51–79). Pfeiffer.

Witkin, B. R., & Altschuld, J. W. (1995). *Planning and conducting needs assessments: A practical guide.* Sage.

16 The Value of Human Performance Improvement in Instructional Design and Technology

T. Logan Arrington, Alison L. Moore, Kaila Steele, and James D. Klein

Chapter Overview

The purpose of this chapter is to provide instructional design and technology students with a broad, yet practical, overview of human performance improvement (HPI). While HPI is often considered an approach more appropriate for business and industry, the systemic and systematic process of the HPI model is a valuable tool for practitioners and leaders who are located in just about any setting where people are working or performing. Within this chapter, we will introduce a case study of HPI applied to a public charter school. By the end of this chapter, you should be able to distinguish between HPI and instructional design and technology, describe the application of the HPI model, and align appropriate interventions to given causes of a performance problem.

Guiding Questions

1. How does HPI connect to Instructional Design and Technology?
2. Why is data collection important in HPI?
3. How do you identify and categorize the causes of performance problems?
4. How do you decide to implement an instructional or non-instructional solution?

Case Study

A non-traditional multi-county public charter school was established to serve at-risk high school students at 18 campuses in the southeastern United States. This state charter school partners with local school systems to serve each community's dropout population and students who struggle to succeed in the traditional high school environment but are still enrolled. The charter school employs mostly part-time staff including administrators, teachers, and student services personnel with one exception: the registrars. As the only full-time employees at each campus, the registrars have an integral role and a significant impact on the culture of each campus. Registrars workday and evening hours and have a variety of responsibilities. Though they are campus-based employees, the registrars are supervised by a central office employee.

During the annual back-to-school meeting, the atmosphere grew tense with a lot of grumbling, complaining, and negative comments made by the registrars. Following the meeting, the Associate Superintendent met with the registrars' supervisor to discuss

DOI: 10.4324/9781003109938-16

concerns about the overall negativity of the registrar department. The negativity within the group had to be addressed.

To explore this issue, the supervisor collected data to quantify the negativity within the registrar department and determine the root causes of this behavior. The central office staff were surveyed and interviewed. An anonymous climate survey was given to the registrars. Finally, the supervisor collected personnel data on the registrars including the rate of pay, years of experience, and education level.

Based on the data, the supervisor determined that 71% of the registrars felt that negativity was a problem. Low morale and job dissatisfaction contributed to the negativity. The supervisor and central office staff identified a desired performance that only 20% of the registrars should feel that negativity is a problem within the registrar department, leaving a performance gap of 51%.

Through data analysis, the supervisor was ultimately able to identify four causes of the negativity:

1. Lack of feedback about behavior;
2. Lack of performance-based incentives or consequences;
3. Insufficient time to get the job done;
4. Lack of knowledge and skills.

To address the causes, the supervisor implemented four interventions:

1. Performance support tools and job aids;
2. Organizational learning;
3. Feedback;
4. Incentives and awards.

After a year, only 14% of the registrars still felt that negativity was a problem. Additionally, the supervisor identified fewer errors during state data collection, noticed increased collaboration across all departments, observed an increase in positivity, and perceived a more supportive team environment.

Theory and Processes of HPI

The purpose of the HPI model is to provide a systemic and systematic method for investigating and solving performance problems (Van Tiem et al., 2012). At a high level, the HPI model roughly mirrors that of the ADDIE framework. Both processes begin by addressing a performance problem and progress through phases (more or less) of analysis, design, development, implementation, and evaluation (Foshay et al., 2014; Rothwell et al., 2007). While both HPI and ADDIE share the same goal of enhanced performance, most instructional designers use ADDIE to focus on gaps in skills and knowledge and use instruction (or job aids) to address them. Practitioners of HPI, on the other hand, focus on many kinds of gaps and consider both instructional (e.g., training) and non-instructional interventions (e.g., increased incentives, upgraded tools/technology, redesigned processes, safer work environment) to support individuals' performance (Stefaniak, 2018). The HPI model is data-driven and iterative, and alignment through all phases and components is

Value of Human Performance Improvement   163

vital to the successful application of the model. This section will outline the main stages of the HPI model, as illustrated by the case study.

Identification of the Performance Problem

When following the HPI model, practitioners first must identify a performance problem to pursue. Oftentimes, stakeholders recognize a problem exists within a workplace through their daily work tasks but identifying and describing the specific problem requires unbiased perspectives. This is where third-party practitioners can leverage their outsider position (i.e., they avoid being too close to the situation), but all stakeholders can engage in the problem identification process by managing their assumptions and maximizing their familiarity with the organization. Sometimes clients experiencing a performance problem will seek practitioners' help but will do so with a predetermined solution already in mind – oftentimes requesting training at the onset of a performance systems analysis (PSA). Despite clients and stakeholders possessing valuable knowledge about the problem and its context, they may not be considering all factors that contribute to the performance problem when they ask for training as a solution. While training can be a beneficial method for improving low performance that stems from a lack of skills and knowledge, instruction is not always the most appropriate solution (Stefaniak, 2018). For example, a new training program would not resolve poor performance caused by inadequate time allotted to complete a task or low motivation of workers. A knowledgeable practitioner of HPI will avoid jumping to a conclusion regarding a solution for a performance problem and will instead rely on data to guide next steps in the PSA. Doing so will ensure alignment throughout the HPI process.

In order to investigate the performance problem fully, HPI practitioners collect data to inform their understanding of the performance problem (Van Tiem et al., 2012). Illuminating a performance problem that is occurring within an organization is a complex task but looking to multiple sources for information allows practitioners to gain insight. Specifically, data should be collected that will inform three facets of the problem: (1) the environment, (2) the performance gap, and (3) potential causes. Practitioners can think of the environment within which the problem is occurring as four levels: worker (i.e., the people doing the work), work (i.e., the job/tasks being done), workplace (i.e., the physical location and the organization in which the work is occurring), and world (i.e., the larger suprasystem in which the organization operates; Rothwell, 2005). The performance gap is the difference between the ideal and current performance, as typically defined by your performers (i.e., current performance) and the key stakeholders (i.e., ideal performance). The causes of the performance problem are the factors that are influencing the problem. Adopting a systems approach will allow practitioners to consider the performance problem holistically (Foshay et al., 2014; Stefaniak, 2018) and avoid omitting valuable data sources.

Sometimes a data source will enlighten more than one facet of the problem, but practitioners should utilize different methods to look to various sources for different purposes (Van Tiem et al., 2012). For example, in addition to surveying individuals from the performer group to gain a firsthand account of the performance problem, practitioners may also look to non-human sources such as extant documents to confirm the current performance (Rothwell et al., 2007). Additionally, supervisors who sit for interviews can clarify expectations of the desired performance, which can be compared with documentation outlining official work requirements. Triangulating data should yield a more accurate picture of the performance problem's context (e.g., conflicting or missing information is just as, if not more, important as common knowledge surrounding the problem). Armed

164　*T. Logan Arrington et al.*

with this updated and unbiased data regarding the performance problem, practitioners are able to move forward in the HPI model.

Gap Analysis

Analysis of the collected data should directly inform the next major milestone of the model, the gap analysis (Van Tiem et al., 2012). A straightforward calculation, the gap analysis quantifies and subtracts the current performance from the desired performance. The difference between the two is the identified gap, or the extent of improvement required to rectify the performance problem (Foshay et al., 2014; Rothwell et al., 2007). Although this is a simple concept, success of this step is contingent on the quality of the data. Vague records or participant descriptions addressed during data collection and analysis may yield inaccurate quantification of the current and/or desired performances. While not all performance problems lend themselves to be quantified easily, care should be taken to seek the best data from the best sources possible.

At this point in the PSA, practitioners have collected data and are able to identify quantified gaps in performance. These previous steps can be considered a type of needs assessment (i.e., verifying that a performance problem exists). The next portion of the PSA involves further investigating the identified needs to assign causes, which can also be referred to as a needs analysis.

Cause Analysis

Once practitioners have established the performance gap, they are now able to identify potential causes of the performance problem. We say "potential" because no investigation is perfect. HPI is an iterative process of continual improvement. This step in the HPI model is the cause analysis, and the goal is to sift through symptoms of the problem and diagnose the root cause(s) (Stefaniak, 2018). Several tools and strategies can assist practitioners at this stage, such as the Behavior Engineering Model (BEM; Gilbert, 1996). Just as the title suggests, the BEM supports practitioners in influencing a specific behavior. Gilbert explained that individuals' behavior is a result of two components: their personal characteristics and the environment in which they work. Additionally, three conditions (i.e., information, instrumentation, and motivation) must be met within these two levels in order for an ideal performance to be possible (Rothwell et al., 2007). Practitioners can identify missing elements (i.e., causes) within the 2×3 matrix and strategically focus improvement efforts. Below are descriptions of what the six cells of the BEM comprise.

> *Environmental/Information (Data).* The environment must provide necessary information in order for performers to conduct ideal performances. This cell from the model is labeled "Data" and can include job descriptions, guidelines for work tasks, and relevant feedback on previous work.
>
> *Environmental/Instrumentation (Resources).* For performers to complete their assigned duties or tasks, the environment must provide the necessary resources. "Resources" includes a variety of things such as tools, materials, or time.
>
> *Environmental/Motivation (Incentives).* Within the environment there must be some incentive to accomplish the targeted performance, which is referred to as "Incentives" in the BEM. Providing monetary and nonmonetary incentives, opportunities for development, and a transparent consequence system are included within this cell.
>
> *Individual/Information (Knowledge).* The individual performers must have the required knowledge and skills to complete their assigned tasks. "Knowledge" ensures that performers are properly trained or require prerequisite knowledge prior to performance.

Individual/Instrumentation (Capacity). Tasks involve specific abilities, and individual performers must possess those abilities in order to complete the tasks, known as "Capacity" in BEM. Performers should be matched with tasks for which they are physically, mentally, or emotionally capable of completing.

Individual/Motivation (Motives). The individual performers must bring a certain amount of personal desire and motivation to the task at hand, which is referred to in the BEM as "Motives". Appropriate recruitment and selection of potential performers demonstrating motives aligned with the task, as well as periodic surveying of current performers, will support performance.

When the criteria for performance within each of these cells are not met, it means that a cause falls within that cell. Essentially, something within the system is lacking from one of these cells (i.e., causing the performance problem; Rothwell et al., 2007).

Intervention Selection

With the root causes of the performance problem identified, practitioners apply the BEM and can confidently target specific areas of weakness. Narrowing focus produces tailored solutions to each unique performance problem. As mentioned earlier, HPI does not limit itself to instruction as a means to support individuals' performance. If a lack of skills is not hindering performance, then additional training will not be a beneficial solution – and may exacerbate the issue. Guided by the identified causes, and with a more robust toolbox at hand, HPI practitioners may recommend learning interventions, which present instruction to build skills and knowledge, and/or non-instructional interventions, which change a work environment, provide additional tools, revise a job title or description, or create new work processes (Foshay et al., 2014; Stefaniak, 2018; Van Tiem et al., 2012). Similar to ADDIE, this stage may involve designing an intervention if an acceptable existing option is not available. A key to selecting a successful intervention is elegance – a simple, tailored strategy of utility.

Evaluation

After the intervention is selected, an implementation plan is put into action. Again, similar to ADDIE, metrics are collected and reviewed regularly to determine the effectiveness of the improvement efforts. Although the HPI model presents a series of steps to be completed in a systematic order, the model is also a highly iterative process (Van Tiem et al., 2012). Practitioners engage in the model and return to previous phases repeatedly to further identify answers and solutions for the problems they are investigating. Marker et al. (2014) suggested that the HPI model is not only iterative, but also can be considered as a spiral. This perspective allows practitioners an almost agile method of conducting a PSA. Because emphasis is on positive outcomes, the intervention should be modified after each round the model is applied based on the most recent performance data.

Professional Practice Revisited

With this background to the HPI model, you can now make connections between the theory and procedures of the model and the case study we presented earlier.

Identification of the Performance Problem

Oftentimes, performance problems present themselves and are noted by leadership within an organization. Within the case, the Associate Superintendent saw the problem and brought it to the supervisor's attention. It is important that the supervisor took a step back and collected data to confirm this problem. An important feature is that those involved saw this as an opportunity for investigation and did not pursue a pre-determined solution.

Within the case, the supervisor employed a selection of human and non-human resources that provided a variety of perspectives. Table 16.1 highlights the intent of each of these sources. Each instrument utilized a systems perspective to collect data on both the characteristics of the individuals and the performance environment.

Table 16.1 Data Collection Alignment Table

Problem Statement	Data Collected		
	For quantifying the performance gap	*For understanding the context or environment*	*For identifying potential causes of the problem*
Registrars felt that negativity was a problem in their department.	Climate survey of registrars Survey of central office staff Interviews with central office staff	Climate survey of registrars Personnel data of registrars	Climate survey of registrars Personnel data of registrars

Gap Analysis

The performance gap was that at least 51% of registrars needed to see a positive change in their work climate. Within the case, the perceptions of the registrars and central office staff were used to quantify the gap. In ideal situations, the gap is usually set by metrics related to the performers' work.

Cause Analysis

Using the BEM, we can see that three of the causes exist within the performance environment and one is related to the individual performers. These causes are communicated in Table 16.2, with the appropriate area of the BEM provided in parentheses. From these causes, we can see that the problem was multifaceted, as most real-world problems are.

Intervention Selection

As outlined in Table 16.2, the solutions were aligned to address the specific causes in an elegant manner (i.e., a simple, tailored strategy of utility). The solutions were efficient

Value of Human Performance Improvement   167

Table 16.2 Solution Alignment Table

Problem Statement	Performance Gaps	Identified Causes	Interventions
Registrars felt that negativity was a problem in their department.	51% fewer of registrars should feel that negativity is a problem within the registrar department.	Lack of feedback about behavior (Data). Lack of performance-based incentives or consequences (Incentives). Insufficient time to get the job done (Resources). Lack of knowledge and skills (Knowledge).	Feedback: Bi-annual reviews with in-depth feedback. Incentive awards: Registrar of the Year Award, Glow-n-grow opportunities. Performance support tools and job aids. Organizational learning.

in that they were low cost to the organization in terms of money and time, which is an important component to remember when selecting interventions.

Also, while considering potential interventions, the supervisor exercised systems thinking and envisioned how the different intervention options may meet resistance when implemented. To avoid barriers to the successful implementation of interventions, the supervisor opted for solutions that were likely to be effective, as well as complemented the registrar community and existing work regulations.

Evaluation

As mentioned above, ongoing evaluation is a crucial point of the HPI process. This iterative process allows for organizations to gauge whether the interventions are successful. The supervisor closed the performance gap in a year. By monitoring and tweaking the interventions based on formative data, the supervisor ensured consistent progress. In a sense, if an organization holds the right frame of mind, performance improvement is never complete.

Connecting Process to Practice

1. Consider the various settings within which human performance improvement takes place (business/industry, healthcare, government, higher education, etc.). Do you see any similarities or differences to applying the process across settings?
2. What are some strategies or techniques that you can use to persuade clients to follow a performance systems analysis when they already have a solution such as training in mind?
3. Considering other aspects of instructional design and technology, what are some strategies that you can use to maintain change and improvement within the organization after addressing a performance problem?

Case 1 – A Small Niche Market Museum in a Metropolitan Area

Scenario: A small museum in a metropolitan region that focuses on the history of a specific product is having issues engaging their customers. The director feels that staff members are able to engage patrons once they are in the museum; however, the director feels that typically the patrons are mostly returning customers. The director knows that the organization is not meeting the expectations when it comes to engaging customers before they visit (i.e., recruiting new patrons) and after their visit.

Discussion Question: Given the information above, how would you determine the performance problem? From your understanding, what do you think an example of the performance problem statement might be?

Case 2 – A Comprehensive University Testing Center

Scenario: The testing center staff at a comprehensive university within a rural setting is struggling with efficiency issues. Specifically, the performance problem statement has been identified as: testing center workers are not checking students in quickly enough (i.e., students' testing windows are being affected). The problem was illuminated by the testing center director after reviewing several student complaints stating that their testing time was cut due to check-in delays.

Discussion Question: Given the performance problem above, what would be the type of data that you would collect to quantify the performance gap? Additionally, what data would you collect to assist in identifying the causes to this problem? *Hint:* Make sure you are collecting data from both the testing center workers (individual level) and the testing center (environmental level).

Case 3 – Cable Installers Encountering Various Issues

Scenario: A PSA was conducted for a problem targeting cable installers at a multiregional cable company. The identified problem was that installers were spending too much time on each installation site (this could be in one or multiple visits). After completing a PSA, the performance consultants identified a variety of causes to the problem based on the data. These problems included a lack of incentives, faulty/inconsistent equipment, poor individual motivation, and unclear performance descriptors.

Discussion Question: Given the previously identified causes, what are some of the solutions you would consider implementing to address these causes? What types of information would you consider prioritizing the causes?

Value of Human Performance Improvement 169

Mini-Cases

For each of the cases below, consider the scenarios through the lens of a practitioner outside of the organization.

References

Foshay, W. R., Villachica, S. W., & Stepich, D. A. (2014). Cousins but not twins: Instructional design and human performance technology in the workplace. In J. M. Spector, M. D. Merrill, J. Elen, M. Bishop (Eds.), *Handbook of research on educational communications and technology*. New York, NY: Springer. doi:10.1007/978-1-4614-3185-5_4

Gilbert, T. F. (1996). *Engineering worthy performance*. HRD Press.

Marker, A., Villachica, S. W., Stepich, D. A., Allen, D., & Stanton, L. (2014). An updated framework for human performance improvement in the workplace: The spiral HPI framework. *Performance Improvement, 53*(1), 10–23. doi:10.1002/pfi.21389

Rothwell, W. J. (2005). *Beyond training and development* (2nd ed.). AMACOM.

Rothwell, W. J., Hohne, C. K., & King, S. B. (2007). *Human performance improvement*. Butterworth-Heinemann.

Stefaniak, J. (2018). Performance technology. In R. West (Ed.), *Foundations of learning and instructional design technology* (1st ed.). Retrieved from https://edtechbooks.org/lidtfoundations/performance_technology

Van Tiem, D. M., Moseley, J. L., & Dessinger, J. C. (2012). *Fundamentals of performance improvement: Optimizing results through people, process, and organizations* (3rd ed.). International Society for Performance Improvement.

17 Preparing Instructional Designers to Apply Human Performance Technology in Global Context

Lisa A. Giacumo and Tutaleni I. Asino

Chapter Overview

This chapter emphasizes key considerations for work across cultures and in global contexts. We share an example of an organizational systems mapping project, which is one way to begin a needs assessment and needs analysis and specifically applicable to performance improvement and instructional design consultants. We provide strategies for consultants who need to work in context that may be new or unfamiliar to them, albeit as an internal consultant on a project situated in a different global location from their headquarters or as an external consultant.

Guiding Questions

1. How can I prepare others to do HPT work in global contexts?
2. What knowledge, skills, and attitudes are required to do HPT work in global contexts?
3. When is it appropriate for individuals to do HPT work in global contexts?
4. What are some adjustments that HPT professional need to make when working across cultures or in cultures different from their own?
5. How do can ethical and methodological consideration guide the data collection and analysis process?

Case Study

A Namibian financial investment organizational client issued a request for proposal (RFP) because the CEO felt employees would benefit from systems thinking training. As experienced HPT consultants, we realized that training alone doesn't usually adequately address an organization's performance improvement gap or opportunity. Further, we realized that the RFP didn't share any information regarding the actual performance gap or opportunity that the CEO was facing to guide the requested training solution design or organizational implementation. In the RFP, we proposed a needs assessment and needs analysis through an organizational systems mapping process. With the process, we promised a bespoke organizational systems model, to deliver the instructor-led training on systems thinking, and in partnership with employees at all levels we would help to identify potential causes and solutions to the desired organizational performance. To ensure solution implementation, we proposed executive coaching to meet the CEO's goals for organizational performance improvement.

DOI: 10.4324/9781003109938-17

> Our proposed partnership approach to meeting their performance improvement and workplace learning needs was accepted. But now what? Yes, we both understood the theoretical underpinnings of instructional design, performance improvement, and working across cultures. We even had experience in doing this kind of work, across other cultures. However, neither of us had ever carried out such a project before in Namibia, which meant we had to find ways to apply our knowledge to a new context.

In this chapter, we present a theoretical framework and considerations for doing ID and HPI work in global contexts and our case study. By the end, you will be able to describe a five-phase needs analysis process and identify the cross-cultural considerations responsible consultants can use in enacting the mapping process across cultures.

It is commonly known that "training alone is not sufficient to address all performance issues and problems" in organizations, even when it is systematically designed to support changes in individuals' knowledge, skill, attitude, or abilities (Abaci, & Pershing, 2017, p. 20). Therefore, while an instructional designer (IDer) may be tasked with a project intended to support organizational or workplace learning they may also be responsible for improving organizational performance through other interventions to create change. IDs accomplish this goal by taking a whole systems problem-solving approach to human performance at the environmental level of any given organization, which can include but is not limited to the design of processes, organizational systems, subsystems, performance supports, feedback loops, job ergonomics, incentives, etc. The study and application of the specific tools and methods that IDs utilize to lead to change and these desired organizational outputs, services, outcomes, and sometimes societal impacts, is called the field of human performance improvement. These tools and methods are often called human performance technology and are most used in businesses, government agencies, military, nongovernmental organizations, and nonprofits. Although, they can be utilized in schools and universities too.

Inevitably, all organizations are characterized by change. Some of that change is external that the organization itself may not have control over but must address. Others are internal changes that impact the function of the organization. Employing a complex systems perspective, one can see that organizations are composed of both constant change and stable structures or levels that exist at the same time simultaneously (Braathen, 2016). Thus, ultimately, organizations are complex systems composed of varied components, such as management, employees or members, stakeholders, procedures, and work products. The interaction of these components (as well as many others) often determines the success of an organization. organizations can encounter conflicts or incongruence whereby different cells of an organism or different parts of a machine are not working fully together which in turn impacts the main mission of the whole. When such a situation arises, different approaches can be employed to realign the needs of the organizations or to maximize the benefit of its human capital as well as output. However, changing one aspect (e.g., system or subsystem) of an organization's performance without considering the larger organization is unadvisable.

Systems Thinking

Saying everything is connected, and that changing one thing has an impact on many other things, is perhaps the easiest way to conceptualize systems thinking. As an approach, system thinking traces its origin to the 1950s work of MIT professor Jay Forrester's system dynamics (Aronson, 1996). As a framework, it emphasizes connectedness and relationships of individual components to a large and often complex whole system, where everything is interrelated and interconnected (Sterman, 2002). Whereas systems are connectedness of parts to a whole, "in contrast *systems thinking* is a more formal, abstract, and structured cognitive endeavor. While not all systems are complex, all thinking is complex, and as such, the process of thinking in a systemic way is complex" (Cabrera et al., 2008, p. 2).

Anderson and Johnson (1997) argue that system thinking is characterized by "thinking of the big picture"; balancing short-term and long-term perspectives; recognizing the dynamic, complex, and interdependent nature of systems; taking into account both measurable and non-measurable factors [and]; remembering that we are all part of the systems in which we function, and that we each influence those systems even as we are being influenced by them (p. 18).

Systems thinking is a powerful multidisciplinary approach to deal with complex problems where the solution of the problem is not known in advance. Bawden et al. (1984) called it a "framework for representing the real world." Complex systems that have high levels of uncertainty, respond to variable conditions, and utilize conflicting perspectives to function (Katina et al., 2014), while the professionals that manage complex systems might have limited understanding of the system or might have incorrect and incomplete information about the variables that affect them (ibid.). Competent engineers and science professionals utilize system thinking skills to identify, evaluate, and solve problems using multiple approaches (Behl & Ferreira, 2014). Godfrey (2014) recommends incorporating systems thinking to prepare engineers using an active learning approach that is "grounded in sustainable development" (p. 112), starting an assignment with an engineering problem instead of a predetermined field to conduct analysis exploring each section to understand their parameters and relationships among them.

Organizational Systems Maps

An organizational map shows the functional areas, relevant contributors in a context, products/services provided and required by each relevant system component, the interfaces between each component (Panza, 1989). In short, it shows the feedback loops in an organization (Panza, 1989). An organizational systems mapping process allows one to create a graphic representation of the relevant feedback loops associated with an organization in both the actual state and desired state. We used this tool because it takes a whole-systems-view, including [internal & external] stakeholders, their contributions (i.e., the products or services provided), and requirements (Panza, 1989). When you collect organizational systems mapping data relevant to the actual state and desired state, you can compare what each component of the system actually provides and needs with what the other components of the system actually provide and need. This is one way to conduct a high-level organizational analysis and environmental analysis, which can help you partner with a client to specify a gap (e.g., an opportunity or need) that is important to address (Dessinger et al., 2012).

Improving Performance in Organizational Systems across Cultures and in Global Contexts is a Growing Concern

Learning and development leaders and instructional designers are increasingly recognizing the importance of culture in organizational performance improvement efforts (Asino et al., 2017; Asino & Giacumo, 2019). While an organization's culture informs

Preparing Instructional Designers 173

learning and development as well as management practices and performance (Giacumo & Savenye, 2020; Bates & Khasawneh, 2005), individuals also influence organizational culture and performance (Kang, 2015). When one understands that [prior] learning is situated and context is critical to the learning process (Breman et al., 2019), one begins to recognize that individuals' culturally situated knowledge, skills, attitudes, and abilities, will influence their subsequent performance in organizations.

Further, harnessing a diverse group of individuals embedded in an organization is a growing concern for leaders (Deloitte Consulting, L.L.P., & Bersin by Deloitte, 2014; Han et al., 2020). In other words, it is no longer sufficient to expect all employees to simply assimilate into the culture of the organization. Today, it's equally important to recognize and address the role of culture in ID and HPI work, such as data collection (Peters & Giacumo, 2020), learning design (Giacumo & Savenye, 2020), environmental assessments, performance gap analysis, cause analyses, and performance support solutions (Breman et al., 2019).

Recently, researchers are beginning to create sources to help emerging IDs and HPT specialists become adequately prepared for this highly nuanced and important work in organizations (Giacumo & Savenye, 2020; Peters & Giacumo, 2020; Asino & Giacumo, 2019; Asino et al., 2017; Young, 2020). In this chapter, we will specifically focus our recommendations to engage in ethical and responsible data collection and analysis across cultures and in global contexts. Further, we illustrate these suggestions through a practical methodology used in needs assessments and a case study about organizational systems mapping.

Ethical and Responsible Data Collection and Analysis

Through our experience working across cultures and later on through our research, Giacumo and Savenye (2020) realized there are specific ethical and methodological considerations that can help facilitate valid and reliable data collection and analysis. Ethical considerations are associated with moral behavioral choices that ensure the project would deliver valued results to all stakeholders, some of which are often invisible in research articles. The four ethical considerations include: building trust, demonstrating respect for cultural beliefs, building additional time into projects, and taking a participatory approach (Peters & Giacumo, 2020). The methodological considerations are focused on more easily observable behaviors and choices often reported to demonstrate logical reasoning and observed evidence that can stand up to scrutiny. The three methodological considerations include communications such as language, translation, and nonverbal cues, sampling decisions, and informed consent (Peters & Giacumo, 2020). While the way you approach each of these considerations may vary across contexts, experienced IDs and HPT specialists working across the globe in a variety of contexts describe their importance (Giacumo & Savenye, 2020).

Building Trust

IDs and HPI specialists report building trust by sharing information relevant to how clients and participants' contributions and engagement in projects may be able to improve their experience in an organization (Peters & Giacumo, 2020). They focus on facilitating a process and relevant experience for all participants that is aligned to the project goal, organizational mission, and strategic objectives. They specify risks and benefits as well as answer any questions authentically (Guerra, 2003). They work hard to transparently address any potential real or perceived threats and conflicts of interest.

Respect for Cultural Beliefs

IDs and HPI specialists develop cultural intelligence and cross-cultural competence through a process of learning and reflection (Peters & Giacumo, 2020). This includes learning about the other culture's social system, norms, and reflection on their own competencies, values, self-identities, assumptions, ethnocentric tendencies, biases, and potential limitations (Guerra, 2006; Levitt, 2015). Through this process, they spend time in the setting (Irvine et al., 2008), allow space to gain new perspective, knowledge, and appreciation for the underlying values, beliefs, and practices of the individuals and organizations they would endeavor to serve (Peters & Giacumo, 2020).

Extra Time for Projects

When we first learned how to scope ID and HPT project work, our mentors suggested that we take whatever amount of time we thought necessary to complete the work and either double or triple it! Well, when we were first starting out this turned out to be a good rule of thumb. These days, while we are better able to come up with an accurate estimate for standard project work through experience, we have also learned that it can take us approximately 30%–50% more time to complete a similar scope of work across cultures and that is not counting the time for translations and materials development in other languages. Peters and Giacumo (2020) give one example of the additional activities that can take up this additional time.

Participatory Approach

A comprehensive participatory approach in HPI means that we include input from stakeholders in all relevant components of the system and at different levels in the organization, from front-line employees to managers and those above them as needed. We work hard to include perspectives from all components of the system and levels in the organization because everyone benefits most when there is a true partnership and exchange of information and ideas (Peters & Giacumo, 2020).

Language, Translation, and Nonverbal Cues

First, be sure to learn about the languages and nonverbal cues of the individuals you would serve as an ID and HPI specialist. It would behoove you to inquire about participants' preferred language for communications, interviews, surveys, focus groups, training, reading, and/or other activities you might plan. It's equally important to avoid assuming organizational members will desire translations into their first language as it is to ensure inquire about their desire for communications in potentially third or fourth languages. If you do need to work with translators and/or interpreters, developing a relationship with a few over a longer period of time is more advantageous than working with a large number who may not already be or become as familiar with the scope of work or context (Liamputtong, 2008; Giacumo & Savenye, 2020). Avoiding colloquial language and jargon will help facilitate better information exchange as well (Peters & Giacumo, 2020).

Sampling

Sampling can be tricky in organizations. You would likely need to partner with your client and/or project sponsor. They can ensure you are able to connect with the individuals who are best suited to share their experiences with the work that is relevant to the performance gap previously identified. Careful selection of representative individuals from specific populations and subpopulations with the goal to avoid individual bias and capture a variety of perspectives can help ensure that your findings are valid and reliable (Peters & Giacumo, 2020). The more relationships you can build in the organization, the more likely you will have a wide network of participants to overcome sample challenges (Liamputtong, 2008).

Informed Consent

The term informed consent is widely known in academic circles and usually includes some ethics review board. However, the concept is also demonstrated in corporate settings too. There, IDs and HPI specialists work hard to ensure the safety, confidentiality, and protect the privacy of individuals who would contribute information to meet their project goals (Peters & Giacumo, 2020). Additionally, participants should be made aware of the potential benefits and limitations of both the outcomes which may result from their contributions and your ability to maintain their confidentiality (Giacumo & Savenye, 2020). The additional challenge of achieving informed consent across cultures, is to ensure the individuals you connect with understand their basic rights, feel safe to share information, your responsibilities to the project and organization, and how you will use, disclose the data they share, and protect their identities. This can be challenging if no such construct exists in the individuals' own culture (Liamputtong, 2008) and also it may take additional time for them to understand after you've built trust.

How to Teach IDs to Do this Important Work

Cognitive Apprenticeships in the Classroom, on Internships, and/or on the Job

A cognitive apprenticeship is a teaching method that emphasizes guided experiences where instructors, managers, or more senior colleagues, explore ideas with less experienced students or professionals through modeling, coaching, scaffolding, and supporting them in reflection (Stefaniak, 2018). In the classroom, instructors can model this by creating instructional activities and providing guidance. The instruction and guidance are designed to share ID/HPI principles and approaches. These can then be selected, applied, and customized, by individual students working on specific, unique projects or deliverables. Additionally, instructors would prompt students or learners to reflect on their learning progress and process. Overtime, the instructor's guidance and feedback can be faded to allow students more responsibility and autonomy in selecting and applying strategies to carry out their projects until the point at which they are responsible for independently delivering status reports, a final set of deliverables, or product, or service, and final self-assessment reflection. This same approach has been shown to be useful when implemented by managers with IDs/HPI specialists in internships or by senior colleagues while less experienced colleagues take on a new project while on the job (Stefaniak, 2018).

We are strong proponents of guided learning through cognitive apprenticeships with real clients in coursework, internships, and/or while on the job. The distinction between each approach is minimal, with a course instructor facilitating the learning with clients while a more experienced colleague can offer similar support through modeling, mentoring, and coaching while the ID/HPI specialist is assigned to a project while on the job. In both cases, the ID/HPT specialist may be provided with templates, past project examples, milestones, specified deliverables, and any other instructions or guidance to undertake a stretch project assignment.

Professional Practice Revisited

We implemented Panza's (1989) organizational systems mapping process. We used this tool because it takes a whole-systems-view, including [internal & external] stakeholders, their contributions (i.e., the products or services provided), and requirements (Panza, 1989). We compared what each component of the system actually provided and needed with what the other components of the system provided and needed.

To enable us to work across cultures, we combined two approaches. First, we integrated a cultural consultant role into our project. In other words, the lead project consultant had a deep understanding of Namibian culture. He adjusted the project approach, instruments, and reports, to best meet the clients' expectations. Additionally, the U.S. consultant relied upon Authors' (2020) ethical and responsible cross-cultural interviewing guidance.

We drew up Chevalier's updated BEM to identify the potential causes of the organizational performance gaps. This tool can help align potential solution sets that go beyond training interventions with each of the causes of the organizational performance opportunity(ies).

Remember our Namibian client? Components of that organizational system were siloed and operating in ways that were not aligned with the organization's mission and vision. The CEO wished to inculcate systems thinking into the organization's culture to promote value addition, achieve the strategic goals, encourage innovation, as well as improve employee efficiency. The CEO's objectives were threefold:

1. To seek congruence between departments, management, and employees in terms of organizational vision, mission and processes;
2. To ignite passion and innovation toward business improvement;
3. To extract untapped value from employees and build a strong organizational culture.

Theoretical Framework

We chose the Dessinger et al. (2012) Human Performance Technology model because it does not assume or advocate training as a sole solution to performance gaps. Instead, it facilitates a diverse set of interventions, and therefore robust approach, to address the root causes of performance gaps and improve performance. We focused on a needs analysis technique (Van Tiem et al., 2005). We also applied a needs assessment technique as described by Watkins et al. (2012) by prioritizing extant data, interviews, and focus groups, with those who are working at all levels and representative areas of the organization. We would rely upon these individuals' working knowledge of the system, organizational culture, and their desire to support change as we worked with them to identify potential solutions to root causes. This approach allows for buy-in at all levels in the organization and a collaborative-design approach toward performance improvement.

Five-Phase Approach: From Discovery to Implementation and Follow-up

We employed a five-step approach that not only helped us get through the process but also scaffolded the client in understanding the proposed solution.

In Phase 1, we partnered with project sponsors to identify an achievement opportunity in measurable terms related to the organization's actual performance, desired performance, mission, and strategic business objectives. This work was meant to define success and the results our partnership would deliver.

During Phase 2, we worked with other executive leaders, and department leaders, to develop a bespoke systems thinking model. We used the first iteration of the model to identify extant data sources related to the achievement opportunity gap in organizational operations and culture. Also, we worked with the client sponsor to begin uncovering the facilitators and barriers perceived by individuals who would be affected by a change to the systems thinking model.

During Phase 3, we facilitated intervention selection and development of a change management strategy for the implementation of the Systems Thinking Model. First, we partnered with key leaders to review the results of Phase 2 and interpret the findings. We then benchmarked potential solutions against industry best practices. Finally, we partnered with the project sponsor and key leaders to rank and prioritize the best intervention package. At the end of this process, we had a solution-set and plan for removing barriers and driving innovation in the organization.

During Phase 4, we planned an implementation of the Systems Thinking Model. At this point, the model and new ways of working are presented to all organizational members at a kickoff event. Then, we step back and allow the organization to take the reins. The organizational leaders would have the knowledge, skills, and experience, of developing and implementing a systems-view approach to seizing opportunities and closing performance gaps across silos in the organization.

During Phase 5, we would provide a follow up executive coaching package. We would meet with executives in a community of practice model, once a month for an hour. During these meetings executives share implementation successes and challenges. Community of practice members ask questions and share experiences that allow the project to move forward.

Conclusion

Applying the 7 evidence-based cross-cultural ethical and methodological considerations and 5-phase mapping process can help consultants work in partnership with clients and stakeholders to gather reliable and valid data from interviews with diverse stakeholder groups for analysis. This approach adds value through higher quality work and better decisions that will ensure solutions' feasibility for implementation. The approach we took to systematically design and modify an interview protocol that intentionally considers diverse stakeholders' input to determine causes, identify solutions, and evaluate results, was welcomed by organizational members at all levels.

Connecting Process to Practice

1. Describe how to adapt an organizational system mapping process to a contextualized location;
2. Practice creating an organizational system mapping process with someone with similar technical expertise and highly contextualized knowledge from living and working in another culture and organization;
3. When would you use an organizational systems mapping process?
4. What considerations do ID and HPT consultants working in a cross-cultural consulting context need to consider?

References

Abaci, S., & Pershing, J. A. (2017). Research and theory as necessary tools for organizational training and performance improvement practitioners. *TechTrends, 61*(1), 19–25. doi:10.1007/s11528-016-0123-7

Anderson, V., & Johnson, L. (1997). *Systems thinking basics* (pp. 1–14). Pegasus Communications.

Aronson, D. (1996). *Overview of systems thinking.* Retrieved from http://www.thinking.net/Systems_Thinking/OverviewSTarticle.pdf

Asino, T. I., & Giacumo, L. (2019). Culture and global workplace learning: Foundations of cross-cultural design theories and models. In V. H. Kenon, & S. V. Palsole (Eds.), *The Wiley handbook of global workplace learning* (pp. 395–412). John Wiley & Sons, Inc.

Asino, T. I., Giacumo, L. A., & Chen, V. (2017). Culture as a design "next": Theoretical frameworks to guide new design, development, and research of learning environments. *The Design Journal, 20*(Suppl. 1), S875–S885. doi:10.1080/14606925.2017.1353033

Bates, R., & Khasawneh, S. (2005). Organizational learning culture, learning transfer climate and perceived innovation in Jordanian organizations. *International Journal of Training and Development, 9*(2), 96–109. doi:10.1111/j.1468-2419.2005.00224.x

Bawden, R. J., Macadam, R. D., Packham, R. J., & Valentine, I. (1984). Systems thinking and practices in the education of agriculturalists. *Agricultural Systems, 13*(4), 205–225.

Behl, D. V., & Ferreira, S. (2014). Systems thinking: An analysis of key factors and relationships. *Procedia Computer Science, 36*, 104–109.

Braathen, P. (2016). Paradox in organizations seen as social complex systems. *Emergence: Complexity & Organization, 18*(2), 1–14.

Breman, J., Giacumo, L. A., & Griffith-Boyes, R. (2019). A needs analysis to inform global humanitarian capacity building. *TechTrends, 63*(3), 294–303. doi:10.1007/s11528-019-00390-6

Cabrera, D., Colosi, L., & Lobdell, C. (2008). Systems thinking. *Evaluation and Program Planning, 31*(3), 299–310.

Deloitte Consulting, L. L. P., & Bersin by Deloitte. (2014). *Global human capital trends 2014: Engaging the 21st century workforce.* Deloitte University Press.

Dessinger, J. C., Moseley, J. L., & Van Tiem, D. M. (2012). Performance improvement/HPT model: Guiding the process. *Performance Improvement, 51*(3), 10–17. doi:10.1002/pfi.20251

Giacumo, L. A., & Savenye, W. (2020). Asynchronous discussion forum design to support cognition: Effects of rubrics and instructor prompts on learner's critical thinking, achievement, and satisfaction. *Educational Technology Research and Development, 68*(1), 37–66. doi:10.1007/s11423-019-09664-5

Guerra, I. J. (2003). Key competencies required of performance improvement professionals. *Performance Improvement Quarterly, 16*(1), 55–72. doi:10.1111/j.1937-8327.2003.tb00272.x

Guerra, I. J. (2006). Standards and ethics in human performance technology. In J. L. Pershing (Ed.), *Handbook of human performance technology* (pp. 1024–1046). Pfeiffer.

Han, J. H., Shin, D., Castellano, W. G., Konrad, A. M., Kruse, D. L., & Blasi, J. R. (2020). Creating mutual gains to leverage a racially diverse workforce: The effects of firm-level racial diversity on financial and workforce outcomes under the use of broad-based stock options. *Organization Science, 31*(6), 1515–1537.

Irvine, F., Roberts, G., & Bradbury-Jones, C. (2008). The researcher as insider versus the researcher as outsider: Enhancing rigour through language and cultural sensitivity. In P. Liamputtong (Ed.), *Doing cross-cultural research* (pp. 35–48). Springer.

Kang, I. G. (2015). *Empirical testing of a human performance model: Understanding success in federal agencies using second-order structural equation modeling* (Doctoral dissertation, Indiana University). Available from ProQuest Dissertations & Theses Global. (1701639415).

Katina, P. F., Keating, C. B., & Jaradat, M. J. (2014). System requirements engineering in complex situations. *Requirements Engineering, 19*(1), 45–62. doi:10.1007/s00766-012-0157-0

Levitt, S. R. (2015). Cultural factors affecting international teamwork dynamics. *International Journal of Knowledge, Culture & Change in Organizations: Annual Review, 13,* 9–23.

Liamputtong, P. (2008). Doing research in a cross-cultural context: Methodological and ethical challenges. In P. Liamputtong (Ed.), *Doing cross-cultural research* (pp. 3–20). Springer.

Panza, C. M. (1989). Picture this ... your function, your company.... *Performance+ Instruction, 28*(1), 10–17.

Peters, D. J. T., & Giacumo, L. A. (2020). Ethical and responsible cross-cultural interviewing: Theory to practice guidance for human performance and workplace learning professionals. *Performance Improvement, 59*(1), 26–34. doi:10.1002/pfi.21906

Stefaniak, J. E. (2018). Employing a cognitive apprenticeship to improve faculty teaching. *The Journal of Faculty Development, 32*(2), 45–52.

Sterman, J. (2002). *System dynamics: Systems thinking and modeling for a complex world.* ESD International Symposium.

Van Tiem, D., Moseley, J. L., & Dessinger, J. C. (2005). *Fundamentals of performance improvement: Optimizing results through people, process, and organizations* (2nd ed.). Wiley.

Watkins, R., Meiers, M. W., & Visser, Y. (2012). *A guide to assessing needs: Essential tools for collecting information, making decisions, and achieving development results.* World Bank Publications.

Young, P. (2020). *Human specialization in design and technology: The current wave for learning, culture, industry, and beyond.* Routledge.

18 Integrating Evaluation in Instructional Design Practice

Philena DeVaughn

Chapter Overview

Evaluation is an essential instructional design (ID) competency. The purpose of this chapter is to challenge faculty of instructional design graduate programs to emphasize the importance of evaluation in best practices in the ID field and to offer instructional designers strategies for explaining the relevance of evaluation in determining the effectiveness of training. The instructional design industry recognizes the importance of validating the effectiveness of instruction. However, that knowledge is not transferring to the various environments in which we work. Studies illuminate the discrepancy between employer expectations for instructional design graduates and the level of skill, and emphasis, placed on evaluation in instructional design programs. Research also reports a paucity of evidence-based literature on the utilization of evaluation models in context. Although the Donald Kirkpatrick four-level model of evaluation has been the leading evaluation model for over 30 years, the reported model of choice for 60% of organizations, the industry is lacking the evidence to support the impact of training on performance change. The challenge to our industry is to create opportunities for instructional design students to immerse in authentic situated learning experiences that support the development of ID competencies, including evaluating instruction.

Guiding Questions

1. What is evaluation in instructional design?
2. How does evaluating instructional products help to increase the effectiveness of individual, and industry best practices?
3. Has the ADDIE acronym primed the instructional design field to place evaluation at the end of the process?
4. How should evaluation be better integrated into instructional design curriculum to increase proficiency in this competency for instructional designers?
5. How do instructional designers ensure the effectiveness of instructional products and programs if evaluation is not considered a critical competency by masters' and Ph.D. degree graduate programs?

DOI: 10.4324/9781003109938-18

Case Study

Three months after graduating with a master's degree in instructional design and technology, Theresa was hired as an instructional designer for the 4X Corporation. Theresa's manager is the Senior Learning and Development Specialist within the Human Resources department. Theresa's employer assumes that she is well-trained, well-informed, and well-prepared for her first position. She is expected to hit the ground running.

The Labor Relations department has requested the design and development of a course to address the inability of managers to address employee concerns and prevent the need for arbitration. Training has been determined as the best intervention to address the performance gap. Theresa is to complete the needs assessment that will guide the development of the learning objectives and evaluation plan. Theresa outlines the needs assessment but realizes the majority of her graduate school experience focused on the design and development of instruction not evaluation.

Theresa meets with the subject matter experts in the Labor Relations department to better understand the impact of the performance gap. She observes several arbitration meetings to assess the managers' approach to the process. Theresa then reviews a representative sample of managers' training transcripts to identify the formal instruction received by managers in the past. Theresa finds several presentations on the topics of negotiation and mediation but no formal training to prepare managers for the arbitration process. Her findings support training as the best intervention to improve the performance of the managers.

Theresa develops the learning objectives and assessments for the instruction. The next step is the evaluation plan. Her boss stresses the importance of documentation that illustrates the positive impact the instruction has on performance improvement. Theresa understands the three levels of evaluation, formative, summative, and confirmative, however, she had no opportunity to practice evaluation in an authentic situation during her graduate training program.

If employers expect instructional designers to conduct formative, summative, and confirmative evaluations, Theresa wonders why evaluation competencies were not considered as predominantly, as design and development skills, in her graduate program.

Theresa calls a few of her previous classmates who are working as instructional designers. During the discussions, she finds that the majority of organizations only require summative evaluations, a trainee reaction sheet (smile sheet) to assess whether learners liked the instructors' teaching style and were satisfied with the learning experience. She also found that several IDs had the opportunity to complete several iterations of courses because they were conducting formative evaluations. Unfortunately, the summative evaluation for their projects was also limited to the smile sheet. Theresa's peers in higher education were more likely to have experience with confirmative evaluation. However, in most cases, faculty rather than instructional designers received the course feedback and guided the formative development of courses. Regardless of which industry the instructional designers worked

182 *Philena DeVaughn*

for, they were expected to craft effective evaluation plans, understand how to use the data collected through evaluation, and make the correct formative changes to their training courses. Theresa recognizes that novice instructional designers lack sufficient training to conduct instruction evaluation.

Theresa decides to contact one of her previous professors, who is also an ID practitioner. She remembered that this instructor stressed the importance of evaluation through every aspect of the design and development process. Theresa is interested in why there was little opportunity to practice the various types of evaluation as she was earning her degree. She also wants to know if this approach to evaluation is common for instructional design programs across the country.

Theresa is raising the important questions that this chapter attempts to address.

Neelen and Kirschner (2020) purport the shortcomings in industry best practices, to address performance change, are caused by the lack of evidence-informed learning design. The authors focus on the learning sciences principles that provide direction for instructional design and development to meet the needs of our audiences. They suggest that the ID industry utilize evidence-informed theories and models to create more effective, efficient, and enjoyable learning experiences. Arguably some of the most widely held instructional systems design theories and models incorporate the importance of prior knowledge and learning transfer, two approaches that are supported by the learning sciences research, e.g., Merrill's First Principles of Instruction (2009, pp. 43–44) and Gagné's et al. Nine Events of Learning (1992). However, the inconsistency of application by practitioners of evidence-informed principles critically impacts the opportunity to determine industry standards.

Learning scientists use the term learning experience design, rather than the nomenclature, instructional design, to connote our inability as instructional designers to control the internal activity or action of the learner during the learning process (Neelen & Kirschner, 2020). The term, experience, suggests that there are numerous approaches to engaging learners through instruction. Our audiences navigate a plethora of contexts, in higher education, students participate in traditional classroom settings, in asynchronous and synchronous online environments, and hybrid classes. The corporate environment offers similar instructional delivery methods, instructor-led training, e-learning, micro-learning, blended instructional experiences, and structured on-the-job training with workers engaged in the activity of performing the roles or tasks of a particular job function. Given the various contexts, how do we convince those in the industry that evidence-informed instructional design is viable for learning audiences in different work environments? Although a sufficient amount of data identifies scientifically based approaches to instructional design, evaluation is the most feasible strategy to achieve the goal. Collecting data to verify the effectiveness of empirically informed design would address the gap in the literature for instruction evaluation and support the development of a standardized approach to evaluation for the instructional design field.

Best Practices for Designing Instruction

A meta-analysis integrating a large number of empirical studies across various training topics including manager, team, cross-cultural training, and other forms of employee training, routinely demonstrated positive results when training was designed systematically and based on the science of learning and training (Salas et al., 2012). The training needs assessment is considered the first and most important step toward the design and delivery of any type of training (Neelen & Kirschner, 2020; Salas et al., 2012).

Conducting a systematic and thorough training needs assessment encompasses identification of expected learning outcomes, guidance for training design and delivery, promotion of ideas for training evaluation, and determination of the organizational factors that will contribute to, or hinder training effectiveness (Salas et al., 2012). The assessment includes a systematic job and task, or contextual, analysis which provides the specifications for the expected performance, and areas requiring improvement. The organizational analysis culminates in the recognition of training priorities, receptivity, and support for the instructional product, culture, norms, resources, and limitations that could impact training effectiveness. Another important step in the needs assessment is the learner analysis. The discovery of the prerequisite knowledge and learner characteristics help to personalize the content and delivery of the training, which leads to increased motivation to participate in the training and transfer of knowledge to the job (Renta-Davids et al., 2014).

The data collected through the needs analysis identifies causal information for the best selection of solution alternatives. The analysis also supports the evaluation of the instruction, as the chosen intervention to resolve the performance gap. The purpose of evaluation is to measure whether the intended results are likely to be achieved through the design and development of the instruction (formative) and whether the learning objectives were attained after completion of the training (summative).

The purpose of the training evaluation should first be identified then evaluation decisions aligned with the purpose. However, the purpose of evaluation is often unstated leading to misconceptions concerning the data that is collected (Kraiger, 2002, p. 340). The Association of Talent Development (ATD Research, 2019) survey of organizations reported that 91% of organizations use trainee reactions or satisfaction surveys to determine instruction effectiveness, however, less than 50% of organizations evaluate whether instructional outcomes were achieved, less than one-fifth measure whether learning was applied on the job (Kraiger, 2002, p. 339; Twitchell et al., 2008). Sitzmann et al. (2008) found that trainee reaction sheets did not reliably predict training effectiveness. The survey found that although the majority of 779 talent development professionals, reported that organizations are using different levels of evaluation, fewer have had success using evaluation to meet goals. Fifty percent of respondents believed their organization's evaluation efforts were effective in meeting learning goals, and fewer (40%) thought those efforts were effective in meeting business goals.

Why are Evaluation Competencies Lacking in Instructional Designers Upon Graduation?

If evaluating instruction and instructional products is important, as purported in the research (Kraiger, 2002; Neelen & Kirschner, 2020; Salas et al., 2012; Thalheimer, 2018), how should instructional design graduate programs better integrate the topic into the curriculum? How should novice instructional designers be trained to better understand the critical nature of evaluation and how to conduct evaluation throughout the ISD process?

Training is often proposed by stakeholders as the intervention to address performance gaps without the completion of a needs assessment (Neelen & Kirschner, 2020; Mager & Pipe, 1997). The instructional designer is then challenged to implement an intervention that may or may not resolve the performance issue, however, the potential success or failure of the instruction is their responsibility (Thalheimer, 2018). The sustainable change in behavior and cognition that is needed to improve performance, requires consideration of the entire ISD process, from needs analysis to evaluation. The activities before and after training that promote the acquisition of knowledge, skills, and attitudes, are imperative to support training effectiveness (Salas et al., 2012, p. 78).

The needs assessment defines success for a student matriculating a course of study: identifying what should have been learned in preparation for the next course or graduation. When considering corporations, the needs assessment or training needs assessment defines the knowledge and skills required to perform at the expected level for the job function. The assessment is critical to the needs analysis which includes the performance gap, learner analysis, job and task analysis, and context or environment analysis. Appropriate learning objectives and evaluation plan development rely on clearly defining the parameters of, and potential obstacles to, performance success.

Purpose of Evaluation

Determining what to evaluate is based on the purpose of the evaluation: decision-making, feedback, or marketing (Kraiger, 2002, p. 337). Decisions associated with outcomes of evaluation may include course retention, course revision, personnel, and supplementing the course with on-the-job aids. Feedback as the purpose for evaluation provides data to instructional designers, trainers, and/or the trainees. Another purpose for evaluation is marketing a training course or program to other organizations, departments, or potential trainees (Twitchell et al., 2008). For example, if the goal of instruction is to increase the level of knowledge, a formative evaluation, during the design would be used to ensure the focus of the instruction is the knowledge needed to achieve expertise in the job function. The summative evaluation should assess training effectiveness, specifically knowledge acquisition, transfer to work tasks, decision-making concerning knowledge application, and task competence (Thalheimer, 2018).

Slagter van Tryon et al. (2018) raise the concern that the plethora of ID models and approaches create challenges for ID educators seeking to teach best practices. The lack of empirical data, concerning best practices for teaching ID competencies, leaves instructors without resources to support a particular approach. The authors raise the question of whether introducing ID novices to a variety of models negatively impacts their decision-making ability. A holistic approach is recommended for teaching the ID process (Botturi, 2006; Shambaugh & Magliaro, 2001). The context must also be considered given the variety of industries in which novice instructional designers will work (Larson & Lockee, 2009).

The perceived obstacles to evaluating organizations are lack of requirement/interest, cost, lack of training in evaluation methods, resources, time, and support (including SME availability and non-instructional design team member resistance) (DeVaughn & Stefaniak, 2020; Twitchell et al., 2008; Williams et al., 2011). Organizations also reportedly hold the misperception that formative evaluation is sufficient and neither summative nor confirmative evaluation are necessary after implementation (DeVaughn & Stefaniak, 2020; Williams et al., 2011). Other studies have reported discontinuity between the perceived value of evaluation for organizations and training departments (ATD Research, 2019; Elliott et al., 2009) It is also suggested that the most frequently utilized evaluation models pose challenges, for the emblematic instructional design practitioner.

In a qualitative study that explored the challenges of evaluating instruction faced by instructional designers, researchers found that formative evaluation is conducted more routinely than summative or confirmative evaluation. Although formal evaluation was conducted more frequently, instructional designers were challenged by lack of support, interest, and ability to create the tools to evaluate ill-defined skills. It was also found that instructional designers were more likely to conduct informal formative evaluations, relying on their expertise or that of team members (DeVaughn & Stefaniak, 2020; Williams et al., 2011). Summative evaluation was more frequently used as a measure for training effectiveness, however, there was reported inconsistency with instructional designer involvement with data collection, or failure of the organization to require evaluation. This perspective supports the discrepancy instructional designers report between instructional design theory and the emphasis placed on evaluation competencies by employers (DeVaughn & Stefaniak, 2020; van Tryon et al., 2018; Williams et al., 2011). Whether preparing instructional designers with the skill to develop evaluation plans, based on empirical data, would help to persuade organizations of the importance of evaluation is unclear. What is certain is the continuing scarcity of data on training effectiveness, in the instructional design field, unless evaluation is promoted across industries. Empirical evidence that supports the value of conducting formative, summative, and confirmative evaluation could provide a vehicle for practitioners to demonstrate the value of instruction and training programs (Neelen & Kirschner, 2020, p. 53; de Leeuw et al., 2019; Thalheimer, 2018; Chochard & Davoine, 2011; Guerra-López & Leigh, 2009).

A teaching approach that potentially addresses this deficit is contextualizing instructional design instruction in authentic complex design problems providing students with the opportunity to integrate theory and practice in preparation for the workplace (Dabbagh & Blijd, 2010). Seventeen of the 18 participants, in a study, suggested that offering real-world practice in their graduate programs would have better prepared them to conduct an evaluation and/or to persuade non-designer stakeholders of the importance of evaluation for instruction improvement or enhancement (DeVaughn & Stefaniak, 2020).

Professional Practice Revisited

Theresa contacts her former professor who is leading a redesign of the foundational courses of her ID graduate program. Although evaluation is introduced in almost 46% of the courses taught in ID programs and recognized as important, Theresa's experience supports research findings that ID graduates lack the essential ID competency for evaluation.

The following table is a recommended revision of a typical ID course outline (Table 18.1). The current foundational course aligns the weekly topics with the chapters of the assigned ID textbook. Note that the outline places evaluation in Week 7. Students are required to create a design plan for a course that will address a performance issue of their choosing. Each assignment aligns with the phases of the instructional systems design process, culminating in a design plan as the final project. The type of evaluation the students would choose for the project is included in the final iteration of the design document, due Week 9.

The revised course outline begins with a foundation of instructional design evidence-based theory. Instructional design graduates report a discrepancy between theory and practice, therefore, an instructional strategy that creates a bridge to authentic practice is critical. Evaluation is introduced and integrated into the student's design plan before course design and development begin. The alignment of evaluation with the needs assessment and learning objectives is then continuously reiterated.

186 *Philena DeVaughn*

Research supports the expectation for evaluation by Theresa's employer. Increased accountability is placed on instructional designers to demonstrate value. The needs analysis should have identified training as the appropriate solution to the performance gap.

Theresa should be prepared to establish an evaluation plan after the needs analysis is completed.

The following strategies may encourage management support of the evaluation plan (Rothwell et al., 2016, p. 236).

- Define evaluation and its relevance to stakeholders with no previous experience with the process;
- Use layman rather than formal terms to avoid confusion, e.g., formative and summative evaluation;
- Determine the best method of evaluation based on the organization's culture;
- Consider timing – are there priorities that may impact when evaluation should be conducted;
- To encourage management support and set expectations for the transfer of knowledge conduct management rehearsals.

A summative and confirmative evaluation should be conducted after implementation. The data should be used to collaborate with decision-makers to identify opportunities for improvement, and continued implementation (p. 251).

Table 18.1 Introduction to Instructional Design Course Outline

	Current Course Outline	*Revised Outline*
Week 1	Topic Selection/Needs Analysis	Instructional Design & Learning Theory
Week 2	Learner and Task Analysis	Introduction to Needs Assessment
Week 3	Content Design-Instructional Objectives	Learner, Contextual, and Task Analyses
Week 4	Instructional Strategies/Sequencing Strategies	Instructional Objectives and Assessment
Week 5	Instructional Message	Formative, Summative, Confirmative Evaluation
Week 6	Considering Technology/Delivery Strategies	Content Sequencing & Instructional Strategies
Week 7	Evaluation	Instructional Message
Week 8	Learning Theory	Instructional Materials
Week 9	Planning for Implementation	Designing for Technology-based Instruction
Week 10	Project Management	Implementation & Team Collaboration
Week 11	Reflection	Reflection

Connecting Process to Practice

1. Consider Identify at least three empirical studies that would help you defend a formative, summative, and confirmative evaluation plan, to your supervisor?
2. Kraiger (2002) explains that there are three purposes for evaluation, decision-making, feedback, or marketing. Identify the purpose of evaluation for a design project that you are working on currently, or could potentially work on in the future? Craft four learning objectives for the project and briefly describe a summative evaluation plan, based on the learning objectives;
3. Creating opportunities for instructional design students to immerse in authentic situated learning experiences is a challenge for ID graduate programs. If you were allowed to redesign an ID graduate program, which instructional strategies would you choose? How would you evaluate the level of mastery achieved by the students, specifically for evaluating instruction?
4. Compare and contrast the principles identified through the learning sciences for best practices designing instruction (Neelen & Kirschner, 2020) with another ISD model. If there is a discrepancy, explain the possible reason this discrepancy exists without correction.

References

ATD Research. (2019). *Effective evaluation: Measuring learning programs for success.* Association for Talent Development.

Botturi, L. (2006). E 2 ML: A visual language for the design of instruction. *Educational Technology Research and Development, 54*(3), 265–293. doi:10.1007/s11423-006-8807-x

Chochard, Y., & Davoine, E. (2011). Variables influencing the return on investment in management training programs: A utility analysis of 10 Swiss cases. *International Journal of Training and Development, 15*(3), 225–243. doi:10.1111/j.1468-2419.2011.00379.x

Dabbagh, N., & Blijd, C. W. (2010). Students' perceptions of their learning experiences in an authentic instructional design context. *Interdisciplinary Journal of Problem-based Learning, 4*(1), 3. doi:10.7771/1541-5015.1092

de Leeuw, R., Westerman, M., Walsh, K., & Scheele, F. (2019). Development of an instructional design evaluation survey for postgraduate medical e-learning: Content validation study. *Journal of Medical Internet Research, 21*(8), e13921. doi:10.2196/13921

DeVaughn, P., & Stefaniak, J. (2020). An exploration of how learning design and educational technology programs prepare instructional designers to evaluate in practice. *Education Technology and Research Development, 68*, 3299–3326. doi:10.1007/s11423-020-09823-z

Elliott, M., Dawson, R., & Edwards, J. (2009). Providing a demonstrable return on investment for organisational learning and training. *Journal of European Industrial Training, 33*(7), 657–670. doi:10.1108/03090590910985408

Gagné, R. M., Briggs, L. J., & Wager, W. W. (1992). *Principles of instructional design* (4th ed.). Harcourt Brace Jovanovich.

Guerra-López, I., & Leigh, H. N. (2009). Are performance improvement professionals measurably improving performance? What PIJ and PIQ have to say about the current use of evaluation and measurement in the field of performance improvement. *Performance Improvement Quarterly, 22*(2), 97–110. doi:10.1002/piq.20056

Kraiger, K. (2002). *Creating, implementing, and managing effective training and development: State-of-the-art lessons for practice.* Jossey-Bass.

Larson, M. B., & Lockee, B. B. (2009). Instructional design practice: Career environments, job roles, and a climate of change. *Performance Improvement Quarterly, 17*(1), 22–40. doi:10.1111/j.1937-8327.2004.tb00300.x

Mager, R. F., & Pipe, P. (1997). *Analyzing performance problems.* Mager Associates.

188   *Philena DeVaughn*

Merrill, M. D. (2009). Experiential approach to instruction. In C. Reigeluth & A. Carr Chellman (Eds.), *Instructional-design theories and models. Building a common knowledge base* (Vol. 3, pp. 117–142). Routledge.

Neelen, M., & Kirschner, P. A. (2020). *Evidence-informed learning design: Creating training to improve performance.* Kogan Page Publishers. ISBN: 13: 978–1789661415.

Renta-Davids, A. -I., Jiménez-González, J. -M., Fandos-Garrido, M., & González-Soto, Á. -P. (2014). Transfer of learning: Motivation, training design, and learning-conducive work effects. *European Journal of Training and Development, 38*(8), 728–744. doi:10.1108/ETJD-03-2014-0026

Rothwell, W., Benscoter, G. M., King, M., & King, S. B. (2016). *Evaluating instructional and nonin-structional interventions. A revised edition based on an adaptation of instructional design competencies: The standards* (5th ed.). John Wiley & Sons, Inc. doi:10.1002/9781119176589.ch14

Salas, E., Tannenbaum, S. I., Kraiger, K., & Smith-Jentsch, K. A. (2012). The science of training and development in organizations: What matters in practice. *Psychological Science in the Public Interest, 13*(2), 74–101. doi:10.2307/23484697

Shambaugh, N., & Magliaro, S. (2001). A reflexive model for teaching instructional design. *Educational Technology Research and Development,* 49(2), 69–92. doi:10.1007/BF02504929

Sitzmann, T., Brown, K., Casper, W., Ely, K., & Zimmerman, R. D. (2008). A review and meta-analysis of the nomological network of trainee reactions. *Journal of Applied Psychology, 93*(2), 280–295. doi:10.1037/0021-9010.93.2.280

Sugar, W., Hoard, B., Brown, A., & Daniels, L. (2012). Identifying multimedia production competencies and skills of instructional design and technology professionals: An analysis of recent job postings. *Journal Educational Technology Systems, 40*(3), 227–249. doi:10.2190/ET.40.3.b

Thalheimer, W. (2018). *The learning-transfer evaluation model: Sending messages to enable learning effectiveness.* Retrieved from https://WorkLearning.com/Catalog

Twitchell, S., Holton, E. F., & Trott, J. W., Jr. (2008). Technical training evaluation practices in the United States. *Performance Improvement Quarterly, 13*(3), 4–109. doi:10.1111/j.1937-8327.2000.tb00177.x

van Tryon, P. J. S., McDonald, J., & Hirumi, A. (2018). Preparing the next generation of instructional designers: A cross-institution faculty collaboration. *Journal of Computing in Higher Education, 30*(1), 125–153. doi:10.1007/s12528-018-9167-3

Williams, D. D., South, J. B., Yanchar, S. C., Wilson, B. G., & Allen, S. (2011). How do instructional designers evaluate? A qualitative study of evaluation in practice. *Education Technology Research and Development, 59*(6), 885–907. doi:10.1007/s11423-011-9211-8

19 Project Management for Instructional Designers

Navigating People, Processes, and Politics

Shahron Williams van Rooij

Chapter Overview

What do the following outcomes have in common?

- The Pyramids of Giza;
- A published book;
- A computer software program;
- A new degree program at an institution of higher education.

Although these outcomes represent different industry sectors (construction, publishing, information technology, higher education), they all involved the application of the practices, principles, and processes of project management by the people involved in producing those outcomes.

The Project Management Institute (PMI), the standards and credentialing body for the project management profession, defines a project as a "temporary endeavor undertaken to create a unique product, service or result" (Project Management Institute (PMI), 2017, p. 4). Nearly all instructional design work conforms to this definition of a project. Instructional design projects are temporary, with a beginning, middle, and end, the outcome of which is one or more products (training, job aids, etc.) or services (assessments, analyses, etc.) to address a gap in knowledge, skills and/or abilities. In educational settings, instructional design projects tend to focus on student learning with an eye toward content mastery; in industry and government settings, instructional design projects are intended to enhance job performance or prepare for advancement.

Regardless of setting, all projects must be completed within agreed timeframes, budgets, and to the quality expectations of the client. That is why the ability to plan, manage, and eventually lead instructional design projects is part of the designer competencies set down by the International Board of Standards for Training, Performance, and Instruction (IBSTPI) and includes the following performance statements: (a) establish project scope and goals; (b) write proposals for instructional design projects; (c) use a variety of planning and management tools for instructional design projects; (d) allocate resources to support the project plan; (e) manage multiple priorities to maintain project time line; and (f) identify and resolve project issues (IBSTPI, n.d.). Similarly, the Association for Talent Development's Talent Development Capability Model™ deems project management to be a foundational ability of all Learning and Talent Development professionals and defines project management as the ability to "to plan, organize, direct, and control resources for a finite period to complete specific goals and objectives" (Association for Talent Development (ATD), n.d.).

DOI: 10.4324/9781003109938-19

Some instructional design textbooks devote chapters to project management (see, for example, Morrison et al., 2019; Reigeluth & An, 2020), and a few case studies (Benson et al., 2013; Mancilla & Frey, 2020) focusing on the application of project management principles to designing instructional events have also gained visibility. Moreover, Internet job ads for early-career designers (less than 3 years of experience) require candidates to be able to coordinate projects from inception to completion and meet specific budget and deadline requirements. These are all reasons why it is essential to start building project management skills along with instructional design skills.

Like instructional design, project management is a distinct profession focused on achieving a specific end result. All projects – including instructional design projects – have a defined scope, a common understanding about the objectives and requirements needed to complete the project, along with factors that define project success. Unlike instructional design, which is grounded in theories drawn from a variety of disciplines, project management has a relatively unique history grounded in processes and best practices with roots well before the Common Era, but formally documented beginning in the early 1900s (for a detailed history of project management, see Garel, 2013; Pollack & Adler, 2015). Over time, a variety of professional associations and certifications have emerged to create a standard set of project management processes. The largest project management associations are the U.S.-based Project Management institute (PMI), representing more than 700,000 project management professionals worldwide, the Netherlands-based International Project Management Association (IPMA), a federation of 50 national associations, and the U.K.-based AXELOS focused on IT project and service management.

PMI's *Project Management Body of Knowledge*, the PMBOK® Guide, provides a common project management vocabulary, along with a body of knowledge requirements that is recognized as good practice by the American National Standards Institute (ANSI), a private, non-profit organization that administers and coordinates the U.S. voluntary standards and conformity assessment system (American National Standards Institute (ANSI), n.d.). You will see frequent references to the PMBOK® Guide throughout this chapter. It should be noted that although the PMBOK® contains a large body of knowledge on the project management profession, this chapter focuses on the basics that you are most likely to need as an early-career instructional designer. Specifically, this chapter will introduce the basic concepts associated with project management; highlight the synergy between instructional design and project management; and identify some key considerations for successful instructional design project management.

Guiding Questions

1. When beginning an instructional design project, what are the top five questions that you would ask about the project?
2. What are some ways to identify the stakeholders in an instructional design project?
3. How does an instructional design team select the project management approach that is most appropriate for a specific project?
4. Why are interpersonal skills as important as design skills for the successful instructional design project manager?
5. When things go wrong – as they sometimes do – what are some steps that the instructional design project manager can take to get things back on track?

Case Study

Aragon Publishing is a 40-year-old company based in Seattle, Washington, that publishes business books, including award-winning titles aimed at students, business professionals, and scholars seeking to build their management and leadership skills. Since its inception, the company has grown to more than 1,100 employees with satellite offices in New York, Houston, and Vancouver, Canada. In addition to the standard publishing company departments (acquisitions, editorial, production, and marketing, etc.), Aragon has a Human Resources (HR) department with three sub-departments: Recruitment, Benefits and Compensation, and Learning and Development. The heads of each of these sub-departments report to the Chief Human Resources Officer (CHRO) who, in turn, reports to the Publisher or Chief Executive Officer. Learning and Development (L&D) was established only 10 years ago but the learning materials they've created for employees have been well received and the manager of L&D has been gaining more and more requests for learning opportunities from various departments in the company.

Samantha has been working as an instructional designer for Aragon Publishing for nearly three years. Although this was her first instructional design job, she had received high ratings on her performance reviews for her knowledge of instructional design as well as her ability to work in teams. At this morning's team meeting, Samantha's supervisor announced that the team has just been charged with revamping the company's process for onboarding new employees. Her supervisor also announced that Samantha would take on a leading role in the project, and her supervisor would serve in a mentoring role. Samantha had expressed her desire to take on more responsibility, with a goal of becoming an instructional design project manager. Now, she was being put into a position of greater visibility and although she had had no formal project management training, she was eager for the challenge and advancement opportunities that this new role would provide for her.

The supervisor noted that of all the departments at Aragon, only the information technology (IT) group followed formal project management methods and processes, so this was an opportunity for Learning and Development to be innovative and increase its visibility. As the team meeting ended, the supervisor added that the other two HR sub-departments – Recruitment, and Benefits and Compensation – were hesitant about changing the current onboarding process and believed that what they were currently doing was working well. Moreover, since revamping of the onboarding program had not been included in Learning and Development's current budget, the team would have to rely on internal resources to complete the work. There was, however, a $5,000 "cushion" available in case of emergency. Finally, senior management had mandated that the revamping project be completed in 90 days, right before the organization's next round of Employee Satisfaction surveys and the sub-department heads' own performance reviews with the CHRO.

Foundations and Concepts

A fundamental question for those new to project management is, how do projects differ from day-to-day operations? Operational work is an ongoing effort that is generally

192 *Shahron Williams van Rooij*

a repetitive process because it follows an organization's existing procedures. For example, weekly updates to a university's Learning Management System (LMS) are part of the existing procedures for the technology group responsible for LMS maintenance and support. In contrast, projects are undertaken to fulfill objectives by producing a unique product, such as a new software application for teaching and learning; a unique service or capability to perform a service (e.g., setting up a new career counseling service for students); a unique outcome, result or document (e.g., a grant proposal for submission to the National Science Foundation); or a unique combination of products, services, and outcomes (e.g., a new software application for teaching and learning, its associated user and technical documentation, help desk services, and training classes). The key word here is *unique*. For example, training courses can be developed with the same or similar materials and by the same teams; however, each training course project remains unique in key characteristics (desired outcomes, target learners, instructional strategies, etc.).

Of course, projects do not operate in a vacuum. There are internal and external factors that affect how challenging projects may be. One internal factor is organizational culture, the collection of assumptions, beliefs, behavioral norms, symbols, values and artifacts that characterize an organization (Sabuhari et al., 2020; Schein, 1984, 2004). If an organization has an established culture of project management, the project is more likely to run smoothly compared with an organization that does not have a steady history of project management. Other internal factors include the organization's technology infrastructure, breadth and depth of talent, and the risk tolerance of the organization's leadership. External factors may include political climate, marketplace conditions, and government or industry sector regulations.

Managing a project involves identifying what it is that has to be done in order to complete the project successfully, as well as addressing stakeholder expectations. Stakeholders are individuals or organizations affected by the project. At a minimum, the stakeholders include the project sponsor/client, the project team, and the project manager. In any organization and in any project, this involves navigating people, processes, and politics.

The People

Project Sponsor

No project can begin without a Project Sponsor. The Project Sponsor is usually a manager or executive responsible for initiating a project and establishing the key project elements of Vision, Governance, and Value/Benefits Realization (Schibi & Lee, 2015). Specifically, the Project Sponsor:

- Provides the business context and business objectives with which the project success criteria must align (the Vision);
- Champions the project throughout the organization to ensure capacity, funding, and priority for the project, including decisions and issues that are beyond the authority of the project manager (Governance);
- Approves project deliverables for overall quality, value and benefits (Value/Benefits Realization).

The Project Sponsor is also responsible for initiating appropriate action should business conditions change during the lifecycle of the project, so the project can remain viable and the project manager can continue to carry out the job of leading the project. Although effective project sponsorship is an important factor for project success, the identity and the role of the project sponsor may vary across organizational contexts (Breese, Couch,

& Turner, 2020). Instructional design projects may be sponsored by an internal manager or by an external client. Examples include the Sales Manager seeking additional training for the Sales Team, or the Product Manager seeking training modules for a new software line to be launched for external clients.

Project Team

The project team consists of those individuals responsible for doing the work of the project. An instructional design team may be led by a senior instructional designer and include individuals with expertise in specific areas, such as graphic design, digital technologies, or proficiency in specific course development software applications. Although research has shown that having people with the right technical and interpersonal skills appropriate for a specific project is essential for project success (see, for example, Bell et al., 2018; Guinan et al., 2019), the instructional design project manager may not always have the opportunity to select the project team members. Some organizations have fixed teams within their Learning and Development units, so that those teams work together on any and all projects assigned to those particular teams. This is not necessarily a disadvantage since members who remain in the same team all of the time gradually develop effective patterns for working together, making decisions, and communicating, as well as sharing knowledge obtained from previous project experiences (Navimipour & Charband, 2016).

Project Manager

The project manager is the person assigned to lead the team that is responsible for achieving the project objectives. For instructional design projects, that could be the most senior instructional designer on a fixed team, or for large, complex projects, an individual with project management experience who also has a firm knowledge of instructional design. A large part of the project manager's role involves dealing with people. The project manager's role has been likened to that of an orchestra conductor, whereby both the project manager and the conductor take a holistic view of their team's products (i.e., a learning initiative and a concert respectively) in order to plan, coordinate, and complete those products. Both leaders begin by reviewing the vision, mission, and objectives of their respective organizations to ensure alignment with their product, establish their interpretation of the vision, mission and objectives involved in successfully completing their products, and use their interpretation to communicate and motivate their teams toward the successful completion of their objectives (PMI, PMBOK®, p. 51).

What makes an effective project manager? First and foremost, (s)he must have a firm knowledge of his/her own organization, particularly in terms of other current or pending projects. Other projects may impact the project manager due to competing demands on the same resources, funding priorities, receipt or distribution of deliverables, and alignment of project goals and objectives with those of the organization. For instructional design projects, that means interacting with other project team leaders and seeking ways to develop relationships that would facilitate the exchange of human resources needed on any given project. The project manager may report to a functional manager, such as a training department manager but also collaborates with other roles such as subject matter experts and those involved with business analysis. Second, the project manager stays informed about trends in the industry in which (s)he is employed. The instructional design project manager working in a healthcare setting, for example, needs to stay current with regulatory issues requiring mandatory training, along with trends in the field of instructional design.

194 *Shahron Williams van Rooij*

The project manager should also have basic management skills (particularly interpersonal or "people" skills) in order to guide, motivate, and direct a team toward achieving the project goals. Lastly, the project manager must have a firm command of project management processes, tools, and techniques in order to apply them to each individual project as needed. This combination of strategic and business management, leadership, and technical project management is the PMI Talent Triangle® or suite of skills required to be an effective project manager in any industry setting, and reflects the importance of the human side of project management (Sivaraman & Raczka, 2017; Tabatabaei et al., 2019; Turner, 2016).

The Processes

The practice of project management involves the application of processes – a series of activities directed toward producing an end result – along with specific areas of technical and interpersonal skills and knowledge areas required to apply the project management processes successfully. A process group is a set of interrelated actions and activities that need to be performed in order to create the product or service that the project is intended to produce. As shown in Table 19.1, the PMBOK® defines five logical process groups: Initiating, Planning, Executing, Monitoring and Controlling, and Closing. Every successfully completed project goes through all five process groups, although smaller projects will complete the process groups faster than larger projects.

The Initiating process groups consists of all of those tasks and activities performed to define a new project by obtaining authorization to start that project. For an instructional design project, that could be a written Statement of Work (SOW) between a vendor/contractor/consultant and a client that describes the deliverables, timelines, and costs; a written Project Charter in which the project sponsor formally authorizes a large project and provides the project manager with the authority to apply organizational resources to project activities; or an internal request for training or other learning opportunity. The Planning process group focuses on establishing the total scope of the effort, defining and refining the objectives, and developing the course of action required to achieve those objectives. For instructional design projects, the Planning process group involves fleshing out the design approach, how, when and who will perform the work and often involves

Table 19.1 Project Management Process Groups

Process Group	Definition
Initiating	Processes performed to define a new project or a new phase of an existing project by obtaining authorization to start the project or phase.
Planning	Processes required to establish the scope of the project, refine the objectives, and define the course of action required to attain the objectives that the project was undertaken to achieve.
Executing	Processes performed to complete the work defined in the project management plan to satisfy the project requirements.
Monitoring and controlling	Processes required to track, review, and regulate the progress and performance of the project; identify any areas in which changes to the plan are required; and initiate the corresponding changes.
Closing	Processes performed to formally complete or close the project, phase, or contract.

Note: Adapted from Section 1.2.4.5 of the PMBOK® Guide, 2017, p. 23. Copyright 2017 by the Project Management Institute (PMI).

Project Management   195

the creation of a formal instructional design document (IDD). The Executing process group consists of those tasks and activities performed to complete the work defined in the IDD or larger project management plan to satisfy project specifications. This process group involves coordinating people and resources, as well as integrating and performing the activities of the project as outlined during project planning. The Monitoring and Controlling process group consists of all the processes required to track, review, and regulate the progress and performance of the project. It is in this process group that project performance is observed and measured regularly and consistently to identify variances from the plan. For instructional design projects, analysis of formative evaluation results for modifications to the instructional product would fall into this process group. Lastly, the Closing process group consists of those processes performed to finalize all activities across the five process groups to complete the project. It includes activities such as obtaining acceptance of the final delivery by the client or project sponsor, a post-project review and documentation of lessons learned, and closeout of any external contracts with vendors or suppliers. For instructional design projects, final approval of and payment for multimedia created by a third-party vendor would fall into this process group.

Knowledge areas refer to the specializations that surround the discipline of project management. The PMBOK® defines ten different knowledge areas; the descriptions of each area are shown in Table 19.2.

Table 19.2 Project Management Knowledge Areas

Knowledge Area	Definition
Project Integration Management	Processes and procedures to identify, define, combine, unify, and coordinate the various processes and project management activities within the Project Management Process Groups.
Project Scope Management	Task and activities to ensure the project includes all the work required, and only the work required, to complete the project successfully.
Project Schedule Management	Processes required to manage the timely completion of the project.
Project Cost Management	Processes and procedures involved in planning, estimating, budgeting, financing, funding, managing, and controlling costs so the project can be completed within the approved budget.
Project Quality Management	Processes for incorporating the organization's quality policy regarding planning, managing, and controlling project and product quality requirements, in order to meet stakeholders' expectations.
Project Resource Management	Processes and procedures to identify, acquire, and manage the resources needed for the successful completion of the project.
Project Communications Management	Processes required to ensure timely and appropriate planning, collection, creation, distribution, storage, retrieval, management, control, monitoring, and ultimate disposition of project information.
Project Risk Management	Processes and procedures for conducting risk management planning, identification, analysis, response planning, response implementation, and monitoring risk on a project.
Project Procurement Management	Processes and procedures necessary to purchase or acquire products, services, or results needed from outside the project team.
Project Stakeholder Management	Processes required to identify the people, groups, or organizations that could impact or be impacted by the project, to analyze stakeholder expectations and their impact on the project, and to develop appropriate management strategies for effectively engaging stakeholders in project decisions and execution.

Note: Adapted from Section 1.2.4.6 of the PMBOK® Guide, 2017, pp. 23–24. Copyright 2017 by the Project Management Institute (PMI).

196 *Shahron Williams van Rooij*

Although experienced project managers draw on all ten knowledge areas, as an early-career instructional designer, the most critical areas with which you should familiarize yourself are Scope Management, Schedule Management, Cost Management, Stakeholder Management, and Communications Management.

- **Scope Management** – defining and controlling what is and is not included in the project to avoid unfunded or unauthorized changes to project deliverables (*scope creep*) – is a critical knowledge area that should be addressed at the beginning of the project. Scope should be defined in a Scope Statement, outlining the need for the project, a description of what features or functions and deliverables are (not) included in the project, any business objectives the project addresses (e.g., increase the number of course offerings for more revenue), and any ingoing assumptions and constraints, such as budget, time, or available resources. A well-defined Scope Statement impacts the instructional design project manager's ability to map out the sequencing and timing of project work (Schedule Management) and thus, stay on top of the defined budget (Cost Management). Consequently, Scope Management also requires clear identification of who has the authority to modify project scope (e.g., sponsor), the process for evaluating a scope change request, and what the trade-offs would be for modifying scope (e.g., longer time to completion, higher costs).
- **Schedule Management** – describing how and when the project team will deliver the products, services, and results defined in the project Scope Statement – serves as a tool for communication, managing stakeholders' expectations, and as a basis for project performance reporting. A project schedule is a timetable that organizes project tasks, activity durations, calendar start and end dates, and sets overall project milestones on a timeline. Project schedules also define the team members and resources needed to complete tasks. For large, complex projects, schedules are created and tracked with project scheduling software (Monday.com and MS Projects) are among the best known for small and large projects), which has key features that allow project managers to monitor the progress of tasks, resources, and costs in real time. They can also assign work, link dependent tasks, view dashboards, allocate resources, and more. Instructional design project teams may not have access to scheduling software and may opt for scheduling templates freely available on the Internet. Using the Scope Statement and the Work Breakdown Structure (WBS), the design team can then establish the sequence of tasks, put the tasks in priority order, identify project milestones (e.g., completion of content storyboards), and assign resources (and costs) to each task. Once the duration of each activity and the required resources are known, the schedule can be developed. Procedures for monitoring schedule performance and for corrective action to be taken if a project is behind schedule or ahead of schedule should be documented as part of Schedule Management.
- **Cost Management** – defining the costs of the resources (human, technical, tools, etc.) needed to complete the project activities – requires collaboration with the organization's Finance Department, since different organizations calculate costs in different ways. Whether working with a fixed budget provided at project initiation, or creating a budget based on estimated costs of resources needed, cost management enables you to track how much you are spending versus how much you thought you were going to spend at a given point in time and/or at a particular task or activity. Instructional design project managers often draw on cost information from previous projects of similar size and complexity, or the experiences of other project managers as a starting point in estimating the costs of new projects. A cost estimate is a quantitative assessment of the likely costs for resources required to complete the activity. It is a prediction that is based on the information known at a given point in time. Once

costs have been estimated and a budget established, the method for tracking costs against budget should be identified and documented. These include monitoring the actual costs spent to date versus the work being accomplished for those costs. There is a variety of data analysis techniques that project management professionals use to monitor and control costs, although Earned Value Analysis (EVA) – a mathematical technique that compares the performance measurement baseline to the actual schedule and cost performance – is the most well-known technique. As an early-career instructional designer, learning which data analysis techniques your organization uses for instructional design projects is your guide for project Cost Management.

- **Stakeholder Management** – identifying the people who will be affected or influenced by your final product and ensuring their buy-in to and satisfaction with the final product – is an extension of the Learner and Contextual Analysis that you conduct as part of your instructional design process, with project stakeholders being a part of the organizational context. At a minimum, you should be able to identify stakeholders by name, business unit, or organizational context, level of interest in the project, level of influence on the project, role in the project (e.g., sponsor, SME, none), project expectations, and any other facts of interest (previous involvement with instructional design projects, desired involvement in the current project, etc.) that would help you to determine how best to manage that specific stakeholder relationship.
- **Communications Management** – getting the right information about the project to the right people at the right time – requires project managers to have solid communication skills so that they can set and manage expectations, share difficult information or news, and facilitate potential conflicts among stakeholders. This can be the most time-consuming part of the project manager's job. Effective communication creates a bridge between stakeholders who may have different organizational and cultural backgrounds, different levels of expertise, and different perspectives and interests that may affect or influence the success of your project. Successful project managers use formal and informal communication methods across various channel to ensure that messages are received and understood by the proper stakeholders, and that relevant feedback is provided to the appropriate project members. The methods and frequency of communication are outputs of your Stakeholder Management plan.

The matrix in Table 19.3 illustrates the interrelationship between the five Project Management Process Groups and the ten Project Management Knowledge areas, along with a sampling of the activities that may take place within each cell.

Project management is grounded in a vast body of knowledge concerning the tools and techniques of individual project practice that can be adapted to the scope and complexity of any given project. The key word here is *adapted*. The project manager and his/her team can choose the appropriate processes, levels of detail, and documentation applicable to the specific project, along with attention to the interpersonal skills essential for communication within the team and with project stakeholders. Next, we will examine the synergy between instructional design and project management.

Instructional Design and Project Management

Project management complements the design process by offering a set of repeatable processes – the five Process Groups – with which to describe, organize, and complete the work required for each phase of the development lifecycle, with deliverable complexity determining how much process is used at each phase. In other words, your instructional design processes set down in your instructional design document describe *what* you are going to do (target learners, desired outcomes, instructional strategies, etc.); your project

198 *Shahron Williams van Rooij*

Table 19.3 Process Group and Knowledge Area Mapping with Sample Activities

Knowledge Areas	*Project Management Process Groups*				
	Initiating Process Group	*Planning Process Group*	*Executing Process Group*	*Monitoring & Controlling Process Group*	*Closing Process Group*
Integration Management	Review SOW/ develop Project Charter	Develop project management plan	Direct & manage project work	Monitor & control project work	Close project, conduct post-project reviews/lessons learned
Scope Management		Define scope, deliverables		Validate, control scope	
Schedule Management		Define, sequence, schedule activities		Control schedule	
Cost Management		Estimate costs, budget		Control costs	

management plan describes *how* you are going to accomplish the work set down in your instructional design document (scope statement describing what is or is not included in the project, resource requirements, scheduling, stakeholder involvement, etc.).

Just as instructional design approaches range from ADDIE to Agile, project management has a range of approaches. There are, however, a few approaches that are recognized worldwide, namely: (a) the traditional Waterfall approach; (b) the Agile Project Management approach; and (c) the Hybrid approach to project management. Examining instructional design through the lens of each of these project management approaches makes the synergy between the two fields clearer.

Waterfall Approach

Waterfall project management defines a series of sequential phases, with each new phase beginning only when the prior phase has been completed (Ajam, 2018; Wysocki, 2011). This approach originated in the manufacturing and construction industries, where environments, processes and procedures were highly structured, inhibiting design changes due to cost. Waterfall project management was adopted by the software development industry in the 1970s to complement engineering practices. Project progress flows in one direction (downward, like a waterfall) through the process groups of project Initiation, Planning, Execution, Monitoring and Controlling, and Closing. The advantages of Waterfall include its worldwide adoption as a well-known approach; it is easy to describe and understand for developers, non-developers, and clients; it is easier to plan and manage because of the emphasis on up front work, documentation, and detail, and it generates stable specifications or requirements. On the other hand, there are some disadvantages. It requires sequential completion of one phase before starting the next; unanticipated risks are identified late in the cycle; delays in coding and integration lead to breakage or bugs late in the design, and the focus on process and documentation does not easily accommodate changes in client requirements and expectations. These disadvantages have been particularly noted in the software development industry where stakeholder priorities are often subject to change, the pre-planning and specification of phases in a linear sequence has proven to be relatively inflexible, and costly, time-consuming revisions have contributed to high project failure rates (for detailed information about IT project failure rates, see PMI, 2020). Figure 19.1 illustrates the synergy between the Waterfall project management approach and the traditional ADDIE instructional design approach. Note that revision and iteration in ADDIE is still accommodated within the linear structure of Waterfall project management.

Agile Approach

An umbrella term for a group of approaches that employ iterative methods, such as SCRUM and Extreme Programming, among others (for a detailed discussion of the various Agile approaches, see Stellman & Greene, 2015), Agile views a project as a series of relatively small tasks conceived and executed as the situation demands rather than as a completely pre-planned process. Agile employs iterative cycles focused on delivering features with the highest priority for the business first, so that the project team can reflect and adapt the process at regular intervals. Greater emphasis is placed on communications and collaboration than on documentation, although documentation is not eliminated completely. Instead, documentation should be sufficient enough to support the development and delivery of a working or "live" high-priority product requirement. Instructional design has adopted Agile techniques in order to take advantage of the flexibility absent from traditional applications of ADDIE, sometimes proposing new naming conventions to differentiate these techniques from ADDIE, particularly when addressing design for online-only delivery modes. Examples include Clark and Gottfredson's (2008) five-step AGILE e-Learning Design (Align, Get Set, Iterate and Implement, Leverage and Evaluate) and Allen's (Allen & Sites, 2012) Successive Approximation Model (SAM), among others. Figure 19.2 provides a graphic illustration of the SCRUM approach to Agile, with the top figure showing the various iterations and the lower figure providing details of an iteration.

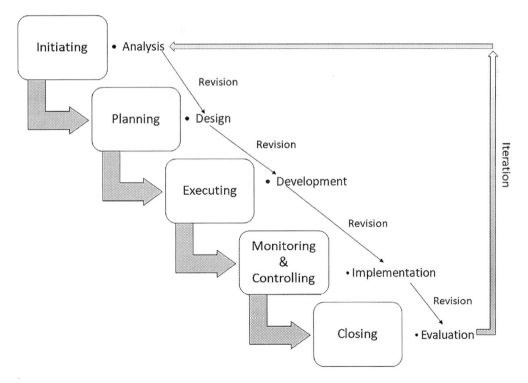

Figure 19.1 Waterfall project management.

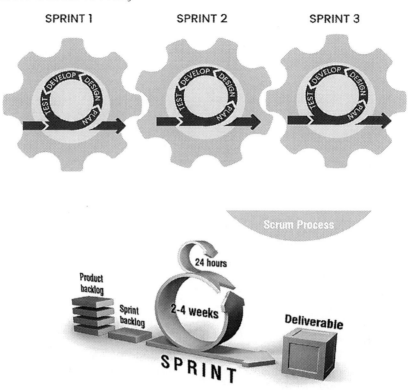

Figure 19.2 Agile approach to project management.

It should be noted that Agile is not a magic bullet. Agile is more than just a set of methods; it is a mindset defined by values, guided by principles, and manifested through many different practices (Denning, 2016). The Agile mindset encompasses collaboration, build, and feedback, is value-driven, welcomes and responds to change, and continuous delivery of must-have product features as small value-added slices. The Agile project manager internalizes the Agile mindset, values and principles, then applies the right practices and tailors them to different situations as they arise. Applying Agile practices without knowing when to tailor and how to select the appropriate processes is a recipe for project failure. Writing in Forbes, Prof. Steve Andriole of Villanova University and one of the founders of Agile, noted that Agile projects fail because Agile approaches are abstract solutions rather than steps to be followed. Consequently, expectations are set too high and thus, the goals are impossible to achieve (Andriole, 2020). In other words, Agile does not in and of itself guarantee project success.

Hybrid Approach

Hybrid project management blends Agile and Waterfall elements to create a custom approach. The hybrid approach enables the project team to apply Agile to uncertain aspects and Waterfall to fixed deliverables in order to gain the benefits of both project management approaches without the weaknesses of either approach (Barbosa & Saisse, 2019; Cooper & Sommer, 2016). Hybrid allows the project team to plan before starting to work on the project, yet allows the team to divide the development cycle into short-term deliverables or sprints. In other words, planning is done using the Waterfall approach, but execution and delivery are done using the Agile approach. As such, the project team can react to market changes and deliver what the market demands in place of what the team planned. Hybrid project management is gaining traction in the software development industry and will no doubt spread to other industry sectors. There is currently little published research about the extent to which instructional designers have adopted hybrid project management.

Project management and instructional design are different but complementary processes and professions, neither of which has a one-size-fits-all approach. It is the nature of the project that determines whether you use one single approach or a combination of approaches. Waterfall project management is best suited when there is project stability, while Agile methods are excellent when there is project uncertainty. If the risks are fairly low but the impact of system failure (think of the space shuttle) is fairly high, then you probably want to stay with Waterfall project management. Conversely, if: (a) your project is suitable to incremental delivery because of changing requirements; (b) you have a very engaged and collaborative customer willing to get down in the weeds and work with you on a regular basis; (c) you work for an organization whose culture is innovate and thrives on near-chaotic dynamism rather than order and structure; and (d) you have team members who are co-located and work together on a regular basis, then Agile methods can work for you. A peer or supervisor may say, "let's go Agile" but you need to ask, "when?" "Always" is the wrong answer. Now, for the political side of project management.

The Politics

No matter how much process is in place, there will always be a human element to project management that involves stakeholder relationship management. Where there are stakeholders, there will be politics:

> Even a project manager who has mastered all the tools of the trade may still struggle to deliver projects successfully due to misinterpreting or even missing the signs of underlying political issues. Politics and the personalities of those involved can be a greater influence in making a project successful than the project management skill base of the team.
>
> (Martin, 2016, p. 1)

An important way for the project manager to mitigate the risks resulting from project politics is to construct and maintain solid working relationships with the project stakeholders, including members of the project team, the project sponsor/client, and any functional managers in your organization who provide resources for the project. Good relationships are developed slowly through consistent interaction and honest behavior. If you have as yet to lead your first project, the following provides the considerations you should explore with your project team leader.

Who?

In instructional design, both scholars and practitioners have stressed the importance of stakeholder analysis for designing and testing instructional interventions (Ertmer et al., 2013; Konings et al., 2014; Rothwell et al., 2015). The Context Analysis helps you to identify the various stakeholders of your project. The identity of stakeholders and their interests in the outcomes of your work may vary from project to project or even during a particular project. Consequently, stakeholder evaluation is a continuous process that helps you to understand the political landscape by: (a) revealing the interests of various stakeholders in relation to your project's objectives; (b) identifying actual and potential conflicts of interest so that you can plan how to engage with a stakeholder who has priorities other than your project; (c) detecting attitudinal and emotional issues that may affect project outcomes; and (d) discovering the relationships between different stakeholders that help to identify a potential coalition of individuals willing to promote project success. Some of the techniques for identifying stakeholders include conducting brainstorming sessions with your team and the client at the beginning of a project, asking known project stakeholders to point out who they think other project stakeholders might be (and why), then determining whether each of the stakeholders has the power and influence to help or hinder the success of your project. Project managers often use a basic spreadsheet – the Stakeholder Register – that lists the names, titles, contact information, interest in the project, power/influence, and project expectations of each stakeholder (for a detailed discussion of stakeholder analysis tools and techniques, see Tran et al., 2020; Williams van Rooij, 2018). Stakeholder identification drives project communication so that the project manager can create a communication strategy that specifies who needs to be informed, what kind of communication will be required, how frequently communication will be needed, what details must be communicated.

How?

All project stakeholders should have a shared understanding as to what business problem the project is intended to solve. A simple way of accomplishing this is to work with your team to craft an elevator speech that: (a) provides the "why" to the listener; (b) constructs a picture of the future state of the business once a solution is implemented; (c) promotes/sells the project to stakeholders at all levels; and (d) creates clarity of direction for a project team. If you're creating an instructional intervention, what are the knowledge, skills, or ability challenges being addressed? How was the need for the project identified? What benefits will project success bring to the organization? The elevator statement allows for consistent messaging for all project team members and enables the early-career instructional design project manager to begin creating a reputation for being competent, knowledgeable, open, and honest in communications. Other forms of verbal communication could include periodic conversations in the team about whether or not the project vision is still in alignment with business needs and if the current vision needs to be updated. Those in-team conversations are also helpful for reviewing and confirming initial project information and team member roles, as well as providing an opportunity to reinforce the value of each team member's contribution to project success. In terms of written communication, deadline dates, procedures and company policies, should all be sent in written form to avoid misunderstandings, especially when parts of your project team or other influential stakeholders are in different locations. Documentation standards and practices in your organization will determine the layout of your documents, along with any technology systems used to capture and archive project documentation. Although project size and complexity determine what is documented and at what level of detail, at a minimum, the following project elements should be in writing:

- Project description, scope, requirements or specifications, and desired project outcomes. Success criteria with metrics, and a formal authorization from the person(s) initiating the project should also be included;
- Resources – people, technology, budget – needed for the projects and how those resources will be secured;
- Potential project risks, frequency of monitoring those risks, and strategies for risk mitigation;
- Stakeholder communication frequency and methods;

Project Management 203

- Formal sign-off on deliverables so that all team members know when the project is completed and the Closing process can be finalized;
- Lessons learned for future projects.

Conclusion

In this chapter, we have explored: (a) the basic concepts associated with project management; (b) the synergy between instructional design and project management; and (c) identified some key considerations around the politics of project management. It should be clear that successful project management lies in the interpersonal skills that enable you to communicate up, down, and sideways, supported by the project management processes and knowledge areas appropriate for each project, to establish and sustain stakeholder buy-in throughout the project lifecycle. Get started by participating in other project managers' reviews, construct a personal checklist for improving your project management competence by performing a SWOT analysis on yourself – your current strengths, weaknesses, how you plan to improve, and what threats there may be to your achieving your personal project management goals. By revisiting your goals and self-reflection throughout your career, you will be able to track your growth from novice to seasoned manager of instructional design projects.

Professional Practice Revisited

Comment on the following aspects of the case study presented earlier in this chapter.

a) As Samantha prepares for this project, what should be her starting point?

b) What is the "why" for this project? Is this in alignment with the "why" that would be articulated by Samantha's supervisor? Aragon senior management?

c) How would Samantha identify project stakeholders and their potential impact on project success?

d) What communication tools would you recommend to Samantha for communicating to the various project stakeholder groups?

e) What formal project management processes would you recommend that Samantha introduce?

f) What success criteria should Samantha used to be able to declare the project completed?

Connecting Process to Practice

1. Think about your most recent project experience, either working in one of your university courses or in the workplace. Describe that project in terms of the following:
   - The people and processes that contributed to project success;
   - The people and processes that contributed to project challenges;
   - The ways in which the project manager/leader established and maintained a shared vision of project outcomes.
2. If you have project management experience, select one project that you have managed and discuss the following:

- Would you consider the project successful or less than successful (and why)?
- What would you have done differently, given the opportunity?
3. List the top five lessons learned from all of your project experiences, including projects that you did not manage yourself. Please explain why each lesson learned made the top five list.

References

Ajam, M. (2018). *Project management beyond waterfall and agile.* CRC Press.

Allen, M., & Sites, R. (2012). *Leaving ADDIE for SAM: An agile model for developing the best learning experiences.* ASTD Press.

American National Standards Institute (ANSI). (n.d.). *ANSI introduction.* Retrieved July 18, from https://www.ansi.org/about/introduction

Andriole, S. (2020). Why no one understands Agile, SCRUM & DevOps & why perfect technology abstractions are sure to fail. *Forbes.* Retrieved from https://www.forbes.com/sites/steveandriole/2020/10/01/why-no-one-understands-agile-scrum--devops--why-perfect-technology-abstractions-are-sure-to-fail/?sh=28d7e77346a5

Association for Talent Development (ATD). (n.d.). *Building personal capability.* Retrieved from https://tdcapability.org/#/personal/project-management

Barbosa, A. M. C., & Saisse, M. C. P. (2019). Hybrid project management for sociotechnical digital transformation context. *Brazilian Journal of Operations & Production Management, 16*(2), 316–332. doi:10.14488/BJOPM.2019.v16.n2.a12

Bell, S. T., Brown, S. G., Colaneri, A., & Outland, N. (2018). Team composition and the ABCs of teamwork. *American Psychologist, 73*(4), 349–362. doi:10.1037/amp0000305

Benson, A. D., Moore, J. L., & Williams van Rooij, S. (Eds.). (2013). *Cases on educational technology planning, design, and implementation: A project management perspective.* IGI Global.

Breese, R., Couch, O., & Turner, D. (2020). The project sponsor role and benefits realisation: More than 'just doing the day job'. *International Journal of Project Management, 38*(1), 17–26. doi:10.1016/j.ijproman.2019.09.009

Clark, T. R., & Gottfredson, C. A. (2008). *In search of learning agility.* Learning Guild Ebooks.

Cooper, R. G., & Sommer, A. F. (2016). The agile–stage-gate hybrid model: A promising new approach and a new research opportunity. *Journal of Product Innovation Management, 33*(5), 513–526. doi:10.1111/jpim.12314

Denning, S. (2016). How to make the whole organization "Agile". *Strategy & Leadership, 43*(6), 10–17. doi:10.1108/SL-09-2015-0074

Ertmer, P., Parisio, M. L., & Warduk, D. (2013). The practice of educational/instructional design. In R. Luckin, S. Puntombekar, P. Goodyear, B. Grabowski, J. Underwood, & N. Winters (Eds.), *Handbook of design in educational technology.* Routledge.

Garel, G. (2013). A history of project management models: From pre-models to the standard models. *International Journal of Project Management, 31*(5), 663–669. doi:10.1016/j.ijproman.2012.12.011

Guinan, P. J., Parise, S., & Langowitz, N. (2019). Creating an innovative digital project team: Levers to enable digital transformation. *Business Horizons, 62*(6), 717–727. doi:10.1016/j.bushor.2019.07.005

IBSTPI. (n.d.). *Instructional designer competencies – Welcome to IBSTPI.* International Board of Standards for Training, Performance and Instruction. Retrieved from http://ibstpi.org/instructional-design-competencies/

Konings, K. D., Seidel, T., & van Merrienboer, J. J. G. (2014). Participatory design of learning environments: Integrating perspectives of students, teachers, and designers. *Instructional Science, 42*(1), 1–9. doi:10.1007/s11251-013-9305-2

Mancilla, R., & Frey, B. (2020). A model for developing instructional design professionals for higher education through apprenticeship. *The Journal of Applied Instructional Design, 9*(2). https://edtechbooks.org/jaid:9_2/a_model_for_developi

Martin, N. A. (2016). *Project politics: A systematic approach to managing complex relationships.* Routledge.

Morrison, G. R., Ross, S. M., Morrison, J. R., & Kalman, H. K. (2019). *Designing effective instruction* (8th ed.). John Wiley & Sons, Inc.

Navimipour, N. J., & Charband, Y. (2016). Knowledge sharing mechanisms and techniques in project teams: Literature review, classification, and current trends. *Computers in Human Behavior, 62*, 730–742. doi:10.1016/j.chb.2016.05.003

Pollack, J., & Adler, D. (2015). Emergent trends and passing fads in project management research: A scientometric analysis of changes in the field. *International Journal of Project Management, 33*(1), 236–248. doi:10.1016/j.ijproman.2014.04.011

Project Management Institute. (2017). *A guide to the project management body of knowledge* (6th ed.). Project Management Institute.

Project Management Institute. (2020). *Pulse of the profession 2020.* Retrieved from https://www.pmi.org/learning/thought-leadership/pulse/pulse-of-the-profession-2020

Reigeluth, C. M., & An, Y. (2020). *Merging the instructional design process with learner-centered theory.* Routledge. doi:10.4324/9781351117548

Rothwell, W., Benscoter, B., King, M., & King, S. B. (2015). *Mastering the instructional design process: A systematic approach.* John Wiley & Sons.

Sabuhari, R., Sudiro, A., Irawanto, D., & Rahayu, M. (2020). The effects of human resource flexibility, employee competency, organizational culture adaptation and job satisfaction on employee performance. *Management Science Letters, 10*(8), 1775–1786. doi:10.5267/j.msl.2020.1.001

Schein, F. H. (1984). Coming to a new awareness of organizational culture. *Sloan Management Review, 25*(2), 3–16.

Schein, E. H. (2004). *Organizational culture and leadership* (3rd ed.). San Francisco, CA: Jossey-Bass.

Schibi, O., & Lee, C. (2015). Project sponsorship: Senior management's role in the successful outcome of projects. In *PMI® global congress 2015 – EMEA*, London, England. Retrieved from https://www.pmi.org/learning/library/importance-of-project-sponsorship-9946

Sivaraman, R., & Raczka, M. (2017). A project manager's personal agility sightings. *PM World Journal, 6*(6). Retrieved from https://pmworldlibrary.net/wp-content/uploads/2017/06/pmwj59-Jun2017-Sivaraman-Raczka-personal-agility-sightings-second-edition.pdf

Stellman, A., & Greene, J. (2015). *Learning agile: Understanding SCRUM, XP, LEAN and KANBAN.* O'Reilly Media, Inc.

Tabatabaei, M., Cuellar, M., & Williams, J. (2019, December 14). *Practitioners' perception of skills in effective project management* [Conference session]. Retrieved from https://aisel.aisnet.org/cgi/viewcontent.cgi?article=1007&context=irwitpm2019

Tran, L., Sindt, K., Rico, R., & Kohntopp, B. (2020). Working with stakeholders and clients. In J. K. McDonald & R. E. West (Eds.), *Design for learning: Principles, processes and praxis.* EdTech Books.

Turner, M. (2016). Beyond the iron triangle: Reflections of an early career academic. *International Journal of Managing Projects in Business, 9*(4), 892–902. doi:10.1108/IJMPB-01-2016-0005

Williams van Rooij, S. (2018). *The business side of learning design and technologies.* Routledge.

Wysocki, R. (2011). *Effective project management: Traditional, agile, extreme* (6th ed.). Wiley Publishing.

20 Supporting Instructional Design Graduate Education through Networked Learning and Institutional Social Media

Enilda Romero-Hall

Chapter Overview

This chapter provides insights on networked learning using institutional social media to support educational technology and instructional design graduate students. Social media is more than just social networking sites such as Instagram, Facebook, Twitter, and Snapchat. Social media also includes web-based and downloadable applications that allow for user generated content such as wikis, blogs, video hosting sites (e.g., YouTube), and text-exchange platforms (e.g., WhatsApp). In this paper, it is argued that social media represents a convivial technology in which individuals are engaging in networked learning. A review of the literature yielded examples of how institutional social media is been used in teaching and learning specifically in instructional design and technology programs. Insights from a case study about an instructional design and technology program that has been actively using different institutional social media to enhance the networked learning experience of the graduate students (and other stakeholders) in the program is shared as a way to connect research with practice. Guiding questions, questions to move the discussion forward, and recommended readings are also shared.

Guiding Questions

1. What is networked learning?
2. What are the benefits and drawbacks of using social media for networked learning?
3. How can you foster networked learning opportunities while using social media?
4. How are instructional design and technology programs using institutional social media to facilitated networked learning?

Case Study

The IDT graduate program at The University of Tampa was established 8 years ago. The program prepares instructional design graduate students to pursue careers in the design, development, implementation, and evaluation of learning experiences to improve knowledge and performance in multiple environments. There were many resources that faculty in our program wanted to share with the graduate students. However, we did not want these resources and information to be contained in a Learning Management System (LMS) that would only be available while the students were enrolled in the IDT program. Instead, we aimed to create affinity spaces that served as professional learning networks. Most of our students were regular users

DOI: 10.4324/9781003109938-20

of social media and often connected with each other in different social networking sites. The instructors in the program also noticed that other IDT programs and professional organizations had a social media presence and would often share resources with members of our field. With this in mind, a year after the program started, I took on the unofficial role of social media coordinator.

As part of this role, I created official social media accounts for the graduate program including a Twitter account, a Facebook page, and Google+ community. These accounts were acknowledged as social media accounts affiliated with the university. These three social media platforms were selected initially because they were the most popular among the graduate students in the program. The Twitter account and Facebook page are both public, while the Google+ community was private.

It has been 8 years since the IDT program has been actively using different institutional social media to enhance the networked learning experience of the graduate students in the program and other stakeholders. Overtime there were changes to the social media platforms used by the graduate students. With the rise in popularity of Instagram, an official account representing the program was created. Then, Google+ communities were discontinued by Google which forced faculty teaching in the program to think about private communities' alternatives for the graduate students. Ultimately, a decision was made to start a LinkedIn group to replace the Google+ community and facilitate a space in which the graduate students could connect, share, and discuss topics among themselves. Today, the number of individuals connected to our program via the public institutional social media has grown beyond our graduate students and alumni.

Many have stated that networked learning comes from engagement in personal or professional learning networks, which are "complex systems of interaction consisting of people, resources and digital tools that support ongoing learning and professional growth" (Trust et al., 2016, p. 35). Through networked learning, learners work to gather, filter, and organize content to make meaning while also sharing resources and their viewpoints (Kennedy, 2018). The Networked Learning Editorial Collective (NLEC) defined networked learning as:

> Involves processes of collaborative, co-operative and collective inquiry, knowledge-creation and knowledgeable action, underpinned by trusting relationships, motivated by a sense of shared challenge and enabled by convivial technologies. Networked learning promotes connections: between people, between sites of learning and actions, between ideas, resources and solutions, across time, space, and media.
> (The Networked Learning Editorial Collective, 2020, p. 9)

One of key aspect of this definition of network learning is the use of the term "convivial technologies," which avoids framing networks in simple oppositions such as a digital or material world. Instead, the re-definition of network learning considers convivial tools that afford networks of people (with common ground or interests) the opportunity to convive regardless of the format of medium (e.g., virtual or in-person networks). In this paper, I argued that social media represents a convivial technology in which individuals are engaging in networked learning.

208   *Enilda Romero-Hall*

There is plenty of evidence that shows that young adults, including undergraduate and graduate students, are spending a significant amount of time using social media (Romero-Hall et al., 2020; Social Media Fact Sheet, 2019). Young adults log in to social media to keep up with their friends, family, and acquaintances, as well as to update others about their daily life. It is rare to find a young adult who is not a member of one of the top five social media platforms (namely, Snapchat, Instagram, Facebook, Twitter, and YouTube). Social media has infiltrated the educational arena (Chen & Bryer, 2012; Gao et al., 2012). There are many research efforts focused on the use of social media in formal teaching and learning (Dabbagh & Kitsantas, 2012; Manca & Ranieri, 2016, 2017; Gao et al., 2012; Romero-Hall & Li, 2020).

The research outcomes on whether young individuals favor using social media in their formal learning experiences are mixed (Greenhow & Lewin, 2016; Garcia et al., 2015). However, researchers believe that social media has the potential to engage users through collaboration, allow connection with educational contexts, and help blur the line between formal and informal learning (Chen & Bryer, 2012; Greenhow & Lewin, 2016). With support from the research literature and a case study, this chapter provides insights on networked learning using institutional social media to support educational technology and instructional design graduate students.

Networked Learning

As a society, we live and work in networked environments (Carvalho, 2018). In educational institutions we engage with others in networked settings, in which staff, students, and instructors are connected via knowledge networks, among others. It makes sense that in higher education, faculty aspire to instill these networked practices in our graduate students we should aim and encourage our graduate students to build personal learning networks (Trust & Prestridge, 2021) in digital environments. "Personal learning networks are unique cultivated systems of people, spaces, and tools that assist educators in improving their teaching and learning (Trust & Prestridge, 2021, p. 1)." Although in this definition Trust and Prestridge (2021) refer to *educators*, personal learning networks are critical in all professions. One probable outcome of a learner's participation in personal learning networks are opportunities for networked learning (Carvalho, 2018). These networked learning experiences foster through social media should constitute practices in which learning has perceived value, there is shared responsibility for the learning process among all stakeholders involve in the network, adequate time is permitted to enable relationship building, learning takes on a collaborative format, there is opportunity for critical reflection, and most importantly, social exchanges support the knowledge, and identity creation (The Networked Learning Editorial Collective, 2020). As stated by social learning theorists, learning is a social, situated, and distributed experience (Trust et al., 2018).

Educators can aim to foster networked learning practices within instructional design and technology programs using social media. Access to social media platforms and their adoption in education have enabled the creation of augmented learning networks that expand opportunities for engagement with digital peers who are accessible across typical temporal, spatial, and institutional barriers (Trust et al., 2018). It is important to state that the use of social media is not the only way in which we can accomplish networked learning, but simply one alternative for instructors in instructional design and technology graduate programs to consider. As previously mentioned, networked learning does not have to be explicitly in a digital format. Rather, it should take place with the assistance of convivial technology. The word technology entails methods, systems, and devices which are the results of knowledge being used for practical purposes.

Social Media

Social media is present in our everyday life. It is important to clarify that social media is more than just social networking sites such as Instagram, Facebook, Twitter, Snapchat, and TikTok. Social media also includes web-based and downloadable applications that allow for user generated content such as wikis, blogs, video hosting sites (e.g., YouTube), and text-exchange platforms (e.g., WhatsApp).

It is fair to say that many have expressed and investigated concerns related to the use of social media. Some of these concerns are related to social media addictions (Szczygieł & Podwalski, 2020), cyberbullying practices (Aydin, 2012), online harassment (Hodson et al., 2018; Veletsianos et al., 2018), effects on self-esteem (Shensa et al., 2016; Whaite et al., 2018), fake news and deep fakes (Chauhan et al., 2021), and the spread of misinformation (Eckberg et al., 2018; Gosse & Burkell, 2020), and context collapse (Dennen & Burner, 2017), among others. Additionally, there are concerns related to the ethical management of data by companies developing these social media applications (Krutka et al., 2019). Controversies have arisen given issues associated to the ethical management of data including lack of data privacy, lack of transparency in user agreements and terms of service, and the use of algorithms of oppression, echo, and extremism (Krutka et al., 2020; Krutka et al., 2019). Despite the concerns and issues that come from using social media, individuals around the world continue to access these outlets of user generated content with an aim to create online communities with others who share similar interest (Romero-Hall et al., 2020).

Social Media in Education

Social media has also been present in teaching and learning in formal, non-formal, and informal education. These experiences have been primarily in post-secondary education at the undergraduate and graduate levels. Instructors have considered creative ways in which social media can serve as a space to discuss, share, generate content, create a sense of community, enhance professional development and/or complement formal instruction (Romero-Hall & Li, 2020). There is a range of learning experiences involving the use of and participation in social media affinity spaces that have been discussed in the literature. An affinity space provides individuals with a physical, virtual, or blended location in which they can communicate and discuss like-mindedness toward a topic (Gee, 2005). Some of the learning experiences that instructors include have considered in social media affinity spaces include the use of course- or topic-related hashtags, the implementation and use of institutional social media accounts (including course related social media groups and communities), and content creation by learners via blogs, vlogs, and podcasts as a course activity.

Hashtags

The use of hashtags in different social media communities has been one of the main ways to supplement classroom experiences, engage in discussion, participate in professional development activities, and cultivate a sense of community. Hashtags are used to create affinity spaces in social media because they aid the categorization, organization, search, and connection of posts. By inserting a hashtag in a public post, the content shared becomes visible to anyone searching for posts with that specific hashtag. In their book *#HashtagActivism: Networks of Race and Gender Justice,* Jackson et al. (2020) discuss the digital labor of African Americans, women, transgender people, and others supporting racial justice and feminist causes to repurpose the use of hashtags such as #BlackLivesMatter,

#MeToo, #SayHerName, #YesAllWomen, and #GirlsLikeUs, among others, in an effort to change national and international consciousness. The hashtag has been used as a method to thread conversations, people, and movements together (Greenhalgh, 2020; Jackson et al., 2020). In education, there are many hashtags that are used as part of formal and informal learning experiences, including general interest education hashtags such as #edchat, #edleaders, and #education. However, hashtags are also created to discuss specific topics such as different types of instructional practices (e.g., #makered, #designthinking), subject areas (e.g., #historyteacher, #SSchat), and trending issues (e.g., #achievementgap, #edequity). It is also common for instructors to create program and/or course specific hashtags for their students. Hashtags have also been used as a key element of Twitter chats (Greenhalgh, 2020). These chats are synchronous conversations between Twitter users with messages that include a specific hashtag to connect the exchanges.

Institutional Social Media

Institutional social media are often created at the department or program level within an institution (Blankenship & Gibson, 2015; Myers et al., 2015). Some of these institutional social media include public and private groups (e.g., Facebook and LinkedIn groups) and resource sharing accounts (e.g., Facebook pages, Instagram accounts, YouTube Channels, Twitter accounts). Institutional social media are often used to facilitate informal socialization among faculty, learners, and other stakeholders. It can serve as an approach for faculty, current students, alumni, and members of the public to stay connected to a department or program. Institutional social media can be formal, non-formal, and informal affinity spaces. These social media groups can also serve for informal chatter and sharing of resources among members of a specific department, program, or course community.

Learning Activities

Social media has also been infused in teaching and learning in higher education through the implementation of blogs, vlogs, and podcasts activities in formal and informal ways (Christie & Morris, 2021; Forbes & Khoo, 2015; La Caze, 2017). Learners are often asked to engage in critical thinking and reflective experiences. These reflective activities are often focused on a specific topic, experience, person, or feeling. The learners' thoughts, ideas, and summaries can be written and shared using a blog (Christie & Morris, 2021). It is also possible to create video blogs, often referred as vlogs, in which the learner can share visuals to illustrate their reflection (La Caze, 2017). Podcasting has become an extremely popular activity for learners to share reflective audio recordings with narration, sounds, and interviews using different podcasting platforms (Forbes & Khoo, 2015).

Institutional Social Media in Instructional Design Graduate Education

A review of the literature yielded examples of how institutional social media are been used in teaching and learning specifically in instructional design and technology programs. In an investigation conducted by Romero-Hall et al. (2018), a crowded source spreadsheet (http://tiny.cc/IDTSocialMediaAccounts) was used to gather information on different types of institutional social media that are used by instructional design and technology programs. A total of 44 departments and/or programs shared information on their public institutional social media. These included: Twitter accounts, hashtags, Facebook groups, YouTube channels, Instagram accounts, LinkedIn groups, and other public social media sites (e.g., Pinterest accounts, blogs, Vimeo accounts). The main purpose of the investigation by Romero-Hall et al. (2018) was on public Twitter accounts of instructional design and technology programs; the researchers conducted a content analysis of a random sample of tweets ($n = 1,023$) by 22 programs (Romero-Hall et al., 2018). The results of the investigation showed that the majority of the tweets aimed to: a) share assets and materials related to instructional design issues and trends (47.41%); b) promote the profile of the program (12.68%); and c) share upcoming or past event information (10.07%). This investigation revealed that institutional Twitter accounts by instructional design and technology graduate programs are seldom used to engage in dialogue or communication exchanges. The great majority of the Twitter accounts by instructional design and technology graduate programs focus on broadcasting messages (Romero-Hall et al., 2018).

In a survey conducted by Romero-Hall (2017a) that examined 77 instructional design and technology graduates' students and their use of their institutional social media revealed that although most graduate students used social media for personal purposes, only a portion of the graduate students actively followed or connected with their respective institutional social media. However, those who did follow the social media spaces of their IDT program expressed tremendous benefits from the experience. Some of these benefits included community building (i.e., getting to know each other outside the classroom, giving each other feedback, keeping everyone in the program up-to-date, and greater social presence compared to the learning management system) and professional growth (i.e., support resource sharing, networking with other graduate students and faculty, opening avenues of knowledge, supporting research collaboration, enabling cross country interactions). This investigation by Romero-Hall (2017a) also served to determine content that the graduate students hope that institutional social media administrators would share, for example: research opportunities, faculty stories, internship opportunities, resources from other programs, graduate students' failure and success stories, events, trends in the IDT field, stories about community impact, and networking opportunities, among others. A key finding of the investigation is that instructional design graduate students use the social media spaces created by their program to share, discuss, exchange, and learn. The content shared can challenge the graduate students' views as instructional designers and expose them to an array of perspectives.

A phenomenological study conducted by Romero-Hall (2017b) helped grasp and elucidate the meaning, structure, and essence of instructional design and technology graduate students' participation in the social media of their program. The results of this investigation shed light on both the benefits and challenges of the use and participation of institutional social media. All the benefits shared echoed those previously mentioned by Romero-Hall et al. (2018) and Romero-Hall (2017a). This benefit included access to resources, feeling connected, access to different perspectives on issues and trends in the field, and participation in informal learning experiences. However, unlike other investigations, Romero-Hall (2017b) shared some insights related to the challenges experienced by graduate students due to their use and participation in institutional social media of their program. These challenges included:

- The time commitment to connect, participate, and use the content shared on the social media affinity spaces of their graduate program;
- The possibility of distraction by going down the "*rabbit hole*" due to the amount of information shared by others;
- Issues of security and privacy in relation to the sharing of ideas, as well as, feeling worried that others would view and read casual thoughts and conversations;
- Resistance by some graduate students to share and participate in the institutional social media due to their personality type, own judgments, or level of caution.

This investigation helped highlight and provide a better understanding of the experiences by instructional design and technology graduate students.

> There are positive and negative experiences. It is important not to overemphasize the positive aspects and overlook the negative experiences. Although there are advantages to adequately implementing social media spaces for teaching and learning, just like any other environments, it presents challenges that should not be ignored.
>
> (Romero-Hall, 2017b, p. 13)

Another investigation by Rosenberg et al. (2016) used a design-based research approach to further investigate the use of social media to support graduate programs. This investigation focused particularly on a program-specific goal of enhancing student learning experiences through the Educational Psychology, and Special Education (EPET) at Michigan State University social media platforms. The *design framework for graduate program social media use* included: a) establish why; b) establish how; c) be authentic; d) respect privacy; e) coordinate platforms; and f) engage volunteers. The design-based research approach helped the researchers identify benefits from the social media initiative in the graduate program. Some of these benefits included that: a) those involved in the social media committee of the EPET program were exposed to a rich context for learning about social media in teaching and learning; b) members of the committee were able to increase their practice of informal academic writing; c) members of the program were afforded opportunities for collaborative scholarship between graduate students and faculty; and d) the lessons learned from the design-based approach were immediately implemented in institutional social media outside the program.

Overall, these research studies highlight how networked learning initiatives using social media can support instructional design graduate education. Through these institutional social media, graduate students can participate in networked learning while engaging on the production and content sharing, discussion and interaction, and collaborative connections (Forbes, 2017). However, before continuing on to the discussion of professional practice (in which these review of the literature is connected with the case study) I would like to: a) reiterate the challenges and issues presented when using social media (Aydin, 2012; Shensa et al., 2016; Whaite et al., 2018; Eckberg et al., 2018; Gosse & Burkell, 2020; Dennen & Burner, 2017); and b) encourage instructors to raise awareness of the issues that graduate students may experience by using social media even in the context of teaching and learning (Krutka et al., 2020; Krutka et al., 2019).

Professional Practice Revisited

In order to facilitate networked learning opportunities using the institutional social media, every semester during the first week of class sessions, as the program coordinator, I send an email to all the enrolled students in the program and our alumni using the program listserv. The email introduces our new graduate students to our institutional social media and serves as a reminder to all students and alumni to please contribute content that they feel would be beneficial to share with others. The email also highlights which institutional social media are public and which as private and everyone is reminded that participation is optional. Content shared in the public social media are contributed by current students, alumni, and faculty, but reviewed and posted by faculty members only. Over the years, some graduate students served as a social media interns. In this role, the social media interns were given permission to review and post professional development links, articles, and videos. The social media interns who were also graduate students of the IDT program would receive independent study credits that could be used as an elective course.

Networked learning using the institutional social media has been facilitated in various ways over the years (see Figure 20.1). First, events and activities are often

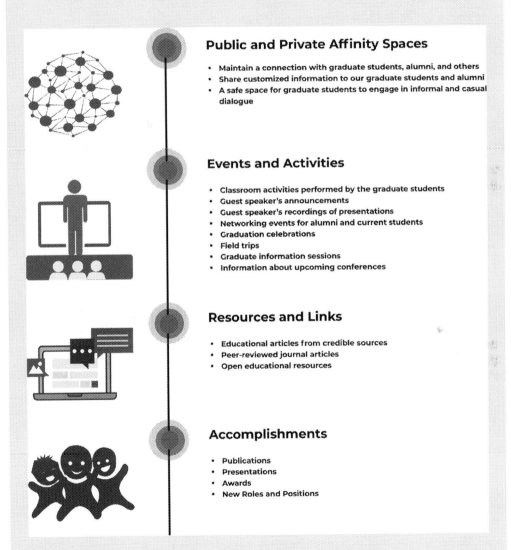

Figure 20.1 Networked learning using institutional social media.

shared. These events include classroom activities performed by the graduate students, guest speaker's announcements, guest speaker's recordings of presentations, networking events for alumni and current students, graduation celebrations, field trips to events within the community or close to campus, graduate information sessions for potential instructional design graduate students, information about upcoming IDT conferences (virtual or in person). Another type of content shared in an effort to encourage networked learning are resources and links to a) educational articles from credible sources, b) peer-reviewed journal articles on key trends and issues on the field, and c) open educational resources.

As previously mentioned, one of the goals of the institutional social media for the programs was to share accomplishments of both the graduate students and faculty including publications, conference presentations, and awards (see Figure 20.2). This

Figure 20.2 Example of Twitter post highlighting our graduates and faculty.

relates very much to what was mentioned in the literature. Instructional design graduate students want to know the successes and failures of other graduates and alumni (Romero-Hall, 2017a). Initially creating a culture of sharing successes and acknowledgments was not easy, since graduate students tend to shy away from the spotlight.

Supporting Instructional Designers 215

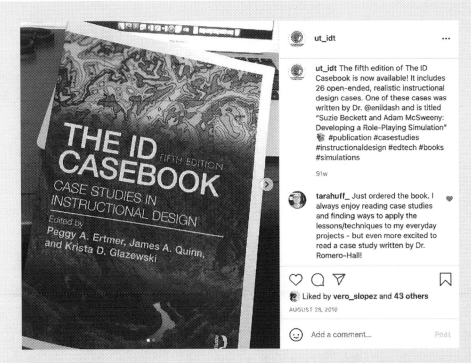

Figure 20.3 Example of content shared in the public Instagram account.

However, with time, sharing these success stories became a way to support and cheer on each other.

Although, job and internship opportunities were initially shared via the different institutional social media. The program listserv made it easier to disseminate this information directly to the email inbox of current students and alumni of the program. Using the listserv gave everyone, including those who are not subscribed to the institutional social media, access to announcements about potential instructional design jobs and internships.

Sharing different types of content via the public institutional social media is the first step to setup a networked learning environment in the graduate program (see Figure 20.3). The next step is to further encourage discussion and exchanges between the graduate students. This has been accomplished and facilitated in the private LinkedIn group (see Figure 20.4). In this group, most of the content shared is provided by alumni and current students of the program.

Figure 20.4 Example of content shared in the private LinkedIn group.

Connecting Process to Practice

1. How would your program or course benefit from having an online social community using convivial technology such as social media?
2. What challenges to you foresee in the pursue to creating and maintaining an online community using convivial technology such as social media for your course or program?
3. What type of networked learning experiences would you aim to facilitate in an online community using social media for your course or program?
4. Who would be the stakeholders in your program or course that would support this networked learning initiative using social media? Describe each of their roles;
5. What strategies can you apply to you stimulate networked learning experiences using the existing institutional social media of your program or department?

References

Aydin, S. (2012). A review of research on Facebook as an educational environment. *Educational Technology Research and Development*, 60(6), 1093–1106. doi:10.1007/s11423-012-9260-7

Blankenship, J. C., & Gibson, R. (2015). Learning alone, together. *Journalism & Mass Communication Educator*, 71(4), 425–439. doi:10.1177/1077695815622113

Carvalho, L. (2018). Networked societies for learning: emergent learning activity in connected and participatory meshworks. In M. J. Spector, B. B. Lockee, & M. D. Childress (Eds.), *Learning, design, and technology: An international compendium of theory, research, practice, and policy* (pp. 1–22). Springer International Publishing.

Chauhan, R. S., Connelly, S., Howe, D. C., Soderberg, A. T., & Crisostomo, M. (2021). The danger of "fake news": How using social media for information dissemination can inhibit the ethical decision-making process. *Ethics & Behavior*, 1–20. doi:10.1080/10508422.2021.1890598

Chen, B., & Bryer, T. (2012). Investigating instructional strategies for using social media in formal and informal learning. *International Review of Research in Open & Distance Learning, 13*(1), 87–104. doi:10.19173/irrodl.v13i1.1027

Christie, H., & Morris, N. (2021). Assessment and emotion in higher education: The allure of blogging. *Research in Post-Compulsory Education, 26*(2), 148–163. doi:10.1080/13562517.2019.1662390

Dabbagh, N., & Kitsantas, A. (2012). Personal learning environments, social media, and self-regulated learning: A natural formula for connecting formal and informal learning. *The Internet and Higher Education, 15*(1), 3–8. doi:10.1016/j.iheduc.2011.06.002

Dennen, V. P., & Burner, K. J. (2017). Identity, context collapse, and Facebook use in higher education: Putting presence and privacy at odds. *Distance Education, 38*(2), 173–192. doi:10.1080/01587919.2017.1322453

Eckberg, D. A., Densley, J., & Dexter, K. (2018). When legend becomes fact, Tweet the legend: Information and misinformation in the age of Social Media. *Journal of Behavioral & Social Sciences, 5*(3), 148–156.

Forbes, D. (2017). Professional online presence and learning networks: Educating for ethical use of social media. *International Review of Research in Open and Distributed Learning, 18*(7), 175–190.

Forbes, D., & Khoo, E. (2015). Voice over distance: A case of podcasting for learning in online teacher education. *Distance Education, 36*(3), 335–350. doi:10.1080/01587919.2015.1084074

Gao, F., Luo, T., & Zhang, K. (2012). Tweeting for learning: A critical analysis of research on microblogging in education published in 2008–2011. *British Journal of Educational Technology, 43*(5), 783–801. doi:10.1111/j.1467–8535.2012.01357.x

Garcia, E., Elbeltagi, I., & Dungay, K. (2015). Student use of Facebook for informal learning and peer support. In *Proceedings of the European conference on e-learning* (pp. 174–182).

Gee, J. P. (2005). Semiotic social spaces and affinity spaces. In D. Barton & K. Tusting (Eds.), *Beyond communities of practice: Language, power, and social context* (pp. 214–32). Cambridge University Press.

Gosse, C., & Burkell, J. (2020). Politics and porn: How news media characterizes problems presented by deepfakes. *Critical Studies in Media Communication.* doi:10.1080/15295036.2020.1832697

Greenhalgh, S. P. (2020). Differences between teacher-focused twitter hashtags and implications for professional development. *Italian Journal of Educational Technology.* doi:10.17471/2499–4324/1161

Greenhow, C., & Lewin, C. (2016). Social media and education: Reconceptualizing the boundaries of formal and informal learning. *Learning, Media and Technology, 41*(1), 6–30. doi:10.1080/17439884.2015.1064954

Hodson, J., Gosse, C., Veletsianos, G., & Houlden, S. (2018). I get by with a little help from my friends: The ecological model and support for women scholars experiencing online harassment. *First Monday, 23*(8). doi:10.5210/fm.v23i8.9136

Jackson, J. J., Bailey, M., & Foucault Welles, B. (2020). *#HashtagActivism: Networks of Race and Gender Justice.* MIT Press Direct. doi:10.7551/mitpress/10858.001.0001

Kennedy, J. (2018). Towards a model of connectedness in personal learning networks. *Journal of Interactive Online Learning, 16*(1), 21–40. Retrieved from http://esearch.ut.edu/login?url=http://search.ebscohost.com/login.aspx?direct=true&db=ehh&AN=133749052&site=ehost-live

Krutka, D. G., Heath, M. K., & Mason, L. E. (2020). Editorial: Technology won't save us – A call for technoskepticism in social studies. *Contemporary Issues in Technology and Teacher Education, 20*(1). Retrieved from https://citejournal.org/volume-20/issue-1-20/social-studies/editorial-technology-wont-save-us-a-call-for-technoskepticism-in-social-studies

Krutka, D. G., Manca, S., Galvin, S., Greenhow, C., Koehler, M., & Askari, E. (2019). Teaching "against" social media: Confronting of profit in the curriculum. *Teachers College Record, 121*(14), 1–19.

La Caze, S. (2017). Changing classroom practice through blogs and vlogs. *Literacy Learning: The Middle Years, 25*(1), 16–27.

Manca, S., & Ranieri, M. (2016). Facebook and the others: Potentials and obstacles of social media for teaching in higher education. *Computers & Education, 95*, 216–230. doi:10.1016/j.compedu.2016.01.012

Manca, S., & Ranieri, M. (2017). Implications of social network sites for teaching and learning: Where we are and where we want to go. *Education and Information Technologies, 22*(2), 605–622. doi:10.1007/s10639-015-9429-x

Myers, L. H., Jeffery, A. D., Nimmagadda, H., Werthman, J. A., & Jordan, K. (2015). Building a Community of Scholars: One Cohort's Experience in an Online and Distance Education Doctor of Philosophy Program. *Journal of Nursing Education, 54*(11), 650–654. doi:10.3928_01484834-20151016-07

Networked Learning Editorial Collective. (2020). Networked learning: Inviting redefinition. *Postdigital Science Education.* doi:10.1007/s42438-020-00167-8

Romero-Hall, E. J. (2017a). Posting, sharing, networking, and connecting: Use of social media content by graduate students. *TechTrends, 61*(6), 580–588. doi:10.1007/s11528-017-0173-5

Romero-Hall, E. J. (2017b). Active user or lurker? A phenomenological investigation of graduate students in social media spaces. *International Journal of Social Media and Interactive Learning Environments, 5*(4), 326–340. doi:10.1504/IJSMILE.2017.10012109

Romero-Hall, E. J., Kimmons, R., & Veletsianos, G. (2018). Social media use by instructional design department. *Australasian Journal of Educational Technology, 34*(5). doi:10.14742/ajet.3817

Romero-Hall, E. J., & Li, L. (2020). A syllabi analysis of social media for teaching and learning courses. *Journal of Teaching and Learning, 14*(1), 13–28. doi:10.22329/JTL.V14I1.6246

Romero-Hall, E. J., Petersen, E., Sindicic, R., & Li, L. (2020). Most versus least used social media: Undergraduate students' preferences, participation, lurking, and motivational factors. *International Journal of Social Media and Interactive Learning Environments, 6*(3), 244–266. doi:10.1504/IJSMILE.2020.109266

Rosenberg, J. M., Terry, C. A., Bell, J., Hiltz, V., & Russo, T. E. (2016). Design guidelines for graduate program social media use. *TechTrends, 60*(2), 167–175. doi:10.1007/s11528-016-0023-x

Shensa, A., Sidani, J., Lin, L. Y., Bowman, N. D., & Primack, B. (2016). Social media use and perceived emotional support among U. S. young adults. *Journal of Community Health, 41*(3), 541–549. doi:10.1007/s10900-015-0128-8

Social Media Fact Sheet. (2019). *Demographics of social media users and adoptions in the United States.* Pew Research Center. Retrieved from http://www.pewinternet.org/fact-sheet/social-media/

Szczygieł, K., & Podwalski, P. (2020). Comorbidity of social media addiction and other mental disorders: An overview. *Archives of Psychiatry & Psychotherapy, 22*(4), 7–11. doi:10.12740/APP/122487

Trust, T., Carpenter, J. P., & Krutka, D. G. (2018). Leading by learning: Exploring the professional learning networks of instructional leaders. *Educational Media International, 55*(2), 137–152.

Trust, T., Krutka, D. G., & Carpenter, J. P. (2016). "Together we are better": Professional learning networks for whole teachers. *Computers & Education, 102*, 15–34.

Trust, T., & Prestridge, S. (2021). The interplay of five elements of influence on educators' PLN actions. *Teaching and Teacher Education, 97.* doi:10.1016/j.tate.2020.103195

Veletsianos, G., Houlden, S., Hodson, J., & Gosse, C. (2018). Women scholars' experiences with online harassment and abuse: Self-protection, resistance, acceptance, and self-blame. *New Media & Society, 20*(12), 4689–4708.

Whaite, E. O., Shensa, A., Sidani, J. E., Colditz, J. B., & Primack, B. A. (2018). Social media use, personality characteristics, and social isolation among young adults in the United States. *Personality & Individual Differences, 124*, 45–50. doi:10.1016/j.paid.2017.10.030

21 Creating and Cultivating a Regional Community of Practice for Instructional Design and Faculty Development Practitioners

Samantha J. Blevins, Tracey W. Smith, Charley Cosmato, M. Aaron Bond, and Emory Maiden

Chapter Overview

This chapter examines the decisions and processes that were taken to establish and support a regional Community of Practice (CoP). The CoP described in this chapter formed in 2014 and generally located in the Mid-Atlantic region of the United States, was conceived to connect practicing professionals in the fields of both instructional design and professional development. The goal of forming this regional network was to allow members to connect locally with others in the profession to promote knowledge and innovation sharing in the fields of teaching and learning. In this chapter, founding members of the advisory board describe the decisions made by those forming the community, as well as the steps taken to sustain the community over time, including the planning and hosting of an annual in-person meeting for community members to attend; built-in opportunities for informal mentorship; and virtual gatherings and professional development offerings designed to connect and sustain community membership and engagement throughout the year.

Guiding Questions

1. What is the value, both intrinsic and extrinsic, of finding and becoming a member of a regional professional learning community?
2. How might individuals who work in higher education and who feel isolated take steps to collaborate with their professional peers at similar regional institutions?
3. What factors influence the successful creation and ongoing sustainability of a regional community of practice?

Case Study

In 2014, in a teaching center located at a rural higher education institution in the Mid-Atlantic region of the United States, two instructional designers hatched an idea. They had been feeling isolated and frustrated, tackling the same problems they sensed were shared among professionals in their field on similar campuses throughout the state. Both were engaged in professional organizations. However, they still did not feel fully connected to the daily practices and practical concerns of instructional designers, technologists, and teaching faculty who are perpetually building learning experiences for students or facilitating training and development for faculty and staff.

DOI: 10.4324/9781003109938-21

In the tradition of Appreciative Inquiry (Cooperrider & Whitney, 2005), they defined their challenge and began to "dream" of the ideal CoP. Given the range of professionals that support students' learning in higher education outside of those in traditional instructional designer roles, the ideal CoP might even include teaching faculty. Rather than charging at silos within their local institution, they instead sought to gather a variety of folks from similar institutions to work out shared challenges in a community setting. They set out to build this sort of inclusive professional community by creating a simple, open invitation to connect.

Working within the field of instructional design can feel isolating, particularly when an Instructional Designer is acting alone at a small institution. Likewise, academic faculty can feel alone when they put on their "course builder" hat prior to the start of a teaching term. Having a regional CoP to tap into can give designers and faculty a way to reach out to their peers for support during the process, or when facing any kind of opportunity or challenge, allowing them to work through or avoid issues that others might have faced.

If we reflect on early universities, we recall that faculty members assumed every non-student role in the institution. These roles included everything from class registration, advising, research, teaching, and supervision in loco parentis. The work of the university rested squarely on the shoulders of the faculty. By 2017 full-time employment in U.S. post-secondary education was 3,914,542. Of that, faculty (teaching/research/public service) made up 1,543,569 (39%) of the total staff (Snyder et al., 2019). While the National Center for Education Statistics (NCES) data doesn't track the composition of the "other" non-teaching academic professionals, it is clear that much of the work in our post-secondary learning institutions is now spread across a range of staff and professionals. Academic librarians, technologists, instructional designers, student affairs leaders and other professionals that support the learning mission of higher education might need a village of their own. In a sense, the IDEAx CoP is a central campfire where rank and role give way to communal story-telling and authentic moments of understanding regarding how our work relates to the work of our colleagues.

Foundational Knowledge

Three areas of foundational knowledge within the literature should be considered and examined when creating a regional community: systems thinking, communities of practice, and mentoring networks. The interplay among these three areas will be evident as we revisit the case at the end of the chapter.

Systems Thinking

Systems thinking is the systematic approach to building understanding of a whole organization and its interdependent parts. Cabrera et al. (2015) identify four components that underlie systems thinking models: distinction, system, relationship, and perspective. To understand a problem, organization, or system, one must understand how to make distinctions between components or ideas, recognize systems in part or whole, identify relationships in action and reaction, and metacognitively take or explore different perspectives or views (Cabrera et al., 2015). Building an understanding of processes, people, culture, infrastructure, and external systems can help leaders make informed decisions and influence change efforts.

Finding ways to influence change often starts with the people who interact with and within the system. Senge (2006) identifies the importance of considering the mental models of individuals in a system as key to changing the larger system. When individuals have a better understanding of systems and the role they play within the system, they are better able to identify the areas of focus that lead to desired outcomes (Senge, 2006; Stroh, 2015). Using social learning engagement strategies can help those affected by new initiatives understand how they are affected by or have influence within the larger system change (Bond & Blevins, 2020). Formal mentoring programs, communities of practice, and other social learning strategies should be designed through a systems thinking lens because people are a critical component of any system, providing social outlets may lead to successful change initiatives.

Though early efforts to form the IDEAx CoP often relied on social learning strategies to recruit, engage, and retain members, there was not an overt use of systems thinking in decision making. However, in our retrospective analysis of how the community formed and was sustained, we realized that systems thinking was unintentionally incorporated into these efforts without any formal planning. Many of the early creators and planners involved in the creation of IDEAx instinctively looked for the whole picture and the individual parts of a local system of instructional designers and faculty developers. Exploring the larger system of higher education, the individuals sought to bring together individual faculty developers and instructional designers to bring changes necessary to improve faculty teaching and ultimately student learning. Topics discussed through social learning engagements helped this specialized group make or influence decisions at their respective institutions.

Professional Community of Practice

CoPs are not often portrayed as systems or subsystems. This connection between systems theory and social learning theory may have implications for how organizations promote growth and change (Bond & Blevins, 2020). Though CoPs are not widely found in systems theory, a CoP is a simple social system characterized by a distinct structure, complex relationships, self-organization, dynamic boundaries, and ongoing negotiation of identity and cultural meaning (Wenger, 2010). A community of practice, as described by cognitive anthropologists Jean Lave and Etienne Wenger, consists of a group of people who share an interest or profession who meet regularly to create and share knowledge together (Lave & Wenger, 1991; Wenger, 1998). CoPs differ from learning communities in that CoPs are centered on learning in apprenticeships with all members taking the role of apprentice or mentor in a given situation with the goal of producing words, tools, concepts, methods, stories, documents, links to resources and other forms of reification (Wenger, 2010).

CoPs also consist of many types of participants. Some members reside on the periphery, learning from the dialog, discourse, and debate that happens naturally inside the social system. Other participants actively participate in the discussion and knowledge creation. The key to a successful CoP is effectiveness and commitment of the core group who organizes and facilitates the events within a given community (Bond & Lockee, 2014). The IDEAx CoP discussed as a complement to this chapter has benefited from engagement by a strong core group of members who are passionate about the field of instructional design and committed to the social learning energy characteristic of IDEAx.

222 *Samantha J. Blevins et al.*

A CoP can take many forms, with small social systems forming naturally or with purposeful intent in a variety of contexts. CoPs are found in a variety of learning fields including K-12 education, industry, the military, nonprofit organizations, healthcare, and higher education (Bond & Lockee, 2018; Enthoven & de Bruijn, 2010; Hurley & Green, 2005; Ranmuthugala et al., 2011; Weller, 2017). Professional associations like the Society for Information Technology and Teacher Education (SITE) have created spaces for CoPs to grow and develop knowledge around a specific topic in the larger field. Rather than organizing interest groups around a specific topic, the IDEAx CoP has been organized for a specific audience and membership who meet regularly to create and share knowledge in order to grow the fields of instructional design and professional development in higher education in their region. Characteristic of CoPs, members of IDEAx participate in knowledge creation and sharing as well as reification efforts through co-created artifacts and learning experiences such as the following:

- Semester-long reading and book group conversations, which sometimes culminate with author visits;
- Process and/or project conversations among community members;
- Hands-on workshops on topics such as using frameworks for course design; building ePortfolios for assessment; bullet journaling for task/project management; facilitating community conversations; and incorporating badging credentials into campus professional development opportunities;
- Zoom meetings during the COVID-19 pandemic to support members through guiding their own campuses during in a time of rapid transition from face-to-face to online course delivery; creating quality video content; use of videoconference tools in the online classroom; round robin sharing session of our different campus situations; and hosting discussions centering around podcasts on various community relevant topics;
- Personal reflections by members through social media posts, journaling, blogging, and ePortfolio entries.

Participation in a CoP such as IDEAx can provide an opportunity for participants to develop a shared knowledge that can be directly applied to real world situations. This direct application enhances both the participation of members within the CoP, as well as their respective campuses.

Mentoring Networks

Mentoring in higher education has traditionally involved a dyadic relationship between a novice and a more experienced professional who transmits knowledge, organizational culture, and experience to increase a novice individual's capacity. However, Yun et al. (2016) argue that the traditional one-on-one mentoring relationship is not flexible enough to support the increasingly complex roles, responsibilities, and needs of individuals who work in higher education environments. Further, they assert that "we live in an era of networks, not hierarchies" (p. 450). In the past several years, Kerry Ann Rockquemore's (2016) National Center for Faculty Development and Diversity (NCFFDD) Mentoring Map has provided an illustration and conversation tool related to an emerging and evolving model of mentoring. The NCFDD Mentoring Map provides a visual representation of a concept that many academics have long experienced and suspected: mentoring doesn't always happen best in pairs. The mentoring map idea has been extended in a model that acknowledges the complexity of those who provide educational development to faculty (Donnell et al., 2018), asserting that educational developers "benefit from identifying and cultivating a constellation of collaborators, resources, and mentors" (p. 3).

A network of mentors (Higgins & Kram, 2001; Rockquemore, 2013), unlike the more traditional mentor/protégé dyad model of mentoring, allows an individual to fashion a support system that provides a rich tapestry of perspectives. This mentoring network perspective allows individuals to identify their community of mentors, those who provide feedback, sponsorship, accountability, professional development, safe space, and intellectual inspiration and stimulation. Mentoring networks highlight both the multiplicity of perspectives that an individual can leverage in a network as well as the significance of the development of the individuals involved in each interaction.

Adult-developmental theorists Kegan and Lahey (2016) describe the characteristics of organizations that are intentionally focused on developing the capabilities of people at work. Kegan and Lahey ask their readers to "imagine so valuing the importance of developing people's capabilities that you design a culture that itself immersively sweeps every member of the organization into an ongoing developmental journey" (p. 5). The organization becomes an "incubator of capability." In such an organization, individuals do not hide their weaknesses; rather, they are encouraged to share them within a trustworthy environment so that they can receive support in their growth.

In supporting each individual, we increase our *collective intelligence* and the capacity of our *innovation ecosystem* (Pór, 2004) to make significant contributions to our local and global communities. Building from this scholarly base, IDEAx, though not an organization, has embraced an identity as an *incubator of capability*. At the outset, IDEAx was established as an intentional mentoring network where people can feel comfortable verbalizing their professional and institutional challenges and leaning on the collective intelligence of the group to brainstorm possible solutions.

Designing a CoP with Systems Thinking in Mind

Those involved in the development and sustainment of the regional CoP addressed in this case study have learned many lessons. Instructional designers interested in developing a CoP of professionals in any capacity should make an intentional effort to incorporate a systems thinking approach from the start. Systems thinking recognizes that the whole is greater than the sum of the parts, that the perspectives or mental models of participants play an important role in the success of any organization, and that all parts of the system have influence in some manner (Cabrera & Cabrera, 2019). With intentional planning, designers can account for each of these common systems thinking ideas.

Those seeking to create a successful CoP can start with an analysis of the needs of the whole system. When planning a regional conference, for example, event planners may conduct an analysis of all of the regional institutions and the different systems of professionals within each institution to determine the many subsystems at play. Some institutions rely on instructional designers to lead faculty development efforts, while others recruit faculty to lead such efforts. Having a critical understanding of the many parts of the whole can lead to better decision making and richer collaborations. One way to operationalize systems thinking is to incorporate the tasks also found in the analysis phase of the ADDIE design model. Bond and Lockee (2014) identify a variety of possible actions in the analysis phase of CoP development: identifying gaps, recruiting and interviewing possible members, and planning evaluation instruments for determining the community's value. Such tasks are an important part of understanding the entire system within which a CoP will reside.

CoP designers should incorporate feedback loops at logical intervals to ensure that stakeholders within the larger regional community are gaining meaning and value from CoP participants. Every potential CoP member has perspectives that represent how they fit within a given context. A new member organization can help participants gain identity and define professional roles that may be helpful in the larger system (Senge, 2006). Systems thinking encourages feedback from stakeholders and participants as well. Professionals working to improve technology adoption within higher education can have positive or negative impact depending on their perception of a given technology or a potential technology adopter (Hall & Hord, 1984).

Wenger (2002) also warns those who are systematically designing a CoP to beware the sway of groupthink. Further, designers should actively look for wrong or inaccurate information that is perpetuated by members. Community members and subgroups that promote bad practice are detrimental to the larger system. Designers can actively seek to understand and correct mental models within the member organization.

Designers should recognize that all parts of the system in which the CoP is situated have influence on and in the community (Cabrera & Cabrera, 2019; Stroh, 2015). This common systems thinking concept is key to a meaningful experience for participants and the regional institutions in which they work. In any system with multiple subsystems, many forces and factors combine to influence the current situation. Designers should look at how these factors intersect within the system and plan to mediate potential obstacles. In the case of a regional CoP, it is important to understand where the community fits within the larger system and the areas where the community can intersect with current subsystems to make meaningful change for the larger system. This concept requires a designer to have a "big picture" understanding of the region, the individual institutions, external/internal pressures, competing organizations, while managing the priorities, strategic direction, and needs of CoP membership. In many ways this sort of thinking is similar to the Design phase in the ADDIE model (i.e., aligning institutional needs with the needs of the professional members). Some considerations or action items include defining goals and objectives and creating plans for knowledge sharing (Bond & Lockee, 2014).

There are many considerations for building and maintaining a regional CoP for instructional design professionals. The case of IDEAx offers some insight into a systems thinking approach to creating and sustaining such regional communities. Though the original community grew out of a grassroots phenomenon, the organizers of IDEAx can see how systems thinking was organically incorporated into the process. As the community continues to grow and thrive, organizers are more intentionally incorporating systems thinking and research-based best practices for cultivating communities of practice into their processes and decision making. Instructional designers who wish to start a similar organization can find many lessons here.

The magic of the IDEAx CoP, as discussed within the case study, has been achieved through combining systems thinking with the intentional (and sometimes unintentional) cultivation of a CoP. In addition, mentoring opportunities among members have emerged throughout the growth of the community. While it might be impossible to replicate this type of CoP in other regions, the founding members of IDEAx agree that the combination of these three constructs (systems thinking, CoP and mentoring network ideologies) have sustained the network among peers, while also allowing flexibility as new members are invited and enter the community.

Professional Practice Revisited

Anthropologist Dorothy Lee (1986) famously differentiated cultural identity as ranging from individualistic to collectivist. She used eggs cooking in a pan as her metaphor. Two soft boiled eggs cook in the same pan (local culture) and remain totally distinct from one another (individualistic identity). Fried eggs, however, remain individual but have blurred and overlapping edges (shared collective identity). The systems view of a professional CoP can be viewed as an extension of this metaphor (see Figure 21.1).

Distinct learning institutions in a region each aim to maximize learning through varied learning supports, which can be supported in different ways at each institution. Faculty members at one university take on some of the instructional design support for their colleagues in partnership with a professional development team. Another university in the region might add a team of technologists to the mix. While individual identities and roles are mixed and varied there are many collective similarities that have the potential to give rise to a regional CoP. This pre-existing condition of loosely knit associations most likely led us to envision learning support for higher education as a regional community and system. This web is indeed the system that we inadvertently stumbled upon. Leveraging what we know about systems and the importance of each part in sustaining the system, we formed a coalition of individuals around a network of overlapping professional concerns.

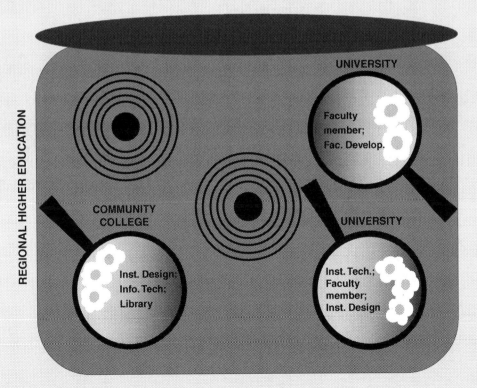

Figure 21.1 Collective identity and systems thinking as the basis of a regional professional learning community

226 *Samantha J. Blevins et al.*

IDEAx founders set to work, inviting the many types of teaching and learning professionals that regularly comprise team membership on instructional design projects, instructional media development, instructional support, and professional training and development for teaching and learning. The invite was literally bounded by a 100-mile circle around a pushpin inserted in the map. Perhaps one of the first lessons that one can draw from this case is this: when starting a movement, start with your neighbors. Your neighbors are familiar, even when you don't know them. Proximity assures that they have the shared contexts of regional norms, governance, demographics, and an array of shared starting points for dialog. This proximity makes the 'getting to know each other' part much easier.

Many elements must be woven into the fabric of a CoP, including discussion, dialog, debate, inspiration, praise, criticism, and sharing. These are the community components consistently cited as reasons for becoming involved and coming back to our annual meeting and virtual offerings. Consider this brief reflection from a regular IDEAx participant:

> [IDEAx is a] vital community of practice for my field. I've been so lucky to be part of a professional CoP [...] for the past 3 years. This regional idea exchange brings together instructional technologists, designers, learning scientists, and teaching faculty for a day-long series of conversations. [...] I'm so energized when I meet new colleagues and old friends –each with an accumulated year of experience to inform conversation on new ideas, problems to overcome, and innovative solutions to the persistent and sometimes wicked problems of teaching and learning.

Connecting Process to Practice

1. Consider how you might identify a regional or other community of practice. Perhaps putting a pin in a map is a good strategy for you as well.
    *   Think about people who work in allied professions that might face similar circumstances and challenges that you face in the workplace. What virtual communities exist (or are missing) that you could either tap into or create?
2. Use the NCFDD Mentoring Map to assess your own Mentoring Community. Reflect on your completed map:
    *   Where is my map most full?
    *   Where does my map seem sparse?
    *   Does this map work for me or others in my profession or community?
    *   Are there categories or other revisions I might make so that I have a more meaningful mentoring network?
3. Consider some of the broader opportunities and challenges your institution is dealing with, and then reach out to neighboring institutions.
    *   Host an online conversational event so that neighboring representatives of institutions can get to know each other;
    *   Host a small conference or "unconference" and invite regional institutions to participate. Unconferences are designed to be more participant-driven meetings and based on discussions on common topics;
    *   Look for ways to include others in the planning and facilitation.

4. Consider follow-up activities from these meetings and leverage technologies to create digital networks to keep the community active.
   - Consider scheduling a virtual book club or coffee chats for the community;
   - Invite participants to lead or help facilitate meetings;
   - Create a Slack channel, Google group, or dedicated listserv to enable ongoing conversations and connections that support community interactions and discussions.

References

Bond, M. A., & Blevins, S. J. (2020). Using faculty professional development to foster organizational change: A social learning framework. *TechTrends, 64*(2), 229–237. doi:10.1007/s11528-019-00459-2

Bond, M. A., & Lockee, B. B. (2014). *Building virtual communities of practice for distance educators.* Springer International Publishing.

Bond, M. A., & Lockee, B. B. (2018). Evaluating the effectiveness of faculty inquiry groups as communities of practice for faculty professional development. *Journal of Formative Design in Learning, 2*(1), 1–7.

Cabrera, D., & Cabrera, L. (2019). What is systems thinking? In M. Spector, B. Lockee, & M. Childress (Eds.), *Learning, design, and technology.* Springer International Publishing.

Cabrera, D., Cabrera, L., & Powers, E. (2015). A unifying theory of systems thinking with psychosocial applications. *Systems Research and Behavioral Science, 32*(5), 534–545.

Cooperrider, D. L., & Whitney, D. (2005). *Appreciative inquiry: A positive revolution in change.* Oakland, CA: Berrett-Koehler Publishers, Inc.

Donnell, A. M., Fulmer, S. M., Smith, T. W., & Bostwick Flaming, A. L., & Kowalik, A. (2018). Educational developer professional development map (EDPDM): A tool for educational developers to articulate their mentoring network. *Journal on Centers for Teaching and Learning, 10*, 3–23.

Enthoven, M., & de Bruijn, E. (2010). Beyond locality: The creation of public practice-based knowledge through practitioner research in professional learning communities and communities of practice. A review of three books on practitioner research and professional communities. *Educational Action Research, 18*(2), 289–298. doi:10.1080/09650791003741822

Hall, G. E., & Hord, S. M. (1984). *Change in schools: Facilitating the process.* Albany, NY: State University of New York Press.

Higgins, M. C., & Kram, K. E. (2001). Reconceptualizing mentoring at work: A developmental network perspective. *Academy of Management Review, 26*, 264–288.

Hurley, T. A., & Green, C. W. (2005). Knowledge management and the nonprofit industry: A within and between approach. *Journal of Knowledge Management Practice, 6*(1), 1–10.

Kegan, R., & Lahey, L. L. (2016). *An everyone culture: Becoming a deliberately developmental organization.* Harvard Business School Publishing.

Lave, J., & Wenger, E. (1991). *Situated learning: Legitimate peripheral participation.* Cambridge University Press.

Lee, D. (1986). *Valuing the self: What we can learn from other cultures.* Waveland Press Inc.

Pór, G. with van Bekkum, E. (2004). *Liberating the innovation value of communities of practice.* Amsterdam: Community Intelligence Ltd.

Ranmuthugala, G., Plumb, J. J., Cunningham, F. C., Georgiou, A., Westbrook, J. I., & Braithwaite, J. (2011). How and why are communities of practice established in the healthcare sector? A systematic review of the literature. *BMC Health Services Research, 11*(1), 1–16. doi:10.1186/1472-6963-11-273

Rockquemore, K. A. (2013, July 22). A new model of mentoring. *Inside Higher Education.* Retrieved from https://www.insidehighered.com/advice/2013/07/22/essay-calling-senior-faculty-embrace-new-style-mentoring

Rockquemore, K. A. (2016, February 3). Why mentor matches fail. *Inside Higher Education.* Retrieved from https://www.insidehighered.com/advice/2016/02/03/most-mentoring-today-based-outdated-model-essay

Senge, P. M. (2006). *The fifth discipline: The art and practice of the learning organization.* Currency.

Snyder, T. D., de Brey, C., & Dillow, S. A. (2019). *Digest of education statistics 2018* (54th ed.). NCES 2020009. National Center for Education Statistics. Retrieved from https://nces.ed.gov/pubsearch/pubsinfo.asp?pubid=2020009

Stroh, D. P. (2015). *Systems thinking for social change: A practical guide to solving complex problems, avoiding unintended consequences, and achieving lasting results.* Chelsea Green Publishing.

Weller, A. (2017). Exploring practitioners' meaning of "ethics", "compliance", and "corporate social responsibility" practices: A communities of practice perspective. *Business and Society, 59*(3). doi:10.1177/0007650317719263

Wenger, E. (1998). Communities of practice: Learning as a social system. *Systems Thinker, 9*(5), 2–3.

Wenger, E. (2010). Communities of practice and social learning systems: The career of a concept. In C. Blackmore (Ed.), *Social learning systems and communities of practice* (pp. 179–198). London: Springer.

Wenger, E., McDermott, R. A., & Snyder, W. (2002). *Cultivating communities of practice: A guide to managing knowledge.* Boston, MA: Harvard Business School Press.

Yun, J., Baldi, B., & Sorcinelli, M. D. (2016). Mutual mentoring for early-career and underrepresented faculty: Model, research, and practice. *Innovative Higher Education.* doi:10.1007/s10755-016-9359-6

22 Developing Consulting Skills in Novice Instructional Designers

Barbara B. Lockee and Miriam B. Larson

Chapter Overview

Samir Parikh, author of the influential "Consultant's Handbook" (2015), defines consulting as "a helping relationship provided based upon expertise and experience" (p. 6), with a primary focus on helping a client achieve a desired outcome. Instructional designers (IDs) typically serve in a consulting capacity regardless of job title, career environment, or whether they are operating within an organization or externally. They use their expertise and experience to solve a wide range of educational and performance challenges, and it is that very expertise and experience that constitutes the value-added they bring to an instructional design project.

What are consulting skills? Across career environments, public and private sectors, and disciplines, the skills that empower IDs to consult are often referred to as "soft skills" or "interpersonal skills." The category includes many different skills, including effective oral and written communication, negotiation and persuasive skills, relationship building and conflict resolution, and a wide range of other interpersonal competencies. These competencies are essential to the practice of good instructional design. Yet, if the mastery of IDT consulting skills requires both expertise and experience, how can IDT programs foster the development of those skills for *novice* instructional designers? While many of the skills and competencies identified as those required for consulting are routinely addressed in IDT programs, there are gaps in coverage that have been noted in the literature, specifically in the area of soft skills of an interpersonal nature.

Guiding Questions

1. What are consulting skills and competencies?
2. How do consulting skills relate to the instructional design process?
3. Which consulting skills and competencies should IDs possess to be effective practitioners?
4. According to the literature, what theoretical foundations and effective instructional practices have been successfully used by IDT programs to foster interpersonal consulting skills?
5. How would the proposed instructional approaches facilitate the teaching of ID consulting skills?

DOI: 10.4324/9781003109938-22

Case Study

Dr. Kamesha Jones has just been assigned the rotating program leader position for the well-established Instructional Design and Technology (IDT) Master of Education (MEd) program. In considering what potential updates may be needed to the program's curriculum, one of her first acts in her new role was to contact the IDT Alumni Advisory Board for feedback on necessary skills and knowledge to be an effective instructional design practitioner. She asked several questions about the competencies and skills they've determined need more attention in the program, based on their experiences in real-world design practice.

The results of the survey surprised Dr. Jones. In general, it looks like the alumni felt well-prepared for practice in a variety of career environments – at least with respect to the hard skills and soft skills like design, analysis, and evaluation. But, just about all of them mentioned that they wished they'd had more opportunities to build their interpersonal skills. Of course, those skills often develop over time and with experience, but the message was clear that this was an issue that needed to be addressed in the professional preparation of the students.

She opened up her email calendar and sent the program faculty a meeting invitation. She looked forward to getting together with her colleagues to explore ways to enhance students' learning of the necessary interpersonal skills identified by their alumni.

Skills and Competencies Necessary for ID Consulting

Consulting tasks are typically included in the job descriptions of all practicing instructional designers, and due to the broad range of topics about which they consult, the list of competencies required is quite long. This presents a prioritization dilemma for IDT programs, especially considering that these programs seek to place graduates in organizations in a wide array of career environments and disciplines characterized by a range of unique content and needs.

It is also important to make a distinction between categories of consulting competencies, and to define the specific nature of the competencies to be addressed, since some of the competencies required to consult with clients are already thoroughly covered in IDT programs. Consider, for example, the competency categories of "hard skills" or technical competencies, and "soft skill" competencies. The category of soft skills is sometimes used to refer to the ID process-related skills of design and analysis, as well as to the broader category of interpersonal soft skills (e.g., communication skills, negotiation skills, relationship-building skills). Both hard and soft skill categories are required to perform and manage the general iterative process of instructional design and to consult with clients, and most of these are categorized as "essential" in the list of competencies for IDs compiled by ibstpi, the International Board of Standards for Training, Performance and Instruction (Koszalka et al., 2013). As a result, the majority of these essential competencies are routinely addressed in the plans of study established by IDT programs. Note, however, that many competencies categorized by ibstpi as "advanced" or "managerial" are *also* necessary to effectively consult with clients (especially when an ID is employed as an external contractor), in part, due to the amount of expertise that clients typically expect of consultants (Gardner et al., 2018; Koszalka et al., 2013). These advanced and managerial skills are not always addressed in IDT programs.

Developing Consulting Skills 231

Hard skills and those competencies identified as ID-related soft skills (such as design and analysis skills) are essential to the ID process, are typically well-defined in the literature, and are generally considered to be teachable. In contrast, there is a lack of consistency in how soft skills are defined in the research literature, not only in the IDT field but across disciplines, stating that "soft skills are cross-disciplinary, independent of job or industry and difficult to define" (Yan et al., 2019, p. 244). Sorana (2013) goes so far as to claim that the "'softest' of the soft skills ... are the hardest to teach and, in fact, they are practically un-teachable" (p. 138). She describes these skills as subtle, deep personality-related skills like "self-esteem, self-confidence, integrity, and ethics ... culminating in what is usually termed as 'Realization of Oneself,' 'Self-Realization' or 'Self-Awareness'" (p. 138). Soft skills are sometimes described as both interpersonal (the ability to manage self) and intrapersonal skills (managing interactions with others) (Botke et al., 2018; Laker & Powell, 2011). Laker and Powell (2011) maintain that soft skills present more of a challenge for transfer (i.e., they are linked to far transfer), in part because their implementation is often dependent on factors in the learners' performance environment. They explain that "the imprecision involved in the application of soft-skill training is due to the uncertainty involved in exactly what the trainee needs to know and in what contexts he or she needs to apply that learning" (p. 116).

Touloumakos (2020) argues that the approach to defining soft skills is problematic because the term means different things to different people in different disciplines, and that this fact impacts the curricula designed to teach those skills and the research designed to study it. She cites Moss and Tilly (2001, p. 44) in tracing the use of the term "soft skills" back to a US Army training document of 1972. Touloumakos goes on to elaborate on how the term has since been expanded in the research literature to comprise one or more of many different categories, including:

- Personal Qualities – including such things as adaptability, flexibility, responsibility, courtesy, integrity, professionalism, and effectiveness, as well as values such as trustworthiness and work ethic;
- Volitions, Predispositions, and Attitudes – such as willingness to learn, self-directed learning, working under pressure or with uncertainty, and working with a good attitude;
- Analytical Skills – including problem solving, decision making, analysis, creativity and innovation, critical judgment, and knowledge manipulation;
- Leadership and Management Skills – including the management of oneself, self-awareness, and coping skills;
- Interpersonal Skills – such as social skills, team skills, effective and productive interpersonal interactions;
- Communication Skills – including negotiation, conflict resolution, persuasive skills, diversity, and articulation or orchestration of interactions with human and non-human resources;
- Emotional Labor – such as that carried out in the service sector;
- Aesthetics, Professional Appearance (sometimes referred to as "lookism"); and
- Other Cognitive Abilities or Processes – including planning and achieving goals.

Yet despite this complexity, there is a consensus across disciplines, job sectors, the design fields, and specifically, the instructional design field, that interpersonal soft skills and lifelong learning are essential for success in the current global climate of change (Botke et al., 2018; Horvitz et al., 2020; DeVaughn & Stefaniak, 2020; Fortney & Yamagata-Lynch, 2013). In fact, while hard skills are necessary for carrying out the design/development process, the research shows that it is the designer's soft skills that significantly influence

232   *Barbara B. Lockee and Miriam B. Larson*

the success and effectiveness of the design/development effort, and these skills are generally acknowledged to be equally or more important to master than hard skills (Yan et al., 2019). Yan et al. (2019) cite a Stanford Institute and Carnegie Melon Foundation study (Fu et al., 2008) that found that "75% of success in long-term work depends on soft skills, with only 25% dependent on technical skills" (p. 243).

Soft skills of an interpersonal nature – like effective communication, negotiation, and conflict resolution skills – are increasingly listed in ID job ads. Yet Solomonson (2008) reports that interpersonal soft skills are often overlooked in IDT practice and research, indicating that they are either not addressed at all or not *explicitly emphasized* in IDT educational programs so that students realize their importance to their future practice. He stresses that the truly fluent ID should attain mastery "of the consultative, decision-making, and relationship management aspects of the client-interaction; that is, within the context of people" (p. 12). Brown (2018) agrees, emphasizing that "preparing individuals for success in the 21st century workplace needs to include instruction and skill development in areas which will best prepare them to effectively collaborate, lead, and work in a community of diversity ... [and] continual, life-long learning is necessary to navigate the changes" (p. 7).

To highlight the potential gaps in the education of IDT graduates, Table 22.1 lists interpersonal or soft skill competencies from the literature that studies indicate are desired by organizations hiring instructional designers. The table also highlights similar terms used to define or elaborate on the basic soft-skill competency identified.

As indicated in Table 22.1, the six most frequently mentioned competencies in the literature include collaboration; communication; metacognition, reflection, and continuous learning; negotiation; relationship and conflict management; and teamwork. Other competencies frequently mentioned include change management and advocacy (Brown, 2018; Grabowski et al., 2016); creativity and innovation (Stierand et al., 2020; Ying & Othman, 2020); critical and systemic thinking (Horvitz et al., 2020; Pedersen, 2020); intercultural competence (Qamar et al., 2019; Yan et al., 2019); decision making (Klein & Kelly, 2018; Stefaniak et al., 2020); flexibility and tolerance of ambiguity (Hartescu, 2020); leadership (Galli et al., 2017; McDonald & Rogers, 2021); problem

Table 22.1 Interpersonal Soft-Skill Competencies Desired by Employers

Competency	ibstpi Statements & Alternate Terms Used	Cited In...
Collaboration	Use effective collaboration and consensus-building skills	Brown (2018)
	Collaborate with production specialists	DeVaughn and Stefaniak (2020)
	Manage partnerships and collaborative relationships	Grabowski et al. (2016)
	Includes mention of collaboration with subject matter experts (SMEs), content experts, disciplinary specialists, faculty, instructors, team members, clients, stakeholders, and production specialists	Guerra-López and Joshi (2021)
	Develop trust and rapport	Halupa (2019)
		Horvitz et al. (2020)
		Kiernan et al. (2020)
		Klein and Kelly (2018)
		Magruder et al. (2019)
		McDonald and Rogers (2021)
		Solomonson (2008)
		van Leusen et al. (2016)
		Wynn and Eckert (2017)

(Continued)

Developing Consulting Skills 233

Table 22.1 (Continued)

Competency	*ibstpi Statements & Alternate Terms Used*	*Cited In...*
Communication	Communicate effectively in visual, oral, and written form	DeVaughn and Stefaniak (2020)
	Effective presentation and reporting skills	Galli et al. (2017)
	Write proposals for instructional design projects	Grabowski et al. (2016)
	Conduct project reviews with design team members and stakeholders	Horvitz et al. (2020)
	Ability to articulate	Kiernan et al. (2020)
	Regular communication, Personal Communication and Interpersonal Communication	Klein and Kelly (2018)
	Dialogue, Constructive conversation; Informal conversation	McDonald and Rogers (2021)
	Listening, Active listening	Qamar et al. (2019)
	Client-facing skills, including interviewing techniques, observation, questioning skills, paraphrasing and summarizing, verification of information, effective facilitation, reading of non-verbal communication, provision of constructive feedback, clarification and explanation of jargon, concepts, and procedures	Sorana (2013) van Leusen et al. (2016) Wynn and Eckert (2017) Yan et al. (2019) Ying and Othman (2020) York and Ertmer (2016)
Metacognition, Reflection and Continuous Learning	Metacognition – "Self-reflection through planning, monitoring and evaluating oneself or the team" (Kiernan et al., 2020, p. 190)	Brown (2018)
	Mindful; Self-aware; Aware of personal strengths and weaknesses	Galli et al. (2017)
	Emotionally intelligent; Emotional strength; Emotional control	Grabowski et al. (2016)
	Developed professional identity; Design mindset	Hartescu (2020)
	Lifelong learner; Continuous learner; Learns from failures; Willing to learn independently; Keeps current; Updates and improves professional skills and knowledge; Curious	Kiernan et al. (2020) Magruder et al. (2019) Qamar et al. (2019) Sorana (2013) Stefaniak (2017) Yan et al. (2019) Ying and Othman (2020)
Negotiation	Use effective negotiation and conflict resolution skills	Hartescu (2020)
	Persuasive and Motivating	ibstpi (2012) Kiernan et al. (2020) Klein and Kelly (2018) Magruder et al. (2019) Patacsil and Tablatin (2017) Solomonson (2008) Stefaniak et al. (2020) Vogler et al. (2018) Wynn and Eckert (2017) Yan et al. (2019) York and Ertmer (2016)

(*Continued*)

234 *Barbara B. Lockee and Miriam B. Larson*

Table 22.1 (Continued)

Competency	*ibstpi Statements & Alternate Terms Used*	*Cited In…*
Relationship Management and Conflict Management	Build and promote effective relationships between the design team and stakeholders	Grabowski et al. (2016)
	Use effective negotiation and conflict resolution skills	Halupa (2019)
	Manage partnerships and collaborative relationships	Horvitz et al. (2020)
	Interface, interact with, and coach clients; Set expectations	Klein and Kelly (2018)
	Conflict resolution; Conflict anticipation; Conflict mediation; Compromise	Magruder et al. (2019)
	Build relationships; Build trust and rapport; Effective client and SME relationship skills; Stakeholder management	Stierand et al. (2020)
	Empathy with perspectives and needs of clients/design peers	van Leusen et al. (2016)
	Diplomacy; Tact	Yan et al. (2019)
	Customer service skills	Ying and Othman (2020) York and Ertmer (2016)
Teamwork	Build and promote effective relationships between the design team and stakeholders	DeVaughn and Stefaniak (2020)
	Conduct project reviews with design team members and stakeholders work well in a team-oriented environment	Grabowski et al. (2016)
	Use interdisciplinary thinking	Halupa (2019) Hartescu (2020) Kiernan et al. (2020) Klein and Kelly (2018) Qamar et al. (2019) Sorana (2013) Ying and Othman (2020)

solving (DeVaughn & Stefaniak, 2020; Qamar et al., 2019); promotion and marketing (Grabowski et al., 2016; Yan et al., 2019), and self-regulation (ibstpi, 2012; Pedersen, 2020; Ying & Othman, 2020). Some articles categorize project management skills as "soft skills;" however, this topic is covered thoroughly in another chapter in this book. In this chapter we highlight the six interpersonal soft-skill competencies most frequently identified in the literature as essential for ID practice. These include collaboration; communication; metacognition, reflection, and continuous learning; negotiation; relationship and conflict management; and teamwork.

Given this background on the nature of interpersonal soft-skill competencies being addressed in this chapter, we offer the following case study to support this discussion. We will revisit this scenario following an exploration of the literature.

Theory and Practical Methods Used by IDT Programs to Foster Consulting Skills

The need for IDT students to develop the kinds of interpersonal consulting skills necessary for successful professional practice was identified decades ago (Hedberg, 1980). Strategies for incorporating engagement in their real-world application have been explored throughout the evolution of our discipline, as well as related challenges for doing so (Bannan-Ritland, 2001; Cennamo & Holmes, 2001; Rowland et al., 1994; Stefaniak et al., 2020). A plethora of pedagogical approaches have been recommended to build awareness of these necessary skills and provide scaffolded learning experiences to apply these competencies in authentic situations. Tracey and Boling (2014) provide a well-researched overview of the methods used to educate IDs in the essential competencies required to practice instructional design. They cite research to report that traditional methods used to train instructional designers include teaching the ADDIE conceptual framework and process model, descriptive and prescriptive theories from multiple domains, methods for analysis, preparation of learning objectives and other process topics, and use of established competencies from the field.

In addition, they report that many programs provide students with opportunities to engage in authentic projects, clinical courses, use of design cases to aid in transfer of design skills to new situations, discussions with expert designers, and experiential learning opportunities. The authors also looked at how designers are prepared in other design professions, including graphic design, engineering, and architecture, finding that these fields emphasize teaching designers to learn to deal with ill-structured problems and uncertainty, and to adapt design models to the context rather than take them literally. Table 22.2 represents teaching strategies to address soft-skill competencies cited in the instructional design and technology literature, as well as methods used these skills in other design disciplines.

Professional Practice Revisited

Dr. Jones prepared a spreadsheet that listed the six most frequently cited soft skills for IDs identified by the Alumni Advisory Board: communication (written, oral, and visual), collaboration, metacognition/reflection/continuous learning, negotiation, relationship and conflict management, and teamwork. For each, she noted existing course and program learning experiences, along with a list of the courses required for the department's Med in IDT.

Dr. Jones presented the lists and asked the faculty to consider whether existing experiences should be "reframed" to explicitly state the competencies targeted by the learning experiences or adjusted to foster the development of the skills more directly. A lively discussion ensued, and everyone seemed pleased with the resulting list of ideas for fostering the targeted interpersonal competencies through both existing avenues and new initiatives:

Existing Course & Program Experiences

Communication skills are currently addressed by:

- Written communication, including design proposals, distinctions between academic and instructional writing, how to write for specific audiences, and job aid and infographic writing, are explicitly addressed in the required program courses: IDT Foundations, Design for Learning, and Program and Product Evaluation. They are also reinforced in the program track elective courses: Educational Research Design, Interactive Learning Design, and Human Performance Improvement;

- Oral communication skills are explicitly taught in College Teaching;
- Communication requirements and process strategies are included in the Design for Learning and Project Management courses.

Collaboration and teamwork skills are currently addressed through in-depth group design projects in Design for Learning, Instructional Video Production, and Audio Production courses.

With the exception of reflective exercises in individual courses, metacognition, reflection, and continuous learning are not currently explicitly addressed. See the next section, New Initiatives.

Negotiation and Relationship and Conflict Management skills are currently addressed by:

- The required course Design Practicum, a problem-based, semester-long design project for individual students;
- Semester-long internships in professional contexts arranged by the student in the career environment of their choice;
- Professional development programming offered through the student-led Instructional Technology Student Association. The student leaders of this group coordinate regular opportunities to hear from expert designers regarding strategies for successful engagement with SMEs. Topics include guidance for developing positive relationships, negotiation of project terms and progress, and resolving conflict when it arises.

New Initiatives

Revisions to Existing Courses

- The addition of weekly design cases (Ertmer et al., 2019) to the Design for Learning course to build conceptual awareness of the consulting skills for ID, as well as provide opportunities for metacognition and reflection as related assessment activities. The cases would represent different contexts and challenging situations, requiring student groups to devise prospective solutions for ill-structured design problems. Faculty will lead guided discussion of the cases and proposed solutions so that all students may benefit from the ideas and feedback for each group;
- A set of four design charrette activities (Edwards, 2009) will be incorporated into the Learning Message Design course, an elective course in which most masters students choose to enroll. The format will facilitate the development of not only of the required interpersonal skills, but also a chance to learn from others and obtain feedback on each design from the instructor and the client;
- Modify the Reflection component of the IDT Student Portfolio to include the six consulting skills as part of the program outcomes that students address. Have students write a self-assessment of these competencies during their first semester and a final self-assessment during their final semester, highlighting changes in their knowledge and application of these key skills. Students may use IDT soft-skill inventories as reflection prompts (Larson & Lockee, 2020, pp. 191–193).

Table 22.2 Teaching Methods Cited in the Literature to Foster Interpersonal Soft-Skill Competencies

Teaching Methods Used to Address Soft-Skill Competencies	Benefits of these Methods	Cited in IDT Literature...	Cited in Other Design Fields or Other Disciplines...
Case-Based Instruction (case studies/design cases)	Small and whole group discussions of situated, real-world cases foster interpersonal skills development and instill confidence in new IDs Cases enable students to use their analysis skills, develop a rationale for design decisions, and learn how to build trust in client-consultant relationships.	Ertmer et al. (2019) Stefaniak et al. (2020) Tawfik (2017) Tracey and Boling (2014)	Solomonson (2012) (Human Performance Improvement)
Traditional Design Coursework	Traditional design coursework that includes group projects, design charrettes, portfolios, and capstone projects situated in real-world contexts, can serve to foster communication, collaboration, teamwork, and negotiation skills	Edwards (2009)	Botke et al. (2018) (Workplace Training)
Interdisciplinary Courses	Interdisciplinary courses designed to incorporate constructive dialogue foster the skills required to work in teams, share information and communicate, collaborate, and negotiate common ground and reach consensus	Tracey and Boling (2014)	Brown (2018) (Global Learning & Development)
Experiential Workshops	Experiential workshops that incorporate design leadership coaching from educators can help participants to be more aware of and to better navigate power dynamics in project relationships	York and Ertmer (2016)	Galli et al. (2017) (Design: Fashion, Architecture, & Other)
Workplace Training and Professional Development	Workplace training that includes interaction between participants and small groups provides employees with opportunities to problem solve with others who possess different personalities, skill sets, and experiences, thus encouraging the development of personal strategies for interaction Workplace professional development programs for soft skills can yield better transfer of learning when designed to consider the effects of work factors (i.e., job-related factors, social support factors, and the organization's facilitation of learning)		Kiernan et al. (2020) (Industrial, Biomedical, & Electrical Engineering; Communication & Media Design; Medicine; Product Design) Lawson and Dorst (2009) (Architecture & Industrial Design) Neuman et al. (2021) (Urban Design) Sorana (2013) (Engineering Design) van Leusen et al. (2016) (Fields of Counseling & Medicine to apply to IDT) Wynn and Eckert (2017) (Software Design, Product Design, Construction Management)

(Continued)

238 *Barbara B. Lockee and Miriam B. Larson*

Table 22.2 (Continued)

Teaching Methods Used to Address Soft-Skill Competencies	Benefits of these Methods	Cited in IDT Literature...	Cited in Other Design Fields or Other Disciplines...
Design Studio Experiences	In both the IDT literature and in other design fields, design studio experiences are credited with contextualizing learning, fostering problem-solving skills, conflict resolution,	Brandt et al. (2013)	Lawson and Dorst (2009) (Architecture, Product & Industrial Design)
	Design studio experiences can act as a bridge to support students in moving from an academic to a professional practice identity	Cennamo and Brandt (2012)	Neuman et al. (2021) (Urban Design)
Entrepreneurship Programs and Boot Camps	Design studios often incorporate desk critiques, group critiques, independent project work, design juries, and design galleries to foster design skills, design thinking, communication skills, and teamwork and collaboration skills. The literature suggests that design studio experiences are most effective when participants have previous background in multimedia development.	Clinton and Rieber (2010) Knowlton (2016) Stefaniak, Reese et al. (2020) Tracey and Boling (2014)	
	Increasingly, entrepreneurship programs and boot camps are being used in the design disciplines to foster soft skills such as innovation, creativity, initiative, teamwork, interdisciplinary thinking, oral and written communication, and self-reliance	Correia (2014)	Qamar et al. (2019) (Engineering Design)
ID Consulting Organizations	ID consulting organizations can provide students and novices with opportunities to work with real-world clients in a variety of contexts, fostering the development of interpersonal soft skills like communication and negotiation	West et al. (2012)	Yan et al. (2019) (Multiple Disciplines)
Communities of Practice	Communities of practice (CoP) can be used to develop communication and interpersonal skills, and a professional identity. CoP's also provide opportunities to keep current on developments and skills through continuous learning, build collaborative practices, and, when the CoP's involve others outside of the profession, to articulate and promote the value of ID	Schwier et al. (2007) Sharif and Cho (2015)	Plack (2006) (Physical Therapy)
Learning from Design Failures	Learning through trial and error can help students perceive how contextual factors (including different stakeholder personalities) can impact designs	Rong and Choi (2019)	Lombardi (2013) (Experience Design)

(Continued)

Developing Consulting Skills 239

Table 22.2 (Continued)

Teaching Methods Used to Address Soft-Skill Competencies	Benefits of these Methods	Cited in IDT Literature...	Cited in Other Design Fields or Other Disciplines...
	Failure-based learning can also support reflection, decision making, creative risk, tolerance for ambiguity, and self-awareness as a designer. Learning experiences should be designed to allow learners to encounter, identify, and classify failures, and should support failure analysis and solution generation for resolution	Stefaniak (2021) Stefaniak et al. (2020) Tawfik et al. (2015) Tessmer and Richey (1997)	
Real-World (Authentic) Projects	Interdisciplinary projects provide practice in using constructive dialogue to work effectively in teams, share information, and communicate, collaborate, and negotiate common ground and reach consensus. Interdisciplinary Project-Based Learning (PjBL) experiences further foster the development of students' professional identities, reflection and teamwork skills	Bannan-Ritland (2001)	Kiernan et al. (2020) (Industrial, Biomedical, & Electrical Engineering; Communication & Media Design; Medicine; Product Design)
Interdisciplinary Projects and Interdisciplinary Project-Based Learning (PjBL) Service-Learning Projects	Service-learning projects that combine community service, academic coursework, and work-based experience, can positively impact personal and social outcomes including skills for client relationship building, teamwork, self-awareness, communication, sensitivity to diversity, and autonomy and independence	Cennamo and Holmes (2001) DeVaughn and Stefaniak (2020) Hartescu (2020) Maddrell (2015) McDonald and Rogers (2021) Stefaniak (2015a) Stefaniak et al. (2020) Tracey and Boling (2014)	Neuman et al. (2021) (Urban Design) Qamar et al. (2019) (Engineering Design)
Authentic projects provide the type of variety and complexity that novices will experience when practicing ID in the real world, and they promote development of problem solving, communication, negotiation, self-directed learning, dealing with unfamiliar contexts and ambiguity, flexibility, and the interpersonal skills required to communicate with and build relations with project stakeholders			

(*Continued*)

240 *Barbara B. Lockee and Miriam B. Larson*

Table 22.2 (Continued)

Teaching Methods Used to Address Soft-Skill Competencies	Benefits of these Methods	Cited in IDT Literature...	Cited in Other Design Fields or Other Disciplines...
Student Internships Coaching Apprenticeships & Cognitive Apprenticeships Mentorships (including from alumni)	Student internships, coaching, apprenticeships, and mentorships all represent opportunities for novices to learn and receive guidance from knowledgeable IDT experts, and to develop communication and teamwork skills. In some cases (e.g., coaching, cognitive apprenticeships, and mentoring), these opportunities can be provided through regular coursework, program advising opportunities, and networking. In others (e.g., internships, apprenticeships, and mentoring in practice), they can be offered through programs that actively build and maintain alumni and community organization relationships	Arrington and Darabi (2018)	Galli et al. (2017) (Design: Fashion, Architecture, & Other)
	When IDT educators adopt a coaching approach as opposed to a teaching approach, the experience can help novices be more aware of and better navigate power dynamics in project relationships, and to successfully fulfill their role as innovative change agents	Rowland et al. (1994) Stefaniak (2015b) Stefaniak (2017) York and Ertmer (2016)	Patacsil and Tablatin (2017) (Information Technology)

Connecting Process to Practice

In this chapter, we have identified the consulting and related interpersonal skills necessary for instructional designers to engage in effective ID practices. It is hoped that the guidance for developing these skills provided herein may inform plans to increase awareness and application of these skill sets in professional contexts upon graduation. In considering ways to apply this information to practice, consider the following questions:

1. What resources and relationships are available within your university that would provide authentic opportunities for students to apply the skills identified in this chapter?
2. How can such experiences be incorporated into coursework or extracurricular programming in ways that are beneficial for students, as well as feasible for program faculty?
3. What consulting skill development opportunities are available to students through professional organizations (i.e., Association for Educational Communications and Technology, Association for Talent Development, the International Society for Performance Improvement)?

In addition to learning and development opportunities for ID students, another recommendation for IDT faculty is to remain a continuous learner in the role of the ID practitioner. Stefaniak et al. (2020) encourage instructional design educators to seek experiences that go beyond their existing skill sets to extend their ability to support novice designers in an ongoing way. Such experiences can inform our own teaching and research activities, as well as serve as important connections to prospective future collaborators for students.

References

Arrington, T. L., & Darabi, A. (2018). Indicators of exemplary programs in instructional design and technology: Faculty and student perspectives. *Educational Technology Research and Development, 66,* 173–189. doi:10.1007/s11423-017-9561-y

Bannan-Ritland, B. (2001). Teaching instructional design: An action learning approach. *Performance Improvement Quarterly, 14*(2), 37–52. doi:10.1111/j.1937-8327.2001.tb00208.x

Botke, J. A., Jansen, P. G. W., Khapova, S. N., & Tims, M. (2018). Work factors influencing the transfer stages of soft skills training: A literature review. *Educational Research Review, 24,* 130–147. doi:10.1016/j.edurev.2018.04.001

Brandt, C. B., Cennamo, K., Douglas, S., Vernon, M., McGrath, M., & Reimer, Y. (2013). A theoretical framework for the studio as a learning environment. *International Journal of Technology and Design Education, 23,* 329–348.

Brown, L. S. (2018). Soft skill development in the higher education curriculum: A case study. *The IUP Journal of Soft Skills, 12*(4), 7–29.

Cennamo, K., & Brandt, C. (2012). The "right kind of telling": Knowledge building in the academic design studio. *Educational Technology Research and Development, 60*(5), 839–858. doi:10.1007/s11423-012-9254-5

Cennamo, K., & Holmes, G. (2001). Developing awareness of client relations through immersion in practice. *Educational Technology, 41*(6), 44–49.

Clinton, G., & Rieber, L. P. (2010). The studio experience at The University of Georgia: An example of constructionist learning for adults. *Educational Technology Research and Development, 58*(6), 755–780. doi:10.1007/s11423-010-9165-2

Correia, A. P. (2014). Creating curriculum within the context of an enterprise. (pp. 113–134) In M. Gosper, & D. Ifenthaler (Eds.), *Curriculum Models for the 21st Century: Using Learning Technologies in Higher Education.* DOI 10.1007/978-1-4614-7366-4_7

DeVaughn, P., & Stefaniak, J. (2020). An exploration of how learning design and educational technology programs prepare instructional designers to evaluate in practice. *Educational Technology Research and Development, 68,* 3299–3326. doi:10.1007/s11423-020-09823-z

Edwards, R. L. (2009, October). Design charrettes as pedagogical method in a multimedia design course. In *Proceedings of the 27th ACM international conference on design of communication* (pp. 181–186). doi:10.1145/1621995.1622031

Ertmer, P. A., Quinn, J. A., & Glazewski, K. D. (2019). The case-learning process. *The ID casebook: Case studies in instructional design* (5th ed., pp. 1–8). Routledge.

Fortney, K. S., & Yamagata-Lynch, L. C. (2013). How instructional designers solve workplace problems. *Performance Improvement Quarterly, 25*(4), 91–109. doi:10.1002/piq.21130

Fu, Y., Zheng, X., & Li, P. (2008). Research progress of soft skills. *Chinese Journal of Nursing, 1,* 20–26.

Galli, F., Pino, B. A., & Suteu, I. (2017). Adaptive thinking for design leadership: Coaching adaptive capabilities to empower next visionary leaders. *The Design Journal, 20*(Suppl. 1). doi:10.1080/14606925.2017.1352917

Grabowski, B. L., Beaudoin, M., & Koszalka, T. A. (2016). Competencies for designers, instructors, and online learners. In N. Rushby & D. Surry (Eds.), *Handbook of learning technology* (pp. 221–241). Wiley.

Guerra-López, I., & Joshi, R. (2021). A study of instructional design master's programs and their responsiveness to evolving professional expectations and employer demand. *The Journal of Applied Instructional Design, 10*(2), 1–11. Retrieved from https://edtechbooks.org/jaid:10_2/a_study_of_instructi

Halupa, C. (2019). Differentiation of roles: Instructional designers and faculty in the creation of online courses. *International Journal of Higher Education, 8*(1), 55–68. doi:10.5430/ijhe.v8n1p55

Hartescu, S. I. R. (2020). *Project-based learning and the development of students' professional identity: A case study of an instructional design course with real clients in Romania* (Doctoral dissertation). Lancaster University, UK.

Hedberg, J. G. (1980). Client relationships in instructional design. *Programmed Learning and Educational Technology, 17*(2), 102–110. doi:10.1080/0033039800170207

Horvitz, B. S., Mitchell, R. L. G., Garcia, L. R., & Singleton, C. D. (2020). Vocational and technical learning. In M. J. Bishop, E. Boling, J. Elen, & V. Svihla (Eds.), *Handbook of research in educational communications and technology* (5th ed., pp. 465–479). Springer.

International Board of Standards for Training, Performance, and Instruction (ibstpi). (2012). *Instructional designer competencies.* Retrieved from http://ibstpi.org/instructional-design-competencies/

Kiernan, L., Ledwith, A., & Lynch, R. (2020). Comparing the dialogue of experts and novices in interdisciplinary teams to inform design education. *International Journal of Technology and Design Education, 30*, 187–206. doi:10.1007/s10798-019-09495-8

Klein, J. D., & Kelly, W. Q. (2018). Competencies for instructional designers: A view from employers. *Performance Improvement Quarterly, 31*(3), 225–247. doi:10.1002/piq.21257

Knowlton, D. S. (2016). Design studios in instructional design and technology: What are the possibilities? *TechTrends, 60*, 350–358. doi:10.1007/s11528-016-0073-0

Koszalka, T. A., Russ-Eft, D. F., & Reiser, R., with Senior-Canela, F., Grabowski, B., & Wallington, C. J. (2013). *Instructional designer competencies: The standards* (4th ed.). Information Age Publishing.

Laker, D. R., & Powell, J. L. (2011). The differences between hard and soft skills and their relative impact on training transfer. *Human Resource Development Quarterly, 22*(1), 111–122. doi:10.1002/hrdq.20063

Larson, M. B., & Lockee, B. B. (2020). *Streamlined ID: A practical guide to instructional design* (2nd ed.). Routledge.

Lawson, B., & Dorst, K. (2009). *Design expertise.* Taylor & Francis.

Lombardi, V. (2013). *Why we fail: Learning from experience design failures.* Rosenfeld Media.

Maddrell, J. A. (2015). Designing authentic educational experiences through virtual service learning. In B. Hokanson, G. Clinton, & M. Tracey (Eds.), *The design of learning experience: Creating the future of educational technology* (pp. 215–229). Cham: Springer. doi:10.1007/978-3-319-16504-2_15

Magruder, O., Arnold, D. A., Moore, S., & Edwards, M. (2019). What is an ID? A survey study. *Online Learning Journal, 23*(3), 137–160.

McDonald, J. K., & Rogers, A. (2021). "I can do things because I feel valuable": Authentic project experiences and how they matter to instructional design students. *The Journal of Applied Instructional Design, 10*(2), 1–14. Retrieved from https://edtechbooks.org/jaid:10_2/i_can_do_things_beca

Moss, P., & Tilly, C. (2001). *Stories employers tell: Race, skill, and hiring in America.* Russell Sage Foundation.

Neuman, M., Perrone, C., & Mossa, A. (2021). Applied research by design: An experimental collaborative and interdisciplinary design charrette. *European Planning Studies,* 1–21. doi:10.1080/09654313.2021.1911956

Parikh, S. (2015). *The consultant's handbook: A practical guide to delivering high-value and differentiated services in a competitive marketplace.* Wiley.

Patacsil, F. F., & Tablatin, C. L. S. (2017). Exploring the importance of soft and hard skills as perceived by IT internship students and industry: A gap analysis. *Journal of Technology and Science Education, 7*(3), 347–368. doi:10.3926/jotse.271

Pedersen, J. (2020). Insights and development of non-cognitive skills. In: Bishop, M.J., Boling, E., Elen, J., Svihla, V. (eds) *Handbook of research in educational communications and technology,* (pp. 301–319). Springer.

Plack, M. M. (2006). The development of communication skills, interpersonal skills, and a professional identity within a community of practice. *Journal of Physical Therapy Education, 20*(1), 37–46.

Qamar, S. Z., Pervez, T., & Al-Kindi, M. (2019). Engineering education: Challenges, opportunities, and future trends. In *Proceedings of the international conference on industrial engineering and operations management* (pp. 629–637), Riyadh, Saudi Arabia, November 26–28, 2019.

Rong, H., & Choi, I. (2019). Integrating failure in case-based learning: A conceptual framework for failure classification and its instructional implications. *Educational Technology Research and Development, 67*(3), 617–637. doi:10.1007/s11423-018-9629-3

Rowland, G., Parra, M. L., & Basnet, K. (1994). Educating instructional designers: Different methods for different outcomes. *Educational Technology,* July/August, 5–11.

Schwier, R. A., Campbell, K., & Kenny, R. F. (2007). Instructional designers' perceptions of their agency: Tales of change and community. In M. J. Keppell (Ed.), *Instructional design: Case studies in communities of practice* (pp. 1–18). Information Science Publishing.

Sharif, A., & Cho, S. (2015). 21st-century instructional designers: Bridging the perceptual gaps between identity, practice, impact and professional development. *RUSC Universities and Knowledge Society Journal, 12*(3), 72–85. doi:10.7238/rusc.v12i3.2176

Solomonson, W. L. (2008). Toward fluent instructional design in the context of people. *Performance Improvement, 47*(7), 12–19. doi:10.1002/pfi.20012

Solomonson, W. L. (2012). Trust and the client-consultant relationship. *Performance Improvement Quarterly, 25*(3), 53–80. doi:10.1002/piq.21123

Sorana, D. (2013). Soft skills for the engineering students. *Synergy, 9*(2), 137–142. Retrieved from http://docplayer.net/29566012-Soft-skills-forthe-engineering-students.html

Stefaniak, J. (2015b). Promoting learner-centered instruction through the design of contextually relevant experiences. In B. Hokanson, G. Clinton, & M. Tracey (Eds.), *The design of learning experience: Creating the future of educational technology* (pp. 215–229). Springer. doi:10.1007/978-3-319-16504-2_15

Stefaniak, J. (2021). Leveraging failure-based learning to support decision-making and creative risk in instructional design pedagogy. *TechTrends,* 1–7. doi:10.1007/s11528-021-00608-6

Stefaniak, J., Reese, R. M., & McDonald, J. K. (2020). Design considerations for bridging the gap between instructional design pedagogy and practice. *The Journal of Applied Instructional Design, 9*(3), 1–7. doi:10.51869/93jsrmrjkmd

Stefaniak, J. E. (2015a). The implementation of service-learning in graduate instructional design coursework. *Journal of Computing in Higher Education, 27*(1), 2–9. doi:10.1007/s12528-015-9092-7

Stefaniak, J. E. (2017). The role of coaching within the context of instructional design. *TechTrends, 61*, 26–31. doi:10.1007/s11528-016-0128-2

Stierand, M., Heelein, J., & Mainemelis, C. (2020). A designer on designing: A conversation with Johannes Torpe. *Journal of Management Inquiry, 29*(3), 350–359. doi:10.1177/1056492619882090

Tawfik, A., Rong, H., & Choi, I. (2015). Failing to learn: Towards a unified design approach for failure-based learning. *Educational Technology Research and Development, 63*(6), 975–994. doi:10.1007/s11423-015-9399-0

Tawfik, A. A. (2017). Do cases teach themselves? A comparison of case library prompts in supporting problem-solving during argumentation. *Journal of Computing in Higher Education, 29*(2), 267–285. doi:10.1007/s12528-017-9136-2

Tessmer, M., & Richey, R. C. (1997). The role of context in learning and instructional design. *Educational Technology Research and Development, 45*(2), 85–115. doi:10.1007/BF02299526

Touloumakos, A. K. (2020). Expanded yet restricted: A mini review of the soft skills literature. *Frontiers in Psychology, 11*, 2207. doi:10.3389/fpsyg.2020.02209

Tracey, M. W., & Boling, E. (2014). Preparing instructional designers: Traditional and emerging perspectives. In J. M. Spector, M. D. Merrill, J. Elen, & M. J. Bishop (Eds.), *Handbook of research on educational communications and technology* (4th ed., pp. 653–660). Springer. doi:10.1007/978-1-4614-3185-5_52.

van Leusen, P., Ottenbreit-Lefwich, A. T., & Brush, T. (2016). Interpersonal consulting skills for instructional technology consultants: A multiple case study. *TechTrends, 60*, 253–259. doi:10.1007/s11528-016-0046-3

Vogler, J. S., Thompson, P., Davis, D. W., Mayfield, B. E., Finley, P. M., & Yasseri, D. (2018). The hard work of soft skills: Augmenting the project-based learning experience with interdisciplinary teamwork. *Instructional Science: An International Journal of the Learning Sciences, 46*(3), 457–488.

West, R. E., Tateishi, I., Wright, G. A., & Fonoimoana, M. (2012). Innovation 101: Promoting undergraduate innovation through a two-day boot camp. *Creativity Research Journal, 24*(2–3), 243–251.

Wynn, D. C., & Eckert, C. M. (2017). Perspectives on iteration in design and development. *Research in Engineering Design, 28*, 153–184. doi:10.1007/s00163-016-0226-3

Yan, L., Yinghong, Y., Lui, S. M., Whiteside, M., & Tsey, K. (2019). Teaching "soft skills" to university students in China: The feasibility of an Australian approach. *Educational Studies, 4*(2), 242–258. doi:10.1080/03055698.2018.1446328

Ying, H. Y., & Othman, A. M. A. (2020). Expected competencies of companies towards designers in Malaysia. *International Journal of Business and Technology Management, 2*(1), 54–65.

York, C. S., & Ertmer, P. A. (2016). Examining instructional design principles applied by experienced designers in practice. *Performance Improvement Quarterly, 29*(2), 169–192. doi:10.1002/piq.21220

Index

Pages in *italics* refer figures and **bold** refer tables.

Abduction-1 form of reasoning 20, *21*
Abduction-2 form of reasoning 21, *21*
accessibility in higher education: medical model of disability 102–103; universal design for learning 103–104
accessible course design 101–102
ADA *see* Americans with Disability Act (ADA) of 1990
AECT *see* Association for Educational Communications and Technology
Al-Kindi, M. **233–234, 238–239**
Allen, D. 165
Allen, M. 199
Altuwaijri, A. A. 23
Alumni Advisory Board 230, 235
American National Standards Institute (ANSI) 190
Americans with Disability Act (ADA) of 1990 103
Anderson, V. 172
ANSI *see* American National Standards Institute
Arnold, D. A. **232–234**
Arrington, T. L. **240**
Association for Educational Communications and Technology (AECT) 9, 123, 139, **140**

Baaki, J. 125
Bailey, M. 209
Baldi, B. 222
Bannan-Ritland, B. **239**
Basnet, K. **240**
Batson, C. D. 60–61, 64
Bawden, R. J. 172
Beaudoin, M. **232–234**
Beck, D. 125
Behling, K. 106
Behling, K. T. 103, 107–108
Benson, A. 123
Boling, E. 22–23, 123, 235, **237–239**
Bond, M. A. 223
Bordonaro, T. 12
Botke, J. A. **237**
Brandt, C. **238**
Brandt, C. B. **238**
Breman, J. 151
Brown, A. **3**

Brown, K. 183
Brown, L. S. 232, **232–233, 237**
Brush, C. G. 65
Brush, T. **232–234, 237**
Buchanan, R. 41

Cabrera, D. 220
Cabrera, L. 220
Cafeteria, O. **3**
Campbell, K. 23, **238**
Carducci, O. M. 92
career outcomes 15–16, **16**
Carey, J. O. 12
Carey, L. 12, 62
case-based reasoning (CBR) theory 49; failure for learning 71–73
case library design 48–49
Casper, W. 183
Cennamo, K. **238–239**
Chen, Y. **3**, 14, **15**
Choi, I. **238–239**
Cho, S. **238**
Clark, K. 107
Clark, T. R. 199
class's diversity 135–136
Clinton, G. **238**
code of ethics 122
community of practice (CoP): collective identity and systems thinking 225, *225*; designing with systems thinking in mind 223–224; IDEAx 220, 226; professional 221–222; regional 219
consulting skills for IDT programs 229–234; foster interpersonal soft-skill competencies 234–236, **237–240**
CoP *see* community of practice
Correia, A. P. **238**
course/course sequence 11
creativity and design thinking: base course elements 42; creative mindset 40–41; definition 39; design mindset 41; ID projects 38–39; inter-team interactions 42–44, *43*; intra-teamwork dynamics 42, *43*; outcomes 44–45; questions and activity 45–46
Cropley, A. J. 40

246 *Index*

Cross, N. 41, 61
Csikszentmihalyi, M. 63
cultural inclusivity in ID process: AECT
  Standards and ISTE Coach Standards 139,
  140; cultural relevant pedagogy 142–143;
  depth levels of **136**, 138–139; design and
  development 141–142; design/image selection
  144; front-end analysis 140–141; multiple
  systems 137–138, *138*; personal culture shapes
  145; surface and shallow elements 143–144

Dagli, C. 23
Daniels, K. 10, 13
Daniels, L. **3**
Darabi, A. **240**
Davis, D. W. **233**
deductive reasoning 20, *20*
Demiral-Uzan, M. 23
Dempsey, J. V. 11
designer's mindset 18, 22
design ethics 23, 25–26
designing for service-learning: assessment and
  student reflection 96; "I"–implementation
  with feedback 93–94, *94–95*, 96; "P"–purpose
  92; purpose–stakeholders–implementation
  91; "S"–stakeholders 92–93
design thinking: case study 18–19; forms of
  reasoning 20–21
Dessinger, J. C. 176
DeVaughn, P. **232–234**, **239**
Dewey, J. 31
Dick, W. 12, 62
disability: in higher education 105; medical
  model 102–103
Dorst, K. 20–21, 61–62, **237–238**
Douglas, S. **238**
Duckworth, A. L. 70
Dweck, C. 69

Eckert, C. M. **232–233**, **237**
Edison, Thomas 69
educational technology: career outcomes
  15–16, **16**; competencies in graduate
  programs *see* educational technology
  competencies; curricula in the ethics of 122;
  definition 9–10, *10*
educational technology competencies: and
  alignment with curriculum 14–15, **15**;
  foundational 10–12, *11*; specialized *11*,
  12–14, **13**
Edwards, M. **232–234**
Edwards, R. L. **237**
Ely, K. 183
empathic design: audience of focus 64;
  collaborative nature 64; process 64; elements
  of ID approach 61
empathy: action for design 61; for audience
  of focus 61; for a learning and performance
  context 62; for oneself 61–62; power of
  observation 65

empathy and empathic design process: be
  empathic toward the audience of focus
  60–61; design with empathy for action 61–62;
  meaningful design deliverable 62–63
Engle, R. A. 80
equity-centered design 3–4
Ergulec, F. 23
Ertmer, P. A. **3**, **233–234**, **237**, **240**
Estes, M. 123
ethical analysis and synthesis: decision
  making 132; learning technology and
  recommendations 132; problem setting/
  framing 124–125; reflection-in-action 125,
  126, *126*
ethics: aspects of 123; as design 126–127, *127*;
  generative learning theory 127–128; issues
  and considerations 124; as the process of
  "reflection 124; social media monitoring,
  framework of 129–131
evaluation: case study 181–182; ID course
  outline 185–186, **186**; instructional design
  industry 180; instruction and instructional
  products 183–184; purpose of 184–185;
  training needs assessment 182–183
Evmenova, A. 107

faculty: development training 108; and
  disability 102–103, 105–106; inclusive course
  design strategy *see* universal design for
  learning
failure: cases 73–74; for learning, using cases of
  71–72; productive 70–71; and success 69–70,
  70
failure-based instructional strategies 67;
  implementation of 68; problem-solving
  experience 73
Finley, P. M. **233**
Finn, J. D. 122
Fonoimoana, M. **238**
Fontaine-Rainen, D. L. 106
form of reasoning: Abduction-1 20, *21*;
  Abduction-2 21, *21*; deduction 20, *20*;
  framing 21, *21*; induction 20, *20*
Foucault Welles, B. 209
foundational competencies 10; design
  and development of instruction 11–12;
  evaluation 12; foundations of instructional
  and performance technologies 11; learning
  theories and principles 12
frame experiments: as a designerly tool 22,
  24–26; design ethics 23, 25–26; design
  judgments 23–26; using in-process design
  failure 23–27

Gagne, R. M. 12
Galli, F. **233**, **237**, **240**
Garcia, L. R. **232–234**
Ge, X. 80, 82
Giacumo, L. A. 151, 173–174
Gilbert, T. F. 164

Glazewski, K. D. **237**
Godfrey 172
Gottfredson, C. A. 199
Grabowski, B. L. 127, **232–234**
Gray, C. 123
Gray, C. M. 22–23
Greene, P. G. 65
Griffith-Boyes, R. 151
Guerra-López, I. **232**

Halupa, C. **232**, **234**
Hammond, Z. 138, 145
hard skills 230–231
Harless, J. 153
Hartescu, S. I. R. **233–234**, **239**
Heelein, J. **234**
Hirumi, A. 184
Hoard, B. **3**
Holmes, G. **239**
Horvitz, B. S. **232–234**
HPI *see* human performance improvement (HPI) model
HPT *see* human performance technology
Huang, K. 80, 82
human–computer interaction (HCI) 48
human performance improvement (HPI) model: and ADDIE 162; case 1–A comprehensive university testing center 168; case 2–A small Niche Market museum in a metropolitan area 168; case 3–cable installers encountering various issues 168; case study 161–162; cause analysis 164–166; evaluation 165, 167; gap analysis 164, 166; intervention selection 165–167, **167**; overview of 161; performance problem identification 163–164, 166, **166**; purpose of 162
human performance technology (HPT): cognitive apprenticeship 175; data collection and analysis, ethical and responsible 173–175; five-phase approach 177; function of the organization 171; organizational systems maps 172; overview of 170; performance in organizational systems across cultures 172–173; request for proposal 170; systems thinking 171–172; theoretical framework 176

IDEAx CoP 220–222
ill-structured problem solving: case study 81–82; iteration and self-regulation 80–81
inductive reasoning 20, *20*
instructional design (ID): competencies 2, **3**; definition 1; design choices 5; designed failure *see* failure; education 39–40; empathy for action in *see* empathy; equity-centered design 3–4; and HPT *see* human performance technology; integrating evaluation *see* evaluation; learner data and feedback 4–5; learning experiences 5–6; learning resources 4; programs 5; systems thinking in *see* systems thinking; UDL guidelines 4

instructional design and technology (IDT) programs 206–207; consulting skills 229; to Foster consulting skills 234–236, **237–240**; interpersonal skills 230; interpersonal soft-skill competencies 230–234, **232–234**
instructional designer and learner contexts 62; and accessible instruction 104; creating meaning 63; dynamic 63; filling spaces 63; interpretation 63; meaning-making 63
instructional design process 81; cultural concepts related to *see* cultural inclusivity in ID process; iterative problem solving in 82–84, *83–84*
International Board of Standards for Training, Performance, and Instruction (IBSTPI) 189
International Society for Technology in Education Instructional Technology Coach standards (ISTE) 139, **140**
interpersonal soft-skill competencies 230–234, **232–234**
ISTE *see* International Society for Technology in Education Instructional Technology Coach standards
iterative problem-solving process 82–84, *83*; analysis phase *84*, 86–87; design and development phases 87–88; matrix of **92**
Izzo, M. V. 102

Jackson, J. J. 209
Jansen, P. G. W. **237**
Jerome, M. K. 107
Johnson, L. 172
Joseph, R. 123
Joshi, R. **232**

Kalman, H. K. 12
Kang, Y. 14, **15**
Kapur, M. 69–71
Kaufman, R. 123
Kaurin, P. S. 124
Kegan, R. 223
Kelly, D. R. 70
Kelly, W. Q. 14, **15**, **232–234**
Kenny, R. F. 23, **238**
Khapova, S. N. **237**
Kiernan, L. **232–234**, **237**, **239**
Kimmons, R. 210–211
Kim, S. M. 44
Kirkpatrick, D. 12
Kirschner, P. A. 182
Klein, J. D. 1, **3**, 14, **15**, **232–234**
Kline, J. **3**
Knowles, M. 12
Knowlton, D. S. **238**
Koetting, J. 122
Koszalka, T. A. **232–234**
Kouprie, M. 59, 61
Kraiger, K. 187
Kumar, S. **3**, 14, **15**

248   *Index*

Lachheb, A. 22–23
Ladson-Billings, G. 142
Lahey, L. L. 223
Laker, D. R. 231
Land, S. M. 80
Lave, J. 221
Lawrence, J. A. 80
Lawson, B. **237–238**
Law, V. 80, 82
learner experience (LX) 50, 52
learner personas 54, 56
learning design 50
learning disabilities 105
learning experience design (LXD):
  characteristics of 51; for instructional
  designers 52; outcomes 54, *55*; principles
  50–51; redesigned case library 52–54, *53*;
  terms and concepts 50
learning/instructional design and technology
  (LIDT) 48, 50
learning management system (LMS) 107, 192,
  206
Ledwith, A. **233–234**, **237**, **239**
Lee, D. 225
Lee, M. **3**
LIDT *see* learning/instructional design and
  technology
Linder, K. E. 106
Lin, H. 123, 125
LMS *see* learning management system
Lockee, B. B. 223
Lombardi, V. **238**
Lui, S. M. 232, **233–234**, **238**
LX *see* learner experience
LXD *see* learning experience design
Lynch, R. **232–234**, **237**, **239**

Macadam, R. D. 172
MacPhail, T. 63
Maddrell, J. A. **239**
Magruder, O. **232–234**
Mainemelis, C. **234**
Marker, A. 165
Martin, F. **3**, 10, 13–14, **15**
Matthews, M. D. 70
Mayfield, B. E. **233**
McAlpine, L. 12
McDermott, R. A. 224
McDonald, J. 184
McDonald, J. K. 41, **232–233**, **237**, **239**
McGrath, M. **238**
Meals on Wheels (MoW) 90
Meiers, M. W. 176
Meloncon, L. K. 62
Merrill, M. D. 12
Mitchell, R. L. G. **232–234**
Moore, J. 123
Moore, S. **232–234**
Moore, S. L. 123, 125, 132
Morrison, G. R. 12

Morrison, J. R. 12
Moseley, J. L. 176
Mossa, A. **238–239**
MoW in Monroe County (MoW-MC) project
  90–91
Murray, A. 102

National Center for Faculty Development and
  Diversity (NCFFDD) 222
NCFFDD *see* National Center for Faculty
  Development and Diversity
Neck, H. M. 65
needs assessment: case study 147–148;
  consultant role in 151–152; instructor
  role in 156–157; models 148–149,
  149; organizational environment 158;
  performance gaps 150–151; project scope
  159; projects range in scale 150; qualified
  projects 152–154, *153*; strategies to support
  instruction 154–156; students interaction
  with client 157–158
Neelen, M. 182
Nelson, H. G. 23
networked learning: NLEC 207; social media
  208; using institutional social media
  212–216, *213–216*
Networked Learning Editorial Collective
  (NLEC) 207
Neuman, M. **238–239**
Nichols, R. 122
Nick's dilemma case 49, 53–54, *55*
NLEC *see* Networked Learning Editorial
  Collective
Nomikoudis, M. 139
Novak, J. 102

Othman, A. M. A. **233**
Ottenbreit-Lefwich, A. T. **232–234**, **237**
Oyarzun, B. **3**

Packham, R. J. 172
Panza, C. M. 176
Parikh, S. 229
Parra, M. L. **240**
Patacsil, F. F. **233**, **240**
performance systems analysis (PSA) 163
Perrone, C. **238–239**
Pervez, T. **233–234**, **238–239**
Peters, D. J. T. 174
Peterson, C. 70
petit design failure 23–27
Pino, B. A. **233**, **237**, **240**
Plack, M. M. **238**
PMBOK® 190; knowledge areas definition 195,
  195; process groups 194, **194**
PMI's *Project Management Body of Knowledge see*
  PMBOK®
Post, T. A. 80
Powell, J. L. 231
Powers, E. 220

Preskill, H. 12
Prestridge, S. 208
problem solving: concepts 79; content analysis 78; ill-structured problems 80–82; iterative *see* iterative problem-solving process
productive failure 70–71; as an outcome 72; applied 72–73
project management: Agile approach 199–200, *200*; case study 191; foundations and concepts 191–192; Hybrid approach 200–201; ID approach 197–198; knowledge areas **195**, 195–197, **198**; process groups 194, **194**; project manager 193–194; project sponsor 192–193; project team 193; stakeholder relationship management 201–203; waterfall approach 198–199, *199*
Project Management Institute (PMI) 189–190

Qamar, S. Z. **233–234**, **238–239**
Quinn, J. A. **237**

Reese, R. M. **238**
reflective practice 29; case study 30; for ethical analysis and synthesis 124–125, **126**, *126*; forms of reflection 34, *35–36*; professional practice 34–35; Russell's phases 33–34; strategies of 33; theory of 31–32
regional community: foundational knowledge 220; mentoring networks 222–223; professional community of practice 221–222; systems thinking 220–221
Reigeluth, C. M. 12
Reimer, Y. **238**
Reiser, R. A. 11
request for proposal (RFP) 170
Richey, R. C. 1, **239**
Rieber, L. 123
Rieber, L. P. **238**
Ritzhaupt, A. 10, 13–14, **15**
Ritzhaupt, A. D. **3**, 14, **15**
Rochberg-Halton, E. 63
Rockquemore, K. A. 222
Rogers, A. **232–233**, **239**
Romero-Hall, E. J. 210–211
Rong, H. **238–239**
Ross, S. J. 12
Rowland, G. 39, **240**
Rozitis, C. P. **3**
Russ-Eft, D. 12
Russell, T. 33–34

Savenye, W. 173
Schank, R. 72
Schön, D. A. 21, 24, 31–32, 124–125
Schwier, R. A. 23, **238**
Senge, P. M. 118, 221
service-learning (SL) 90; designing for *see* designing for service-learning; pedagogy 91; types of project **92**
Sharif, A. **238**

Singleton, C. D. **232–234**
Singleton, K. 107
Sinnott, J. D. 80
SITE *see* Society for Information Technology and Teacher Education
Sites, R. 199
Sitzmann, T. 183
SL *see* service-learning
Snyder, W. 224
social media: in education 209; Hashtags 209–210; institutional 210–212; monitoring 129–131; networked learning using institutional *see* networked learning; in teaching and learning 210
Society for Information Technology and Teacher Education (SITE) 222
soft skills 229–234, **232–234**
Solomonson, W. L. 232, **232–233**, **237**
Sorana, D. 231, **233–234**, **237**
Sorcinelli, M. D. 222
specialized competencies: instructional materials development 12–13; other competencies **13**, 13–14; performance and management 13; teaching with technology 13
Spector, J. M. 11
Stanton, L. 165
Starr, M. 139
Stefaniak, J. 2, 149, **232–233**, **237**, **239**
Stefaniak, J. E. **233**, **239–240**
Stepich, D. A. 165
Stierand, M. **234**
Stolterman, E. 23
Stroh, P. 118, 120
Stufflebeam, D. L. 12
Sugar, W. **3**
Suteu, I. **233**, **237**, **240**
Svihla, V. 124
systems thinking: archetypes 116, **117–118**; feedback loops 118–119, *119*, 120; general systems theory 113; information 119; and instructional design 114–115; mindset 114; procedures in bookstores 114; simple system 113; stakeholders 116; theory and process 115–116; university library 112–113

Tablatin, C. L. S. **233**, **240**
Tan, V. 23
Tateishi, I. **238**
Tawfik, A. A. **237**, **239**
Tennyson, R. D. 12
Tessmer, M. **239**
Thompson, L. 46
Thompson, P. **233**
Tillberg-Webb, H. 125, 132
Tims, M. **237**
Tobin, T. J. 103, 107–108
Touloumakos, A. K. 231
Tracey, M. W. 1, 125, 235, **237–239**

250   *Index*

Trust, T. 208
Tsey, K. 232, **233–234**, **238**

UCD *see* user-centered design
UDL *see* universal design for learning
universal design for learning (UDL): activities
for instructional design course 108–109; in
designing accessible online courses 103–104;
faculty development training 108; guidelines
4; and reframing accessibility 107–108; shared
responsibility and institutional support 108
university library 112–113
Ursavas, Ö. F. **3**
user-centered design (UCD) 48, 50
user experience design (UXD) 49–50
UXD *see* user experience design

Valentine, I. 172
van Leusen, P. **232–234**, **237**
Van Tiem, D. M. 176
van Tryon, P. J. S. 184
Veletsianos, G. 210–211
Vernon, M. **238**
Villachica, S. W. 165
Visser, F. S. 59, 61
Visser, Y. 176
Vogler, J. S. **233**
Von Bertanlanfly, Ludwig 113
Voss, J. F. 80

Wang, X. **3**, 14, **15**
Warren, S. 125
Watkins, R. 176
Wenger, E. 221, 224
Weston, C. 12
West, R. E. **238**
Whitbeck, C. 123, 126
Whiteside, M. 232, **233–234**, **238**
Williams van Rooij, S. W. **3**
Wilson, E. 46
Winzeler, B. 13
Wolfe, C. R. 80
Wright, G. A. **238**
Wynn, D. C. **232–233**, **237**

Xu, M. 2

Yalçın, Y. **3**
Yanchar, S. C. 41
Yan, L. 232, **233–234**, **238**
Yasseri, D. **233**
Yeaman, A. 122–123
Yinghong, Y. 232, **233–234**, **238**
Ying, H. Y. **233**
York, C. S. **3**, **233–234**, **237**, **240**
Young, M. F. 81
Yun, J. 222

Zimmerman, R. D. 183

Printed in the United States
by Baker & Taylor Publisher Services